MW00561306

BLACK MARKET BUSINESS

Studies of the Weatherhead East Asian Institute, Columbia University

The Studies of the Weatherhead East Asian Institute of Columbia University were inaugurated in 1962 to bring to a wider public the results of significant new research on modern and contemporary East Asia.

To my loves: Mike, Chiara, and Ezra

BLACK MARKET BUSINESS

SELLING SEX IN NORTHERN VIETNAM, 1920–1945

CHRISTINA ELIZABETH FIRPO

CORNELL UNIVERSITY PRESS
Ithaca and London

Copyright © 2020 by Cornell University

All rights reserved. Except for brief quotations in a review, this book, or parts thereof, must not be reproduced in any form without permission in writing from the publisher. For information, address Cornell University Press, Sage House, 512 East State Street, Ithaca, New York 14850. Visit our website at cornellpress.cornell.edu.

First published 2020 by Cornell University Press

Library of Congress Cataloging-in-Publication Data

Names: Firpo, Christina Elizabeth, author.
Title: Black market business : selling sex in Northern Vietnam, 1920–1945 / by Christina Elizabeth Firpo.
Description: Ithaca [New York] : Cornell University Press, 2020. | Series: Studies of the Weatherhead East Asian Institute, Columbia University | Includes bibliographical references and index.
Identifiers: LCCN 2020011449 (print) | LCCN 2020011450 (ebook) | ISBN 9781501752650 (cloth) | ISBN 9781501752667 (epub) | ISBN 9781501752674 (pdf)
Subjects: LCSH: Prostitution—Vietnam, Northern—20th century. | Prostitution—Law and legislation—Vietnam, Northern—20th century. | Human trafficking—Vietnam, Northern—20th century. | Women—Vietnam, Northern—Social conditions—20th century. | Vietnam, Northern—Colonial influence.
Classification: LCC HQ242.5 .F57 2020 (print) | LCC HQ242.5 (ebook) | DDC 306.7609597/3—dc23
LC record available at https://lccn.loc.gov/2020011449
LC ebook record available at https://lccn.loc.gov/2020011450

Contents

Acknowledgments ix

A Note on Terms and Translations xiii

Introduction: Late Colonial Vietnam
and the Development of the
Black Market   1

1. The Geography of Vice: Spatial
   Dimensions of Clandestine Sex Work   20

2. Venereal Diseases: Policing the
   Sources of Infection   59

3. Unfree Labor: Debt Bondage and
   Human Trafficking   90

4. Adolescent Sex Work: Poverty and
   Its Effects on Children   113

5. Ả Đào Singers: New Ways to Police
   Female Performance Art   136

6. Taxi Dancers: Western Culture and
   the Urban-Rural Divide   162

Conclusion: Patterns of Clandestine
Sex Industries into the
Postcolonial Era   187

Notes 195

Bibliography 235

Index 249

Acknowledgments

From the bottom of my heart, I would like to thank countless individuals and institutions for helping this book come to print. The research for *Black Market Business* was made possible by grants from the American Philosophical Society and the Dutch Royal Society for Asian and Caribbean Studies (KITLV) as well as numerous grants from my home institution, California Polytechnic State University. At Cornell University Press, I would like to express my deep appreciation to Emily Andrew, Alexis Siemon, Karen Hwa, Don McKeon, and the faculty board for all the hard work that they put into this manuscript. I am especially grateful for the thoughtful feedback from the two external readers, Charles Keith and Micheline Lessard. This book would not be what it is today without the help of the readers and the Cornell staff.

Cal Poly University in San Luis Obispo, California, has proven to be a warm home while I worked on this book. My students, the staff, and my fellow faculty, have enriched my work significantly. In particular, I am grateful to the history department chair and my close friend Kate Murphy, as well as the administrative assistant, Sherry Miller, Dean Philip Williams, College of Liberal Arts librarian Brett Bodemer, library data specialist Russ White, the staff of the interlibrary loan office, the women's and gender studies department, and my colleagues in the history department. The hard work of my research assistants, Solange Khielbach, Sophie Rosales, Kim Adams, Katie Romero, James Cecil, Darby Leahy, and Hoa Thi Nguyen, has been indispensable and must be heartfully acknowledged. While working on this book, I regularly taught a class on the history of prostitution in Asia, which was often the brightest part of my workday. Not only were the students a delight, they were engaged and asked critical questions that forced me to think about this topic in new ways.

I have the great fortune of being part of a vibrant group of scholars and archivists. In my countless research trips to Vietnam, I have received tremendous help from the archivists at the National Archives, especially

Hòang Hằng, who is also a dear friend. I have also been lucky to work with and become friends with professors Đặng Thị Vân Chi and Trần Phương Hoa. I am especially appreciative to my colleagues in the Vietnam Studies Group and in the French Colonial History Society. I cannot thank the following colleagues enough for diligently reading drafts of chapters and offering valuable feedback: David Ambaras, David Biggs, Olga Dror, Jason Gibbs, Agathe Larcher-Goscha, Stephanie Limoncelli, Kate Norberg, Barley Norton, Keith Taylor, Mike Vann, and Peter Zinoman. I would like to extend a special thank you to Jennifer Boittin and Elisa Camiscioli. Boittin and Camiscioli are perhaps the sharpest minds in the field, and, even better, they are amazing friends. I thank my lucky stars for these two. I am particularly indebted to David Del Testa and Micheline Lessard for not only reading chapters but also for providing sound professional advice, writing letters of recommendation, and offering great friendship. I can only hope the final product meets their standards.

In addition to colleagues and friends mentioned above, I would like to thank Pascal Bordeaux, Brad Davis, Katie Dyt, Claire Edington, Chris Goscha, Philippe Papin, Isabelle Tracol-Huynh, Thu Huong Nguyen-Vo, Tom Hoogervorst, Philippe Peycam, Hue Tam Ho Tai, Michele Thompson, Neetu Bali, George Cotkin, Hoàng Lan Hương, Alyson Holob, Meme Lobecker, Hong Anh Ly, Nguyễn Thị Hồng Hạnh, Nguyễn Thị Hoa, Marta Peluso, Suzie Smith, Kate Norberg, Reggie Allen, Julie and Jay Bettergarcia, Maggie Bodemer, Devin and Don Kuhn-Choi, Jane Lehr, Kate Murphy, Preston Moon, Andrew Morris, Elvira Pulitano, and Jay Singh.

I like to reserve a bit of space in each book to show my deep appreciation for Shawn McHale and Ron Spector, to whom I am forever grateful. Shawn and Ron introduced me to Vietnamese studies as an undergrad at The George Washington University, and they went over and beyond their job descriptions and continued to teach me long after I graduated. I will always be thankful to them for their support and friendship.

I am extremely fortunate to have a loving, supportive, and very patient family. David and Cecilia, and Andrew, Su-Wen, Adrian, and Amelia Chen gave me and the children lots of love and fascinating conversations about Chinese etymology. I am forever grateful to my mother-in-law and father-in-law for watching Chiara and Ezra so I could log in some extra hours of work. On the Firpo side, I thank my sisters Patrice Guitreau and Erica Firpo, my brothers-in-law Darius Arya and the late Joe Guitreau, my nephew Jack Guitreau, and my nieces Emilia Arya, Audrey Guitreau, and Xanthe Arya. I owe a special thanks to the gynecologist Dr. Patrice Firpo and the internist Dr. John Firpo for answering all of my explicitly detailed questions about venereal diseases. Finally, I am extremely lucky to have the most loving parents that one could ever ask for. John and Kathy Firpo have cheered me on since the inception of my academic career. Over the years, they have challenged me to think beyond accepted ideas and they are by far the most important influence in my intellectual life.

I dedicate this book to my husband, Mike, and my children, Chiara and Ezra, who are my everything. The best decision I ever made was to marry Mike. I especially feel this way when reflecting on the days when I wrote this book, as Mike did everything he could to make sure I finished it on time. I started the writing phase of this project while pregnant with Chiara, and I finished my last edits while nursing Ezra. If there are any good ideas in this book, they came from Chiara and Ezra, as both children were with me—in my belly or nursing at my breast—while I worked. Of course, all mistakes came from me. Thank you, Mike, Chiara, and Ezra!

A Note on Terms and Translations

Readers will notice that I use the terms "sex worker" and "the sale of sex" over the historical terms "prostitute" and "prostitution." Although "sex worker" is a modern term, I have chosen it in an effort to avoid the negative connotation that comes with the term "prostitute" and "prostitution." I do, however, use "prostitute" and "prostitution" when directly quoting from primary sources, when using historically specific legal definitions, and when sentence grammar or syntax makes it necessary.

French language sources rarely include full diacritics for Vietnamese names and often misspell them. To avoid incorrectly guessing at the diacritics and spelling, I will use the spelling given in the primary sources. In colonial-era Vietnamese language sources, names are frequently abbreviated. For example, "Nguyễn" might be written as "Ng."; but, to avoid incorrectly assuming the last name, I follow suit.

I refer to newspapers by their full Vietnamese names, preceded at first mention by "the newspaper" to identify them for non-Vietnamese reading audiences. For example, there is "the newspaper *Đông Pháp*" and "the newspaper *Việt Báo*," even though "*báo*" means newspaper.

Regarding music terms: The musical form is called *hát ả đào*, the venue is called *nhà hát ả đào*, and the singers are called *cô đầu*. To simplify these terms for anglophone audiences and emphasize their commonality, I refer to "*ả đào* music," "*ả đào* singing houses," and "*ả đào* singers."

BLACK MARKET BUSINESS

Introduction
Late Colonial Vietnam and the Development of the Black Market

In 1936, Đặng Thị Như, a sixteen-year-old girl from Thái Bình Province, grew bored of laboring in the rice paddies for meager pay and little food. Like many young women in the late colonial period, she left the countryside to look for work and a more glamorous life in the big city. When she arrived in Hanoi, she met an elderly woman who offered her a job and shelter in the Cầu-Giấy neighborhood, a suburb just outside the city limits. Never having been exposed to urban crime or corruption, Đặng Thị Như, who, according to the newspaper *Đông Pháp*, "couldn't tell the good from the bad," had no way of knowing that the old lady would soon be selling her to an *ả đào* singing house that was actually a clandestine brothel. When Đặng Thị Như attempted to leave the *ả đào* house, the owner refused to let her go, insisting that the girl was responsible for working off the debt incurred in purchasing her as well as any interest that had accrued. Even when Đặng Thị Như's family traveled to Hanoi to rescue her, the owner of the *ả đào* house refused to let her go. The family appealed to authorities, and her story made the news soon after she was freed.[1]

Đặng Thị Như was one of many adolescent girls and young women who sold sex in Tonkin's black market during the interwar years and the early years of World War II. While illicit markets for sex work predated French rule, during the interwar years a black market for clandestine sex work had developed in response to a regulated, legalized system intro-duced by the colonial government to combat the spread of venereal dis-eases. State regulations required sex workers to register their names on a police roster of prostitutes, taxed sex workers' earnings, set minimum-age requirements for sex work, mandated invasive venereal exams, and institutionalized those who tested positive for a venereal disease. Work-ers who wished to quit the profession had to meet stringent requirements before they could clear their names from the police list of prostitutes. Not surprisingly, these requirements deterred sex workers from registering with colonial police, and a second, *illicit* sex industry for unregistered sex work developed parallel to the licit sex industry.

Tonkin's informal economy for clandestine sex work operated in the cities and the countryside, in the lowlands and near remote military bases, in border towns, and in centers for transportation or industry. Unregistered sex workers operated out of the privacy of their homes, from seedy boardinghouses (*nhà xăm*)—often Chinese- or Vietnamese-owned, that one could rent for the hour, the half day, the whole day, or for multiple nights—and from public venues such as dance halls and ả đào singing houses. In some ways, the black market offered women more freedom by enabling them to sell sex unencumbered by the state regulation system; in other ways, it left them vulnerable to being tricked or trafficked into sex work or shackled in a state of unfree labor by exploitive debt-bondage contracts, abused by pimps, madams, and customers, and stricken with untreated venereal infections.

Black Market Business explores the underground market for clandes-tine sex work in late colonial Tonkin. This book begins with the imple-mentation of a 1921 law to uniformly regulate sex work in the French concessions of Tonkin and ends during World War II, which greatly changed daily life in Tonkin, including the nightlife. The interwar years were a time of remarkable economic and social change in Tonkin. The protectorate experienced a volatile economy that boomed in the 1920s, busted in the 1930s, and enjoyed a brief recovery in the late 1930s (at least in urban areas) until the war began in the 1940s; each downturn of the economy plunged peasants further deeper into poverty and barely recovered before the next economic crisis. Rampant and persis-tent poverty and overpopulation in the countryside resulted in a major demographic shift as peasants migrated around the Red River Delta, as well as toward sites of industry, and into the cities. The economic disparities between Tonkin's rural and urban areas, along with the new

Western -influenced cultural trends that were sweeping the cities, created a sharp urban-rural divide.

I argue that the interwar black market sex industry thrived in what I characterize as spaces of tension, which were created by the confluence of economic, demographic, and cultural changes sweeping late colonial Tonkin. Tension occurred where there was inequality and discord, most of which, in the case of Tonkin, was brought about by colonial policies. These tensions typically developed in sites of legal inconsistency, cultural changes, economic disparity, rural-urban division, and demographic shifts. Certain designated areas of Tonkin were governed by colonial law, while other areas were governed by Vietnamese law. Venereal diseases spread faster than state health services could control. Colonialism brought Western culture and new ideas about the individual's role in family and society. Landless peasants in the countryside were falling deeper into poverty, while a small middle class was thriving in the cities. Cultural changes together with economic disparity intensified the rural-urban divide, and peasants flooded the cities and provincial capitals looking for employment. Such spaces of tension proved fertile for illicit activity. In interwar Tonkin, sex workers, pimps, madams, and traffickers artfully evaded colonial police by moving between the administrative boundaries separating French and Vietnamese territories. Those infected with a venereal disease fled mandatory quarantine. Pimps, madams, kidnappers, and traffickers found their workforce among impoverished peasants and new migrants to the cities, provincial capitals, military bases, and border towns. With relative wealth accumulating in urban areas, border towns, and military bases, residents pursued new forms of leisure, including a hopping nightlife for dancing and music. The clandestine sex industry developed for the most part as an entertainment-focused industry. Businesses that were fronts for clandestine sex work, such as dance halls and å đào singing houses, marketed sex work to customers who embraced cultural change as well as those who preferred tradition. As a nexus of the many tensions besetting late colonial Tonkin, the black market sex industry serves as a useful lens through which to examine these tensions and the ways they affected marginalized populations.

More specifically, an investigation of this black market shows how a particular population of impoverished women—a group regrettably understudied by historians—experienced the tensions. Marginalized by the colonial economy and swayed by new cultural trends, these women came to participate in black market sex work by choice, by force, or,

more often, by some combination of the two. When I began researching this book, I envisioned a very different project. For one thing, I had
hoped to explore cases of both male and female, and homosexual as
well as heterosexual, sex work. While homosexual and male forms of
sex work certainly existed, historical documentation of them is scant
aside from a few anecdotal cases. Given the limited source material,
I have focused this story on female heterosexual sex work. I had also initially assumed that I would be writing story about women who sold sex
because they were shrewd businesswomen and because they enjoyed
expressing their sexuality. As it turned out, while I did find some cases
of women who sold sex for the glamour of it, the overwhelming majority of women in the historical sources entered the sex industry because
it was the only or the best option for earning money—or because they
were coerced into some degree of unfree labor. Likewise, I had hoped to
write about the ways that sex workers prevented pregnancy and dealt
with unplanned pregnancies as well as to learn about the fate of their
children. With few exceptions, stories of contraception, pregnancy,
abortion, and children are largely absent from the historical sources
that I consulted.

That the black market flourished outside the law was inherent in the
product it sold: sex. The colonial state's failure to regulate the black
market sex industry stemmed, to a large extent, from the larger challenge of controlling a behavior that is generally private and negoti-
ated in innuendos. What made the illegal sex industry *sexy* was that
it offered more than the straightforward business transactions found
in state-sanctioned brothels: it wheeled and dealt in hints, double
entendres, nuance, and, of course, the taboo. The line between seduction as a romantic endeavor and seduction as a business activity could,
in short, be exceedingly blurry. The ambiguity was heightened by the
fact that clandestine sex workers typically hid their illegal operations
within legitimate industries. While many of the women who worked as
å đào singers, taxi dancers, waitresses, or bar girls did not engage in sex
work, clandestine sex workers used these positions as a front for their
sex work. For their part, customers were attracted to pretty women
and girls who were open to sexual relations yet were not registered
sex workers. In other words, customers liked the thrill of the chase—
something decidedly absent in the sterile transactional sex offered in
state-run brothels.

The ambiguity of clandestine sex work is evident in the primary
sources. Notwithstanding the plethora of historical sources on the sex

industry in late colonial Tonkin, few of these sources actually define the term "prostitution." This was the case even as the first regulations on the selling of sex were established in the 1880s in Hanoi and Hải Phòng. In the 1921 law that instituted a uniform regulation system in the French concessions, prostitution was defined simply as "giving one's body" and implicitly as being associated with two or more venereal infections. Throughout the interwar years, neither French governmental or health-related sources nor Vietnamese newspapers specified whether sex acts beyond vaginal intercourse and anal sex were prostitution. I have done my best to respect the ambiguity of the sources. The pages that follow tell the story of the various forms of clandestine sex work that flourished in Tonkin during the interwar years, the colonial state's attempts to police and regulate them, and the ways that sex workers, their managers, and clients managed to flout the law.

This book focuses on Tonkin, the northernmost protectorate of French-colonized Vietnam. Tonkin was home to Hanoi, the colonial capital; Hải Phòng, the second largest port in Indochina; military bases; a diverse natural geography; and the border with China. The particularities of Tonkin's political and geographical landscape created legal tensions that enabled black market economies, including sex work and human trafficking, to flourish. Per the 1884 Patenôtre Treaty (Treaty of Huế), which established French protectorate status on Annam and Tonkin, Tonkin was officially under the jurisdiction of the Vietnamese emperor in Huế, who maintained sovereignty over most domestic affairs while remaining subordinate to the French colonial government. While Tonkin was only indirectly under colonial rule, an 1888 royal ordinance had conceded the cities of Hanoi and Hải Phòng, as well as provincial capitals and military bases, to the French.[2] Creating "not only municipal, but also and above all true national borders"[3] between cities and their suburbs, the treaty left Tonkin a messy patchwork of Vietnamese territories and French concessions—and, by extension, two separate legal systems. The resulting ambiguity in turn enabled a fair amount of lawlessness. In Tonkin, sex workers aiming to escape the regulation system set up shop just outside city limits and military bases to profit from the urban and military customer population while evading colonial laws.

Since the early nineteenth century, the sale of sex had had a nebulous legal status in northern Vietnam. For one thing, the areas that would come to make up Tonkin were governed haphazardly by multiple, different legal codes established by the Lê dynasty, the Mặc family, and the

Nguyễn Dynasty, among others.[4] The 1812 Nguyễn legal code, the most prominent of the various codes governing the North, never explicitly prohibited the sale of sex but did mandate the punishment of officials who frequented ả đào singing houses.[5] In the 1880s, as part of an international trend to stymie the spread of venereal diseases among military troops,[6] the French colonial government of Tonkin established a series of municipal-level ordinances to regulate the sale of sex in Hải Phòng (1886) and Hanoi (1888), both French concessions.[7] These laws placed the regulation system under the authority of colonial police, and, in 1907, the city of Hanoi created a vice squad (Đội Con Gái, or Police des Moeurs). By the end of World War I, the French colonial government faced skyrocketing rates of venereal diseases, which had become one of the colony's top health threats, particularly in the military. Doctors identified sex workers as the primary source of contagion, and colonial officials enacted public health regulations designed to limit transmission.

At the end of World War I, as colonial troops crisscrossed the globe to return to their countries of origin, the skyrocketing rates of venereal diseases became a pressing concern for French officials. In 1921, the resident superior of Tonkin, the highest ranking French official governing the protectorate, took the additional step of promulgating a uniform legal code for sex work throughout the French territories of Tonkin, the history and details of which will be discussed in detail in chapter 2.

The 1921 law, which had originated in the metropole as the "tolerance" system, required sex workers to register with the state, but its stringent requirements discouraged many of them from registering in the first place. The law taxed the sale of sex and required sex workers to submit to regular gynecological exams to check for venereal diseases; those who tested positive were sequestered in venereal disease clinics until the infection passed and lost out on valuable income as a result. Moreover, once women had registered with police, it was difficult for them to have their name removed from the police roster of prostitutes. A 1926 amendment to the law set the minimum age requirement for selling sex at eighteen years old. With its strict regulations, the oppressive nature of the tolerance system drove many sex workers to operate underground. The result was a dynamic black market for sex work that existed alongside the legal, regulated tolerance system. While sex work outside state control was nothing new to Tonkin, the 1921 law and the major economic, cultural, and demographic trends taking place in interwar Tonkin shaped the character of the black market.

Women looking to evade colonial regulations sold sex without registering with the police. Some worked in the cities. Others moved their business beyond the reach of colonial law to the suburbs, where they were subject to the less stringent Vietnamese law. They sold sex in many places, most commonly dance halls, å dào singing houses, private homes, or boardinghouses. Some came to the black market willingly; others were tricked, trafficked, or coerced into sex work. It is impossible to estimate how many unregistered sex workers operated in Tonkin during the interwar years, and few estimates were made by authorities at the time. In 1938, Roger Charbonnier, a medical student who wrote his doctoral thesis on venereal diseases in Hanoi, estimated that in Hanoi, a city of 120,000 residents, there were six hundred registered sex workers and five thousand clandestine sex workers. Charbonnier's claim, however, is questionable, as he never stated his methodology for quantifying sex workers. Nor is it clear whether he counted only women who regularly sold sex, or whether he included those who occasionally sold sex and/or those who had originally registered with the state and were currently *en fuite* (on the run)—registered sex workers who had been diagnosed with a venereal disease but fled mandatory quarantine in the dispensary and continued to sell sex on the black market. As black markets are secretive by design, their participants work hard to conceal their activities; moreover, sex workers are wont to come and go at will. It would thus have been impossible to estimate with any accuracy how many women sold sex on the black market during the interwar years.[8]

Unregulated sex work was not illegal per se in Vietnamese-governed areas. Nonetheless, French officials still categorized the sex industry in those areas as "clandestine" or "illegal." This and the fact that many sex workers chose to move to these areas to escape French regulations made these areas part of the black market sex industry. Tonkin's black market, therefore, spanned areas where unregistered sex work was illegal as well as areas where it was not technically illegal at all. Moreover, as we shall see in chapter 2, colonial officials were not concerned about unregistered sex work for moral or legal reasons; it was rather the spread of venereal diseases that alarmed them and made unregistered sex work both inside and outside of colonial jurisdiction a preoccupation. For this reason, I identify the black market as a disorganized informal economy for unregistered sex that spanned both the French concessions, where unregistered sex was illegal, as well as the Vietnamese territory, where it was not.

While unregistered sex work was only a misdemeanor in colonial Tonkin, the black market sex industry was nonetheless vexing for the colonial government in many ways. For one thing, given that clandestine sex workers evaded the tax on the sale of sex, the colonial government missed out on valuable revenue. Clandestine brothels were, moreover, associated with crime, violence, and criminal networks. Most problematic of all for the colonial state was the association between clandestine sex work and venereal diseases, which had the ability to immobilize whole military units and was known to cause birth defects.

In the late 1930s, a confluence of events changed the colonial government's approach to policing clandestine sex work. Since the late nineteenth century, the international antitrafficking movement had pressured France to consider banning sex work outright. According to participants in the movement, the legalized system was only bolstering the market for illegal sex trafficking by providing buyers and sellers alike. After decades of refusing to comply with the movement's request that France abolish the tolerance system, in the late 1930s, the French colonial administration in Indochina drew from the rhetoric of the antitrafficking movement but used it only to make the case for cracking down on the black market, where unfree labor was common.[9] Meanwhile, colonial officials—concerned that the regulation system was inadequate in preventing the spread of venereal diseases—enacted localized public health measures that focused on punishing those who knowingly transmitted the diseases. These measures taken to prevent human trafficking and the spread of venereal diseases enabled the state to police clandestine sex work in ways that the 1921 law did not. Nonetheless, unregistered sex workers continued to evade the police.

The success of the clandestine sex industry in Tonkin can be attributed in large measure to the economic disparity between Tonkin's urban and rural areas that characterized the late colonial era. Widespread and persistent poverty in the Tonkin countryside triggered mass migration, thereby supplying an ample workforce for the sex industry; a concurrent economic boom in urban areas fostered the emergence of a middle class that formed the bulk of the consumer market. Moreover, the large military presence needed to pacify the countryside resulted in an eager customer base with a reliable income in the countryside.

When France made Tonkin a protectorate, the colonial government built a modern export sector that proved devastating for the Vietnamese economy. In the early days of colonization, the colonial government seized land from peasants and villages in fertile areas of the Red River Delta and

mineral-rich areas such as the Hòn Gai coal fields. The state redistributed land concessions to French companies and colonists as well as
to those Vietnamese who collaborated with the French.[10] With land thus
concentrated in the hands of wealthy landowners and French companies,
Tonkin soon changed from a subsistence economy to an export-driven
one. The transformation not only deprived the Vietnamese peasant class
of financial autonomy but also left them vulnerable to the whims of the
international market.

Poverty had grave effects on the peasants, providing an incentive for
some women to seek extra income selling sex. Food scarcity combined
with low peasant income resulted in widespread hunger.[11] Many peasants could scarcely afford more than two meals a day; within two months
of a harvest, their ration was closer to one meal.[12] The period between
harvests was especially difficult, as tenant farmers did not earn a living then. Peasants often survived the periods between harvests through
debt-bondage agreements in which they borrowed money that was to be
paid back through labor. For many women, debt-bondage agreements
were often paid off through sex work, and, as we shall see in chapter 3,
debt bondage was a common arrangement in clandestine brothels.

By the end of World War I, a large class of impoverished, landless peasants had developed in the Red River Delta. Although Tonkin maintained
a system of communal land much longer than did China or Japan, by
1930 only 21 percent of the land in Tonkin was communal.[13] Communal
land ownership and subsistence agriculture was giving way to individual
ownership and monocrop farming.

Rural poverty was exacerbated by a series of catastrophic events in the
region. Excessive rains in the mid-1920s led to poor harvests, and floods in
1924 and 1926 breached the badly neglected dikes in Tonkin, causing extensive flooding and an ensuing outbreak of cholera. A few years later, when
the Great Depression hit, rice prices fell, plunging farmers further into
debt. Those who still owned their land were forced to sell it to larger
landowners or corporations, further concentrating land ownership in the
hands of a few. In 1935, another flood devastated the region, destroying
homes and crops and leaving peasants unable to pay their taxes.[14]

Seeking refuge from rural poverty, landless peasants—including
women and orphaned children—migrated around the delta and to the big
cities in search of better opportunities.[15] Although no accurate statistics
are available to illustrate the scale of migration around Tonkin during the
interwar years,[16] population statistics on Hanoi's long-term growth provide a basis for understanding the rural-to-urban migration in Tonkin.

The city's population nearly doubled from 1918 to 1928—increasing from 70,000 to 130,000 in just ten years. By 1939, the population had reached 200,000, and by 1945 there were 276,000 recorded inhabitants.[17]

Migrants arrived in the cities to find a volatile economy. As the economy adjusted to the end of the war, Tonkin experienced a brief economic downturn in the early 1920s, but the economy picked up again in 1924 and thrived through 1928.[18] In the 1920s, an economic boom in the rice and rubber industries had fostered the development of Hanoi and Hải Phòng cities,[19] yet their economies came to a screeching halt with the Great Depression. A 1931 article in *Đông Pháp* warned that widespread layoffs sometimes left women in the position of needing to support their husbands and family. Increasingly, such women began resorting to sex work.[20] In the mid-1930s, as the economy recovered in urban areas, a middle class with disposable income grew—a middle class that would become the customer base of the burgeoning entertainment industry for which migrant peasants, largely women and girls, provided the primary workforce. Customers flooded entertainment hot spots, including ả đào singing clubs and dancing halls, both of which were well-known venues for clandestine sex work.

Black market sex work proved to be an attractive choice for some migrant women and orphaned girls as clandestine brothels offered food, shelter, and a quick source of income while enabling the women to avoid officially registering with the state. For many women, registering with the police as a prostitute was not an option, as it would bring shame to their family if word got back to their village; additionally, deregistering from the police list was notoriously difficult. However, although black markets afforded participants a degree of anonymity and freedom from state regulation, they also left participants without the protection that may have otherwise have been provided—in theory, at least—by government regulation. Many women within the clandestine sex industry were forced into working as unfree laborers and endured violence (including rape), theft, and exploitation. The clandestine market for sex work also provided a market for traffickers, kidnappers, and other tricksters, putting women at risk of being sold into clandestine brothels. Moreover, a dark market for sex with juveniles existed.

During the interwar era, the cities where migrants arrived were undergoing a major cultural transformation. Among the cultural changes sweeping urban Tonkin were four related trends: Europeanization, modernism, individualism, and materialism. Although these trends were popular more or less exclusively among Tonkin's literate middle-class urbanites—a group that rarely included sex workers themselves—they played a key role in the ways that sex work was marketed to middle-class male clients and understood by Vietnamese thinkers.

The Europeanization trend, also known as the Westernization trend, was an obvious biproduct of French colonization and the *mission civilisatrice*, the colonial government's strategy for imparting French culture to its colonial subjects. A key component of this strategy was the Franco-Annamite school system, which introduced students to French literature and other aspects of French culture, including attitudes toward romance and sexuality.[21] In 1919, the colonial state also put an end to the Confucian exam system, thereby diminishing the social status of the mandarin class and, by extension, of å đào singers. As we shall see in chapter 5, this decline in status played a role in the utilization of å đào houses as venues for sex work during the interwar period.

Along with imparting French culture through the education system and ending the Confucian exams, the colonial state also introduced *quốc ngữ*, romanized script, which facilitated the spread of Western cultural trends among the Vietnamese. Literacy rates increased exponentially, and a thriving print culture blossomed in Tonkin. As was the case in other areas of Asia, including China, Japan, and Burma, the media in Vietnam featured lively debates about gender equality, female education, the "modern girl," and the role of young women in choosing their marriage partners.[22] With a flurry of newspapers being introduced, European and American companies quickly bought up advertising space in which to market their products. Materialism and a mania for Western cultural expressions, including art, cinema, fashion, music, and language, swept Tonkin's cities.

New ideas spread rapidly through media. The closely related trends of individualism and modernism were especially popular among French-educated youth. In the 1930s, two important literary movements developed that would become important sources in the study of the colonial sex industry. Tự Lực Văn Đoàn (Self-Strengthening Literary Group) eschewed traditional Vietnamese culture and espoused independence, self-reliance, and the freedom to determine one's own destiny. Tonkin's educated youth picked up on these ideas. They questioned the practice of parents arranging their children's marriages and explored French notions of sexual freedom. A second group, the social realists, published reportage-style journalism (*phóng sự*) that investigated Tonkin's social problems and exposed problems stemming from traditional cultural expectations. Reportage journalists and members of the Self-Strengthening Literary Group themselves conducted thorough investigations of unregistered sex work and venereal diseases leaving historians with a wealth of information about the black market sex industry.[23]

Cultural tensions emerged between urban, French-educated youth and their parents' generation. The youth generation, David Marr famously wrote, put "tradition on trial."[24] This new generation was deeply influenced—whether consciously or subconsciously—by intellectual questions about tradition and society. The new generation of middle-class urban youth not only had ideas that differed dramatically from those of their parents but looked different and behaved differently as well. The urban youth cut their hair, sported Western clothes, caked on makeup, and left their teeth white rather than blackening them per Vietnamese tradition. They enjoyed new European leisure activities, including cinema, fashion, music, and dancing. The change in youth culture was so shocking that journalist Nguyễn Đình Lạp dubbed the new generation "the depraved youth" (*thanh niên trụy lạc*). In his reportage of the same name, Nguyễn Đình Lạp investigated the lives of such youth—young men in particular. They disrespected teachers and parents alike, drank alcohol, smoked cigarettes, romanced young women into sex before marriage, frequented clandestine sex workers, and stayed out late in dance halls, where they got a chance to publicly explore physical touch and sexuality outside of marriage—a taboo in Vietnamese culture at the time.[25]

Yet it was young women, even more than young men, who experienced the most striking changes. Until the interwar years, girls, for the most part, were expected to obey their parents without question, parents had arranged marriages, young brides had moved in with their husband's family, and mothers-in-law were known to abuse their daughters-in-law. With this new generation, however, changes in gender roles and attitudes toward sexuality led young women to break from their families in search of an independent life. While this change influenced only a minority of young women, the change was shocking to Vietnamese society. French-educated youth, who had been exposed to Western individualism, rejected obligatory arranged marriages in favor of romantic love. Stories abounded of young people challenging their parents' choice of a husband or wife and of girls committing suicide when their parents denied them permission to marry their true love. Literary writers criticized abusive mother-in-law–wife relationships. And young women escaped strict parents or abusive in-laws by running away to big cities.[26] Some of these young women who rebelled—often by necessity—against traditional expectations found themselves living independently of their family and with little emotional or financial support. Some chose to support themselves through clandestine sex work; others were coerced or forced into the black market.

The cultural changes of the interwar years also contributed to growing tensions resulting from Tonkin's urban-rural divide. For one thing, there were substantial economic disparities between cities and the countryside. With urban economies recovering much faster in the cities, a middle class developed with sufficient disposable income to enjoy a few material luxuries and pursue entertainment and leisure activities such as cinema, music, dancing, and an exciting night on the town. As these opportunities were rarely available to peasants in the countryside, they exacerbated the cultural divide between city and country. Yet one must also be careful not to overstate the cultural divide, as there was a fair amount of interaction between urban and rural areas. The suburbs, for example, were a place where city and country and Vietnamese culture and colonial French culture met and mingled. Entrepreneurs in the black market sex industry artfully deployed the cultural intermingling, as on the infamous Khâm Thiên Street outside of Hanoi, an entertainment spot that included venues catering to aficionados of Western culture and others for those who preferred Vietnamese tradition.

The role of these new cultural tensions in contributing to the clandestine sex industry was not lost on Vietnamese thinkers. Vũ Trọng Phụng identified the growth of individualism and the influence of European culture on women's sexuality as one of the main reasons that some women were selling sex. In the introduction to his novel *Làm Đĩ* (To whore), Vũ Trọng Phụng pointed to "the encounter of the East and West" as triggering major social changes—including the emergence of dance halls—that made young people more open to experimenting with their sexuality.[27]

Vietnamese intellectuals of the late colonial period also claimed that materialism, a byproduct of capitalism, was a contributing factor in women's decision to sell sex. Nguyễn Đình Lạp warned that with materialism, "youth worship an ideal: money. . . . Young people have only one intention: material satisfaction, and they trample upon all others in order to attain that goal. Now, the sacred nouns of Honor, Country and Humanity are to them just smoke and laughter."[28] In *Làm Đĩ*, a novel by Vũ Trọng Phụng, the narrator points to materialism as a factor that led her into sex work: "Materialism, also known as progress or modernization . . . has the power to deceive people. . . . I believed I was modern or civilized. It was too late when I became disillusioned. . . . I was—a whore."[29] Vũ Trọng

Phụng, Peter Zinoman writes, "suggests that colonial capitalism fosters the generalized growth of an acquisitive mentality that fuses a desire for commodities with a wanton craving for sex."[30] In his study of the Hanoi Dispensary, which treated patients afflicted with venereal diseases, journalist Thao Thao interviewed women from poor families who had been lured into a life of materialism. They turned to sex work after enjoying attention from wealthy young men and used sex work to support their shopping habits. Ironically, the work they did in their quest for glamour led them to contract venereal diseases and left them quarantined in the dispensary.[31]

It is important to note that the role of individualism, Westernization, and materialism in women's decision to sell sex on the black market may have been overstated by phóng sự authors. An examination of the hundreds of individual cases of clandestine sex work found in the historical sources reveals that while some women did go into sex work to live fast and glamorous lives—which some were probably able to enjoy—the majority of them sold sex to escape poverty, and many soon became disillusioned with sex work and returned to their lives in the countryside. In his investigation on ả đào singers and taxi dancers, journalist Trọng Lang found that most women came to clandestine sex work out of a desperation to escape poverty[32].

The aforementioned cultural tensions were, nonetheless, an effective marketing strategy to sell sex. Madams operating out of private homes and pimps selling women from boardinghouses dolled adolescent girls up in Western clothes. "Modern girls" wearing slinky dresses and French lingerie sold sex from art deco dance halls, which offered upbeat Western tunes and appealed to soldiers and sailors of the French forces nostalgic for Western culture, as well as colonial-educated youth chasing the cult of modernity. And for those less comfortable with these cultural changes that Tonkin was experiencing, ả đào singers in traditional garb set classical poetry to tune and flirted with customers in a venue with few—if any—Western men in sight. It should be noted that neither ả đào singing houses nor dance halls were making political statements; instead, the two venues were merely marketing sex to cater to certain men's taste and thereby maximize their own profit.

During the colonial period, much ink was spilled over the issue of clandestine sex work. Colonial-era French scholars looking to solve medical and social problems in the colony wrote prolifically about sex work. Because venereal diseases were a group of contagious infections that spread mainly by sexual contact, the social aspects of transmission were as important to doctors as the scientific aspects. As a result, doctors and public health officials looking to prevent further transmission of venereal diseases critiqued a range of societal behaviors, specifically the ways that venereal diseases spread within the black market for unregistered sex work.[33]

The prevalence of kidnappings and human-trafficking networks was another matter of international concern, and international antitrafficking organizations commissioned studies of trafficking networks, including those in Indochina. Additionally, French scholar André Baudrit wrote multiple articles about the market for people in Indochina who were trafficked to sex industries in China.[34]

The most thorough studies of the clandestine sex industry come from Vietnamese journalists who published during the colonial period. During the interwar years, phóng sự journalists explored the darker effects of the rapid social and economic changes on the people of Tonkin, especially sex work.[35] As Shawn McHale has shown, in some cases newspaper editors even encouraged writers to cover stories about sex to sell more papers.[36] As a result, today's historians have a wealth of writing about the sex industry at their disposal. There was a proliferation of reportage stories, which were serialized articles—many of which were later published as books—investigating the grittier side of Vietnamese society, including sex work.[37] The authors of these reportage pieces had day jobs as conventional journalists covering quotidian life in Tonkin and, in the process of their investigations for their longer reportage stories, they regularly published news articles about events they had witnessed in clandestine brothels.[38] With these articles, the Vietnamese-language newspapers of the late colonial era provide a vast collection of detailed reporting on life inside the brothels. These sources include detailed cases of juvenile sex work, human trafficking, and debt-bondage arrangements in sex work as well as cases of clandestine sex work in Tonkin's nightspots such as singing houses and dance halls.

Twenty-first-century historians have begun reflecting back on colonial-era clandestine sex work. International concern about sex trafficking led to a renewal of interest in the sex industry in Vietnam and debates about the existence of a contemporary human-trafficking network. Sociologists such as Thu Huong Nguyen Vo, Kimberly Kay Hoang, and Nicolas Lainez have written impressive studies of the contemporary sex industry.[39] Given this renewed interest in the sex industry, scholars are beginning to investigate the sex industries of the French colonial period and during the Second Indochina War (1955–75), also known to Americans as the Vietnam War and to others as the US-Vietnam War. Much work needs to be done on the Vietnam War–era sex industry. Aside from brief discussions of the sex industry in studies of that war, the most thorough investigations of the mid-twentieth-century sex industry are Heather Stur's book on gender and the war, Sue Sun's study of anti-venereal-disease measures taken by the US military, and a forthcoming dissertation by Nguyễn Bảo Trang.[40]

The three most comprehensive studies on colonial sex work are by Isabelle Tracol-Huynh, who writes about the French regulation system in Indochina, Ben Tran, who analyzes reportage stories about sex and the sex industry in the late colonial period, and Shaun Kingsley Malarney, who explores the French colonial approach to preventing the spread of venereal diseases in the introduction to his translation of Vũ Trọng Phụng's 1937 classic reportage story Lục Xì (The dispensary).[41] In 2012, the Journal of Vietnamese Studies published a special issue, "Commodified Women's Bodies in Vietnam and Beyond," which included a study on the colonial regulation system by Tracol-Huynh and a study on Japanese sex workers in colonial Tonkin by Frédéric Roustan.[42] The colonial sex industry has also been explored in articles, book chapters, and dissertation chapters by Đặng Thị Vân Chi,[43] Lê Thị Hồng Hải,[44] Kimberly Kay Hoang,[45] Marie-Corrine Rodriguez,[46] and Haydon Cherry.[47]

Only recently have historians begun to investigate human trafficking in colonial Vietnam. Leading the field of historical trafficking in colonial Vietnam is Micheline Lessard's rich study Human Trafficking in Colonial Vietnam.[48] Likewise, Erica Peters, Julia Martinez,[49] and Nicolas Lainez have also published articles on colonial human-trafficking networks in Vietnam, and Stephanie Limoncelli devoted a chapter of her very impressive book on the First International Anti-Trafficking Movement to the French Empire, and a large portion of it focused on Indochina.[50]

Drawing from the important scholarship on the colonial-era regulation system and human-trafficking networks, this book explores the clandestine market for unregistered sex work in late colonial Tonkin. The challenge of this book has been, among other things, the difficulty of studying a black market, which, as an informal economy, leaves behind no official archives or documents. Given that unregistered sex work violated the law and was potentially damaging to their reputation, participants in the black market sex industry were motivated to conceal every last trace of their activities. Moreover, many of the actors in the black market sex industry were illiterate and thus unable to leave behind any written documentation of their work in the first place. As black market industries thrive on disorganization, tracking historical sources is challenging.

Although the secretive nature of black market sex industries typically results in a dearth of historical record, I have found more than a thousand cases of clandestine sex work covered in hundreds of articles printed in twenty-four newspapers published from 1920 to 1945 or in files tucked away in archives in Hanoi, Ho Chi Minh City, and Đà Lạt in Vietnam and in Aix-en-Provence in France. Stories of clandestine sex work appeared in local crime reports in colonial-era Vietnamese newspapers; among those available in the National Library of Vietnam at the time of my research (2008–11), I chose certain newspapers for their descriptive coverage of local crime and gossip. Many of the articles were written by reportage journalists who were researching larger investigative stories. Transcripts of colonial court cases on forced sex work and daily vice squad reports on surveillance and raids of clandestine brothels offer detailed descriptions of the black market business and testimonies from sex workers, victims of trafficking, madams, and pimps. Epidemiological studies, public health records, and medical reports from both venereal disease clinics and military doctors provide important details about clandestine sex workers who came to the attention of authorities while being treated for venereal diseases. A historian's dream, all these sources are rich in "thick description" information about how the business of clandestine sex work operated, where sex was sold, how business transactions were hidden, how sex workers were recruited and customers solicited, and how sex workers evaded authorities as well as about sex workers' lives, their home towns, their reasons for migrating from rural areas to urban centers, and their interactions with managers, clients, and police.

Of course, with so few voices from the clandestine sex workers themselves, it is difficult to know with any certainty what motivated those women to enter the industry voluntarily. I draw from testimonies by sex workers and trafficking victims found in court records, interviews of sex workers conducted by reportage authors and police, and letters that sex workers wrote to newspapers or state officials. Vietnamese journalists and French authorities offered varied thoughts as to why women became sex workers. Some of their thoughts were based on interviews with the sex workers themselves, while others appear to have been mere conjectures. While their reasoning does not represent that of the women involved in the sex industry, it nonetheless provides a window into the general problems facing impoverished women in the interwar years as well as ideas and stereotypes associated with sex work.

Instead of focusing solely on the lives of women whose voices are largely unattainable, this book will focus on the business of selling sex. During the colonial period, the clandestine sex industry consisted of many different forms of sex work, including male prostitution, European prostitution,[51] prostitution of *métisses* (Franco-Vietnamese girls and women), Chinese prostitution,[52] streetwalking, clandestine unregistered sex work carried out in registered brothels, sex work conducted at homes or in opium dens, and sex work by *filles en fuite*. Because there is scant documentation on the operations of such forms of clandestine sex work, this book will instead focus on the forms of sex work most frequently discussed in the surviving historical sources. There is an overwhelming amount of surviving historical sources that cover trafficking, debt bondage, underage sex work, sex work in singing houses, and sex work in dance halls. The prominence in the historical sources of references to these particular forms of clandestine sex work suggests that they were the most common—or at least that they were considered by journalists and French administrators to be the biggest threats to civil society.

I have arranged the chapters of this book topically to investigate the business of selling unregistered sex and to explore the various forms of clandestine sex work discussed in the primary sources. Although the chapters focus on a single distinct form of sex work, many women in colonial Tonkin participated in multiple forms.

Chapter 1, "The Geography of Vice," is a spatial analysis of Tonkin's black market sex industry. It investigates how the area's physical, administrative, economic, and political geography shaped the ways that unregistered sex was sold in Tonkin. Chapter 2, "Venereal Diseases," considers how the treatment of venereal diseases guided the colonial policing of sex work. Colonial policies designed to slow the spread of venereal diseases by policing ended up backfiring—inadvertently driving women underground to sell sex on the black market, where infection spread all the more easily. In the late 1930s, venereal disease prevention became a useful tool for policing unregistered sex work in ways that were not permitted under the 1921 law. Chapter 3, "Unfree Labor," examines two forms of unfree labor—debt bondage and human trafficking—in which sex workers were not recompensed for their labor and, for a variety of reasons, remained stuck in their place of employment.

Chapter 4, "Adolescent Sex Work," delves into the dark market for juvenile sex work, which to a large extent was a function of Tonkin's extreme poverty. This chapter explores the operations of the market for adolescent sex workers, including the various ways that girls were recruited to sex work, who their managers were, how these managers kept their operations secret, and which industries served, in part, as fronts for juvenile sex work.

Chapter 5, "Å Đào Singers," is a study of the sale of sex in å đào singing houses, a form of female performance art dating back to the fourteenth century. In its twentieth-century iteration, sex work in å đào singing houses appealed to those with a taste for traditional culture in an era of dynamic cultural change. The success of clandestine sex work in å đào venues lay in the ability of sex workers and their managers to capitalize on both the sensuality inherent to this genre of female performance art and the legitimacy associated with a revered traditional art form. The result was that å đào venues operated as ambiguous spaces that blurred the traditional lines separating art, sex, and commerce.

Chapter 6, "Taxi Dancers," explores the clandestine sex work that occurred in dance halls. Whereas sex work in å đào singing houses was marketed to men who sought comfort in traditional culture, the sex work that occurred in dance halls appealed to men excited—even titillated—by modernization and Western culture. As their success derived from both an image of urban sophistication and a mostly peasant workforce, dance halls exemplified the urban-rural divide in colonial Tonkin.

This book follows cases of black market sex work into the early years of World War II, when the violence and economic displacement of war changed the nature of the black market sex industry. In June 1940, the Japanese military invaded and occupied Tonkin. Initially life in Tonkin—and its clandestine businesses—continued as usual, but as the war in the Pacific heated up and Allied forces bombed Hai Phòng, its inhabitants fled to the countryside. It was no longer a site for fast times and entertainment. On September 2, 1945, after Japan officially surrendered, Hồ Chí Minh declared Vietnam's independence, and, by March 1946, Tonkin had descended into the First Indochina War. While clandestine sex work certainly continued through the war years, the nature of the black market changed due to the war.

CHAPTER 1

The Geography of Vice
Spatial Dimensions of Clandestine Sex Work

During the interwar years, a busy market for unregistered sex work animated the shadows of Tonkin. Traffickers smuggled women and girls from rural areas to the cities and provincial capitals, from lowlands up to highland border towns and to military bases. Mẹ mìn (old lady kidnappers) fanned the countryside looking for naive young women and girls to lure into accepting work in the city; they drugged or kidnapped others. Mẹ mìn took women and girls to urban areas for the purpose of selling them to brothels or out to Hải Phòng's port, where they sold their victims to gangs of Chinese traffickers. Junks dodged customs officials among the thousands of islands dotting Hạ Long Bay; small ships carrying trafficking victims hugged the coast, from port to port, all the way to China, where the victims were sold to brothels, dance halls, or men looking for a wife.

Meanwhile, back in Tonkin, droves of peasant women and adolescent girls voluntarily set out for the protectorate's urban areas, provincial capitals, border towns, and military bases in search of income. Some stayed only for the short periods between harvests; others remained for the long term or permanently. Many of these migrants ended up joining the intimate labor force, whether intentionally or through manipulation

and trickery. To avoid ruining their reputations by officially registering as sex workers, most worked on the black market. They operated in
annexes to registered brothels, out of their homes, in dance halls and ả
đào singing houses, or in one of the many seedy boardinghouses that
sprung up to cater to the sex industry.

In the margins of the sex industry was an ultrasecretive market for
underage girls. Some daughters and orphans were sold into the sex
industry; in other cases, migrant girls arriving in the city seeking work
and shelter were tricked or forced into sex work. Men looking for underage girls surreptitiously approached market vendors, itinerant flower
vendors, or rickshaw pullers, the latter of which played a particularly
crucial role in the clandestine sex industry.

Clandestine sex workers of all ages crisscrossed the city streets. In the
late-night hours, sex workers hunted for clients from the back of rickshaws. Men hailed rickshaws and then solicited the puller to find them
an underage girl, and madams called on pullers to transport underage
girls to secret locations to meet customers.

Sex workers looking to avoid harassment by the colonial vice police fled
to the provinces. They set up camp near military bases, coal mines, border towns, and train depots to profit from the large male customer base
at these sites. Others stayed close to the cities, enabling them to access
city amenities and benefit from the wealthy urban customer base. They
moved their operations just outside of the colonial-governed cities and
provincial capitals, forming a ring of illicit sex work in the suburbs. As a
result, de facto "entertainment neighborhoods" developed in the suburban areas outside of Hanoi, Hải Phòng, and the provincial capitals.

This chapter explores the relationship between space and the evolution of the black market sex industry. The physical, political, economic,
and urban geography of the interwar years all shaped this industry.
The physical geography provided hiding spaces, routes, and barriers
for smuggling women and girls. The political geography created spaces
of legal order and disorder, which sex workers, their managers, human
traffickers, and clients artfully used to their advantage. The economic
geography made for places of need and places of opportunity, leading
women to migrate in search of a better life—sometimes afforded through
sex work. And the urban geography, marked by the rapid growth of big
cities, simultaneously attracted migrant sex workers and provided a substantial customer base.

Tonkin's Landscape

The geographic and political landscape of Tonkin enabled traffickers and clandestine sex workers to evade colonial police. Tonkin bordered China to the north, mountains leading to Laos to the west, the French protectorate of Annam to the south, and the South China Sea to the east (see figure 1). For centuries, there have been established trade routes— through the highlands in the west, south into Annam, and by sea— connecting the Viet people and other ethnic groups in Tonkin and Southeast Asia. Traffickers used these established land routes to transport young women and girls from the highlands to the lowlands, from the countryside to the cities, and across the border into China.

Inside the administrative boundaries of the French protectorate, Tonkin was mostly mountainous highlands to the north and west, with a lowland valley that formed the Red River Delta, which opened to the sea on its eastern border. Among the cases of sex work that I was able to track, the overwhelming majority happened in the lowlands, with the exception of military bases and border cities, for reasons discussed later in this chapter.

The most salient feature of Tonkin's geography was waterways, which served as the basis for much of its transportation in the lowlands. Operators within the clandestine sex industry used these riverways, ports, and islands to smuggle kidnapped women around Tonkin and north to

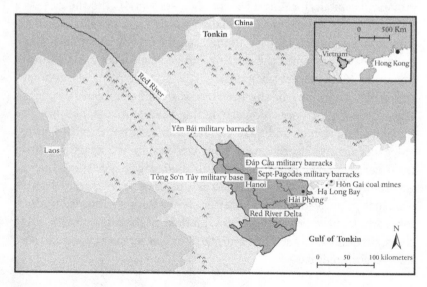

FIGURE 1. Tonkin

China. At roughly 750 miles (1,200 kilometers) long, the Red River starts in southern China and flows through Tonkin. To the northwest of Hanoi, the river branches into tributaries, forming waterways that make up the Red River Delta, a lowland floodplain in the western coastal part of northern Vietnam. The delta itself forms a triangle whose legs extended from the inland to the coast and whose third side runs along the coast, with Hải Phòng as its northernmost point. The network of waterways connected villages with each other and with the big cities and, as they flowed southeast into the Gulf of Tonkin, provided access to the coast. At the northern portion of the Gulf of Tonkin is Hạ Long Bay, home to almost two thousand small limestone islands. Covered in jungle brush, many of the limestone islands had caves. Traffickers easily evaded maritime police by hiding among the islands and taking cover inside the caves.

During the colonial period, the treaty structure that determined the degrees of Vietnamese sovereignty over Tonkin in turn shaped the landscape of the sex industry. In June 1884, the French and Vietnamese governments signed the Treaty of Hué, also known as the Patenôtre Treaty. As discussed in the introduction of this book, the treaty established Tonkin and Annam as French protectorates, meaning that they were indirectly governed by France and Vietnamese law prevailed in most domestic situations. Initially, Vietnamese viceroys appointed by the court in Hué administered the provinces, and villages remained under Vietnamese imperial law. In 1897, the colonial government took control of selecting the Vietnamese officials for the royal government while still maintaining indirect control. Villages and provinces were under the legal jurisdiction of the Vietnamese emperor.[1]

A royal ordinance of October 3, 1888, ceded the cities of Hanoi, Hải Phòng, and Tourane to France. As French concessions, these cities were subject to direct colonial rule, and French law prevailed. Military bases were also subject to French law. As a result, Tonkin was Vietnamese territory with proverbial islands of French rule.[2] Under French law, the sale of sex was tolerated and loosely regulated in the French concessions, but beyond the city limits sex workers were free to operate outside of colonial law. The suburbs thus would become a major site for clandestine sex work.

As the French colonial government established control over Tonkin, it developed the region's transportation infrastructure. The state improved existing roads and canals while also building new ones that connected the provinces to Hanoi, the capital of Tonkin and, by the 1890s, the administrative seat of Indochina. In 1887, the colonial government began developing the port of Hải Phòng, which expanded opportunities for international commerce. In the 1890s, under Governor-General Paul Doumer, construction began on the railway linking Hanoi to Saigon. In 1902, the railway connected Hanoi to the sea by way of Hải Phòng. Two years later, the state began the construction of the railway connecting Hanoi to China, in Yunnan. These transportation-related innovations facilitated the migration—voluntary or forced—of women and girls around the delta, from the countryside to the cities, out to the port, and north to China. Improved roads enabled sex workers to become more mobile, making it easier for sex workers to flee the vice squad or abusive bosses. The labor force required to build and maintain the roads, railroads, and port provided a large customer base.

However much transportation was being developed in Tonkin, the provinces still lacked reliable transportation infrastructure for the most part. Rural areas continued to rely on dirt roads and waterways for transportation, thereby influencing trafficking patterns. Of the more than 250 cases of smuggling of women and girls that I examined, I found that human-trafficking activity decreased significantly in rural areas during the spring and summer months, while city abductions maintained the same rate. This is likely because spring and summer saw the highest rainfall, leaving dirt roads muddy and waterways flooded and difficult to navigate. Moreover, because summer months are the harvest months for rice, women were employed and families would have been less likely to resort to selling their daughters, who were needed to labor in the fields, during that season.

The Red River Delta

Poverty, overpopulation, and environmental disasters in the Red River Delta led women to migrate around the delta or into urban areas, where some joined the clandestine sex industry. The majority of the sex workers whom I identified in my research came from the rural areas of the Red River Delta, notably the overpopulated areas of Tonkin—Nam Định and Thái Bình in the southern area of the delta as well as Hưng Yên, which was inland. (see figure 2).[3] The poverty that these women were escaping was caused in part by the overpopulation of the delta.

Fertile land, as well as colonial medical and technological advancements, made the Red River Delta the most densely populated area in

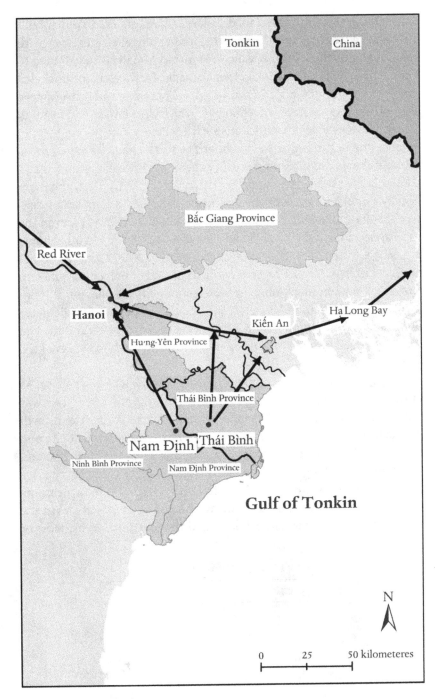

FIGURE 2. Red River Delta: Migration of sex workers

Indochina. Irrigation projects led to larger harvests, and French-built dikes allowed for food to be transported for famine relief. Moreover, with medical and technological advances, French colonialism contributed to a population increase in Tonkin. French medical advancements included smallpox vaccine and malaria control.[4] The French colonial government also introduced sanitation technology, which decreased the mortality rate of previously deadly afflictions such as cholera and plague.

Since the beginning of the twentieth century, the delta experienced considerable population pressure, but there was little expansion of cultivated lands aside from minor irrigation projects.[5] By 1921, the more heavily populated areas of the Red River Delta had a population density of 800 to 1,200 inhabitants per square kilometer.[6] In 1931, even the rural areas of the delta had a population of 6,500,000, or 380 inhabitants per square kilometer.[7] The delta, approximately 15,000 square kilometers, consisted of just 0.2 percent of the total land of Indochina but, with almost 7.5 million inhabitants in 1936, contained 32.6 percent of Indochina's total population.[8] By 1945, the population per square kilometer of the Red River Delta was double that of the Mekong Delta, and the Red River Delta had become one of the most densely populated areas of the world (see table 1.1).[9]

There was a fair degree of migration around the Red River Delta. As Li Tana has shown, during the colonial period, migration in Tonkin was multidirectional. Male and female peasants migrated back and forth between rural and urban areas. They also moved around the delta and from small farms to plantation zones, mining areas, or border towns. Migrations were long-term or seasonal, following the timing of the rice harvest.[10] As rice was harvested at different times in the delta, peasants migrated to follow the harvest.[11] Growing seasons drew workers to the high delta, then to the central delta and the low delta areas. Most of

Table 1.1   Population of Tonkin

YEAR	
1906	5,896,000
1911	6,120,000
1921	6,871,000
1932	7,325,000
1936	7,471,000

Source: Ng Shui Meng, "Population of Indochina," 33.

the migrating workers came from the southern coastal part of the delta, in particular Nam Định, Thái Bình, and Ninh Bình, the most populated areas of the delta. Such migration was facilitated by the new colonial transportation network of roads, fluvial streams, and railways.[12] Many migrants moved to plantation areas. In the late 1930s, the French government instituted a planned migration program that, among other things, exported workers from the delta to Annam and Cochinchina to address a perceived problem of population overload.[13] Other peasants migrated to urban areas. During the interwar years, Hanoi and Hải Phòng developed rapidly, and labor was in constant demand. From 1926 to 1930, 7,400 to 18,000 workers were recruited from Tonkin and Annam annually.[14] Stories of sex work follow these migration patterns. In the many cases of clandestine sex work and trafficking that I found in the sources, the most commonly traveled route was a triangle formed between the southern coastal area of Nam Định and Ninh Bình, the capital city Hanoi, and the major port at Hải Phòng. Consistent with this finding, records from the Hanoi Dispensary show that sex workers were often migrants from the rural poor areas of Tonkin.[15]

Colonial land policies further impoverished peasants, leading women to seek alternative income through sex work. Before colonization, Vietnamese land was largely communal. When the French took over Tonkin, they introduced a system to convert much of the village land to private property, though it was never fully realized. The colonial government rewarded French colonists with 198,000 hectares of land "concessions" in the northern section of the Tonkin Delta. The state also appropriated formerly village lands and rewarded the land to collaborating mandarins, some of whom, in turn, sold it off. Former inhabitants of the land were relegated to sharecroppers.[16] These landless peasants were impoverished and would regularly migrate with the growing seasons. They also took out large debts, many of which were repaid through debt bondage of themselves or debt bondage and prostitution of their daughters.[17]

Further impoverishing peasants were two colonial economic strategies. The colonial tax system directly taxed individuals and villages.[18] Moreover, colonial-imposed export-oriented monocrop farming had largely supplanted substance agriculture. By the twentieth century, rice was Tonkin's main agricultural product, and the colonial state exported more rice than it had for its peasantry to consume, shipping rice grown in Tonkin to less fertile areas of Annam and off to the international market.[19] Despite French efforts to prevent famine, the Red River Delta was plagued with a chronic food shortage, leaving women and girls desperate for money and subsistence. While the colonial government frequently shipped in rice from the Mekong Delta, high population density and poor distribution of food left many peasants malnourished. Peasants survived from harvest to harvest. Many borrowed money to make it through the next harvest, only to be paid through debt bondage. Others pawned their children's labor. Families often survived on as little as a bowl of soup per day.[20] The ranks of clandestine sex workers increased and decreased according to the harvest, according to French public health officials: with a good harvest, officials observed less sex work; with a feeble harvest, officials observed women approaching known madams for work or renting rooms for a few days in seedy boardinghouses (nhà xăm, nhà săm) where they would sell sex.[21]

Environmental and economic disasters during the interwar years led to large-scale migration to the cities, where many female migrants entered the sex industry. In the summer of 1926, flooding in Tonkin decimated the harvest and caused cholera outbreaks.[22] In 1928, rubber prices fell; the following year saw the deflation of the French franc. Bankruptcies and wild speculation followed. Rice exports decreased, and, by 1932, rubber prices had fallen to an all-time low. Tonkin, like much of the world, succumbed to the Great Depression, and the colonial government responded with only minor short-term or midterm solutions. Small planters were hit especially hard, and many lost their land. Peasants suffered disproportionately, and malnourishment abounded. Peasants flooded Hanoi in search of work, including desperate young women who moonlighted in the clandestine sex industry to avoid being forced to officially register on the police list of sex workers. Indochina only began to recover from the Depression in 1934, when Cochinchina's rice harvest boomed, enabling it to export rice to Tonkin, France, and various other foreign nations.[23] Yet economic recovery was uneven across Indochina and within Tonkin. Cities recovered more quickly than the countryside, leading more migrants to inundate the cities.

Hanoi

During the colonial period, the clandestine sex industry grew along with the rapid urbanization of Hanoi. On the Red River, the city was the center of riparian trade linking it to other areas of Tonkin. With roads connecting to the provincial capitals and trains arriving from Yunan, Lào

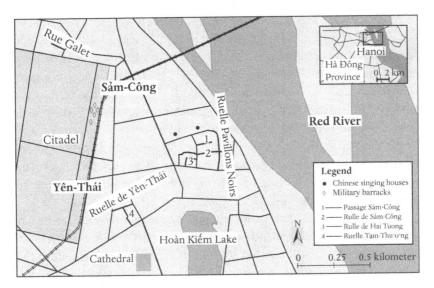

FIGURE 3. The 36 Streets section of Hanoi, also known as the Indigenous Quarter

Cai, Lạng Sơn, Vinh, and Annam, Hanoi was the transportation and trade nexus for Tonkin during the colonial period.[24]

Not surprisingly, Hanoi became a magnet for migrants. In 1880, just before the French established a concession of the city, there were roughly 50,000 inhabitants. France took Hanoi as a protectorate in 1885 and established it as a concession in 1888. In 1902, Hanoi was designated the capital of Indochina.[25] As the city developed its infrastructure, there was a demand for laborers to work at the construction sites, in factories, and on the railroad. By 1913, Hanoi had a population of 85,000 inhabitants, with an additional 30,000 in the surrounding suburbs.[26] The population of Hanoi proper reached almost 127,000 people in 1928,[27] and by 1940 it had grown to 200,000.[28]

From 1885 to 1895, the colonial government planned Hanoi to be a modern city, well-known for its grand hotels and elegant shops as well as simple luxuries of electricity, running water, sanitation, and electric tramways that crisscrossed the town. As the administrative capital of Tonkin as well as Indochina at large, Hanoi was the seat of the governor-general and other administrative officials, along with foreign embassies. Thanks to its proximity to natural resources and its large population base, Hanoi was the economic and industrial center of Tonkin.[29] By the 1920s, it had all the accoutrements of a modern city, including paved roads lined with ornate concrete buildings, as well as theaters, hotels, and cinemas.

As Hanoi was a French concession, French law tolerated and regulated sex work in the city. Although the city never had a reserved quarter for sex work, its government restricted locations in which sex could be sold. For example, it forbade registered brothels from setting up shop near schools or public edifices. Because landlords preferred not to rent to sex workers, brothels ended up operating out of dilapidated houses with poor sanitation and rent that was four to five times the market value.[30] The sex industry grew rapidly during the interwar years. In 1930, there were only twenty licensed brothels in the city;[31] by 1938 there were, by Roger Charbonnier's estimation, six hundred registered sex workers in the city and five thousand clandestine sex workers.[32]

Colonial Hanoi had two major population centers. On the northeastern end of the city was the Indigenous Quarter, north of Hoàn Kiếm Lake. The quarter was overpopulated: by 1907, it comprised 40 percent of the city land but housed 80 percent of the city's population.[33] This indigenous section of town had been walled until the 1920s, when the colonial government knocked down most of the walls; only two gates to the quarter remained standing. As Michael Vann writes, while other areas of Hanoi were modernizing rapidly, the colonial government "initiated a policy of neglect [of the Indigenous Quarter] in the name of preservation."[34] The buildings were left dilapidated, sanitation was poor, and traffic was often at a standstill.

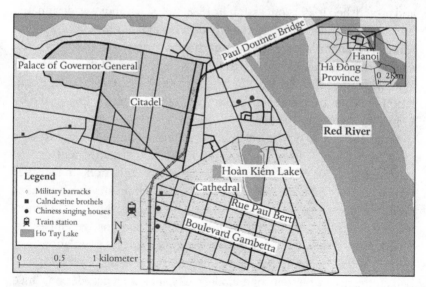

FIGURE 4. Hanoi: French Quarter

The Indigenous Quarter was also known as the 36 Streets section, with each street named after the products sold on it, including silk, rice, silver, sugar, and so forth. Residents of the Indigenous Quarter were mostly Vietnamese or Chinese. Its reputation as a center of clandestine sex work dated back at least to the 1890s. French colonists ventured into the Indigenous Quarter in hopes of fulfilling their erotic fantasies, what Vann called "the Chinatown Syndrome," where Asian enclaves in colonial cities "combined an alluring Oriental otherness and a titillating potential danger with the power of the white man to do what he liked."[35]

In 1930, there were two major centers for brothels in the Vietnamese section. The first section of registered brothels was in the Yên Thái area, including Ruelle de Yên Thái and Ruelle de Tạm Thương. The second section was the Sầm Công area, including Ruelle des Pavillons Noirs, Passage de Sầm Công, Ruelle de Sầm Công, Rue de Galet, Voie 18, and Ruelle de Hài Tượng.[36] Ả đào singing houses, many of which operated as clandestine brothels, were located on Hàng Đậu[37] and Rue de Papier, where there were sixteen houses in 1930, and on Route de Huế, where there were twenty-five houses in 1930.[38] In the 1930s, a considerable number of dance halls were located inside the Hanoi city limits, but a steep tax instituted in 1934 limited their profitability and drove them to the suburbs, where the regulation system did not apply. In 1938, Hanoi considered lowering the tax to lure them back after officials realized the tax had been an important source of revenue.[39]

To the south of Hoàn Kiếm Lake was the French Quarter, whose boundaries extended to the southern limit of the city and, in the 1920s, to the train station in the west and the Red River in the east (see figure 4). French colonists quickly populated the area south of Hoàn Kiếm Lake. In 1889, there were fewer than four hundred French residents in the city; by 1901, the number had risen to one thousand, and, by 1908, it had quadrupled to four thousand.[40] Although the area was known as the French Quarter, it housed a diverse group of Europeans, as well as some wealthy Asians, including Indians, and mixed-race families.[41]

Lined with ornate-façade buildings, meticulously manicured gardens, and arching trees, the French Quarter's chicest streets, Boulevard Gambetta and Rue Paul Bert, were said to be comparable in elegance to those of Paris.[42] The French Quarter also included a much less fashionable neighborhood in the vicinity of the train station. With its dodgy hotels and Chinese singing houses cramped into close quarters on Route Mandrine and Rue des Voiles,[43] clandestine brothels abounded. In 1930, the brothels were located on Ruelle de Nam Ngư, Ruelle de Hàng Thịt, and Passage de Sơn Tây.[44]

The northwestern section of the city was the site of the old Vietnamese citadel, but during the colonial period this section came to be known as the "new European Quarter."[45] This was the seat of Indochina's government, with the palace of the governor-general, government buildings, and foreign embassies. Here also were the city's lush botanical gardens and vibrant zoo. During the colonial period, this area of three hundred acres was occupied by the colonial military and surrounded by clandestine sex workers looking to take advantage of the large military customer base.[46]

Crowding the streets of Hanoi was a large itinerant workforce that helped shape the business of clandestine sex work. At all hours of the day, peddlers and vendors circumambulated the streets selling soup, hotcakes, rice porridge, sweets, flowers, kitchenware, and handicrafts from nearby villages. Barbers and tailors set up street stalls every few blocks, shoe shiners hovered in doorways, and flower vendors wandered about hoping to stumble on romantic customers or women looking to brighten a room in their home. As they were poor and often migrants from the countryside,[47] itinerant vendors often sought extra income in the criminal underworld stealing, smuggling contraband alcohol, and participating in the clandestine sex industry.[48] Some worked as sex workers themselves; others earned money by acting as intermediaries to connect clients with sex workers. Many itinerant vendors provided sex workers with support services, selling them food, transporting them around town, and, in some cases, serving as confidants of those who were being mistreated.

A particularly influential contingent of itinerant workers were rickshaw pullers. Introduced to Tonkin from China and Japan in the 1890s, rickshaws were sedan chairs set upon wheels in the back, with two poles held by the puller (coolie-pousse), typically a man twenty to forty years old, in the front. Rickshaws were initially intended for European customers, but as a Vietnamese middle class emerged, they came to be used by colonizer and colonized alike. Given their practicality, rickshaws quickly became ubiquitous throughout Hanoi, which by 1925 had twelve thousand rickshaw pullers. Yet the life of a rickshaw puller was notoriously difficult. The rickshaws they pulled weighed approximately two hundred pounds, not including the passenger. As they had to rent their rickshaws from a rickshaw company, pullers were left in debt if they failed to find customers or if customers could not pay the amounts due. In 1938, a puller netted only ten to fifteen cents per day after paying the rent on his rickshaw. Pullers often could not afford three meals a day and slept in their sedans between turns pulling customers at night.[49]

With their meager income, it is not surprising that many rickshaw pullers became involved in the clandestine sex industry.[50] They transported sex workers to boardinghouses to meet clients or pulled them around town looking for clients on the streets. Rickshaw pullers even introduced customers to pretty women and girls and found clients for madams. Pullers were particularly useful for the juvenile sex industry, an industry shrouded in secrecy. As clients had to be in the know to find adolescent girls, rickshaw pullers became intermediaries who introduced clients to the madams who controlled these girls.[51]

Some rickshaw pullers unwittingly participated in the search for clients. This scenario was captured in Nguyễn Công Hoan's 1931 short story "Người Ngựa Ngựa Người," in which he details the hardship of an impoverished rickshaw puller in Hanoi's 36 Streets section. A woman hired the puller by the hour, initially telling him she was looking for an acquaintance, but it turned out that she was searching for customers. The sex worker refused to pay him until she found a client, so the rickshaw puller ran her from boardinghouse to boardinghouse while she promised to pay him. In the end, she found a customer but skipped out on her payment.[52]

Another consequence of the unfettered urbanization that influenced the character of Hanoi's clandestine sex industry was the prevalence of cheap boardinghouses.[53] With the rapid development of Hanoi, there was not enough housing for all the workers who migrated to the city. Moreover, the French had torn down the city's many small wooden shacks in an effort to beautify the city according to French standards.[54] In response to the housing crisis, cheap boardinghouses popped up throughout the city; in 1938, one could rent a room in one for anywhere from one to three piastres.[55] They were ubiquitous, with one on every road in certain sections of the city.[56] Clusters of boardinghouses were located near Hanoi's train station and the citadel.[57] They were also commonly found near ả đào singing houses, dance halls, and markets. Although it was impossible to estimate how many unregistered boardinghouses were in business, by 1938 there were one hundred registered boardinghouses in Hanoi, with an average of six rooms each.[58] Only the street-facing rooms had windows, and ventilation was poor. The rooms were just big enough to fit a small bed, a nightstand, and a chamber pot or, in nicer boardinghouse, a sink; guests used common shower rooms or outdoor showers. Boarding-houses had a reputation for being squalid and rodent infested.

With their transient guests, cheap prices, and sketchy living condi-tions, boardinghouses quickly earned a bad reputation.[59] Those who stayed at them were seen as untrustworthy and associated with subver-sive activities. Some, such as the Thin Zel boardinghouse, were rumored to shelter revolutionaries with ties to the Chinese Kuomintang (KMT) and the Việt Nam Quốc Dân Đảng (VNQDĐ), a nationalist revolution-ary party.[60] More often, boardinghouses were associated with sex, with young unmarried couples renting a room for a day or night to escape the moralizing of their parents while exploring the pleasures of their bodies.[61] One member of the Hanoi municipal council called such board-inghouses a "dangerous instrument" that enabled youth to live a life of debauchery.[62]

Boardinghouses were also associated with sex work. One source described them as "veritable clandestine brothels."[63] The bellhops who worked at them, called *boys* in both French and Vietnamese what-ever their age, frequently served as intermediaries for clients and sex workers. Clients would request an introduction to a sex worker from a boardinghouse boy, who ran a prostitution ring himself or had business relationships with sex workers, madams, or rickshaw pullers, who in turn also had connections with sex workers. The process also worked in the reverse: clandestine sex workers found clients on the street, through rickshaw pullers, or at singing houses or dance halls and took them back to a boardinghouse.[64] Take, for example, the 1926 story of Minh Huong, a fifteen-year-old orphan who had taken refuge in a Miss Chung's house in Hải Phòng. Miss Chung forced her and another woman into sex work. Instead of receiving clients at the house, where they could be easily caught by the vice police, they went to a boardinghouse when a rick-shaw puller or boardinghouse boy had notified Miss Chung that there were clients waiting.[65] Many boardinghouses were located near markets so as to attract a large customer base, thereby enabling peasant women who took day trips to sell their vegetables in the market to earn extra income by serving as sex workers or as informal brokers. A customer signaled to a vendor that he was looking for a woman, the vendor con-nected him to one for a small fee, and the customer and sex worker car-ried out their business in a nearby boardinghouse.[66] So common was sex work in boardinghouses that from January to August 1922, 115 women were arrested in Hanoi for clandestine sex work in boardinghouses;

100 of them were infected with a venereal disease.[67] Similarly, in 1926, the majority of the 266 sex workers arrested in Hanoi were found working from boardinghouses.[68]

Boardinghouses were also sites of debt-bondage work. Women who went to meet lovers but could not pay the room bill frequently ended up being forced into sex work.[69] In 1937, journalist Thao Thao published a story in the newspaper *Việt Báo* about a Miss Lan, a beautiful woman from a poor family. Her one dream was to escape poverty. A wealthy man swept her off her feet with promises of riches and gifts of fashionable clothing. They had sex in a boardinghouse, and in the morning she awoke to find him gone—having taken all her clothes with him and leaving her with the bill. The owner of the boardinghouse forced her to pay off the debt through sex work.[70]

The colonial government had limited means of policing boardinghouses. As Hanoi's chief of police explained to the mayor in 1922, they were protected by French privacy laws, and state interference would violate the "principle of liberty of industry." Acknowledging that boardinghouses were prohibited from renting rooms to sex workers under paragraph 2 of article 475 of the penal code, he also noted that the penal code did not explicitly prohibit renters of rooms from bringing in sex workers as their guests. The vice police did stake out some of the city's boardinghouses to track sex workers, but they were often outsmarted by owners, guests, and sex workers who hid their operations with legal savvy or foiled police by privacy laws.[71]

On multiple occasions, the city government attempted to police boardinghouses by other means. In 1922, Hanoi's chief of police advised the mayor to order arrests of youth under twenty-one who had committed acts of debauchery and of those who had corrupted women and girls against their will, a reference to debt bondage and trafficking.[72] In 1926, the mayor considered restricting the number of boardinghouses allowed to operate in "respectable" neighborhoods.[73] In 1927, the resident superior of Tonkin, René Robin, admitted to trying to shut down boardinghouses or at least limit the number of boardinghouses within the city limits. He found that legally he could not do so, but he sent a warning to owners to remind them that it was illegal to rent to sex workers.[74] In 1930, city sanitation workers regularly inspected boardinghouses for public health code violations that would serve as justification to shut down establishments that were suspected sites for clandestine sex work.[75] In 1934, Dr. Bernard Joyeux, head of the Hanoi Dispensary, characterized boardinghouses as "a bastion of prostitution" and suggested they be closed "en masse" to conform with city sanitation laws.[76] In late 1937, the resident superior of Tonkin considered using antipimping laws to punish boardinghouse boys involved in promoting sex work, but he never had the legal power to close boardinghouses.[77]

With clandestine sex work taking place in boardinghouses, private homes, and other unsanctioned locations throughout the city, colonial authorities flirted with the idea of creating a reserved quarter in the city designated for sex work, as they had in Casablanca.[78] Such "reserved quarters" were easy to police and, as Julia Scriven Miller argues in the case of Morocco, medical surveillance of the sex industry was a form of political control and a means of ensuring the health of the colony's workers.[79] Moreover, as Manuel Aalbers and Magdalena Sabat have shown, sex industries themselves benefit from zoning measures for red-light districts. Most saliently, centralizing sex work in one area makes the industry visible and enables customers to locate the services they desire.[80] Colocating businesses would not have been outside the norm for Hanoi, as the 36 Streets section of the Indigenous Quarter was already organized by business product.

Colonial-era proposals for a reserved quarter called for a location close to the city's military barracks, train station, or tram station, areas already known for sex work. According to colonial proposals, the reserved quarter would have two rows of simple houses, where sex workers would be obligated to live and pay rent. They would pay subsidized rent, and the area would have telephones and be hygenic, with running water. Each room would include a bed, chair, sink, and toiletries with the necessary prophylactics. Posters would hang on the walls teaching sex workers and clients how to identify venereal infections and how to prevent contamination. The quarter would include a police station at one end and a military post at the other. Such a reserved quarter would allow the Bureau of Health Services to apply prophylactic measures and "rid the population" of the "embarrassing neighborhood" where sex workers intermingled with respectable residents.[81]

The idea for a reserved quarter was brought up multiple times during the colonial period. In 1926, the vice squad proposed a reserved quarter on the grounds that it would be easier for the vice police to regulate sex workers more effectively if they were colocated in one or two sections of the city, rather than in brothels spread out randomly throughout the city. In 1931, the resident superior of Tonkin formed a commission to consider creating a reserved quarter near the military barracks of the citadel.[82] In 1932, the Vietnamese charity society Hợp Thiện (literally, Charity) cited Morocco as an example when they proposed a building project of apartments for sex workers, presumably to help the sex workers avoid exploitative debt-bondage contracts (to be discussed in chapter 3).[83] In 1934, the city of Saigon established a reserved quarter.[84] That same year, at the meeting of the Subcommittee on Venereal Disease Prophylaxie, Dr. Joyeux suggested creating a center of entertainment with a brewery, surrounded by boutiques and registered brothels, by Rue Lambert.[85] In 1943, after Vietnamese residents complained about the prospect of a registered brothel in their neighborhood, the Commission for Disease Prophylaxis returned to the idea of a reserved quarter.[86]

A reserved quarter never came to fruition in Hanoi for multiple reasons. In 1932, Hợp Thiện's proposal was rejected on grounds that sex workers living in close proximity might exacerbate the spread of venereal diseases. Of course, colocating sex workers would only result in the spread of venereal diseases if sex workers shared clients, and because men experience long refractory periods that typically rendered them unable to have sex with more than one partner in a night, this scenario was no more likely than if the brothels were located separately.[87] The 1934 proposal was rejected because officials feared that military men would not frequent reserved quarters and instead continue to frequent clandestine sex workers.[88] The 1943 proposal, for its part, was rejected on the principled grounds that a reserved quarter would limit individual liberties.[89]

Hanoi's Suburbs

As Hanoi's population grew, exacerbating its housing crisis, the population spilled over to form a suburban ring around the city (see figure 5). The 1884 Treaty of Huế designated the provinces as protectorates; as such, they were governed by Vietnamese law. However, per the royal ordinance of 1888 that ceded Hanoi to the French, the city was under direct colonial rule. The boundary between the city and its suburbs thus resulted in different laws governing the two realms. As Philippe Papin points out, a Vietnamese person in the city was not subject to the same laws that governed his cousins in the countryside.[90] This fact was not lost on suburbanites, many of whom had settled just outside the city limits in order to access the city's amenities while evading colonial law.

As the colonial government never invested in the suburbs, they became rundown sites of poverty, lacking the beautification and modern amenities afforded to Hanoi proper.[91] Without Hanoi's carefully manicured

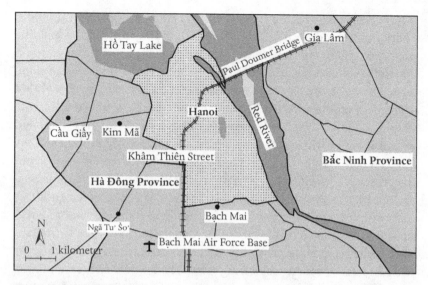

FIGURE 5. Hanoi and suburbs

canopy of trees shading the streets, suburban pedestrians baked in the summer sun and choked on dust kicked up by cars traveling into and out of the city. Yet the suburbs were not a wholly distinct realm; they were instead a liminal space, a hybrid where what was deemed as "modern," cosmopolitan, wealthy city life coexisted or even melded with what was deemed as "traditional" culture and rural poverty. Those living on the edge of urban life participated in traditional, rural life as well as modern, urban life. They had constant interactions with their wealthy city neighbors: they ventured into the city to buy imported goods or for the nightlife, and city folk came out to the suburbs to do likewise. Denizens of the suburbs artfully deployed either traditional or modern culture to their advantage.[92] This is apparent in the sex market where sex workers capitalized on both "tradition" and "modernity," according to clients' sexual preferences. Take, for example, Khâm Thiên Street, where a "traditional" á đào house featuring songstresses crooning lyrics from ancient Chinese poetry could be found right next door to a modern-style, art deco–inspired dance hall blasting the latest songs from Europe and America. A mere outfit change enabled sex workers to pop in and out of singing houses and dance clubs, which were often under the same ownership.

Since French rule was limited to the concessions, the suburbs were a haven for those seeking to avoid French law, notably unregistered sex workers. As Vann notes, by creating two separate legal realms, the colonial administration limited its ability to control Hanoi's suburbs in the same way it controlled Hanoi proper.[93] To the colonial government, the suburbs were a frontier zone, a "threat to the social order" of the city, much as the Paris suburbs were to that metropolitan city.[94] Policing the suburbs was complicated. Hanoi had the most advanced police force in Tonkin, stacked with bilingual officers who had access to modern technologies and freely deployed French law to herd the urban population into French norms of civility. The city also had a vice squad that arrested clandestine sex workers, followed leads for venereal disease infections, and verified the age and registration of brothel workers. Because French law extended only to the city limits, however, the provinces were run by a different police system, the gendarmerie, a form of military police that enforced Vietnamese law. While some provincial gendarmerie had vice squads, they were poorly funded and minimally staffed, often with only a couple of officers. Moreover, clandestine sex work was not enough of a priority for colonial police to find alternative means to pursue cases into the provinces, as they did for more serious political matters such as anticolonial activities or alcohol bootlegging.

As land outside the Hanoi city limits was ruled by Vietnamese law and hence not subject to French laws or policing, savvy sex workers set up shop just outside the city to benefit from the urban center's large customer base while avoiding its laws. Moreover, the suburbs, on the edge of a large city population, provided the necessary anonymity for women looking to lead double lives in which they temporarily sold sex without tarnishing their reputation back in their home village. It also allowed for city folk to travel to the edge of the urban sprawl, where they could keep the darker side of their sex lives private. With so much sex work in the suburbs, one public health inspector referred to the suburbs of Hanoi as "the belt of Venus that crowns the suburbs of Hanoi and the other urban zones of Tonkin."[95] A similar phenomenon of sex workers surrounding cities appeared in French colonial Morocco.[96] In 1938, Dr. Joyeux identified six main neighborhoods for sex work in the suburban areas of Hanoi: Bạch Mai, Khâm Thiên Street, Ngã Tư Sở / Vĩnh Hồ, Gia Lâm, Kim Mã, and Cầu Giáy (see table 1.2).

Directly south of Hanoi's Hoàn Kiếm Lake, just seven hundred meters outside the city gates, was the Bạch Mai neighborhood, which includes the crossroads of Bạch Mai and Trung Kiên in Hà Đông Province. This area was near the Bạch Mai Air Force Base, home to Indochina's first squadron, thus providing a built-in clientele for sex workers.[97] Congested with traffic and known as an area of "urban anarchy," the Bạch Mai neighborhood was considered one of the most important zones for clandestine

Table 1.2 Clandestine sex work in Hanoi's suburbs, 1937–38

	1937	1937	1938	1938
	CLANDESTINE BROTHELS	SEX WORKERS	CLANDESTINE BROTHELS	SEX WORKERS
Khâm Thiên	41	244	35	201
Bạch Mai	47	226	71	310
Ngã Tư Sở / Vĩnh Hồ	59	248	75	261
Gia Lâm	36	181	35	186
Total	183	899	216	958
Increase in 1938			33	59

Source: Virgitti and Joyeux, *Le péril vénérien,* introduction.

sex work and was frequented by French, Vietnamese, and Chinese men alike. It was also known to authorities as a market for "goods forbidden by the health services," likely meaning condoms and other forms of birth control that were contraband in French territory.[98] The neighborhood was congested with traffic, the streets were dirty, and the shacks and buildings, made of brick, cob, and palm leaves, were dilapidated. In 1938, the neighborhood included thirty-five å đào houses and two boarding-houses, the Mai Vien and the Sinh Loi. Only two hundred meters down the road at the corner of Trung Hien Street were a few houses with iso-lated sex workers, some small shacks where singers lived, and a board-inghouse, the Mai Lam. A little farther down the road were twenty-two more houses. At the next intersection were fifty-seven more brothels. In total, there were roughly 400 women living in clandestine brothels and another 250 sex workers operating in the area, not including singers or taxi dancers.[99]

Farther westward along Hanoi's border, in Hà Đông Province, was Khâm Thiên Street, the infamous "good times street" (*phố ăn chơi*) known for å đào singing houses as well as dance halls, casinos, opium dens, and boardinghouses (see figure 6).[100] Khâm Thiên ran one kilometer from the buildings south of the train station to Thái Hà Ấp, at the crossroads of Ô Chợ Dừa. On the maps since 1831, Khâm Thiên Street originally ran through agricultural hamlets that would become the twenty-six alley-ways that darted off the main road.[101] By the early colonial period, it had become a busy road roaring with traffic that resulted in thick dust clouds. With few trees to provide shade, summers on Khâm Thiên were unbearable. Electric cables propped up on poles lined both sides of the

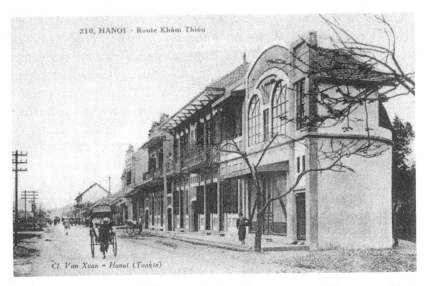

FIGURE 6. Undated postcard showing Khâm Thiên Street, with rickshaws on and along-side it. From author's personal collection (purchased at a flea market in Paris).

road, along with row after row of two-story houses. The houses were narrow—only six to seven meters wide—possessed neither street-side doors nor sewers, and failed to meet sanitation codes. The majority lacked running water; residents gathered at street corners, where water taps were located, to bathe or drink.[102]

Khâm Thiên was the most famous district for colonial-era ả đào singing houses that offered sex work. During that time, the road was described as an "unbroken line of [singing] houses." In 1938, Mayor M. H. Virgitti and Dr. Joyeux estimated that there were forty houses with two hundred singers as well as five dance halls (Casino, Déesa, Étoile, Feéric, and Pagode) with fifty taxi dancers, dance schools, and two boarding-houses. The price to listen to ả đào singing was much higher on Khâm Thiên than in any other neighborhood.[103]

During the day, the buildings on Khâm Thiên Street appeared unas-suming, but when the sun set each day, the street quickly grew animated. Houses that had been silent during the day flicked on their lights and opened their doors. Street hawkers descended upon the road, selling peanuts, rice porridge, and steamed cakes—all typical late-night drink-ing snacks.

Chauffeur-driven automobiles dropped off wealthy customers—typically mandarins or French civil servants or businessmen—then parked in a line, waiting until the early hours of the morning to return the men home to their respectable neighborhoods in the city or to their manors in the country. Shoe shiners huddled by the cars, hoping to nab a rich client. Walking down the street, one could smell patrons' opium and the cheap perfume of ả đào singers who performed to the beat of a drum and accompanying lute. Drunk, sweaty couples stumbled out of dance halls, their faces smeared with lipstick. From the street, one could hear Western songs such as "J'ai deux amours" or "Nuit chinoise" playing on gramophones inside the dance halls.[104] French Foreign Legion soldiers tried to convince—or pay—singers and taxi dancers to spend the night with them. Young unmarried couples trying to preserve their reputation attempted to slip unnoticed inside the doors of Khâm Thiên's many boardinghouses, and men looking to hire underage girls were ushered into secret back rooms.

Moving west along the city's edge in Đống Đa, along the intersection of Route Soeur Antoine and Route Thái Hà Ấp (Colonial Route 6), joining Khâm Thiên Street, was the Ngã Tư Sở / Thái Hà Ấp neighborhood. The area was formerly part of the verdant residence of Hoàng Cao Khải, who, in the late nineteenth century, was granted a land concession and viceroy position by the French after he helped suppress the royalist Cần Vương movement.[105] By the 1930s, Ngã Tư Sở / Thái Hà Ấp had become a bustling neighborhood, crowded with boardinghouses out of which clandestine sex workers operated. A center for black market sex work developed along Route Thái Hà Ấp, near the traffic circle. According to public health reports, in 1938, the Thái Hà Ấp neighborhood had fifty-eight ả đào singing houses made of brick, as well as a number of surrounding shacks that housed more than two hundred singers. This area drew an upper-middle class Vietnamese clientele, including civil servants and shop employees. By 1943, the Ngã Tư Sở / Thái Hà Ấp neighborhood was home to 126 ả đào houses.[106]

Farther southwest were the Kim Mã and Cầu Giấy neighborhoods in Ba Đình, southwest of the citadel and the "new French Quarter." In 1938, Kim Mã had twenty ả đào houses with seventy-five singers. The Cầu Giấy neighborhood had five clandestine brothels with twenty sex workers. Due to its proximity to a military post, it was frequented by European civilians and military personnel. Poorer Vietnamese men reportedly avoided brothels in this area, not wanting to interact with European military men.[107]

Across the river from Hanoi and over the Paul Doumer Bridge, in Bắc Ninh Province, was Gia Lâm, the railroad gateway to Hanoi. Rail lines coming from the east, north, and west met at Gia Lâm before slowly making their way over the river into the capital. Gia Lâm was also the point where the Yunnan and Lang Son lines separated. As a nexus for rail lines, Gia Lâm was a site for traffickers looking to transport victims by rail to China. Because the area was an important train depot, there was a high population of railroad workers, who formed the bulk of the clientele of sex workers in the villages of Thường Cải and Gia Quất. Thường Cải was the site of twelve brothels and eighty sex workers; Gia Quất had eighteen singing houses, with eighty singers.[108]

Hải Phòng City

The rapid industrialization and urbanization of the port city of Hải Phòng made it a hot spot for clandestine sex work and human trafficking. With access to both the coastal and inland water networks, it was a site of strategic importance in colonial Vietnam (see figure 7). The port itself was on the Cửa Cấm tributary of the Thái Bình River, twenty miles inland from the mouth of the Cửa Cấm, where it opens to the Gulf of Tonkin. Originally a fishing village called Ninh Hải, it became a French possession under the treaty of March 15, 1874, which gave France a concession of thirteen hectares of land between the Cửa Cấm and Tam Bạc Rivers and opened the port to foreign trade. Hải Phòng began to grow, but in 1881 a typhoon devastated the area, leaving the colonial government to rebuild the city.

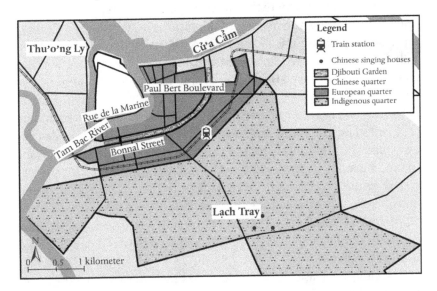

FIGURE 7. Hải Phòng and suburbs

In 1884, the French military founded a base at Hải Phòng, whose sailors would form the bulk of the clientele for local brothels. In 1886, the French colonial government began constructing the first docks on the port, and, in 1888, a Vietnamese royal ordinance established Hải Phòng as a concession of France and thus subject to French laws. The sale of sex, therefore, was legal and regulated in the city of Hải Phòng, but, as in the case of Hanoi, a ring of unregistered brothels in the provincial suburbs encircled it, just out of the reach of colonial jurisdiction.[109]

With its rapid urbanization, Hải Phòng attracted migrant labor. In the process of rebuilding the city in the 1880s, the colonial government dug a network of canals to drain the marshland on which the city was built and to connect Hải Phòng to the Thái Bình River. That same year, the city built the Bonnal Canal, which connected the Tam Bạc River with the Cửa Cấm River.[110] But the Cửa Cấm River and its port were prone to building up silt, requiring constant dredging, a laborious job that attracted many migrants from the Tonkin countryside. The dredgers, who were both male and female, provided a male clientele base along with female sex workers looking to supplement the meager income offered for manual labor.[111]

With Hải Phòng's strategic location and port, as well as its proximity to the Hòn Gai coal mines, the city quickly grew to become Tonkin's industrial center. In the city and its environs were a brewery, an electric company, glassworks, a button factory, rice and textile mills, a cement factory that employed more than four thousand workers, and the Tonkin Shipping Company (Companie Tonkinoise de Navigation).[112] Further enriching Hải Phòng was its status as a transportation hub. In 1902, a railroad connected it to Hanoi and Yunnan. In the 1930s, three trains ran daily between Hanoi and Hải Phòng, a three-hour trip. Streamliners took passengers to Hong Kong and Saigon, from which they could connect with steamers headed to Europe.[113] Connected by waterways to important cities and provincial capitals, the city developed into a trade center,[114] and the port quickly grew to become the second most important in Indochina, after Saigon. Hải Phòng became the hub for coal transportation, connecting the Hòn Gai coal mines to the rest of Indochina and elsewhere in East Asia. By 1923, the port of Hải Phòng was responsible for 23 percent of Indochina's international trade.[115] Import-export trading companies brought wealth to the city's many international banks and lending companies.

The city's population grew rapidly, making it the second most populated city in Tonkin. In 1877, there were only a little more than 6,000 residents in Hải Phòng. By 1885, the city had grown to 10,000 residents, and, by 1900, there were more than 16,000 residents. By 1926, with 100,473 residents, the population of Hải Phòng was roughly equal to that of Hanoi and slightly smaller than Saigon's.[116] In 1931, Hải Phòng's population was recorded at 124,000, but because the city was hit particularly hard by the Great Depression, the population fell to 70,000 by 1936.[117] Aerial bombings by Allied forces during World War II led Hải Phòng's residents to flee for shelter in the countryside, and by 1941 the city's population had fallen to 65,413.[118]

Migrants to Hải Phòng found a bustling city. The city rebuilt after the 1881 typhoon had European architecture, running water, and electricity. As Tonkin's center of industry and commerce, Hải Phòng was a wealthy town, and its international residents made for a cosmopolitan city, with consulates representing England, Siam, Norway, Russia, and Belgium.[119] The city was rather diverse, with a majority Vietnamese population, a small European population, sailors from all corners of the French Empire, and a sizeable population of both resident and temporary Chinese. The city's architecture included a mosque and a Hindu temple in the center of town, hinting at a considerable South Asian population and migrants from Island Southeast Asia.

Newcomers found work at the shipyards, in the factories, or on any of the constant public works projects to dig canals or dredge shipping lanes. Yet this manual labor, for which women as well as men were employed, was arduous. Laborers shivered in the damp winter and baked in the summer sun, and employees at the cement factory periodically fell to an entombed death. It is not hard to see why some women chose sex work over manual-labor jobs.

The city also had a reputation for late-night debauchery. Hải Phòng was well known for its ả đào singing houses and dance halls.[120] In 1930, Dr. Paul Bodros, director of the Hải Phòng Bureau of Health Services, reported that there were 136 registered sex workers and 2,000 clandestine sex workers.[121] In 1934, there were twenty-one registered brothels.[122] In 1943, the city considered creating a reserved quarter called a *centre d'attractions*, for singing houses, cafés, and dance halls, but, as in the case of Hanoi, this never came to fruition.[123]

The city itself comprised three zones. The Indigenous Quarter was in its northern section, between the roads leading to Đồ Sơn and Kiến An.[124] The Thương Lý neighborhood, on the edge of the Indigenous Quarter, was home to ả đào singing houses.[125] The European Quarter was located near the Canal de Ceinture, flanking Paul Bert Boulevard. Named for its architecture, the European Quarter was actually quite diverse, with a majority European population but also numerous Vietnamese, Chinese, Indian, and mixed-race residents. Situated at the site of the original village of Ninh Hải, the European Quarter was the administrative center of Hải Phòng. There one could find all the amenities of a French colonial city, including a mayor's office, an elaborately decorated theater, a hospital with a venereal disease clinic out back, schools, banks, and markets. Central to the European Quarter was Paul Bert Boulevard, which presented a striking contrast to the poverty-stricken native quarter. It was a "handsome, modern street, both sides of which [were] lined by European buildings, including a Catholic church, the government house, the chamber of commerce, law courts, and barracks."[126]

The European Quarter, however, did have its poverty and black market sex work. Avenue de Belgique, which stretched from the train station to the docks, was home to the city's poorest residents, including Vietnamese coolies, street hawkers, and small shop owners.[127] It was well-known for legal as well as clandestine brothels, many of which held kidnapped women.[128] Sex workers who lived on Avenue de Belgique went to wealthier parts of the French Quarter, such as Bonnal Street and Caron Bridge, to solicit rich customers on the street.[129] As in Hanoi, in downtown Hải Phòng, itinerant vendors and rickshaw pullers circulated the streets, connecting sex workers and clients under the police radar. South of the train station and just outside the colonial-era city limits, the neighborhood of the Lạch Tray River was home to the city's many ả đào singing houses.[130]

The other nexus for sex work, Rue de la Marine,[131] was located in the Chinese Quarter, which encompassed the area between the wharves of the Tam Bạc River and the Bonnal Canal. It was a loud, busy section of town crowded with "forests of boat masts, . . . [and] a multitude of *junk* ships and small boats,"[132] and it smelled of newly caught fish, cigarettes, and the opium smoke that wafted from its many clandestine dens. In 1932, Rue de la Marine was home to 127 known sex workers.[133] That same year, Dr. Bodros identified clandestine sex workers on Rue de Marine as the source of an outbreak among French military troops stationed in the city.[134] Two years later, a public health report listed the brothels on Rue de la Marine as catering to "the lowest class of the population," including rickshaw pullers, ferry captains, boat men, and longshoremen.[135]

Venereal diseases were rampant in the Hải Phòng area. As a port city and naval base, Hải Phòng had a large military population. The transient nature of military personnel, naval commerce, and travelers increased

Table 1.3 Venereal disease exams in Hải Phòng, 1940–42

	REGISTERED SEX WORKERS	AFTER RAIDS OF CLANDESTINE BROTHELS
1940	538	360
1941	400	840
1942	150	1,300

the circulation of venereal infections. After World War I, as the French military repositioned its forces, new sailors arrived in Hải Phòng, some of whom introduced fresh venereal infections to the city, while others were infected by local women. Venereal infections in Hải Phòng proliferated so quickly that in 1920 the mayor of Hải Phòng alerted the resident superior of Tonkin, thereby helping set in motion the drafting of a law later that year establishing a uniform prostitution code (discussed in chapter 2).[136] Statistics from 1930 and 1934 show colonial doctors treated almost thirteen thousand cases of venereal diseases per year.[137] From 1940 to 1942, the mayor's office reported a decrease in the number of sex workers visiting the dispensary for their regular venereal exams but also an increase in the number of women arrested in raids of clandestine brothels and forced to submit to venereal exams (see table 1.3).[138] Desperate to stop the spread of venereal diseases, in 1942, authorities required waitresses in tea houses in suburban Hải Phòng to submit to venereal exams.[139]

Maritime Networks of Trafficking in Coastal Tonkin

Unique geological features, busy international ports, and proximity to China made the Gulf of Tonkin a central location for trafficking for sex work. Situated along the coast of Tonkin and southern China, the Gulf of Tonkin includes the deepwater ports of Hải Phòng and Cẩm Phả, Hạ Long Bay, as well as the towns of Hạ Long, Cẩm Phả, and Móng Cái, on the border with China (see figure 8). Along the northern coast of the gulf are roughly two thousand limestone islands, many of which have long, deep caves providing ample cover for those looking to hide from authorities.

In the late colonial period, traffickers crisscrossed the gulf, transporting victims from port to port and eventually to markets in China.

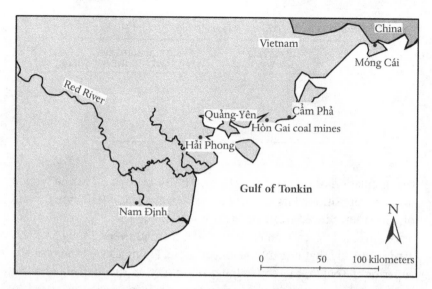

FIGURE 8. Hạ Long Bay area

Traffickers with larger ships hid among the islands in Hạ Long Bay; smaller boats could not survive in the rough waters and needed to hug the coast. They made multiple stops along the coast, often to pick up more victims.

Kidnappers abducted women not just in Hải Phòng but also in rural coastal provinces such as Quảng Yên and Nam Định,[140] subsequently transporting them to Hải Phòng. From Hải Phòng, kidnappers took victims by boat to other coastal ports such as Cửa Ông,[141] Cẩm Phả,[142] or Móng Cái, ultimately selling them to markets in China. In 1928, the newspaper *Trung Hoà Nhật Báo* printed a story about the "epidemic" of people being kidnapped, especially along the road to Móng Cái, and then being trafficked north to China.[143] A 1930 article from the same newspaper reported that police had arrested Trần Văn Tẻo for kidnapping a child whom he then sold to Chinese traffickers.[144]

In 1936, *Việt Báo* covered case of a twenty-two-year-old woman, Nguyễn Thị Lợi, and an eight-year-old girl, Thị Hoà, a case that illustrates the clever use of maritime geography. Like many peasants from the overpopulated and poverty-ravaged Red River Delta, the pair migrated to Nam Định City in search of employment, hoping to find shelter with a relative. Soon, however, they found themselves destitute and desperate for income. Their fortunes seemingly took a turn for the better when they met Nguyễn Thị Nghĩa and Nguyễn Thị Tý, two kindly older women who offered Nguyễn Thị Lợi a job as a domestic servant and promised to adopt Thị Hoà. As it turned out, however, Nguyễn Thị Nghĩa and Nguyễn Thị Tý were mẹ mìn, and the group was about to embark on a long and arduous journey to China where Nguyễn Thị Lợi and Thị Hoà would be sold into the sex industry. The older women transferred the young pair onto a boat to Hải Phòng. The group continued north in a small boat, hugging the coast to avoid being questioned by French maritime customs officers and occasionally taking cover among the islands of Hạ Long Bay. They stopped at Cẩm Phả, the busy coal-mining port, where they were transferred to a boat piloted by Chéong Sy Tche. The three traffickers then took Nguyễn thị Lợi and Thị Hoà to Móng Cái, the last port on the Tonkin side of the border with China. There, the traffickers aimed to sell them to one of China's many networks for trafficking women and girls. The victims only came into luck when authorities intercepted the boat, arrested the kidnappers, and set Nguyễn Thị Lợi and Thị Hoà free.[145]

Hải Phòng, a junction port for railroad and maritime transportation, was a central location for trafficking. In 1937 alone, more than 1.2 million tons of goods passed through the port on ships and trains.[146] Meanwhile, women from the countryside were kidnapped and brought into the city to be trafficked on the many trains and ships arriving and departing each day.[147] Newspapers of the day sounded the alarm about the frequency with which young girls went missing.[148] For its part, the colonial government deployed maritime customs officers to search ships from the port for trafficking victims, but, as we shall see in chapter 3, crime syndicates seemingly always managed to evade authorities.

The center of Hải Phòng's trafficking market was the Djibouti Garden. Located at the site of the former Bonnan Canal, which had been filled in 1925, it was a long strip of land that ran between Rue Courbet and Rue Bắc Ninh, snaking through the center of town. The place was a gathering spot for those looking for work and a first stop for migrants from the provincial countryside coming to the city. In the Djibouti Garden, workers could find jobs as day laborers for construction projects, household servants, wet nurses, rickshaw pullers, servant girls in wealthy houses, or servant boys in hotels.[149] But it was a garden in name only. With its rock-hard dirt, garbage, horse manure, frequent sewage floods, and nary a flower in sight, Djibouti Garden was best avoided. In his memoirs of growing up in Hải Phòng, author Nguyên Hồng described it as a gathering place for thieves and clandestine sex workers.[150] Men preyed on young girls, unregistered sex workers propositioned potential clients, and mẹ mìn trolled for victims to abduct.[151] The so-called garden, an easy half-mile walk from the port, was so notorious for human trafficking that it was nicknamed *chợ đưa người*, meaning "the market to trade people," and newspapers regularly warned readers about instances of older women—likely mẹ mìn—scouting the market, looking for prey.[152] Girls such as seventeen-year-old Bùi Thị Bảo, whose story was reported by *Ngọ Báo* in 1935, were kidnapped there and forced into sex work.[153]

Leaving Hải Phòng and traveling to Hòn Gai, one follows the Cửa Cấm River, where, as a 1920 source described, "the banks sometimes come close together, reducing the stream to a very narrow channel, while the river runs in an S-shaped course, making many meanderings and thus cutting its way through an extensive delta plain, covered by a thick growth of brushwood."[154] These murky backwaters proved to be an ideal route on which to surreptitiously transport trafficked victims. By the late 1930s, at the site of the Quảng Yên coal basin, more than forty thousand workers were mining the coal pits in Hòn Gai, providing a client base for sex workers. Unlike Hanoi, Hải Phòng, and military bases, which were French concessions per the 1888 treaty, Hòn Gai had remained a Vietnamese territory and thus not subject to the 1921 French law regulating sex work. However, shortly after the passage of that law, authorities attempting to regulate sex work and police trafficking made the case that the mining center at Hòn Gai, insofar as it was privately owned by the Société Française des Charbonnages du Tonkin (French Coal Company of Tonkin), was actually French territory. By this same logic, mining centers at Hòn Gai, Hà Tu, and Cẩm Phả, as well as Cẩm Phả port, were likewise argued to be French territory and thus subject to the 1921 law regulating sex work.[155]

Coal from Hòn Gai was transported to Cẩm Phả, a busy deepwater port nearby, from which it was transported all over the world. Although equal to Hải Phòng in shipping volume,[156] Cẩm Phả was mainly a commercial port and thus lacked the police scrutiny of Hải Phòng, a busy immigration port. With fewer security forces, Cẩm Phả was an important site for trafficking women, both out of Tonkin and into China, and also into Hòn Gai to serve the miners in the coal fields.[157]

Still farther north along the coast was the seaside city of Móng Cái, closest to the border with China. Because of its proximity to the border, Móng Cái was typically the last stop that traffickers made before crossing into Chinese waters. In 1930, for example, police apprehended two mẹ mìn transporting five young women from Quảng Yên to China through Móng Cái.[158] Similarly, in 1936, vice squad agents arrested a mẹ mìn who had stopped in Móng Cái on her way north to sell a girl into the sex markets in China.[159] Traffickers also took women and girls from the streets of Móng Cái. So frequent were abductions in Móng Cái that parents in that city were afraid to let their children play outside.[160]

Military Bases

Military bases were popular sites for sex workers to gather. For one thing, the influx of military men resulted in a severe gender imbalance in regions where the bases were located. Sex workers, of course, benefited from the large clientele that resulted. The gender imbalance quickly reversed itself as women flooded into the military zones. Vietnamese journalist Vũ Trọng Phụng, who wrote prolifically about sex work on military bases, estimated that for every three hundred soldiers or sailors, there were three hundred and fifty women, fifty of whom were "unemployed," indicating the volume of sex workers who flocked to military bases.[161] Although they were not wealthy, military men did have a steady income with paid housing and food, leaving them with some disposable income. Moreover, late nights of drinking, entertainment, and flirting with women were a regular part of life for soldiers and sailors stationed in Tonkin.

Given that military bases were considered French territory, they were subject to the 1921 law that regulated sex work.[162] The colonial state permitted brothels on bases, provided the brothels were located more than five hundred meters from villages. For example, when a local man petitioned to have a brothel opened at the base in Chapa in 1933, the French resident rejected the request on the basis of its proximity to a village.[163]

As for military commanders, they welcomed the presence of registered brothels and even invited brothel owners to set up shop at bases. The idea was that registered brothels that catered to an exclusive military clientele would forestall the spread of venereal diseases by carefully monitoring registered sex workers and preventing personnel from having sex with clandestine sex work. The following story illustrates the lengths to which military would go to keep on-site brothels in business. In 1932, a military commander asked businessman Henri Delevaux to open a brothel to service an exclusively military clientele in the Tông–Sơn Tây area.[164] In 1934, when Delevaux was considering closing the brothel due to financial problems, a General Verdier, the commander of the indigenous troops, stepped in to save his business. General Verdier appealed to the resident superior of Tonkin, warning that without government aid to help Delevaux maintain his registered brothel, clandestine sex work would proliferate—as would venereal diseases. The general requested a tax exemption for Delevaux's business and insisted that the colonial government take "extreme measures" to crack down on the illicit sale of sex.[165] It was not clear from the historical sources what—if any—measures were taken.

Sex workers who wanted to avoid the regulation system set up clandestine brothels just outside the limits of military bases, where they could enjoy the benefits of a nearby clientele without the regulations of French law. In 1937, when a military unit arrived at Tiên Yên, a group of sex workers and alcohol traffickers immediately flooded the area outside of the military camp.[166] Similarly, in late 1938, Route de Ngọc Hà, located just outside the Hanoi city limits and near a military barracks, was home to a handful of clandestine brothels as well as 125 Vietnamese wives of military men, women whom Mayor Virgitti and Dr. Joyeux assumed were sex workers.[167]

Paid sex was popular among military men. As one French medical student observed in 1938, "the unmarried soldier, on a thin salary, far from home, could still ... find these young women done up with makeup, sweet talking, with their crepe paper turban, the illusion of this nonchalant Far Eastern beauty that is extoled in novels."[168] Soldiers from Europe, French African colonies, and Martinique frequented brothels just outside the bases, often arriving in large groups after a night of drinking. They were known to be a "terror" for sex workers: they arrived drunk, yelling and screaming, shoving and breaking furniture. They frequently lost their temper when they could not find the woman they wanted or when the language barrier rendered them unable to communicate with brothel owners or sex workers. Some soldiers and sailors reportedly demanded "abnormal sex," a euphemism for anal sex. Some women acquiesced because the men paid well; those who resisted were brutally raped.[169] Military bases and the surrounding villages had high rates of venereal diseases. Particularly bad outbreaks, such as a 1924 outbreak among legionnaires in Yên Bái and a 1936 outbreak among European troops throughout Tonkin, were reported up the chain of command to the resident superior of Tonkin.[170]

A serious concern for the military were *me tây*, Vietnamese women who lived with European soldiers as temporary wives. Although me tây, whose existence was made famous in Vũ Trọng Phụng's book, *Kỹ nghệ lấy tây* [The industry of marrying Westerners],[171] did not technically engage in the kind of sex regulated by the 1921 law, colonial authorities believed that unmarried cohabitation between a Vietnamese woman and a European or African military man was tantamount to sex work, with one French resident justifying this claim on grounds that me tây were "at the service of European soldiers."[172] A military doctor named Augier warned colonial officials that me tây were women of "dubious origins" who had likely worked as prostitutes and been infected with a venereal disease before settling down with their respective soldiers.[173] The vice squad reported that "concubines" of Europeans and Africans "live in prostitution": when their partner was away on temporary assignment, they received clients in their home or at a local boardinghouse in urban areas. According to the vice squad, such women frequented the local dispensaries.[174] Similar complaints were made about me tây in Việt Trì, Đáp Cầu, and Yên Bái.[175] It is likely that some me tây engaged in sex work, but it is incorrect to generalize that temporary wives were sex workers. In my previous research on Eurasian children, many of whom came from military families like these, I found that many of the relationships between me tây and soldiers were based on love and that their households operated as families.[176]

While some authorities acknowledged that the stability of cohabitation relationships had the potential to deter soldiers from seeking clandestine sex workers,[177] officials still blamed military wives for spreading venereal diseases among troops. A 1931 medical report from Yên Bái accused me tây who lived with legionnaires of being "an inexhaustible reservoir of the virus that escapes our control."[178] Likewise, after a 1936 outbreak of venereal diseases among European and African troops stationed in Quảng Yên, military officials blamed me tây for infecting soldiers, accusing them of being clandestine sex workers, not wives.[179]

Colonial officials considered ways to police the me tây. In 1934, the doctor located in Sơn Tây suggested regulating concubinage as sex work and considered requesting that the military only recruit married men to become soldiers. The idea was that men would not, in theory, seek temporary wives if they had a wife waiting for them at home.[180] Weeks after the February 10, 1936, decree requiring sex workers to carry a work booklet, called a *livret de travail*, that included their name, age, photograph, home village, medical history, and the name of their place of employment and that verified their official registration as sex workers—the French resident at Quảng Yên and military suggested placing me tây under surveillance and requiring them to register them with police as sex workers, carry work booklets, and submit to regulations[181] A 1939 document marked "confidential" revealed that the military requested that the director of medical services for troops stationed in Indochina report all me tây who were infected with venereal disease. The doctor was obliged to reject the order on grounds of doctor-patient confidentiality but nonetheless assured his superiors that "it's not that I do not recognize that *me tây* are prostitutes."[182]

We know the most about sex work that occurred near the military encampment at Tông, near the provincial capital Sơn Tây and forty-five miles northwest of Hanoi. Established in 1928, Tông was flanked by Ai Mô and Sơn Lộc, once simple farming towns that had turned into commercial towns focused on supplying the military with bars, opium dens, dance halls, and boardinghouses.[183] The base was home to an artillery unit, a marine infantry company, a company of assault tanks, and a unit of Tonkinese infantrymen. In total, more than twelve hundred European men were stationed at Tông at any one time.

French authorities classified three types of sex workers in the vicinity. The smallest group was registered sex workers. In 1938, there was only one registered brothel, which housed twenty-five sex workers. The brothel closed that year, leaving the women to sell sex out of their homes. According to one military doctor, registered sex workers were typically undesirable women: "women with flaws (ugliness, age, ineptitude)."[184]

The second form of sex worker that authorities identified at Tông were me tây, the cohabiting girlfriends of soldiers, discussed earlier. Of the 713 legionnaires stationed at Tông, 281 reported having a me tây. The temporary wife situation was ideal for legionnaires from Africa, many of whom sought a family-like environment while stationed far from their home countries. The me tây in Tông reportedly lived quite well, in small houses serviced by a maid. In 1938, legionnaires reportedly gave their me tây an average of half of their monthly salary, the payout amounting to twenty to twenty-five piastres per month.[185]

The third form of sex worker that authorities identified at the Tông base was unregistered sex workers, of whom there were approximately three hundred in 1938, according to estimates by military doctors. Clandestine sex workers were of all ages—some as young as thirteen years old. Others were so old that, in the words of Dr. Marcel Piere, the head physician of the Foreign Legion's Fifth Regiment, they were "markedly senile." [186] Sex workers came to Tông for a variety of reasons. Some were local girls from the countryside looking to make money in this new military city. Others were sex workers from Hanoi who were fleeing that city's vice squad or a debt-bondage arrangement with a brothel owner or creditor. Many were hiding from contaminated clients looking for revenge. They had fallen on hard times or were working to help pay off a family members' debt. Military doctors noticed correlations between the volume of sex workers and the harvest output of a given season. According to doctors Piere and Joyeux, the numbers of clandestine sex workers increased during the agricultural lending periods of the first and fifteenth of each month, on holidays, and between rice seasons. Those numbers further increased with bad harvests and decreased with plentiful ones.[187]

Sex work occurred in multiple spaces at Tông. Roughly half of the area's clandestine sex workers operated out of small dilapidated shacks with poor sanitation. They solicited clients on the road at night. Others worked in bars and cafés. Clandestine sex workers were an asset for bar and café owners, as they enticed customers to buy more drinks.[188] Another popular spot for clandestine sex work in Tông was the ubiquitous boardinghouses. In 1938, there were eighteen registered boardinghouses and another fifty to sixty clandestine boardinghouses. Boardinghouses were used by singers and taxi dancers looking for a place to take their clients for the night. They were also useful for women from nearby villages who wanted to remain discreet and preserve their reputations. Such women only occasionally engaged in sex work, often to pay off debt, and the method used to procure sex work in the boardinghouses was ideal for such discretion. Customers looking for clandestine sex workers approached boardinghouse boys, who acted as mediators to locate sex workers. As for unregistered sex workers, they remained hidden, thus preserving their reputations in their nearby home villages. While on one hand this method allowed women who only occasionally sold sex to avoid embarrassment, it also facilitated the darker side of the black market sex industry, including the trafficking of women and juvenile sex workers—a subject that will be discussed in the coming chapters.[189] Clandestine sex work in dance halls and opium dens was less common at Tông. As á đào singing houses were not popular among Europeans, there were few to be found around the base. Instead, singing houses were located in the city of

Sơn Tây on Rue de Đông Tác and Rue de Hanoi.[190] Authorities estimated that there were twenty clandestine opium dens near the base at Tông. But because opium was a sedative and often rendered men temporarily impotent, the "true smokers had little concern with women."[191]

Border Towns

The towns along the Tonkin-China border were famous for clandestine sex work. For one thing, border towns were major transportation hubs and thus were constantly refreshed with new customers. Such towns had a vibrant night life complete with ả đào singing houses and dance halls. In 1939, the newspaper *Đông Pháp* described the mountain pass towns of Lạng Sơn, Móng Cái, and others along the Chinese border as party towns where one could hear the music and feel the beat of the drums all night long (see figure 9).[192]

As Eric Tagliocozzo's work on British colonial frontier zones shows, artificially created colonial borders were a haven for smugglers.[193] Prime sites of smuggling, border towns enjoyed a continuous cash flow. In the fiscal year 1937–38, the vice squad thwarted more than twenty cases of trafficking. Most of the trafficking took place in Hải Phòng or Lạng Sơn, both of which were major transportation hubs and the last stops before China.[194]

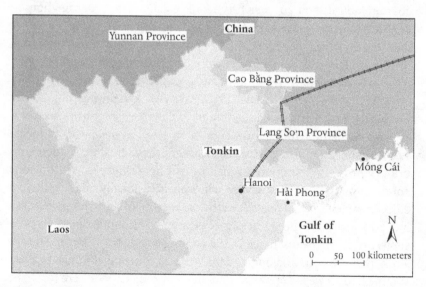

FIGURE 9. Tonkin-China border

Nestled up in the mountains on the northeastern border with China, Cao Bằng was notorious for its sex industry—and human trafficking. Visitors stopped in Cao Bằng on their way to and from China. It was a sin city with a military garrison, a casino, and singing houses. The presence of a trading company, Commerce d'Abrasin, brought wealth to the city, thus attracting sex workers.[195] By 1931, Cao Bằng had earned a reputation for a clandestine sex industry—and venereal diseases.[196] In 1941, there were more than 150 clandestine sex workers in the city center.[197] There one could find Vietnamese women, ethnic Thổ women, and Chinese women, all "beautiful girls sashaying back and forth."[198] The clientele drew from all kinds of men, particularly Western soldiers who had the "love sickness."[199] Police frequently raided entertainment spots hoping to find clandestine sex workers and arrested couples kissing in the alleys at night, as well as women who were in cars or walking on the road, with the presumption being that they were of dubious morals and sold sex.[200]

Place matters. Physical, political, and economic geography shaped the way the clandestine sex industry operated in Tonkin during the interwar years. The physical geography provided passages and hiding spots for smugglers to conceal human cargo en route to sex markets in the big cities or China. Political boundaries designating French concessions amid a Vietnamese-ruled protectorate made for suburban frontier spaces that fostered black market sex work. And the economic landscape resulting from colonial policies created intense rural poverty and rapidly developing cities, the combination of which resulted in large-scale migrations around the Red River Delta region and into the cities. Migrant women came to constitute the majority of the clandestine sex workers in the cities and in Tonkin more generally.

In urban spaces such as Hanoi and Hải Phòng, itinerant vendors and rickshaw pullers connected sex workers with clients, taking them to one of the hundreds of boardinghouses dotting the cityscape. Outside the cities, a suburban belt of prostitution work developed as a haven for clandestine sex work. Waterways formed a network that connected Hải Phòng to the smaller coastal cities of Hồn Gai and Móng Cái, a commonly traveled route among traffickers heading north to China. With their large population of single men looking for a good time, military bases attracted sex workers, and border towns, with money flowing in from both legal and illicit trade, fostered a lucrative sex trade.

The administrative geography, economic trends, and demographic changes gave rise to an interplay between city and country in Tonkin. Poverty in the countryside and rapid urbanization drew migrants into the cities, the urban-rural divide became more pronounced during the interwar years, and the suburbs developed as a site where urban and rural cultures were artfully deployed—and crime syndicates flourished. In the chapters that follow, we will explore the different forms of sex work that the geography shaped, including human trafficking, adolescent sex work, ả đào singing houses, and dance halls.

CHAPTER 2

Venereal Diseases

Policing the Sources of Infection

In 1928, the annual report from Indochina's inspector general of health services declared that venereal diseases (syphilis, gonorrhea, and chancroids likely caused by Haemophilus ducreyi) were the most problematic pathology in Indochina, citing both the rapid increase in the transmission of infection and the proliferation of birth defects.[1] That year, state medical professionals in Indochina treated almost ninety thousand patients for venereal diseases.[2] These statistics are a conservative estimate, as they reflect only those patients who sought treatment from Western-trained doctors and do not include individuals who sought treatment from Sino-Vietnamese medical practitioners or those who evaded treatment for what the Vietnamese language press nicknamed the "private" illness (*bệnh kín*).[3] With statistics continuing to be reported at a high rate, French general Gaston Billotte made a stunning statement at the 1934 meeting of the Commission for the Prophylaxis of Venereal Diseases: "The most fearsome enemy in Indochina is not the Chinese, nor the Germans, nor the [anticolonial] rebels, it is venereal infections."[4]

It would not be until the mid-1940s, when antibiotics were developed as a potent antidote against syphilis and gonorrhea, that venereal diseases no longer posed a threat. Before the development of antibiotics, venereal diseases were potentially devastating for a society and its

59

military. They were highly contagious through sexual contact and, if left untreated, could lead to severe itching, pain, blindness, neurological damage, transmission of infection to fetuses, birth defects, and, in rare cases, death.

Women, particularly sex workers, were considered the main source of transmission.[5] As a result, preventing the spread of venereal diseases would be the driving force behind colonial efforts to control unregistered sex work. Since the beginning of the nineteenth century, the French state had identified the sale of sex as a victimless crime, legalized it, and regulated it in the capital city of Paris.[6] By the late nineteenth century, when France colonized Tonkin, the sale of sex was neither a felony nor the moral issue that it had become in Anglophone countries. Yet because of its association with venereal diseases, the French state still regarded sex work as a threat and, consequently, aimed to maintain control over the sex trade by regulating, taxing, and policing sex work. French concerns about sex work were therefore rooted neither in criminality nor morality but instead in the potential transmission of venereal diseases.

In the 1880s, as part of an empire-wide effort to slow the spread of venereal diseases among French troops, the new colonial government established municipal ordinances to regulate the sale of sex in the French concession cities of Hải Phòng (1886) and Hanoi (1888).[7] Most of the subsequent laws and ordinances pertaining to sex work were designed to prevent the spread of venereal diseases. But the black market for unregistered sex work continued to boom in Tonkin, leading one of the most famous doctors in Indochina to conclude that "it is not registered prostitutes who are dangerous to European soldiers; it is the clandestine prostitutes."[8] Nonetheless, the colonial state lacked the legal means to regulate unregistered brothels or force women to submit to venereal exams unless they were caught in the act of selling sex.

This chapter explores the patterns of infection transmission, the ways that the colonial government attempted to prevent the spread of venereal disease among clandestine sex workers, and the reasons that such efforts backfired. Colonial health-care professionals were concerned with two major consequences of venereal diseases. Most important to French health-care professionals was the potential for a venereal disease outbreak to cripple their military units, as soldiers frequently contracted the diseases. (Indeed, French doctors believed that venereal diseases were more virulent and frequent among Europeans than among the Vietnamese.[9]) Second, French and Vietnamese doctors—as well as

Vietnamese intellectuals—feared that the birth defects caused by venereal diseases could lead to racial degeneracy among both the French and
the Vietnamese populations. By the 1930s, venereal disease prevention
would be the leading justification for policing clandestine sex work in
ways not permitted through the regulation system.

While studies of sex work typically treat venereal diseases as an outcome of sex work, this book will use the spread of venereal diseases as
a starting point for understanding the state concern with the clandestine sex industry as well as sex workers' preference for operating in the
black market. The interplay between these two trends triggered a downward spiral whereby greater regulation ironically became associated
with a proliferation of the diseases. The state's efforts to curb venereal
diseases—through regular, invasive gynecological exams and, if infection
was found, quarantine—led many sex workers to operate in a clandestine, unregulated market in which venereal diseases continued to spread.

The Making of the 1921 Law

Since the early nineteenth century, sex work had been legal but regulated under French metropolitan law to prevent the spread of venereal
diseases. Venereal diseases were a particular threat to the French government as they had potentially devastating effects for the national
population, particularly the military. State concerns with sex work, therefore, lay not in the perceived morality of selling sex or the criminality
of evading laws; instead, the French state was preoccupied with the transmission of venereal diseases. As there was a large and important presence of military troops stationed in Tonkin—many of whom frequented
brothels—the colonial state was particularly concerned with rates of
contagion. In response, the colonial government developed laws to
police sex work, mainly to prevent the spread of venereal diseases.

During the colonial era, "venereal disease" was an umbrella term
referring to sexually transmitted infections, specifically syphilis, gonorrhea, chancroids, and other less common infections. Although the three
predominant infections came from different forms of bacteria, their
mode of transmission through sexual contact led medical professionals to classify them as part of the "venereal trident."[10] In reality, it was
very difficult for doctors then to differentiate among the various infections that afflicted genitals; indeed, many could not detect syphilis. I will
nonetheless take this clinical ambiguity seriously, as the diagnosis itself
was political.

In the years leading up to World War I, venereal diseases were a growing problem among French military troops stationed in Indochina, many
of whom frequented unregistered brothels. The circulation of troops
between the colony and the metropole only exacerbated the problem. In
1915, the general commander superior of the Indochina troops reported
that venereal diseases were the main contagious diseases afflicting the
French troops stationed in Annam and Tonkin—and warned that those
troops could potentially spread venereal diseases back in France when
they returned home.[11] Less than a year later, the French minister of
war alerted the general commander superior of Indochina that troops
originally stationed in Hải Phòng, Hanoi, or Saigon were indeed arriving in the metropole infected with venereal diseases (see table 2.1).[12]
Conversely, soldiers and workers returning home from service in the
metropole contributed to the proliferation of venereal diseases when
they arrived back in Indochina.[13] With more than 43,000 Vietnamese
soldiers and 49,000 Vietnamese workers returning from the war,[14] the
problem was potentially calamitous.

Beyond the circulation of troops, colonial policing measures also inadvertently resulted in the proliferation of venereal diseases. For example,

Table 2.1 Percentage of the troops from
the Ninth Regiment, Colonial Infantry,
infected with venereal disease

1903	8.29
1904	16.87
1905	19.99
1906	32.94
1907	45.83
1908	39.18
1909	27.49
1910	26.14
1911	23.82
1912	24.66
1913	41.98
1914	74.66

Source: Minister of War to the General Commander Superior
of Troops, Group Indochina, December 20, 1916, Centre des
archives nationales d'outre mer (CAOM), RSTNF 3856.

after a 1920 outbreak of venereal diseases in Hải Phòng, police expelled infected sex workers who had been deemed incurable and sent them back to their province of origin, where they could freely spread infections.[15] That same year, public health officials reported more than 25,000 cases of venereal diseases in Tonkin alone (including 14,127 men, 4,825 women, and 6,318 children).[16] In 1921, the protectorate reported more than 27,000 venereal examinations, including 13,927 men, 5,632 women, and 7,982 children.[17] As noted in a 1928 "Annual Report of Health Services," public health statistics, which did not account for unreported cases of venereal diseases, underrepresented the problem.[18]

Prominent French doctors identified sex workers as the main vector of disease transmission and called on the colonial government to enact stronger laws to control the sex industry. In 1920, Tonkin's local director of health, Dr. A. Le Roy des Barres, informed the Committee for the Hygiene of Tonkin that the standing municipal regulations for sex work were insufficient. He urged the committee to draft stricter measures requiring sex workers to carry identity cards with photographs and the results of their medical exams, accompanied by a doctor's signature.[19] On February 3, 1921, the resident superior of Tonkin adopted a metropolitan law that established a uniform regulation system for sex work occurring in the French-controlled concession areas of Tonkin, including the capital, Hanoi, the major port of Hải Phòng, provincial capitals, and military bases. Per the 1884 Patenôtre Treaty, the rest of Tonkin fell under the indigenous legal code.

The law of 1921, a critical law in the history of prostitution in Tonkin, originated in the metropole.[20] The law as it applied in Tonkin after World War I allowed indigenous women to register as sex workers and carry an identity card that included a photograph, their name, place of birth, most recent address, past profession, and workplace or brothel. This law also required sex workers to carry a work booklet of medical records listing the results of their recent medical exams, including any past infections. The law permitted registered sex workers to operate state-sanctioned brothels or from their homes but prohibited public solicitation on the streets or from balconies. The 1921 law also restricted travel for registered sex workers. The law allowed sex workers to leave their city of residence only if they tested negative for venereal diseases, and it mandated they notify police of any change of address within twenty-four hours. Women caught clandestinely selling sex were given a chance at redemption after the first offense. Unregistered women caught more than once engaging in clandestine sex work or those who tested positive more than once for a venereal disease would be forcibly registered by police, with the burden of innocence placed on the women themselves. Those who sought to strike their names from the police register of sex workers had to prove that they maintained a steady and honorable source of income or prove that they would be reclaimed by an "honorable" person who would bear financial responsibility for them.[21]

Crucially, the 1921 law also required registered sex workers to submit to weekly pelvic exams and bacteriological tests. Unannounced medical visits to registered brothels could be mandated if it was declared to be in the public interest (article 17). All medical test results would be registered with the police and recorded in their work booklets. Sex workers who tested positive for a venereal disease had to notify police within twenty-four hours and admit themselves to a dispensary (also known as a lock hospital or prison infirmary) or regular hospital that same day. Infected European sex workers were treated at a European hospital; indigenous women went to the dispensary, where they were quarantined until they were cured of the disease—or at least appeared to be cured.

This system proved financially devastating for some women, who could not earn a living while at the dispensary.[22] For this reason, many sex workers avoided registering with the state and submitting to its regulations, choosing instead to operate in the black market. Ironically, the 1921 law, with its strict regulations designed to prevent the spread of venereal diseases, would only drive many sex workers deeper into the clandestine market, where the lack of regulations led to an increased transmission of venereal diseases.

The 1921 law also created problems in policing. For one thing, it did not define acts that constituted sex work. It also effectively allowed for only registered sex workers to be investigated for compliance with regulations. Women not registered could not be investigated. Perhaps most important, it defined prostitution narrowly as "making a profession of one's body to all [customers] and without [discrimination], for a monetary renumeration."[23] As we shall see in the chapters that follow, the phrase "making a profession" would come to limit policing efforts to those women who had already registered as sex workers or those who tested positive more than once for a venereal disease.

Patterns of Venereal Disease Transmission in Tonkin

In spite of, and to a large extent because of, all the regulations put in place under the 1921 law, venereal diseases continued to spread in Tonkin and posed a real threat to the local population. Given that venereal diseases are transmitted through sexual contact, their proliferation was influenced by geography, transportation, and the interactions that occurred among various ethnic groups. Rates of venereal diseases were high in the cities that attracted migrants, many of whom moonlighted as clandestine sex workers and evaded venereal exams or quarantine in the dispensary. In his 1937 investigation of the Hanoi Dispensary, journalist Thao Thao joked that for every hundred people living in Hanoi, ninety-nine were infected with syphilis or gonorrhea.[24] The following year, Roger Charbonier claimed no more plausibly that 96 percent of those arrested for clandestine sex work in Hanoi were found infected with a venereal disease.[25] While these figures were likely exaggerated, it is likely that rates were extremely high among sex workers and even the general population during the interwar years. In 1938, a doctor who had tested women in singing houses in Nam Định found that 90 percent of them were infected with a venereal disease.[26] The overpopulated lowland areas of the Red River Delta had high rates of venereal diseases. Transportation hubs were also notorious for clandestine sex work. Military bases were particularly vulnerable sites of transmission. Shrewd businesswomen set up shop just outside the territorial limits of military bases, where colonial law did not apply. For example, Cao Bằng, a military garrison and transportation hub on the way to cross the border to China, was infamous for clandestine sex work—and venereal diseases.[27]

Indeed, rates of venereal diseases were high for multiple reasons. The French military would not use antibiotics to treat venereal infections until World War II, and condoms, with their nebulous legal state, were not popular. The problem of venereal disease prevalence, according to a 1941 article published in *Đông Pháp*, was a lack of education about the symptoms of sexually transmitted infections among the general public. The average person, the article argues, did not know how to identify venereal diseases and thus unwittingly spread the infection. Since syphilis, in its primary stage, appears as a small, painless sore on the lower abdomen, those infected typically mistook it for scabies, another affliction prevalent in Tonkin during the colonial period. As that small sore appears twenty to thirty days after the initial exposure, the infected person was unlikely to connect the sore with a past sexual experience and realize they were infected with a venereal disease. Once the sore had scabbed over, the infected person typically assumed that the bout of scabies had run its course and did not realize that the venereal infection remained latent in the body. Patients often felt no pain for a few years—sometimes up to a dozen—after which point they entered the third stage of syphilis, in which the nervous system is attacked. Until then, patients were unwittingly spreading the infection through sexual contact.[28]

Some areas of Tonkin's highlands bucked this trend. Colonial public health authorities reported low rates of venereal diseases among ethnic minority groups in the highlands, likely because these areas were geographically isolated, local officials did not report cases, or because some ethnic minority groups practiced mostly endogamous sex. For example, authorities from the mountainous province of Hòa Bình reported no cases of venereal diseases among ethnic Mường people and reported that the few cases that appeared in Hòa Bình tended to originate among ethnic Vietnamese traveling from the Red River Delta area.[29] Similarly, in 1930 and 1931, authorities reported that although there were high rates of venereal diseases near the Yên Bái Garrison and in Nghĩa Lộ, areas with a significant population of ethnic Chinese women, there was little sex work or venereal diseases among the Mãn, Tai, Mèo, Mường, Nùng, and Xa Cao groups in Yên Bái, in the highlands northeast of Hanoi.[30] Authorities reporting in 1922 from Lào Cai and in 1930 from Bảo Hà, also in the highlands, noted only a handful of infections.[31]

Throughout the interwar years, French and Vietnamese sources from all over Indochina were rife with lurid stories of untreated venereal diseases. In one such story from 1923, a woman in Hà Nam found herself paralyzed in the limbs just two months after discovering that she had syphilis and had to be transported by hammock to the hospital.[32] In 1927, the newspaper *Văn Minh* recounted a story of a man in Mỹ Tho in Cochinchina who could not afford treatment for an unspecified venereal disease; within two years the symptoms had worsened until he died.[33] In 1941, the newspaper *Việt Báo* reported another case in which the symptoms of an unspecified venereal disease resulted in a fever that left eighteen-year-old Nguyễn Văn Thuất, from Ninh Bình, bedridden for days. The symptoms were so painful that he eventually committed suicide by drowning himself in a pond in nearby Yên Mẫn village.[34]

In a 1937 impassioned speech to the Overseas Commission of Inquiry, Đỗ Văn Nam, representing Canton de Minh Huê (Bến Tre, Cochinchina), declared that "without a doubt the government knows that this terrible illness is without equal." He continued: "Venereal microbes are the enemy. They are dreadful killers: they announce the arrival of death, a death that only comes after it causes long pain and suffering." He described villages stricken with a disease that was left untreated and families ruined because the adults became too weak to work. In Đỗ Văn Nam's own family, two of the three brothers had a venereal disease. His uncle lost an arm, and his cousin's wife was wasting away and suffering from insomnia and nerve damage, all attributed to an untreated venereal disease. Another man in their village, once robust in his youth, contracted a venereal disease and found his bones beginning to "bend." They decomposed, and he eventually died of a combination of osteitis and periostitis, infection of the bone and surrounding membrane around the bone, a complication of secondary syphilis.[35]

Particularly alarming for French officials, Vietnamese officials, and journalists alike were the effects of that venereal diseases had on young children. Mothers and wet nurses who had gone untreated went on to infect children by giving birth or breastfeeding. The director of the Bureau of Hygiene in Hanoi told Vietnamese journalist Vũ Trọng Phụng that in one study of four thousand infant deaths, one thousand were found to have resulted from syphilis.[36] A French public health report from 1928 deemed syphilis the primary cause of newborn mortality (through miscarriage, stillbirth, or infantile death) as well as child mortality generally.[37] The official deemed syphilis more virulent than gastrointestinal problems, which is significant considering the medical problems caused by poor sanitation and untreated water in the colonial period. According to the report, the hardest-hit regions were the urban centers of Tonkin, including Hanoi, Hải Phòng, and Nam Định.[38] Mothers with gonorrhea risked infecting—and blinding—children in the process of giving birth. A Dr. Keller, who ran the Hanoi Ophthalmological Hospital, told Vũ Trọng Phụng that 70 percent of those who were blind in one or both eyes had likely been infected with gonorrhea at birth.[39] In his 1937 address to the Overseas Commission of Inquiry, Đỗ Văn Nam reported that in his village there remained only a few people who were not infected; most had been infected by their parents. An infected woman in Đỗ Văn Nam's hamlet gave birth to "a bizarre child that looks like a monster. Everyone is afraid to look at it because it does not resemble a human form." Đỗ Văn Nam's own nieces and nephews, who had likewise contracted a venereal disease at birth, suffered from bone deformities.[40] Another case reported in 1941 in the newspaper Đông Pháp was a premature birth in which the baby had webbed hands, a small head, and a distended stomach. Both parents had a venereal disease.[41]

Due to the widespread effects of venereal diseases on adults and children, French and Vietnamese alike viewed it as a threat to colonial society and the Vietnamese race. When addressing a Franco-Vietnamese commission on venereal diseases in 1939, one Vietnamese doctor labeled them "disastrous disease[s] inundating the world today" that were detrimental to the race [nòi giống].[42] A 1941 article in *Đông Pháp* describes the fight against venereal diseases as "a war that is massacring humanity" and implores readers "we need to fight [this war] in order to preserve mankind, as this is a war of humanity versus syphilis."[43] Similarly, French public health officials called it "the principal factor of the physical degeneration of the race, along with malaria and malnutrition,"[44] a source of concern for "the future of the race." As Julia Christine Scriven Miller shows, much of the French concern about venereal diseases originated in a widespread fear that France was at risk for depopulation, and venereal diseases would only render more couples infertile or put them at risk for miscarriage. By the 1930s, metropolitan concerns about venereal diseases focused on the potential effects of infections on the future of the French people.[45]

While anyone could transmit a venereal disease, French officials and Vietnamese journalists identified sex workers as the most common source of infection. As a 1938 *Thời Vụ Báo* newspaper article read, "Everyone knows that the profession of prostitution and the epidemic of venereal disease has bad effects: bad for the body, bad for the family, and bad for society and the city. The bigger in number it gets, the wider it spreads."[46] Indeed, the spread of venereal diseases occurred in a kind of downward spiral, with sex workers infecting clients and clients, in turn, infecting other sex workers. Dr. Bernard Joyeux noted that it was not registered sex workers who were dangerous to European soldiers—it was the clandestine sex workers.[47] In 1933, the newspaper *Ngọ Báo* reported that when colonial police raided clandestine brothels, they forced all the women present to submit to venereal exams.[48] Their searches frequently found that most—if not all—of the women in these clandestine brothels were infected. In 1938, the newspaper *Đông Pháp* reported that in a raid on an unregistered brothel on Lò Đúc street in Hanoi, every single woman working at the house was found to be infected[49] In 1939, the newspaper *Quốc Gia Nhật Báo* reported that the prevalence of venereal diseases among á đào singers who moonlighted as clandestine sex workers led one Vietnamese journalist to refer to singers as the front line in the war against venereal diseases.[50]

Sadly, women who were trafficked or forced into sex work frequently contracted venereal diseases. For example, in 1933, *Ngọ Báo* reported the story of Nguyễn Thị Na, a fourteen-year-old girl who had been coerced into sex work in Hanoi and contracted a venereal disease from a client.[51]

Similarly, in 1938, *Đông Pháp* ran a story about eighteen-year-old Ng. Thị Bình, from Thọ Bạc village near Đông Sơn, who also contracted a venereal disease after being forced into sex work.[52]

To evade colonial medical examiners and avoid repelling customers, sex workers resorted to extensive measures to hide their infections. Sex workers in Hải Dương used makeup to cover syphilis rashes to conceal them from customers and medical examiners.[53] To eliminate visible traces of infection for required medical examinations, registered sex workers flushed their vaginas with a mixture of water and alum, according to journalist Vũ Trọng Phụng. They then applied pressure to their abdomens to expel pus and inserted cloths to soak up any that remained pus before the doctor arrived.[54] According to journalist Thao Thao, some sex workers even used pig blood to give the impression that they were experiencing menses and to disguise any visible sores on their vagina.[55]

Military troops were particularly vulnerable to contracting venereal infection. Clandestine brothels formed around the perimeter of most military bases, just beyond the limits of French legal control. Many enlisted men frequented clandestine brothels, and some went on to transmit the infections to the local women with whom they lived in long-term relationships. French colonial officials were particularly concerned about the effects of venereal diseases on military troops. Marcel Piere, a military doctor, and Dr. Joyeux warned that "in Indochina, venereal disease is a plague for European troops that [spreads at] a markedly catastrophic pace." Claiming that European troops were contracting venereal diseases at a much higher rate than indigenous ones, Piere and Joyeux deemed venereal diseases a question of "the security of national defense."[56] With their painful symptoms, venereal diseases could hinder troops' ability to fight.[57] The Hanoi Prophylactic League viewed venereal diseases in terms of eugenics, noting the negative repercussions of French soldiers, "who are the future of our race," contracting them.[58] In one telling statement, an official revealed the public health service's fundamental priority: "It appears that this rough and vain battle that we are carrying out at the dispensary is for the principal purpose of protecting the military men of the garrisons."[59]

French and colonial soldiers tried various methods to avoid contracting venereal diseases, but most of these only exacerbated its spread. Dr. Joyeux claimed that some soldiers, incorrectly assuming venereal diseases were contracted only through sexual encounters with women, engaged in homosexual sex to avoid infection.[60] Others demanded— and sometimes forced—sex workers to engage in anal sex, erroneously believing that this constituted a safe alternative to vaginal intercourse. According to Dr. Joyeux, brothel madams forced registered sex workers to accept anal sex, whereas unregistered sex workers—who in theory could flee a clandestine brothel—had the power to reject it.[61] In 1934, Joyeux estimated that 30 percent of venereal hospitalizations were due to anal-rectal infections, which could be quite dangerous.[62] It was not uncommon for the dispensary to treat women for multiple infections in the vagina, anus, and mouth.[63]

Venereal diseases spread quickly in Tonkin with the development of the colonial transportation infrastructure and lack of sexual education among the general public. Sexually transmitted infections had devastating effects on Vietnamese society, especially if left untreated or passed from pregnant mothers to their children. Most concerning for the colonial government, however, was the transmission of venereal diseases to military personnel. Until antibiotics were developed in the 1940s, the colonial state, which prohibited the sale of condoms, would remain otherwise powerless to prevent the spread of the diseases.

The Fight against Venereal Diseases

The colonial government fought the spread of venereal diseases by making therapeutic treatments more widely available to the public. Before antibiotics were introduced during World War II, French-trained doctors treated syphilis with arsenic benzene, a poison to the lungs, kidney, and liver if used in large quantities.[64] After 1923, they added bismuth to treat both syphilis and gonorrhea. Not as toxic as arsenic benzene, bismuth nonetheless causes liver and gastrointestinal tract damage.[65] Military doctors also offered prophylactic measures, distributing tubes of calomel ointment, which contained mercuric chloride, and was put on the skin to destroy the bacteria associated with venereal diseases. The military sequestered infected soldiers in cabins equipped with soap and tubes of Metchnikoff's pomade, which was made with mercury chloride mixed with benzene and lard and was to be applied externally in order to eliminate bacteria from venereal diseases. These treatments were minimally effective and potentially toxic if overused.[66]

Traditional Sino-Vietnamese medical practice treated syphilis and gonorrhea with mercury, which could result in mercury intoxication, causing oral ulcers and nephrotoxicity.[67] French officials dismissed traditional practitioners. In his doctoral thesis on venereal diseases in Hanoi, Roger Charbonnier derided doctors of traditional medicine as "destitute of scientific knowledge," as they lacked official training and diplomas. Pharmacists who made their own potions and pills, they were, he wrote, as "ignorant as water." Nonetheless, the colonial government failed to prevent the public from seeking medical advice from traditional practitioners.[68]

While registered sex workers were required by law to consult with colonial doctors, most other victims of venereal diseases consulted with Sino-Vietnamese medical practitioners, who often agreed to maintain patient privacy and not to report their infections.[69] Although a 1909 law required herbalists to report cases of venereal diseases, the newspaper Thông Tin reported that herbalists refused.[70] In 1934, the colonial state implemented a project to regulate traditional Sino-Vietnamese medicine,[71] but reports reveal that even as late as 1943 the colonial government was struggling to get herbalists to comply.[72]

In the spring of 1936, the Agency to Eradicate Venereal Disease opened in the 36 Streets section of Hanoi, also known as the Indigenous Quarter. The agency, made up of Sino-Vietnamese medical practitioners, drew from medical cures used throughout Vietnam, as well as cures employed by the Mường and Mãn people. Doctors and midwives saw patients seven days per week and charged a fee of three piastres. Treatments lasted three months beyond the last reoccurrence of the symptoms.[73]

Beyond its mandatory regular testing of registered sex workers, French officials' primary strategy to slow the proliferation of venereal diseases was to set up dispensaries to treat the indigenous population. In 1921, Sơn Tây, Bắc Ninh, and Lào Cai Provinces all reported having dispensaries. A dispensary was built in Hải Dương in 1922. Although Quảng Yên had no registered sex workers, the town did have a place where public health officials could examine and treat clandestine sex workers. Officials in Thái Nguyên examined women in shacks but requested funding to build a modern dispensary. In 1922, Nam Định had plans to build a dispensary. Hòa Bình, Cho Bo, Kiến An, Ninh Bình, Bắc Kạn, and Hà Đông reported no registered sex workers, so officials in these provinces felt no need to build dispensaries.[74] Provinces with no dispensaries frequently hospitalized infected patients in wards with prisoners and lepers.[75] Lạng Sơn, which in 1926 had no dispensary, sent infected sex workers to be treated at the local hospital. Because the hospital did not imprison patients as the dispensary did, women were free to leave. French military officials soon discovered that when soldiers approached madams to find sex workers, the madams would prematurely check patients out before they finished treatment and pimp out the sick women.[76]

The historical records are most detailed for the Hanoi Dispensary, known to locals as the "Girls' Hospital" (*nhà thương con gái*).[77] Hanoi's first dispensary was built in 1886, and in 1926 the last iteration of the colonial dispensary was located on Rodier Street, near the courthouse.[78] The hospital staff consisted of a French male doctor, who concurrently served as the director of the Hanoi Municipal Service of Hygiene, a French female chief supervisor, who managed the affairs of the dispensary, and Vietnamese male and female nurses. The dispensary treated only Vietnamese, Chinese, and ethnic-minority women. French women who contracted a venereal disease through clandestine sex work or other means enjoyed the privilege of being treated at home or the Hospital for Europeans in Hanoi.[79]

Shrouded in secrecy, the dispensary had high walls and tight security. "Because of this 'private illness,'" [bênh kín] journalist Thao Thao wrote—mockingly using a slang term for venereal diseases—"we must have a private building."[80] Thao Thao described the mystery of seeing both fashionable modern girls and rough, dirty brothel women who emerged from the shadows of dank, filthy alleys such as Ngõ Sầm Công, Ngõ Hàng Mành, and Đâu Hàng Đẫy walk past the courthouse to the dispensary and quietly slip behind its big doors. He watched this daily, wondering what went on inside. The dispensary was so secretive that Thao Thao considered posing as a female sex worker and getting himself "caught" and quarantined in the dispensary to find out.[81] He would eventually be granted entrance in 1937.

In Hanoi, the madams of registered brothels took sex workers to be tested at the dispensary twice a week. Registered sex workers also submitted to semiannual Bordet-Wassermann reactions, an antibody test for syphilis. As for women arrested for clandestine sex work, they were required to submit to a venereal exam; if they tested positive, they were mandated to be treated at the dispensary. After the first offense, they were set free; after the second offense, they were required to register as sex workers, effectively making venereal diseases a component of the definition of prostitution. Registered sex workers who were caught fleeing the brothel system without official permission to deregister from the list of local sex workers were automatically sent to the dispensary as a public health—and punitive—measure.[82]

The majority of the cases at the Hanoi Dispensary were syphilis, 25 percent to 33 percent were gonorrhea, and few were chancres.[83] The 1930 "Annual Report on the Functioning of the Hanoi Municipal Hygiene Service" noted the painful irony that women were "undoubtedly" being contaminated through the unsterile process of being examined at the dispensary.[84] Registered and unregistered sex workers who tested positive or had symptoms of a venereal disease were retained at the dispensary until they recovered (typically a three-month stay).[85] It was not uncommon for patients to cycle in and out of the dispensary due to improperly treated infections or repeat exposure from their clients. Those women deemed "incurable" were sent indefinitely to the Lanessan Hospital.[86]

The Hanoi Dispensary had strict regulations for its interned patients. Women were expected to wake at 6:00 a.m., bathe, and promptly be examined. Authorities at the dispensary put patients to work cleaning, sewing, or doing laundry. Alcohol, opium, gambling, arguing, and shouting were prohibited; cigarettes and betel nut were permitted but only with special permission. Those who failed to comply with the rules were punished by the withholding of meals or by solitary confinement.[87] At the dispensary, women were taught skills to protect them from becoming reinfected, such as personal hygiene, prophylactic treatment, and how to identify signs of a venereal disease in men. Interned sex workers also learned skills to prepare them for alternative professions, including sewing and reading.[88]

It is not hard to understand why sex workers did their best to avoid the Hanoi Dispensary. The French officials and Vietnamese journalists who visited it reported that it felt like a jail.[89] The building itself had little ventilation, thereby exacerbating cold winters and sweltering Hanoi summers. Dr. Joyeux himself expressed concern that the poor health conditions at the dispensary were impeding the recovery process.[90]

Abuse, physical as well as emotional, was common at the Hanoi Dispensary. Adolphe Blanchon, a dispensary employee, was the subject of multiple complaints, including one report that he left a patient to starve.[91] The colonial archive in Hanoi includes a large file on abuses committed by a Madame Frass, the chief supervisor at the dispensary from 1931 to 1937. In 1933, after a nurse informed Frass that the dispensary was out of menstrual napkins, Frass did not believe her and slapped her in front of the patients. In 1935, Frass was found to have taken bribes and dubious gifts from registered sex workers. One sex worker who tested positive for a venereal disease told authorities that Frass had allowed her to break out of the dispensary in exchange for a bribe of thirty piastres.[92] That same year, Frass reportedly cut one woman's hair as punishment, slapped another woman in the face, and beat another with a piece of wood when she voluntarily returned after escaping. Frass punished another woman who tried to flee by forcing her to take ice baths for more than thirty minutes during the winter. Frass was suspected of poisoning patients' food with petrol after three patients were hospitalized.[93] She was also accused of taking the child of a registered sex worker, falsely claiming that the woman had abandoned it.[94] In a 1935 report to the mayor of Hanoi, the police commissioner wrote that the sex workers being treated in the dispensary "literally live under the terror of this authoritarian woman."[95]

Collaborative Efforts to Reduce Transmission in the Countryside

Because the colonial government was not responsible for governing the internal affairs of the countryside—and thus did not regulate sex work in those areas—venereal diseases spread easily in the provinces. The provinces also lacked manpower and authority with which to regulate registered or clandestine sex work. For example, the province of Ninh Bình reported in 1921 that even though venereal disease rates were high, there was no state mechanism for the surveillance of sex work.[96] Likewise, reports from 1923 reveal that neither the towns of Phát Diệm nor Hưng Hóa had any surveillance mechanisms.[97]

Because there was limited regulation of the sex industry in the countryside and, by extension, few measures to prevent the spread of venereal diseases, venereal infections had grave effects on the military units stationed there. In 1922, public health officials from the military garrison of Móng Cái reported that their efforts to regulate sex work and reduce the spread of venereal diseases were futile. The source of the problem, according to public health officials, was the garrison's proximity to Tang Hung, a popular location for clandestine sex work and the origin of many cases of gonorrhea.[98] Similarly, the 1923 annual public health report for Tonkin revealed that indigenous troops in Thái Bình and Hải Dương had high rates of venereal diseases, most of which had been contracted from clandestine sex workers who worked as singers or vendors or from registered sex workers who somehow escaped mandatory venereal exams.[99] In 1926, officials in Ninh Bình lamented that women from ả đào singing houses located just a few meters from the city limits—and thus outside of French jurisdiction—had infected indigenous military troops.[100] That same year, military officials in Bắc Ninh complained that venereal diseases had become so prevalent that military men were reportedly making weekly visits for treatment at the local dispensary.[101]

Colonial officials collaborated with local Vietnamese authorities to try to halt the spread of venereal diseases. Together they raided known unregistered brothels and forced unregistered sex workers to submit to venereal exams.[102] Most of the raids targeted ả đào singers, who were rumored to moonlight as clandestine sex workers. In 1935, authorities in Bắc Ninh raided a few singing houses and mandated singers on Phủ Từ Street undergo to venereal exams. When other singers showed up at the local mandarin's house to complain, the police responded by carting away these women, who by this point were yelling and crying, to get venereal exams themselves. A journalist who reported on the incident for Ngọ Báo mused, "You never know if the doctor will find germs in whichever places."[103] In 1937, Việt Báo reported that singers in Hà Đông were forced to submit to pelvic exams,[104] and in 1938, Đông Pháp reported that singers in Nam Định and Ninh Bình were likewise forced to be examined.[105]

Vice squads and colonial health authorities sometimes learned of clandestine brothels and unregistered sex workers through complaints from those infected with venereal diseases. In 1926, when a twenty-three-year-old soldier tested positive for a venereal disease, he revealed to doctors the identity of the clandestine sex worker who had contaminated him. The doctors promptly went to the police.[106] In 1937, Đông Pháp reported that customers led authorities to the clandestine brothel where they had contracted a venereal disease. Upon investigating, the police found not only that there had been violations of the venereal code but also that at least one of the women had been trafficked into sex work.[107] In 1939, Việt Báo reported that the Vietnamese wives and concubines of Western men alerted authorities in Quảng Yên of the clandestine sex workers who had infected their husbands, who in turn had infected the wives. The local mandarin ordered a sweep for all known clandestine sex workers and forced them to submit to venereal exams. Of the hundred women arrested, twenty-eight tested positive for infection and were held at the venereal clinic.[108]

Anti-venereal-disease health measures often targeted women who were only rumored to have "loose morals" but were not necessarily sex workers. In 1931, Ngọ Báo reported that after an outbreak of venereal diseases that had detrimental effects on European soldiers in Cao Bằng, the French resident, the highest-ranking colonial official of the province, ordered officials to track down any and all women involved in the entertainment business. Police arrested women who worked in bars and dance halls, young women who rode in cars with men (presumably an indication of low morals and, by extension, sex work), and couples found having any form of sexual contact—including mere kissing—in back alleys. Police arrested the women, forced them to submit to venereal exams, and registered them as sex workers. Authorities expelled the women from Cao Bằng or notified their families to claim them at the dispensary, surely an embarrassment to the women and their families. When the family members arrived, they found their loved ones in shackles.[109] As reported in *Ngọ Báo* in 1933, police in the suburbs of Hải Phòng conducted a raid of alleyways and sent suspected clandestine sex workers to the venereal clinic.[110]

Me tây, the Vietnamese wives and live-in girlfriends of French or Foreign Legion soldiers, were a frequent target of police harassment. While French law tolerated interracial relationships and even marriages, not all colonial officials privately approved of them. Assuming that all me tây sold sex when their husbands or boyfriends were absent on military assignment, authorities blamed them for outbreaks of venereal diseases. Of course, those authorities never considered that the wives and girlfriends may have contracted the venereal disease not from customers but from their own husbands. After a 1936 reoccurring outbreak of venereal diseases in Quảng Yên, authorities accused me tây of spreading the infection through clandestine sex work.[111] Military police arrested soldiers' wives and girlfriends, photographed them, and registered them as sex workers. The women protested in a letter to the resident superior of Tonkin, explaining that many of them were legally married to soldiers— marriages for which had been vetted and approved by the military. As evidence of their family values and loyalty to the colonial state, the wives even reminded the resident superior of Tonkin that some of their children attended military schools or served in the French military.[112] Nonetheless, authorities considered putting me tây under surveillance or requiring them to carry a work booklet, as required of registered sex workers, but such measures violated French privacy laws.[113] The violation did not stop authorities from trying again. In 1939, me tây in Việt Trì were forced to submit to venereal exams; those who tested positive for a venereal disease had to register as sex workers.[114] In 1939, police in Sept Pagodes / Móng Cái and Sơn Tây raided the homes of me tây who were suspected of being clandestine sex workers and forced them to submit to weekly exams.[115]

Records reveal that provincial authorities sometimes resorted to expelling infected women from the province where they were caught.

In 1933, authorities from Hòa Bình expelled infected women from that province,[116] and, in 1939, the military commander at Sept Pagodes / Móng Cái issued a similar directive.[117] Expelling infected women served multiple purposes. It eased the strain on local public health officials and venereal disease clinics, and it eliminated the carriers of recurring infections, a common problem before the development of antibiotics as a cure. This policy, however, was myopic, as infected women would simply go on to transmit venereal diseases in their new location.

As one can imagine, accusations of prostitution, forced venereal exams, and expulsion from the province were traumatic for the women experiencing them. One particularly sad case from 1937 involved Nguyễn Thị Hải, a pretty seventeen-year-old who was unmarried and lived with her parents, owners of a popular bar in Hà Đông. One crisp December day, a French messenger delivered a note summoning her to Văn Yên military base in Hà Đông. Thinking it was a simple business matter, her father allowed her to go accompanied by a cousin.[118]

When Nguyễn Thị Hải arrived, the military commander insisted that she alone come into his office while her cousin waited outside. As Nguyễn Thị Hải would later recount, the room looked more like a bedroom than an office, with a bed, chair, mirror, comb, a pair of shoes, and a table strewn with papers. The man invited her to sit down in the chair. He went to the mirror, adjusted his tie, and casually told her that she would have to have a pelvic exam to check for the presence of venereal diseases. She protested, telling him she was not yet married, a Vietnamese way of implying that that she was a virgin. He explained that he heard that she had a venereal disease and assured her that he only wanted to settle the truth of the matter. The exam would be for her own good, he insisted, and if she was indeed a virgin there would be no cause for concern. As he steered her to the infirmary for the venereal exam, a panicked Nguyễn Thị Hải managed to desperately yell to her cousin to notify her parents. Her cousin rushed back to the house for help, but her parents could not make it to the doctor's office in time to help their daughter.[119]

In the doctor's office, Nguyễn Thị Hải screamed and thrashed about in an effort to prevent the exam. Perhaps a morsel of sympathy led the doctor to whisper that to her that he was only acting on military orders. The doctor tried three times to force the speculum and other instruments into her vagina. Nguyễn Thị Hải fought him for half an hour and even bit the doctor's hand. He eventually overpowered her, conducted the exam, and briefly consoled her before he left her to cry alone in the room.[120]

When Nguyễn Thị Hải's parents arrived, they demanded to know why the battalion commander had forced their daughter to submit to a venereal exam. He dismissed them as *nhà quê*, an insulting term for peasants, told them not to question his authority, and directed a subordinate to remove them. The distraught parents returned home without their daughter. Not long afterward, she stumbled back home in tears and refused to let her parents see her clothing. They eventually found her underwear soaked with blood.[121] Nguyễn Thị Hải's father immediately reported the incident to a military superior and a civilian French official, demanding them to rectify the situation, which he characterized an "act of oppression" (*sự ức hiếp*).[122]

Nguyễn Thị Hải's story continued to spiral downward. The military doctor, a Dr. Theill, concluded that she had tested positive for a venereal disease and gave orders to expel her from the Hà Đông—even though it was quite possible that he was lying to justify the invasive exam or that she had contracted the disease from unsanitary equipment used during the forced exam,[123] a problem so common that French administrators themselves acknowledged it.[124] Nguyễn Thị Hải went on to become the object of multiple unsubstantiated accusations on the part of the military officer. When the resident superior of Tonkin looked into the matter, military officials in Hà Đông claimed that Nguyễn Thị Hải was a known sex worker who went by the name "Little Peanut."[125] The resident superior referred to what he claimed was a two-year-old rumor that Nguyễn Thị Hải had transmitted a venereal disease to a soldier but conspicuously offered no detail or evidence that such a claim was ever made.[126] Dr. Theill called into question the morality of Nguyễn Thị Hải on the grounds that she worked at a bar, but he ignored the fact that the bar was owned by her father and, moreover, that Vietnamese children were expected to help with a family business. He insisted it was Nguyễn Thị Hải herself who was suspect for having brought a complaint against the battalion commander who, he argued, was only taking proper measures to protect his troops from venereal diseases.[127] In retaliation against the family, another military officer directed that the father's license to own a bar not be renewed.[128] Eventually, the damage to the family business and the pressure on Nguyễn Thị Hải's father was so great that it forced him to rescind his complaint against the military commanders and doctor.[129]

Given the frequent abuse of women accused of sex work, as well as the persistently high rates of venereal diseases in rural and urban areas alike, colonial officials would experiment with various reforms in their approach to fighting venereal diseases.

Informal Reform of the Regulation System

In the 1930s, a debate among doctors and public health officials about the effectiveness of the regulation system in preventing the spread of venereal diseases led to changes in the way sex work was policed in Tonkin. With the rise of clandestine sex work and venereal diseases, many public health officials saw the regulated sex industry not only as a failure of policing but also a failure to prevent the spread of the diseases. The medical community's desire for an alternative to the regulation system, along with the rise of the socialist Popular Front government in France, led to a shift away from the policing of sex work and a move toward the monitoring of the spread of venereal diseases itself. Increased medical surveillance resulted in greater state authority over clandestine sex work—authority that had been inadvertently curtailed by the 1921 law.

At the heart of state-level policy on the prevention of venereal diseases was a debate about the efficacy of the regulated prostitution system. In this debate, which dated back to the mid-nineteenth-century metropole, those who supported the regulation system were pitted against those who sought to abolish it. Those who argued for the regulation system, known as regulationists, supported existing state laws requiring sex workers to register with the state, to submit to venereal exams, and to cease work if found to be infected with a venereal disease. Regulationists were primarily police and military doctors. They supported the use of vice police and lobbied for the creation of reserved quarters for sex work.[130]

Regulationists in the military issued new measures specific to military bases. Military authorities in Quảng Yên requested that all brothels be situated within the confines of the base, thereby making them subject to the French regulation system and enabling military doctors to monitor the spread of venereal diseases.[131] Military leaders ordered troops to undergo sex education about the spread of venereal diseases, and doctors armed soldiers with tubes of prophylactic creams whenever they left the base. Troops were subject to frequent unannounced medical exams, and those who contracted a venereal disease were required to register with a military doctor who would maintain their medical confidentiality but closely monitor the progress of their infection.[132] In 1933, officials suggested following the Moroccan and Syrian protectorate models of *bordels militaire de campagne*, mobile military brothels whose sex workers were under close medical surveillance and virtually guaranteed to be free of venereal diseases. These mobile brothels would travel alongside military units and service the troops. "There are already canteens, cooperatives, stores, and ice cream parlors. . . . They will have their women, so why not?" read a 1933 medical report considering allowing sex work near military bases.[133]

On the other side of the debate were abolitionists. Founded in the metropole in the 1870s, the abolitionist movement was modeled after the antislavery movement. Abolitionists did not seek to ban the sale of sex, as they valued privacy.[134] Instead, abolitionists argued that with forced registration and forced venereal exams, the registration and brothel system was tantamount to slavery and did little to stop the spread of venereal diseases.[135]

In Tonkin, abolitionists recognized that the problem was a repressive anti-venereal-disease regime that was leading sex workers away from the registration system and into the black market, where they received no treatment and thus continued to transmit venereal infections at an alarming rate. Abolitionists were led by public health officials and doctors working in the dispensaries, who sought to eliminate the regulation system and allow sex workers to operate in a free market. Abolitionists argued for the importance of maintaining the liberty and dignity of all individuals, including sex workers, by treating venereal diseases just like any other illnesses instead of as a source of shame and a scourge on society. Their basic motivation, however, was more practical than idealistic: they felt that the current regulation system was too draconian and hence ineffective.[136] Sex workers infected with a venereal disease would, abolitionists contended, voluntarily seek medical treatment if they could do so without the fear of incurring legal or financial consequences.[137] Abolitionists further maintained that the regulation system addressed only part of the problem—monitoring sex workers while allowing their infected clients to spread venereal diseases to other sex workers and non-prostitutes alike. Dr. Le Roy des Barres, a leading abolitionist, called for making the transmission of venereal diseases—by anyone—punishable by law.[138] He also called for disbanding the vice squads, abolishing the practice of pimps and madams to make sex workers independent workers, and promoting sex education. He made the case for closing dispensaries, which stigmatized infected women, and instead allowing sex workers to voluntarily seek treatment at indigenous hospitals.[139] Another abolitionist physician agreed that the regulation system constituted an assault on individual liberties and that it was in "the public's primary interest" to protect these liberties.[140] Similarly, the Medical Surgical Society of Indochina declared to the resident superior of Tonkin that measures of administrative coercion vis-à-vis sex workers were ineffective and insisted that it would be best for colonial officials to handle venereal diseases no differently than ordinary illnesses.[141] In addition to the points made above, Dr. Joyeux called on the colonial government to increase sex education in both the French and Vietnamese languages and to create a prophylactic institute and laboratory for bacteria and serology in lieu of dispensaries.[142]

A third faction, which held a middle ground, comprised representatives who sat on the Hanoi municipal council. Members of this faction called for a reform of the regulated sex industry, the introduction of zoned quarters for sex work, and the consolidation of the Hanoi Dispensary and the Indigenous Hospital. They also called on the state to increase the number of vice squad agents, to remove the vice squad from the administrative control of the Sûreté (the police detective force), to place it under the authority of the city police, and to establish vice squads in the countryside. According to middle-faction members, vice squads should be granted the legal authority to enter clandestine establishments, including ả đào singing houses, dance halls, and bars, and ả đào singers should be required to submit to venereal exams.[143] Roger Charbonnier, also called for the reform of the regulation system, which he argued was wise to maintain. To reform the system, he suggested improving policing and treatment. He recommended a larger vice squad, with two French inspectors and ten Vietnamese agents. He called for improved communication among the vice squads in Tonkin's cities to enable police to catch sex workers who fled their venereal exams. He made the case for a larger dispensary and creating a prophylactic institute.[144] To fight the spread of venereal diseases in the military, he suggested a collective prophylaxis for military men, including improved education about the diseases, periodic venereal exams for soldiers on leave, health instructions, sanitary cabins at the door of military quarters, and a wider distribution of ointments with which to treat infections.[145] For the provinces, he called for increasing the number of doctors trained in French medicine.[146] Finally, he implored the colonial government to dedicate more money to research and education. This plan would include more scholarships for Vietnamese students to study French medicine as well as the regulation of teaching of traditional medicine by instituting an official "modern, scientific" approach to herbal medicine in which students would study the medicinal plants of the country.[147]

As a result of these debates, colonial administrators and doctors collaborated throughout the 1930s to find legal ways for the colonial state to control the spread of venereal diseases. In a decree of December 2, 1933, the governor-general founded the Indochina Council for the Eradication of Venereal Disease to research ways to suppress the transmission of venereal diseases and prevent them from spreading, especially to military sites.[148] The council met in Hanoi and comprised the governor-general, the resident superior of Tonkin, the head of economic services, the head of the military health service, Mr. Tissot (a councilman who would become the mayor of Hanoi), Dr. Le Roy des Barres, Dr. Simpon, and a representative from the Vietnamese royal government.[149] The council aimed to develop a treatment that would be freely available at dispensaries and considered offering sex education in schools to teach children about the dangers of venereal diseases.[150]

On May 2, 1934, the council was replaced with the Prophylactic League, whose goal was to find solutions for the eradication of venereal diseases in Hanoi and its suburbs. Headed by Hanoi mayor M. H. Virgitti, the league comprised doctors and colonial administrators who would meet throughout the rest of the 1930s with the aim of controlling the spread of venereal diseases in Tonkin. It renovated the city's dispensary and founded a school dedicated to the promotion of sexual prophylaxis.[151] The league also urged French military leaders to consider following the American model of distributing condoms to troops.[152]

In the mid-1930s, metropolitan France saw a renewed movement to abolish the regulation system,[153] which was bolstered by the 1936 rise of the socialist Popular Front government. One of the projects of the Popular Front was a law proposed by French minister of health Henri Sellier on November 5, 1936, but never passed. The Sellier proposal called for the eradication of the system that sequestered registered sex workers to brothels (while still allowing for legalized sex work), making solicitation an offense, obliging those infected with a venereal disease to seek treatment, and criminalizing the transmission of venereal diseases. While this proposal was never codified into law, Sellier's idea to make the transmission of venereal diseases a punishable offense was supported in Tonkin.[154] Authorities in Tonkin began to realize that policing the transmission of venereal diseases was the key to give colonial authorities the means to police clandestine sex work while making clandestine sex workers more comfortable with seeking treatment for sexually transmitted infections.

The metropolitan Popular Front government ordered an empire-wide study of the social, economic, and political problems facing each colony. The study, called the Guernut Mission, sent representatives to the French colonies and territories to research and interview colonial subjects about the major issues complicating local politics. In January 1937, Justin Godart, a representative of the mission charged with conducting the study, arrived in Indochina to research the needs of colonizers and colonized alike. Godart and his team interviewed medical experts, police, and both French and Vietnamese local officials about their struggle to combat the spread of venereal diseases and their suggestions for improving the situation in the colony. Many of the recommendations about sex work later made by locals to the Guernut team focused on regulating the ả đào singing houses around the Khâm Thiên neighborhood, known for clandestine sex work. The director of health in Hà Đông suggested grouping singing houses in one central location so as to facilitate police regulation.[155] To address the problem of venereal diseases, which was reportedly rampant in the ả đào houses, the French resident of Hà Đông recommended that a medical "consultation room" be installed on Khâm Thiên Street, just outside Hanoi's city limits. To avoid shaming the singers, this medical facility would be billed as serving the public but would actually be devoted exclusively to the singers.[156] Đỗ Văn Nam, the representative of the Canton de Minh Hue in Cochinchina, recommended that the state punish not only sex workers but all who transmitted a venereal disease, including the male customers who frequented clandestine sex workers.[157]

Guernut Mission representative Godart would leave Indochina convinced that the colony's regulated sex industry was flawed. In his final report to the commission, he reasoned that with an estimated 60,000 people infected in Saigon-Cholon, a city of only 250,000, the regulation system had a "pitiful medical-policing design." He concluded that the regulation system was "insufficient, harmful, and costly."[158] In 1938, a meeting of the colony's Commission on Venereal Diseases referenced Godart's desire to end coerced treatment for venereal diseases and replace it with voluntary treatment.[159]

In February 1937, on orders from the Guernut Mission before Godart's departure, Hanoi mayor Virgitti and Dr. Joyeux invited journalists from Việt Báo and Đông Pháp to tour the Hanoi Dispensary. The goal was to showcase recent renovations and to work with journalists to promote the dispensary in a way that would encourage infected sex workers to feel comfortable seeking treatment.[160] The renovations, which made the dispensary less prison-like and possibly more humane than most hospitals, were intended to raise the morale of the patients while equipping them with the medical knowledge to avoid reinfection.[161]

Vũ Trọng Phụng and Thao Thao were two of the journalists permitted to report on the dispensary. Both had attempted to conduct first-hand research on the infamous facility in the past and had been turned down. Yet once Justin Godart and the Guernut Mission had arrived in Indochina, the mayor allowed the two journalists to tag along for the commission's tour of the dispensary.[162] In his famous 1937 series of newspaper articles that were eventually compiled into a book, *Lục Xì* (The dispensary), Vũ Trọng Phụng found that the newly renovated dispensary did indeed offer medical and social programs to help its patients. As evidence of its hygienic conditions, he cited a sterile examination room with stark white walls and spotless counters.[163] In 1935, a classroom was added to the dispensary to teach former sex workers skills that would enable them to assimilate into alternative professions. In the classroom, Vũ Trọng Phụng observed forty women sewing and learning to read and write quốc ngữ. The lessons were strikingly effective; Vũ Trọng Phụng noted that most women left their stay at the dispensary literate in quốc ngữ.[164] In another classroom, women learned sex education and measures to prevent the contraction of venereal diseases. Outside was a garden for patients to grow vegetables.[165]

While the dispensary was indeed reformed to a degree, the journalists also witnessed a harsh and even dangerous side of its environment that belied any remotely pleasant firsthand impressions. Treatment at the dispensary included a wash with acid-infused hot water so painful that patients took opium to endure the pain. Thao Thao claimed—exaggerating for effect—that for every hundred women at the dispensary, ninety-nine of them were addicted to opium.[166] Such high rates of opium addiction among women in the dispensary may have been a form of pain management or could have been a symptom of rampant drug use in the clandestine sex industry. Moreover, the living conditions were dismal. The dormitory where the women slept had a "dreary look of a prison."[167] In the summer, patients slept in beds without the protection of mosquito nets; winters were cold, as the windows had no curtains and the beds had minimal blankets.[168] Vũ Trọng Phụng observed that one hundred women were crammed into a room appropriate for only sixty.[169]

Fighting was common among patients and typically centered on the issue of officially registering with the police as a sex worker.[170] Relations between registered and unregistered sex workers were particularly tense. Thao Thao described it as two classes of women, "like a divided world."[171] Since the 1921 law did not require women to register as sex workers until the second time they were caught, registered sex workers resented first-time offenders who remained unregistered. Stories abound of registered sex workers bullying—or even beating—first-time offenders into registering. In an effort to stop it, dispensary officials divided the dormitory with bars, "like a tiger cage."[172] Yet the constant surveillance and tiger bars did little to subdue the conflicts. According to Thao Thao, patients frequently fought in the middle of the night after the lights went out. They pulled each other's hair and tore at their clothes. One could hear screaming throughout the night. One woman told Thao Thao that certain registered sex workers would regularly burn the bed sheets of a clandestine sex worker while she slept.[173] Another woman, a first-time offender, recounted to Vũ Trọng Phụng a disturbing story in which registered sex workers beat her and sodomized her with a hair pin. The fear of further violence led her to surrender and register as a sex worker, even though she knew how difficult it would be to get her name removed from the police roster.[174]

Thao Thao wrote of a dispensary full of women with tragic stories. In interviewing the patients, he listened to stories of naive girls from poor families becoming seduced by the lure of materialism, agreeing to sleep with men to pay for fancy clothing and high heels, only to be stiffed with the hotel bill and then, when forced to work off debt at a brothel, contracting a venereal disease. In a particularly heartbreaking case, Thao Thao wrote about a Miss Tuyết, pregnant at the time, whose life was derailed when the actions of a jealous neighbor resulted in the death of Miss Tuyết's lover. Miss Tuyết's child was born soon after that, but she lacked the funds to support the baby and resorted to clandestine sex work to make ends meet. The vice squad arrested her and imprisoned her in the dispensary. With no one to care for the nursing baby while its mother was quarantined, the child died.[175]

Although the Sellier proposal to eliminate the oppressive registration system and criminalize the transmission of venereal diseases never passed in the metropole, officials in Tonkin considered ways to implement Sellier-style measures in Tonkin. One administrator suggested eliminating state regulations on the sale of sex and instead offering free, discreet medical care for anyone—man or woman, sex worker or private citizen—affected by a venereal disease.[176] The Vietnamese press supported this measure. Writing for *Thời Vụ Báo* in 1938, journalist Tô Ân called to "eradicate the venereal disease epidemic and introduce science," imploring the state to "carry out [these measures] in a way that is humane." He called on the colonial government to follow the model of the "civilized countries" that "have cast aside the strict laws pertaining to the restriction of sex work and returned to the cures that follow science."[177]

In the spirit of the Sellier proposal, the Tonkin government bolstered public health measures to make venereal disease treatment accessible in a nonoppressive way so clandestine sex workers would trust the system and seek treatment. The state opened new venereal disease clinics and made treatment more accessible to the local population. In 1936, public health officials discussed transforming the Hanoi Ophthalmological Institute into a clinic to treat dermatological disorders and venereal diseases. They also considered opening a wing in the Indigenous Hospital specifically for the treatment of married women so as to protect their reputations.[178] That year, officials also established a special ward in the René Robin Hospital in Bạch Mai to treat cases of venereal diseases.[179] In 1937, the Prophylactic League of Hanoi called for expanding services, opening more dispensaries, and offering twenty-four-hour treatment to those afflicted with a venereal disease.[180] Specifically, officials planned to construct new dispensaries in Đáp Cầu, Tông, and on Khâm Thiên Street outside of Hanoi and recommended that visiting nurses circulate within Hải Phòng and Nam Định.[181]

The Tonkin government also launched public education campaigns to prevent the spread of venereal diseases. In the late 1930s, the state embarked on a program to teach prophylaxis and treatment to sex workers.[182] By 1938, sex workers in Hanoi had multiple options for venereal treatment. They could go to official hospitals such as the René Robin Hospital, the Polyclinique on Rue Miribel, local municipal consultations posts, or private clinics. Each of these offered clandestine sex workers an opportunity to obtain treatment without having to register as professional sex workers.[183] At meeting of the Anti-Venereal Disease League on January 11, 1939, officials came up with a multipronged strategy for fighting the spread of venereal diseases: a public awareness campaign disseminated in newspapers, books, and leaflets to teach people how to prevent venereal diseases; free treatment and the establishment of a special hospital for the poor; and, for those who lived just above the poverty line, reduced prices on treatment and medicine.[184]

Officials in Tonkin instituted provincial-level decrees modeled after the Sellier proposal that allowed clandestine sex workers to remain unregistered yet also provided means for the state to punish those who knowingly transmitted a venereal disease. By making public health needs predominant, these laws effectively allowed authorities and doctors to police clandestine sex work in places where they had previously had no jurisdiction, including ả đào singing houses, dance halls, bars, and other establishments that were not covered by the 1921 law or were located outside of colonial jurisdiction. Hanoi mayor Virgitti and Dr. Joyeux laid out a plan that would allow ả đào singers, taxi dancers, and the girlfriends of military men to avoid registering as sex workers but called for these women to have periodic venereal exams and to carry booklets in which to log the results of their checkups. Those who tested positive, Virgitti and Joyeux argued, would presumably submit to treatment voluntarily.[185]

In some cases, unregistered women were forced to submit to venereal exams. In 1939, Việt Báo reported a story about ả đào singers outside of Hanoi who were required to undergo pelvic exams. The singers protested, arguing that the exams themselves, reputed to be unhygienic, would lead to infection.[186] In 1940, Đông Pháp reported the case of a customer in Thanh Hóa who had contracted a venereal disease from an ả đào singer and led authorities to seek out other cases of transmission originating from the same ả đào house. The local government dispatched a nurse to inspect eight houses in Cửa Hậu, Quán Đò, and Cầu Thanh (Thanh Hoá). Of the twenty-one singers who were subjected to venereal exams, eighteen tested positive.[187] The following year, authorities required singers on Khâm Thiên Street withstand venereal exams and immediately arrested those who tested positive.[188] In 1942, the colonial-controlled city of Hải Phòng enacted a law mandating singers, taxi dancers, and waitresses at tea houses and cafés to allow doctors to examine them twice a month.[189] This change in the state's approach from policing sex work to policing venereal disease transmission proved to be an effective means of controlling sex work among women and establishments that were not officially registered with police.

Rather than being motivated by moral outrage, colonial policing of sex work in Tonkin was driven by the need to arrest the spread of venereal infections. With increased migrations around the Red River Delta and into the cities, the venereal trident of syphilis, gonorrhea, and chancroids was rampant in the lowlands of Tonkin. As the Tonkinese population remained largely ignorant about the symptoms of venereal infections and their modes of transmission, those infected with the diseases unwittingly continued to spread it. The French colonial government, meanwhile, grew ever more concerned that the high rates of venereal diseases would be devastating for the colonial population, as untreated infections resulted in serious neurological problems, miscarriages, and birth defects. Even more alarming for colonial officials were the high rates of venereal diseases among soldiers and sailors, which in some cases jeopardized whole military units.

Authorities identified sex workers as the primary source of contagion. In 1921, the Tonkin government adopted a metropolitan law that regulated sex work and made venereal exams mandatory. This law was uniformly applied in the few French concessions of Tonkin but could not be applied in Vietnamese-ruled areas, which made up the majority of the protectorate. Moreover, due to the oppressive nature of the regulation system—with its prescribed invasive pelvic exams and mandatory imprisonment (and concomitant loss of wages) for those requiring venereal disease treatment—the 1921 law had the unintended effect of discouraging women from registering as sex workers and leading them to operate on the black market, where they continued to transmit venereal infections unabated. Over the course of the interwar years, the colonial state collaborated with local authorities, built dispensaries to treat sex workers, and attempted to police clandestine sex workers. Yet venereal infections continued to proliferate, in part because of strict metropolitan privacy laws curtailing the operations of police in the clandestine industry.

Political trends from the metropole in the late 1930s led colonial authorities to reconsider the regulation system. As policing was proving ineffective, colonial officials introduced a twofold approach that sought to reduce the spread of venereal diseases through public education while aiming to make clandestine sex workers more comfortable with seeking treatment. Local-level laws passed in the 1930s that criminalized the transmission of venereal diseases led to new ways of policing clandestine sex work. Whereas the 1921 law had given authorities the ability to police registered sex workers, the law's emphasis on protecting individual liberties had inadvertently prevented authorities from policing clandestine sex work in ả đào singing houses, dance halls, bars, and other private establishments. New public health measures introduced in the 1930s allowed sex workers to seek treatment without forcing them to register with the state, while transferring a certain amount of authority from the police to the medical industry. In other words, the new regulations allowed clandestine sex workers to remain unregistered while effectively granting public health administrators authority to monitor their role in the spread of venereal infections. The following chapters will show how colonial authorities used the fight against venereal diseases as a means of justifying the policing of á đào singers and taxi dancers in ways that had not been permitted under the 1921 law.

CHAPTER 3

Unfree Labor

Debt Bondage and Human Trafficking

In 1940, the newspaper *Đông Pháp* published an article with the headline "[She] No Longer Wants to Live a Life of Misery." The article recounted the tragic story of Lê Thị Cúc, a young woman from the countryside who was attracted to what she thought would be the "luxurious and fun" lifestyle of an ả đào singer.[1] Ả đào singers, who will be discussed in chapter 5, had a reputation for being beautiful women who lived fast lives and often moonlighted as clandestine sex workers. Lê Thị Cúc found a job at an ả đào singing house in Hanoi owned by a Miss Thị Thuật.

Arriving in the city broke, homeless, and without the support of her family, Lê Thị Cúc took out a sixty-piastre loan from Miss Thị Thuật to help her get started. The women agreed to a debt-bondage arrangement in which Lê Thị Cúc would pay the loan back through labor. Arrangements like this were common in many sectors of early twentieth-century Tonkin's labor force, including among plantation workers, domestic servants, and service industry workers. Debt-bondage arrangements enabled workers who had little money and no place to live to bargain for an advance on their salary, room, and board. The arrangement thus offered a degree of social mobility for the poor—and independence for young women who were looking to start new lives away from their family. Workers who accepted the advance payment or room and board were bound by the debt-bondage arrangement to pledge their wages to the employer—and forgo a salary—until the debt was paid off.

Despite the advantages of debt-bondage arrangements, they were frequently exploited by employers. In this case, Miss Thị Thuật forced Lê Thị Cúc to sign a contract stating that she had taken a loan for one hundred piastres—in other words, 166 percent of the actual initial loan of sixty piastres. The longer it took for Lê Thị Cúc to pay off the debt, the more interest would accrue. All the while, the money that Lê Thị Cúc would otherwise have been earning from her labor was given to Miss Thị Thuật. Given that Lê Thị Cúc earned no salary and could not leave her job for a better situation due to the debt she owed Miss Thị Thuật, she was effectively "unfree."

Unfree laborers—those who earned no wages for their labor—were common in the colonial black market sex industry. Unfree labor situations such as debt-bondage agreements helped impoverished women to get a start living independently in the big city while avoiding registering on the police roster of sex workers. Thus, working outside the regulation system meant that clandestine sex workers could not benefit from legal protection, however meager it may have been. Consequently, many of these women were left vulnerable in situations of unfree labor. Underpaid, they were forced to take out loans and tied to jobs they could not leave—sometimes for years. Some were left in what Rhacel Salazar Parreñas describes as "a paradoxical position of coercion and choice."[2] Others were forced into sex work or trafficked.

Ashamed of selling sex, Lê Thị Cúc wanted to leave, but she was trapped by the hundred-piastre debt agreement that Miss Thị Thuật had forced her to sign—and the interest that accrued as Lê Thị Cúc struggled to work it off. She considered running away before the debt contract was satisfied, but Miss Thị Thuật learned of her plan and repeatedly beat her into subordination. Lê Thị Cúc eventually became so traumatized by the beatings that, according to an article in *Đông Pháp*, she "went mad" and was admitted to the René Robin Hospital. Knowing that returning to the á đào singing house would mean being forced to take more customers to pay off her debt, Lê Thị Cúc appealed to police. Her "life of misery" eventually made the news, though the outcome was never reported.[3]

This chapter explores two forms of unfree labor in Tonkin's black market sex industry: debt bondage and human trafficking. Women involved in debt-bondage arrangements exchanged work for room, board, and a cash loan, thereby temporarily forgoing their salary and being forced to remain at their jobs until the debt was worked off. Trafficked women were typically tricked or abducted and sold against their will to brothels in Tonkin or China, linking the sex industries of both countries. The two forms of unfree labor were not mutually exclusive. Sex workers in debt-bondage agreements could be trafficked against their will, and women and girls who had been kidnapped and trafficked could be forced to work off the debt incurred when brothel owners bought them.

In the early years of colonialism, French officials failed to effectively police exploitative debt-bondage arrangements and human trafficking. The problem continued, and, by the late colonial period, the prevalence of unfree sex work proved to be an embarrassment for the Third Republic French government, which prided itself on its respect for human rights and its antislavery stance. Meanwhile, a League of Nations special committee on the trafficking of women and girls was pressuring the French government to close brothels, including those that employed voluntary sex workers, as the committee claimed that the mere existence of brothels created the market for trafficking women and girls. Yet the metropolitan and colonial French governments resisted. In the late 1930s, pressure from the international community, as well as the need to regulate the black market, would finally lead the colonial government to enact measures to limit the trafficking of women and girls. As this chapter will show, the governor-general drew from the rhetoric of the anti-trafficking movement to make the case against all forms of unfree labor, including trafficking and debt bondage (consensual as well as nonconsensual). Measures proposed by the governor-general would enable the colonial state to police clandestine sex work in ways it could not before.

Debt Bondage

Debt bondage in the sex industry was part of a larger practice of debt-bondage arrangements that was ubiquitous throughout Southeast Asia. Under debt-bondage agreements, the indebted paid off a monetary debt through labor for a definitive period of time. Such agreements existed in many sectors of the economy, and debts originated from a variety of factors. Between growing seasons, landless peasants entered into debt-bondage arrangements to pay off debts that had accrued in the farming process.[4] Some were forced into bondage due to usury scams that targeted the poor. Others owed money from gambling debts or loans taken out to pay for expensive social obligations, including weddings and funerals.[5] Debts could be transferred among family members. For example, parents could designate their children to complete the labor required to satisfy a debt. Likewise, creditors could sell the debt of laborers, thereby requiring laborers to complete the debt-bondage agreement for another boss. For many people, debt bondage was preferable to starvation or begging. In theory, debtors had the option to pay off their loans and buy their freedom before the original time table of the debt-bondage agreement.[6] And it was a means for impoverished workers—both men and women—to obtain an advance of capital, pay off a family debt, or secure food and shelter, all in return for labor.

Those who could not repay their debt were able to request to have the debt reduced, though the request could be denied. Those who failed to pay were pursued by a debt collector (nặc nô), who, more often than not, intimidated the indebted family and threatened violence. When caught, debtors were tried by a local Vietnamese magistrate and forced to sell their possessions to pay off the debt. Any leftover debt was settled through further bondage arrangements, which could be met by the debtor or a family member.[7] In theory, debt-bondage arrangements were transactional, with debt being erased through a predetermined amount of labor. Yet, in practice, debt-bondage agreements could be easily exploited or manipulated, thus prolonging the period of labor.

It would be erroneous to conflate twentieth-century debt bondage with Western ideas of chattel slavery. Conflating debt bondage and chattel slavery elides an important distinction: whereas slaves had no choice in the matter, debtors could, in many cases, chose to satisfy their debt through work, thereby earning their freedom.[8] Debt bondage was a common choice for women like Lê Thị Cúc, whose story opened this chapter. The choice was made for social as well as economic reasons. For example, an advance of money or promise of shelter could help the indebted migrate to a new city or, as we shall see in the case of the clandestine sex workers studied in this book, escape the traditional gender expectations imposed on young women.

When taking social factors into account, it is more useful to describe debt-bondage agreements as unfree labor rather than as slavery. As Elisa Camiscioli argues in the case of French women who migrated to Argentina, it is more useful to look at sex work as a continuum of coercion and agency. Similar to Camiscioli's findings in Argentina, in interwar Tonkin, it was not uncommon for those owing or borrowing money to willingly enter debt-bondage agreements with full or incomplete information about the terms of the work agreement that they were entering. In fact, for some women, debt-bondage agreements were a temporary step toward greater freedom. Full information gave them a degree of agency; incomplete information left them vulnerable to exploitation and coerced work.[9] The complexity of their stories of debt bondage and kid-napping becomes apparent when contextualized in a larger history of colonial poverty, urbanization, and migration.

During the late colonial period, debt bondage was common in the major cities of Indochina, which were rapidly developing, resulting in a high demand for labor. Meanwhile, the turbulent economy left people in the rural provinces financially unstable. A wave of male and female peasants seeking financial security migrated to the cities to fill the demand for labor. Migrants, most of whom arrived with little money and nowhere to stay, were desperate for work. Cities such as Hải Phòng had well-known—but often illegal—markets for laborers, the most notorious of which was the Djbouti Garden (discussed in chapter 1). Workers sat-isfied demands in sectors including construction, household labor, and unregistered sex work. The volatile capitalist economy and its resulting impoverished class made conditions ripe for exploitation, leaving some workers in a state of unfree labor.

Debt bondage had long been a prevalent practice in sex industries across Asia. Trude Jacobsen found that laws governing debt bondage in early modern Cambodia enabled creditors to demand sexual labor from women who were in debt, and that right was transferred when the debt was bought out or transferred to another party.[10] In the early modern period, colonial economic policies in Island Southeast Asia drove increas-ing numbers of Southeast Asians into debt, which was often repaid with their daughters' labor.[11] In the late nineteenth century, as colonial gov-ernments introduced the European-style brothel system to Asia, brothel owners offered debt-bondage arrangements because, according to Bruno Lasker, it was their business "to keep the laborer in debt."[12] A similar debt-bondage agreement played out in China: families lent their daugh-ters to a madam in exchange for an advance on a loan, an arrangement where daughters became "pawned prostitutes" (baozhang).[13]

In Tonkin, debt-bondage sex work provided the necessary capital and resources for women to strike out on their own. In early twentieth-century Vietnam, it was rare—and very difficult—for women to break free of the family structure to live independently. Women were expected to remain with their family until marriage, after which they moved into the home of their husband or with his family. Women who did leave their family for an independent life faced problems finding landlords to rent to them, as single women were often suspected of selling sex. This was a common problem for rural peasant women migrating to the big city, where they had no family or social structure in place. Women's employment options were limited to low-paying positions such as maid, market vendor, street hawker, manual laborer, shop girl, and child-care provider, among other professions. For those with little access to capital, debt bondage functioned as an alternative to borrowing from unscrupulous moneylenders. Debt-bondage agreements in the clandestine sex industry usually included a cash advance, clothing, and room and board, all of which were to be paid off through labor.[14] For example, Ng Thị Đào and Ng Thị Thu borrowed money from a dancing house owner to pay off former petty debts and buy fancy clothing to attract customers.[15] In short, while debt bondage was a form of unfree labor, for some women it was the first step toward an independent, self-supporting life.

For nineteen-year-old Nguyễn Thị Ch., whose situation was covered by the newspaper *Việt Báo* in 1939, debt bondage was an attractive means of breaking free from her family. As the daughter of a prominent deputy mandarin, she felt constrained by the traditional expectations for a daughter in a family of such status and ran away to the big city. When she arrived in Hanoi, she found work in an ả đào singing house that was also a clandestine brothel. She reached an agreement with the owners for room and board, as well as a cash advance of thirty piastres to pay for the fashionable clothing needed to attract customers. The three piastres that she earned with each customer went directly to the brothel owners to pay off her debt.[16] Similarly, when Lê Thị Cúc, whose 1940 story opened this chapter, looked for a way to leave her simple life in the countryside and ended up becoming an ả đào singer in Hanoi, she was able to do so by taking out a sixty-piastre loan from the owner of a singing house.[17]

While most women entered into informal contracts, some signed formal loans to be repaid through employment. In 1936, the newspaper *Trung Hoà Báo* reported, Thị Cúc and Thị Tình signed contracts to borrow fifty piastres in exchange for working for a Miss Tòng, the owner of a dancing hall in Hải Phòng.[18] In 1937, *Đông Pháp* ran an article about Ng Thị Đào, a migrant from Thái Bình, and Ng Thị Thu from Hà Nam, who signed contracts stipulating that they would pay off loans of one hundred piastres in return for three years of work in a dance hall.[19]

Unscrupulous managers used debt bondage to exploit sex workers. Two common scams were to add compounding interest to the loan or devalue the earnings the debtor made with sex work, thereby increasing the time it took to pay off the loan. Brothel managers, like the one who ran the singing house where Thị-Cúc worked, used these tricks to retain employees who were looking to leave.[20] Other managers at clandestine brothels forced workers to take out loans—even when the workers did not need or want one—as a condition of employment. These loans served as a way for owners to prevent employees from leaving. Given the high interest rates associated with these loans, the workers became indebted to the owners and had no choice but to extend their stay at the brothel. Take, for example, the 1938 case, reported in *Đông Pháp*, of the owner of an ả đào singing house and clandestine brothel who forced employees Hồng and Bảo to take out loans of fifty piastres in cash and seventy-two piastres in gold. The women's meagre eight-piastre monthly income went to paying off the debt, but after nearly a year—well beyond the amount of time needed to pay off their debts—the owner still refused to pay them or let them go.[21]

In another scam, women willingly took out loans and entered into debt-bondage agreements thinking they would be working in another profession, only to find that they had been tricked into selling sex to pay off the loans. In 1931, the newspaper *Ngọ Báo* reported on Thị Ty, a migrant from Thái Bình. When she arrived in Hanoi, she found herself tired, lonely, and hungry. A Madame Th. lent her twenty piastres and offered her room, board, and a job so that she could embark on her newly independent life. The two agreed that she would work at a clothing store, but when Thị Ty showed up for her first day of work, she discovered that Madame Th.'s "clothing store" was actually an ả đào singing house and clandestine brothel. To make matters worse, interest accrued on the initial twenty-piastre loan, doubling her debt and requiring her to work without salary for twice as long as she had anticipated.[22]

Some managers claimed debt bondage to hold workers against their will even when no cash advance had ever been given to the worker. Take, for example, the 1936 *Đông Pháp* story about Đinh Thị Hiếng, a migrant who worked at Thị Nghĩa's ả đào singing house in Hanoi. Hiếng asked for permission to leave the singing house to attend a funeral in her home village, but Thị Nghĩa refused, claiming that she had not yet worked off a debt of ten piastres. Hiếng denied ever borrowing the money and claimed to have been made to perform sex work without pay.[23]

Some women were forced into the clandestine sex industry in order to pay off debts incurred elsewhere. In 1936, *Việt Báo* covered the case of two young women from the village of Kim Sơn in Ninh Bình Province who hired a rickshaw to take them from the Phúc Nhạc market up to the provincial capital. When they arrived, the young women did not have even a few loose coins to to pay the twenty-five *xu* rickshaw fee. The rickshaw puller then took the two women to the local ả đào singing house on Cầu Lim Street and made them work off their debt there, subsequently claiming their earnings for himself.[24] In 1937, *Việt Báo* ran another story in which Miss Lan, covered in chapter 1, was forced into debt bondage by the owner of a boardinghouse after getting stiffed for the bill by a lover who also robbed her.[25]

Women got out of their debt-bondage contracts in a myriad of ways. In 1936, *Trung Hoà Báo* reported, Thị Cúc and Thị Tình, mentioned above, borrowed fifty piastres and agreed to be taxi dancers in Miss Tòng's dance hall. To escape their debt, they ran away with a French customer who frequented the hall.[26] A few months later, *Đông Pháp* again reported on Đinh thị Hiếng—mentioned above with regard to the dispute over whether or not a manager had lent her ten piastres—who likewise ran away in order to escape being forced into sex work.[27] Some women found legal channels to fight unfair contracts. In 1938, Hồng and Bảo, mentioned earlier, sued their manager for not paying their salary and asked for their freedom. When they left, the owner countersued them for not having paid their debts. The outcome of these lawsuits was not reported in the newspapers.[28]

Other women got out of debt bondage when their families intervened to free them. In 1936, as the newspaper *Đồng Pháp* reported, N., a migrant from Thái Bình, was tricked into debt bondage at an ả đào singing house. When singing house's owners refused to release her from the debt, her brother appealed to authorities, who eventually freed her.[29] The mandarin parents of Nguyễn Thị Ch., mentioned above, searched tirelessly for their runaway daughter. They eventually found her working in an ả đào singing house, whereupon they paid off her debt and brought her back to the countryside.[30]

Employers also turned to authorities to enforce debt-bondage contracts. Although unregistered sex work was illegal, brothel owners likely either lied to police about the nature of the work in question or paid them off. When Nguyễn Thị Đào and Ng Thị Thu—mentioned above in the 1937 story about their contracted loan of one hundred piastres—skipped town before meeting the terms of their contracts, the brothel owner, Trịnh Thị Ý, appealed to police, who subsequently helped track down the women in another dance hall and arrested them.[31]

While in theory debt bondage offered women the first step toward an independent life, in many cases debt-bondage contracts were exploited. Employers tricked women into sex work, misrepresented the loan amount, and devalued sex workers' labor, leaving them in a state of unfree labor. Despite these abuses, it would not be until the late 1920s that the colonial government would take measures to stop debt-bondage agreements, though without specifically targeting the black market sex industry. In the late 1930s, the governor-general would cite the abuses that had been reported in this industry to make the case that debt bondage was a form of human trafficking and in turn use this argument as pretext for policing clandestine sex work.

Trafficking

The second type of unfree labor in Tonkin's black market sex industry was human trafficking. Early twentieth-century trafficking was a broad industry that encompassed both voluntary and forced migrations of men, women, and children who were sold into a number of sectors of the work force, including plantation labor, factory work, domestic labor, and the sex industry. In her study of trafficking in twentieth-century northern China, Johanna Sirera Ransmeier identifies a "reproductive economy" in which women and girls were sold—voluntarily and involuntarily—as wives, concubines, child brides, sex workers, and adoptive children.[32] While anecdotal evidence suggests that a similar reproductive economy may have existed in the countryside of Tonkin, more research is needed on this topic.

Trafficking networks in Tonkin long vexed the colonial government. As Micheline Lessard writes, although human-trafficking networks in Vietnam predated the arrival of the French, the problem was exacerbated by the colonial wars and French monopolies on opium.[33] Tonkin's location and geographical landscape facilitated smuggling, and Vietnamese women and children were trafficked internationally by land and by sea throughout the colonial period. Trafficking networks in Tonkin shuffled women around the Red River Delta, from the countryside to the cities, and to international human-trafficking markets in Asia.

The land route sent women to China, Phnom Penh, and Bangkok;[34] the sea route, controlled for the most part by Chinese pirates, sent women to Hong Kong, Shanghai, and Singapore.[35] Most of the trafficking occurred near one of Tonkin's well-traveled trade routes or many waterways. Traffickers used the land routes to transport women and children to Lào Cai and Lạng Sơn and the water routes to transport them to Hồn Gai, Cát Bà, or Móng Cái, from which sites they traveled easily to China.[36] Border towns were well-known spots for trafficking. Due to their proximity to the Tonkin border, the Chinese port of Pak Hoi and neighboring city of K'intcheou were major markets for buying and selling people. By the 1880s, the trade of women and children in Pak Hoi had become commonplace, and the

French consulate at Pak Hoi warned colonial authorities in Tonkin that the market thrived in part because local authorities tolerated the buying and selling of Vietnamese women and children.[37]

Micheline Lessard shows that the late nineteenth-century transnational anticolonial rebellions that straddled the Sino-Vietnamese border were supported, in part, by human trafficking insofar as the sale of Vietnamese women and children funded the anticolonial rebels' supply of weapons. "In a perverse way," Lessard writes, "the trafficking of women and children was practiced in the name of patriotism and nationalism."[38] In the first decade of the twentieth century, the rebel highland areas of Guangxi in China and Thái Bình in Tonkin were hotbeds of raids, kidnappings, and sales of people.[39]

The prevalence of trafficking was a thorn in the side of the colonial government. In a complicated legal history, slavery and the slave trade had been completely abolished in France and its territories since 1848,[40] and the Third Republic government took pride in its motto "Liberty, Equality, Brotherhood," however hypocritical that may have been in the context of colonialism. The colonial government used customs agents, working from fortified posts in strategic spots on Indochina's waterways and maritime borders, including one in Hạ Long Bay, to spot-check ships in order to police the movement of goods and people across the border.[41] Nonetheless, trafficking of women and children prevailed—and it was a great embarrassment for the colonial government. The French resident of Bắc Kạn warned the resident superior of Tonkin in 1904 that trafficking was "a political question that has not escaped us."[42]

Colonial policing of traffickers was complicated by Tonkin's status as a protectorate. As those living and committing crimes outside the French concessions were subject to the indigenous legal code, the bureaucratic geography rendered it impossible to prosecute traffickers in those areas under the French legal code. Colonial authorities cooperated with local Vietnamese authorities to prosecute traffickers under Vietnamese laws that deemed slavery and trafficking illegal, but they rarely succeeded.[43] Articles 209 and 210 of the indigenous code set the punishment at from six months to three years and a fine of twenty to a thousand piastres, article 211 condemned those who sold family members to traffickers to a prison time of six months to two years, and article 212 outlawed buying women and girls. Officials also drew from a French metropolitan decree of December 1912 that punished traffickers for six months to three years or up to five years if the trafficked person was younger than fourteen. This decree was also applicable to French subjects in Tonkin.[44]

As the prevalence of human trafficking belied French Third Republic values, the colonial government historically faced pressure from within France to stop the trafficking networks. In 1906, the French League of Human Rights implored the Ministry of Colonies to develop a legal code reflective of that implemented in France's West African colonies and in the French Congo to punish traffickers who, the league wrote, "lived in impunity."[45] In 1907, the resident superior of Annam lamented the limits of colonial jurisdiction, urging the governor-general of Indochina to enact a decree to punish such traffickers by expanding French jurisdiction into areas governed by the Vietnamese royal government. Frustrated by insufficient resources devoted to catching traffickers and by the colonial juridical code, the League of Human Rights in 1910 suggested that the French government establish special jurisdiction that would enable it to prosecute traffickers who operated in areas outside the jurisdiction of the French legal code. France was unable to follow through with the request.[46]

The international community also pressured France to collaborate with Vietnamese officials to put an end to trafficking. As slavery was being abolished around the world in the mid-nineteenth century, the international community turned its attention to rumors of global trafficking networks.[47] As Stephanie Limoncelli shows, the movement, which emerged in England, grew out of the movement to end transatlantic slavery, Christian missionary activity, and the "desire to help 'distant others.'"[48] Along with other European, North American, and South American states, France joined the first international antitrafficking movement at the turn of the century. Initially, the antitrafficking movement was solely concerned with "white slavery": forced sex work among white women.[49] Rumors of foreign men trafficking white women to the colonies inspired European and North American activists.[50] Over a series of agreements, the international community organized resources and synchronized laws against trafficking. The 1904 agreement coordinated international communication about traffickers, called for policing at ports and rail stations, and established legal means for foreign women to be repatriated.[51] A second agreement of 1910 set the age of consent for transport and sex work to twenty years old. It established legal measures by which to punish procurers who transported young women—with or without their consent.[52] The 1912 conference called for the suppression of trafficking in the colonies.[53] And the 1921 convention, administered by the League of Nations, replaced the term "white slave trade" with "traffic of women," explaining that "it was never intended that we should concern ourselves with only white women." Thus did the antitrafficking movement turn its attention to indigenous women in the colonies.[54]

The 1921 convention was particularly damning for France. Members of the commission identified licensed brothels, including those that housed voluntary sex workers, as "the principal cause of the trafficking of women" and condemned France's system of tolerating regulated sex work. The "disappearance" of licensed brothels, according to the convention, was "an essential condition for the absolute suppression of the traffic."[55] For its part, France made the case for tolerating the sale of sex, arguing that regulations would prevent the spread of venereal diseases.[56]

Although French representatives participated in the 1904, 1910, and 1921 international antitrafficking meetings, France never adhered to the final agreements.[57] The French government—and much of the metropolitan French population—regarded the measures proposed at the conventions to be an attack on the French-regulated prostitution system and an imposition of Anglo-Saxon sexual mores, as the regulation of sex work was "an important locus in the struggle to define modern French identity."[58] Nonetheless, in the 1920s, the French colonial government did introduce minor measures to thwart trafficking networks in Tonkin. In 1923, it expelled foreign sex workers, many of whom were believed to be trafficked, and customs agents searched ships that were potentially carrying women and children from Tonkin. Yet French boats were too slow to catch traffickers who were shuffling victims to China.[59]

The strength of the trafficking network was, ironically, its disorganization. Because networks in Tonkin relied on multiple, loosely organized, smaller networks and lone-wolf actors instead of any single group of kidnappers or buyers, colonial authorities could not disrupt the logistical system simply by arresting random perpetrators or banning foreign ships from entering and exiting Vietnamese ports. Meanwhile, the very amorphousness of trafficking networks made them all the more terrifying to a public that never knew who would be kidnapped next.

During the interwar years, stories abound of women and children being abducted and sold into trafficking networks, where they were destined to be sold off as sex workers, concubines, or household servants. The colonial-era scholar André Baudrit estimates that in Tonkin, from 1933 to 1936, there were 180 reported kidnappings of Vietnamese women and children per year—an average of one every other day.[60] Files from the 1941 Hanoi police department log showed that dozens of women and girls aged ten to twenty years old were reported missing each month.[61]

The Vietnamese media expressed outrage at what they referred to as an "epidemic" (*nạn*) of missing people; a 1928 *Ngọ Báo* headline declared that "Truly [Human Trafficking] Is a Huge Detriment to the Vietnamese Race [*giống nòi*]," and a 1929 *Trung Hoà Nhật Báo* newspaper headline asked, "Why Are So Many Children Going Missing These Days?"[62] Journalists saw it as their moral obligation to print stories that called attention to the epidemic and urged authorities to take action.[63] Yet the articles expressed certain contradictory sentiments—a sense of defeat over the ubiquity of trafficking along with the feeble hope that the French government would somehow fix the problem. A 1928 *Trung Hoà Nhật Báo* article headlined "Why Do Kidnappers Do This?" expressed tepid optimism: "Hopefully officials will track down, arrest and punish them severely; hopefully they will eradicate this group [of kidnappers]."[64]

Women and girls found themselves entangled in trafficking networks in many ways. In some cases, their own families handed their daughters over to traffickers—wittingly or unwittingly. Families in desperate situations entrusted daughters to friends or family to guarantee their survival, never imagining that the trusted friend or family member would turn around and sell the girls into trafficking networks. In times of famine, families gave their children to family friends or someone claiming to adopt the child. Unbeknown to the family, the trusted loved one sold their child off to become a household servant, a concubine, or a sex worker in Tonkin's cities or abroad. Large families too poor to feed their children sometimes sold their daughters on the rationale that selling a few children was preferable to letting all of them starve and that the children who were sold would be at least guaranteed food and shelter. In times of poverty, some families married off their daughters to rich men, only to learn that they were traffickers. Other families knowingly sold their daughters into the sex industry.[65]

In some cases, women and girls were abducted by mẹ mìn—the old ladies who roamed the countryside in search of women and children whom they would kidnap and sell either to clandestine brothels in the big cities or to traffickers who would take them to China. The term "mẹ mìn" (女眠) is from Chinese, "mẹ" (女) meaning woman and "mìn" (眠) meaning sleep, which may have been a reference to the use of sedatives by mẹ mìn in capturing their victims.[66] Scholars of trafficking in China found similar figures in trafficking operations. In his research on the Shanghai sex industry, Christian Henriot references elderly women who, for survival, engaged in illegal activities, including kidnapping women and children for the purposes of reselling them to middle men. Likewise, in her work on Shanghai, Gail Hershatter found references to old lady traffickers called *bai mayi*—literally "white ants" because locals saw them as pests in society. In her work on human trafficking in Beijing, Johanna Ransmeier noted that women played an integral role in the buying and selling of people and found trafficking was the most common major crime committed by women.[67]

Described as "a class of people who specialize in selling women and girls to China,"[68] mẹ mìn were notorious in Tonkin, and newspapers were abuzz with the dangers they posed. According to a 1928 article in *Trung Hoà Nhật Báo*, "these days, everywhere you go people talk about the mẹ mìn, especially outside of the city gates."[69] An article printed in the newspaper *Ngày Nay* deemed 1929 to be "the year of mẹ mìn" due to the frequency of kidnapping.[70] The mere mention of "mẹ mìn" reportedly struck terror in parents and made children abandon their sidewalk games to run and hide.[71]

Public fear of mẹ mìn was so great that vigilante violence was not unusual. A strange woman appearing in a market was enough to elicit accusation of her being a mẹ mìn, as explained in *Ngày Nay*. All that was needed was for one person to point a finger and yell, "Mẹ mìn!" before parents yanked their children close and a mob gathered around the suspected mẹ mìn to intimidate her into leaving. In some cases, the mob would attack the woman.[72]

A mẹ mìn was typically an unmarried Vietnamese woman, usually in her forties or fifties.[73] Kidnapping may have been the one of few ways for single or widowed older women to make an income. While mẹ mìn usually worked alone, in 1939, journalists reported on a group of mẹ mìn. Hoàng Thị Tự and Trương Thị Lan, both forty-seven, and Lương Thị Xuân, sixty, from Hạ Lý, lived and worked together to traffic women and girls. The three called themselves *bà ba*—literally "the three women"— and *Đông Pháp* described them as being in the "profession of luring people."[74] In 1931, the presses reported on a *bố mìn*, a male form of the mẹ mìn kidnappers.[75]

Mẹ mìn abducted women and girls in a variety of ways. Being older, mẹ mìn may have lacked the physical strength and stature to take their victims forcibly.[76] Instead, mẹ mìn reportedly looked and acted like decent people. When kidnapping children, if parents were present, a mẹ mìn would befriend the parents in order to gain their trust and permission to take care of the children.[77] Otherwise, mẹ mìn typically preyed on unsupervised children.[78] They were known to invite children to play and offer them treats or a cool towel, which would have been much appreciated in the tropical summer heat but was also a way to administer ether and thus render a victim unconcious.[79]

In reports on kidnapping, the archetypal mẹ mìn had a special ability to "lure" (dỗ) her victims.[80] Rumor had it that mẹ mìn bewitched their victims by putting them under a spell. After thirteen-year-old Đào Thị Yến of Ninh Bình Province disappeared, Ngọ Báo reported in 1936, friends of the family spotted her following a strange old woman. Family members suspected that the lady was a mẹ mìn and had cast a spell on the young girl, leaving her semiconscious and "bewitched" (bị bỏ bùa mê) by the old woman.[81] The more pedestrian explanation was that such kidnappers rendered victims unconscious or made them docile by slipping them sedatives via food or sweets.

Indeed, reports abound of mẹ mìn drugging their victims. They were rumored to administer potent sedatives manufactured in China.[82] A 1924 article in Trung Hoà Nhật Báo noted that a mẹ mìn gave victims an intoxicant that put them into a state where they "obsessively followed" her. In another case, harbor police caught a mẹ mìn in a small boat in Hạ Long Bay, on her way to sell three Vietnamese women in their twenties who were drugged unconscious.[83] The same paper printed a story in 1933 of group of five women in their mid-twenties and a six-year-old girl, all found drugged and unconscious in a trafficker's boat traveling from Hồn Gai to Cẩm Phả.[84] In a 1938 case, also reported in Trung Hoà Nhật Báo, Vong A Si, a Chinese mẹ mìn, offered Vũ Thị Tý and Thị Lăng fruit dosed with an intoxicant that rendered them unconscious.[85]

Mẹ mìn took advantage of family problems to lure young women away, particularly young women who were fighting with their families or were fed up with social expectations for women.[86] In 1931, Trung Hoà Nhật Báo reported on a case of a mẹ mìn who targeted women who had been arguing with their husbands or mothers-in-law and then prostituted the young women to Foreign Legion soldiers.[87] Later that same year, Ngọ Báo covered the case, mentioned above, of twenty-year-old Thị Ty, from Thái Bình, who ran away to escape regular whippings from her parents. She met an old lady who promised to take care of her. Little did she know that the lady would end up selling her to an ả đào singing house that turned out to be a clandestine brothel and that she would be forced into sex work.[88] In 1937, Đông Pháp printed the story of an eighteen-year-old woman from Kiến Xương (in Thái Bình Province) who found herself vulnerable to the charms of a mẹ mìn during a point when her stepmother was trying to force her to marry a man she did not love. She met a woman who, unbeknown to her, was a mẹ mìn. The woman helped her run away, but once she left home, the mẹ mìn sold her to a brothel.[89] The following year, *Đông Pháp* ran another story about eighteen-year-old Ng. Thị Bình, who also encountered a mẹ mìn after fleeing an abusive family. The woman offered to take her to a restaurant for a warm meal, but when they arrived the old lady sold the woman to a man named Ng V. Chiêu, who forced her into sex work.[90]

Migrants were particularly susceptible to being trafficked into the clandestine sex industry. Coming from the countryside, most migrant young women were naive and unaware of the common crime schemes in Hanoi and Hải Phòng. Exacerbating their situation, most migrants were poor, disoriented by the chaos of the big cities, and in need of food, shelter, and work. In 1935, *Ngọ Báo* published a story about Thị Bảo, a young migrant who took a shortcut through the Djibouti Garden in Hải Phòng as she made her way to her aunt's house. In the garden, a notorious spot for kidnappings, she met an elderly lady named Trần Thị Lan, who offered her shelter for the night. Instead of taking Thị Bảo home as promised, the old lady sold her to a man who forced her into sex work.[91] In 1937, *Việt Báo* ran a story about Thị Đào, a migrant from Thái Bình to Hải Phòng, who was lured by a mẹ mìn who ended up selling her to a brothel. The *Việt Báo* article presented the case in terms of the standard narrative for country people traveling to the debauched city: "A country girl who left the province, Thị Đào never even knew of this horror of trapping of people."[92] Similarly, in 1938, Đặng Thị Nuột and her aunt went to Hải Dương to see the Bastille Day parade, *Đông Pháp* reported. They got separated in the crowd, and Đặng Thị Nuột wandered around for hours looking for her aunt. A woman eventually approached her, offering to help and give her a place to stay. But when she went back to the woman's home, the woman tried to pimp her to an African guard from Shell Oil Company. Đặng thị Nuột refused and managed to escape and find police.[93]

Mẹ mìn used bait-and-switch promises of employment to trick young women into sex work. In a common scheme, a mẹ mìn lured naive country girls with jobs serving drinks in the big city. When the migrants reached their destination, they would find that the mẹ mìn had sold them to a clandestine brothel.[94] In 1937, *Việt Báo* covered a case in which a mẹ mìn promised seven ethnic Chinese women from the Tonkin countryside jobs at a weaving factory in Chợ Lớn, in Cochinchina. When the women arrived in Chợ Lớn, she prostituted them to a group of men who brutally gang-raped the women.[95]

Mẹ mìn drew on preexisting relationships with owners of clandestine brothels—usually ả đào singing houses and dance halls—to sell girls and

young women into sex work. Such was the case for fifteen-year-old Thị
Ngân and seventeen-year-old Thị Oanh, whose 1941 case was reported
in both of the newspapers *Tin Mới* and *Đông Pháp*. A mẹ mìn promised the
girls a waitress job, but when the girls arrived at the establishment, they
learned that the mẹ mìn had a preexisting agreement to sell girls to the
owner of an ả đào house.[96] In some cases, ả đào house owners even forced
women into debt bondage to pay off the debt they had incurred when
buying them from a mẹ mìn. In other words, such women worked to pay a
debt for money that went to someone else and they never received in the
first place. Đặng Thị Như, the migrant from Thái Bình whose story opened
this book, found herself in such a situation. She met an unassuming and
helpful old woman who lured her with the promise of employment in
Hanoi. Little did Như know, the lady then sold her to an ả đào singing
house, where she was made to sell sex to pay off her purchase price.[97]

Those not sold to brothels in Tonkin or other areas of Indochina were
sold to traffickers who transported them to China. In this scheme, kidnapped young women and girls were drugged and taken to Hải Phòng,
where they were likely held until the mẹ mìn had gathered enough victims to make her efforts to transfer them across international waters
profitable. In some instances, multiple mẹ mìn collaborated in their
sales.[98] Once at the port, the mẹ mìn took her collection of victims—
usually five or six at a time—out on small boats to one of the small islands
in Hạ Long Bay. In a 1923 *Trung Hoà Nhật Báo* report, harbor patrol found
a group of kidnapped women being held on a small island near the island
of Madeleine. With their limestone caves providing cover, the islands
were located at a convenient meeting point near the border with China,
where mẹ mìn could sell young women and girls to gangs of Chinese
pirates, who trafficked them to China.[99]

In another version of the scheme, mẹ mìn took their victims to a border town and sold them to Chinese traffickers, who would then transport
them across the border by road, rail, or sea. A 1937–38 vice squad report
lists the case of two Tonkinese mẹ mìn and two Tonkinese men who took
a thirty-four-year-old woman to Lạng Sơn, where they sold her into a
trafficking network leading to China. Similarly, another case involved
a Tonkinese man and a mẹ mìn who tried to sell a Tonkinese woman to
a Chinese trafficker who would smuggle her north of the border. The
operation was botched in the process, and the traffickers ended up mur-
dering the woman.[100]

Gangs of ethnic Chinese pirates (*giặc khách*), who roamed the Tonkin
countryside and the Gulf of Tonkin, trafficked women to China.[101] There

was already a long history of Chinese bandits and pirates running human-trafficking networks along the Sino-Vietnamese frontier and in the South China Sea.[102] In the late nineteenth century, the trafficking of Vietnamese women to China was a by-product of the political and economic turbulence in China.[103] As Tracy Barrett has shown, Chinese theater groups and caravan peddlers regularly crossed the border and may have provided a front for traffickers.[104] With the 1911 revolution in China, army deserters-turned-bandits earned their living by kidnapping.[105] In the years following the revolution, when the warlord military had disbanded, many soldiers had side gigs trafficking women. As a result, rates of trafficking increased after battles.[106]

The prevalence of Chinese trafficking gangs likely fed into public hostility toward ethnic Chinese in Tonkin. During World War I, the Chinese community gained a stronghold on Tonkin's economy. Resentment built up among ethnic Vietnamese, leading to anti-Chinese demonstrations in Hanoi and Hải Phòng and eventually riots by the summer of 1927.[107]

The success of Chinese trafficking gangs in Tonkin partly stems from special rights granted to Chinese in Indochina as part of various Franco-Chinese diplomatic agreements.[108] For one thing, the colonial state gave Chinese migrants special immigration status that enabled them to enter and leave Indochina with only a valid passport or membership in one of the protectorate's Chinese congregations, which were state-registered economic and mutual aid organizations for ethnic Chinese in Indochina.[109] In 1913, the colonial government offered temporary Chinese immigrants special residency permits, a pass to travel around Tonkin, and exemption from travel departure taxes for those intended to return to Indochina within a year. Moreover, Chinese fishing ships—the cover frequently used by Chinese trafficking gangs to transport victims— were permitted to spend six months off the coast of Tonkin.[110] The 1930 Convention of Nanking, which went into effect in 1935, made Chinese in Indochina subject to French law and afforded them the almost all of the same rights as French men and women, including criminal defense rights.[111]

The special status minimizing migration constraints on Chinese allowed for large-scale migrations in and out of Indochina.[112] Trafficking gangs traveling by land or sea easily blended in with legitimate migrants. Because China had no birth registry until 1929—and thus no way of proving or disproving family relations—traffickers passing across the border or traveling by boat easily passed off young women and girls as their own children. Traffickers instructed victims to remain silent around authorities, who would otherwise have picked up on the fact that victims were Vietnamese speakers or spoke Chinese dialects with a different accent than the traffickers posing as their parents.[113]

The trafficking of women across the border went both ways. Traffickers also shuffled Chinese women and girls south to Tonkin. For example, in 1920, Vong A Kiou was brought from Pak Hoi, China, to Móng Cái, Tonkin, by junk. Because junks were routinely searched by customs agents looking for contraband and trafficked women and girls, when they reached Móng Cái the traffickers then transferred her to an unassuming rowboat and quietly smuggled her into Hải Phòng, where they sold her into sex work.[114]

Chinese trafficking gangs also sold Vietnamese women and children north into one of China's many human-trade networks. Markets for women and girls thrived in Beijing and in Shanghai, which Christian Henriot identifies as "the greatest market for women."[115] Vietnamese women and children who were trafficked to China were particularly vulnerable because their lack of familiarity with Chinese languages, culture, and terrain made it difficult for them to flee their kidnappers. In his 1941 study of human trafficking, André Baudrit suggested that, for racist reasons, the Chinese would only buy or sell people who were not ethnically Chinese. For the same reason, it was much easier to procure a Vietnamese woman than a Chinese woman for sex work, as Vietnamese women were less respected in China. Finally, because racism against Vietnamese was culturally acceptable, traffickers could be more violent toward, and demand more of, a Vietnamese victim than a Chinese victim.[116]

Young women and girls trafficked to China were rumored to enter the country's sex industry. In 1930, *Trung Hoà Nhật Báo* warned that Vietnamese girls were becoming mere "merchandise to sell to an old Chinese man."[117] In 1931, *Ngọ Báo* lamented that "[Vietnamese] girls from good homes . . . enter into filthy establishments."[118] In the trafficking network that led to China, traffickers sent women to brothels, tea houses, dance halls, or *bateaux de fleurs*—floating brothels that were developed to evade prostitution restrictions on land.[119]

Colonial Efforts to Stop Abuses of Unfree Labor

Traffickers were extremely difficult to police. Colonial authorities made genuine—though anemic—attempts to stop trafficking. In 1932, the customs office of the colonial government placed Chinese ships entering and departing Hạ Long Bay under surveillance.[120] Some of these efforts proved fruitful. In March 1936, *Trung Hoà Báo* reported, police in Hải Phòng arrested a mẹ mìn selling people at the port.[121] That December, the same newspaper reported that the vice squad had arrested a woman for trafficking young women by boat to sell to a brothel in China.[122]

Under 1937 metropolitan law, those caught trafficking would be punished with a six-month to three-year prison sentence.[123] Yet, as estimated by a Hải Phòng city council member in 1938, only 1 percent of trafficking cases were ever brought to the police. To encourage people to turn in traffickers, the city offered rewards commensurate with the number of traffickers caught.[124] The Sûreté also placed agents around Hanoi to catch mẹ mìn and Chinese traffickers in an effort to halt trafficking at its inland sources.[125]

Little information has survived about those who were caught trafficking. When found guilty, they were punished with both prison time and fines. In 1926, after a customs agent caught a Chinese trafficker trying to smuggle a young girl by boat under the veil of night, the court in Hải Phòng sentenced the trafficker to six months in jail and a 4.24 piastre fine for "luring a minor into debauchery."[126] The 1937–38 fiscal year report of the vice squad cites more than twenty cases of traffickers who were caught. Most of the traffickers were mẹ mìn who had plans to sell their victims to brothels. Traffickers were sentenced to anywhere from three months to three years in prison; fines ranged from twenty to thirty piastres, to be paid to the victim or her parents. When two mẹ mìn along with two male accomplices were caught trafficking a woman to China, they were sentenced to two years of prison and a fine of twenty piastres to be paid to the victim. In the case mentioned above of a woman who was murdered while trafficked, the male traffickers were condemned to death, and the mẹ mìn was sentenced to six months in prison.[127]

In the late 1920s, the colonial government began to enact policy to limit unfree labor in Indochina. The League of Nations launched its Slavery Commission to address debt bondage, among other issues.[128] The French colonial government cooperated with the league's directive, outlawing debt-bondage agreements in all sectors of the economy and eliminating punishment by labor.[129] Yet with the social contract of debt bondage in legal limbo, debtors lost any legal protection they had previously enjoyed, in theory at least.[130] Realizing that the lack of available credit for the poor was what had been causing debt bondage in the first place, the colonial government in 1927 set up the Crédit Populaire banking program to offer small loans at 10 percent interest, which was considered low at the time. The program was mostly successful, although there was some abuse. Some used the money to pay off Chettier lenders, Nagarathar migrants from India who were known to be involved in informal, small-scale lending; others borrowed at a low interest rate, only to turn around and lend out that money to another peasant for a higher interest rate.[131]

In the 1930s, the international antitrafficking movement pressured France to abandon the brothel system and thus eliminate what the movement perceived as a market for trafficked women. In 1934, a Commission of Social Questions established by the League of Nations adopted an abolitionist stance and advised countries to abandon regulated prostitution. In February 1937, the League of Nations held a Conference of Central Authorities of Eastern Countries on the Traffic of Women and Children in Bandung in the Dutch Indies, which was attended by representatives from the Malay Federated States, the Straits Settlement, Macao, the Dutch East Indies, Hong Kong, China, and Indochina. The participants called for the abolition of brothel systems "once and for all," specifically calling out France.[132]

The meeting embarrassed the colonial government in Indochina. Governor-General Jules Brévié, appointed by the socialist Popular Front government, reconsidered the colonial government's approach to human trafficking. But, instead of acquiescing to the international anti-trafficking movement's demands for France to eliminate the whole state-regulated sex industry, Brévié maintained the state regulation system and redirected the conversation to a discussion of trafficking in clandestine brothels, particularly dance halls and ả đào singing houses, both of which will be discussed in later chapters.

In response to the 1937 League of Nations meeting in Bandung, Brévié appropriated the language of that meeting and warned local administrators about the trafficking of ả đào singers, which will be discussed at length in chapter 5. He cited examples of trafficking in singing houses that occurred in the form of debt-bondage schemes and mẹ mìn tricking or abducting young women and girls and selling them to the singing houses known for clandestine sex work. The singers, he wrote, were "a miserable group who are at the will of patrons of the establishments or an intermediary without scruples," insinuating that singers were controlled by pimps, which was illegal in France and sure to stir up popular emotions.[133]

Governor-General Brévié had other motives besides altruism when it came to the victims of trafficking. He and other French officials had long wanted to police the ả đào singing houses but had been unable to do so. For one thing, á đào singers did not meet the 1921 definition of prostitutes; moreover, as many of the á đào singing houses were located outside of the French concessions, they were outside of French legal jurisdiction. The governor-general artfully reframed the issue of policing á đào singing houses from one of cracking down on clandestine sex work to one that emphasized trafficking and humanitarian concerns. Brévié's move, in short, gave authorities justification to police á đào singing houses.

Brévié's warning successfully riled up administrators, who interpreted trafficking broadly, often focusing on pimping of voluntary clandestine sex workers. In a letter to the resident superior of Tonkin, one administrator, Roy Mourer, agreed to follow the terms of the 1937 treaty, fight all international trafficking, and protect women from pimping, "even if they are consenting adults and are not sent abroad."[134] Brévié announced in a subsequent letter to the resident superior that Indochina would follow the 1937 convention and punish anyone who ran an illegal brothel and anyone who, "in the spirit of profit," exploited sex workers.[135]

That December, the French representative to the League of Nations suggested modifying France's position such that it would support the league's call to end trafficking to a degree.[136] In response, the minister of foreign affairs wrote to the minister of colonies, noting that the French tolerance system was a point of criticism in the international community and directing him to end the sale of sex by foreign women in a good-faith effort to reduce trafficking.[137]

In April 1939, Brevié informed local administrators that Indochina had to maintain the same approach to prostitution as France and thus could not follow the league's call to abolish the brothel system. Nonetheless, he wrote, the colonial government in Indochina could make exceptions when there were "particular local considerations," specifically the á đào houses, where the French regulation system had proven ineffective.[138] In May 1939, the resident superior of Tonkin issued a decree on the working conditions of singers and dancers. The decree, which will be discussed in more detail in later chapters, took measures to protect á đào singers and taxi dancers from trafficking and debt bondage by forbidding cash advances or jewelry as well as the paying off of debt through work.[139]

As the clandestine sex industry operated outside the law, many women in the black market often found themselves in situations of unfree labor, including debt bondage and human trafficking. However, unfree labor in Indochina belied France's values of liberty and equality. Moreover, the League of Nations Special Committee on Trafficking identified the French brothel system as a source for women to be trafficked. Instead of heeding the committee's calls to end the brothel system, the governor-general of Indochina artfully reappropriated the rhetoric of the anti-trafficking movement to police the unfree labor rampant in clandestine brothels. As we shall see in chapters 5 and 6, this approach proved especially useful for policing á đào singing houses as well as dance halls.

CHAPTER 4

Adolescent Sex Work

Poverty and Its Effects on Children

One spring day in 1925, fifteen-year-old Thi Tuyen told Hải Phòng police about her harrowing experience of being forced into sex work. Thi Tuyen was born in Thái Bình Province to parents she never knew. She was adopted by a family that owned a restaurant and had forced her to work long hours to earn her keep.[1] Fed up with the arduous labor, Thi Tuyen ran away to Hanoi, where life was easier—or so she had heard. Like many other orphaned migrant children who arrived in the city with no support system, she found shelter in a pagoda, where she slept at night. During the day, she worked for a jeweler. Soon her boss became verbally and physically abusive, and after enduring multiple beatings, Thi Tuyen quit.

Wandering the streets in search of work, Thi Tuyen met Nguyen Thi Lieu, a twenty-four-year-old woman from Hà Đông with whom she shared a common experience. Like Thi Tuyen, Thi Lieu was an orphan who had migrated within the Red River Delta in search of employment, eventually making her way to the city. Thi Lieu befriended the young girl and offered her a job as a domestic servant in Hải Phòng. Desperate and hungry, Thi Tuyen eagerly accepted the job, and the pair left for Hải Phòng that same day.

When they arrived in the port city, Thi Lieu brought Thi Tuyen to a room in a boardinghouse near the train station where Thi Lieu worked as a maid and her husband was a boardinghouse "boy." The next day, Thi

Lieu took Thi Tuyen to a Japanese hotel where, she was startled to learn, an Indian man was waiting for her. Thi Lieu locked the girl in a room with the man. He turned off the light, climbed on top of Thi Tuyen, overpowered her, and sodomized her. (Humiliated, Thi Tuyen would later confess to the police, "I should tell you, I did not resist.") So brutal was the rape that Thi Tuyen could not stop crying from the pain for days afterward. Angered by what she perceived to be weakness in an industry where only the toughest survive, Thi Lieu scolded her for her naiveté and locked her in a room as punishment. After two days—time for Thi Tuyen to heal just enough to see more customers—Thi Lieu proceeded to bring more men to the room, including four Europeans, one of whom was a military officer. The Europeans attempted to "commit acts against nature" (a euphemism for sodomy) on her, she later told the police, but stopped "not because I resisted, but because I cried when they hurt me."

When Thi Tuyen was finally permitted to leave the boardinghouse, she confided in an itinerant soup vendor about the violent rapes. The vendor urged her to go to the hospital. Upon examining her injuries, the doctor hospitalized her for a few days to treat her for a deep tear that extended from her anus to her vulva, ripping through the perineum. The doctor notified authorities, who interrogated Thi Lieu, her husband, and the owner of the boardinghouse. Thi Lieu was arrested, tried, and convicted for leading a minor into debauchery.

Thi Tuyen was just one of many adolescent girls who were forced or tricked into sex work in late colonial Tonkin. As this chapter shows, juvenile sex work was a function of the extreme poverty that was endemic to this time and place. Children and adolescents were particularly vulnerable. Some were orphaned when their parents died unable to afford medical care; others were abandoned as infants or, as children, sold into what their parents presumed was domestic servitude. Orphaned and abandoned children migrated to other parts of the Red River Delta and into the cities in search of employment and shelter. Like Thi Tuyen, many of them found shelter at night in one of the cities' many pagodas and churches or in abandoned houses. During the day, they wandered the streets looking for work. Alarmed by the growing numbers of young vagabonds showing up in the cities, the colonial government developed programs aimed at alleviating child poverty, but the problem only continued to worsen. Unaware of common scams and desperate, many adolescent migrant girls were forced or manipulated into performing sex work or chose to do it as a last resort.

Colonial authorities took juvenile sex work seriously, arresting, convicting, and punishing those involved in the trafficking of underage sex workers. Yet they had little success in policing juvenile sex work due to the highly secretive nature of the market for adolescent girls. Unlike sex work among ả đào singers or taxi dancers, which will be discussed in subsequent chapters, juvenile sex workers did not operate out of centralized locations such as dance halls or singing houses; instead, they were hidden in private apartments or rented rooms of boardinghouses, making it harder for police to track them. Pimps and madams never advertised their adolescent sex workers; men looking for underage girls had to seek out those in the know—usually boardinghouse boys, itinerant vendors, or rickshaw pullers—to connect them to juvenile sex workers.

The shadowy nature of the market for underage girls makes it difficult for historians to investigate this industry. Yet authorities' zeal in pursing justice for victims resulted in court records that are rich in details about adolescent girls' experiences in the underage sex industry, often told in their own voices. In the sources that I found, underage girls were typically adolescents from ten to seventeen years old. Although I found many cases involving the kidnapping of prepubescent girls, there are scant details of their experiences. Of course, this does not mean that prepubescent sex work did not occur in colonial Tonkin; it may instead mean that the market for prepubescent girls was so secretive that pimps, madams, and customers were rarely caught. While the legal age of eighteen for adulthood was artificially imposed by the colonial state, I nonetheless use the state-imposed legal age to delineate the line between adolescents and adults. This approach places adolescent sex work within a legal framework, which is especially relevant to a study of a black market economy. Moreover, the illegality of adolescent girls is, to a large extent, what drove the market demand in the first place. This chapter will investigate the markets for adolescent girls aged ten to seventeen.

Poverty and Its Effects on Children

The juvenile sex industry in Tonkin was a consequence of the area's high rates of rural poverty—poverty that was itself largely a consequence of radical economic changes introduced by the French. In the early days of colonization, the colonial government seized land from peasants and redistributed land concessions to French companies and colonists as well as those Vietnamese who collaborated with the French.[2] Land, therefore, gradually became concentrated in the hands of wealthy landowners or French companies. Further exacerbating the problem of rural poverty, the state forced peasants to pay heavy taxes, often in cash. Overpopulation and chronic food shortages in the Red River Delta resulted in widespread hunger, especially during the periods between harvests. In the 1920s, peasants in the Red River Delta were dealt additional blows in the form of excessive rains, crop failures, and floods.[3] The Great Depression sent the price of rice plummeting, driving rural farmers further into debt. Although the cities were able to climb out of the economic crisis by the mid-1930s, the countryside was much slower to recover.

Children felt the effects of poverty the most. Families with too many mouths to feed abandoned or sold their children. Older children migrated to the cities in search of new sources of income, either to support their family between harvests or to try to make it on their own. Poor health care in the countryside led to high rates of morbidity and mortality. Malaria, cholera, tuberculosis, dysentery, and neglected infections left children orphaned or neglected by infirm parents. Poor maternity care led some mothers to die in childbirth. Fathers who were unable to take care of their children sold them, gave them up for adoption, or abandoned them.[4]

Vietnamese society had multiple social safety nets with which to care for the many orphaned and abandoned children. Villages organized mutual aid societies in which village members paid into a sort of insurance pool that came to the aid of those struck by disaster.[5] Two types of mutual aid organizations assisted families and orphaned children: giáp and phúng. The giáp helped members in emergencies such as family deaths or famine. The phúng assisted with care of descendants, among other things.[6] Community-funded programs, called nhà dưỡng tế, provided temporary aid and shelter for the village's poor and orphaned.[7]

Adoption, often by distant family members or friends, was another social safety net. In some cases, the adoptive couple would pay the biological parents a regular sum of money in exchange for the child's domestic labor. In other cases, desperate parents sold their children outright—into domestic servitude, manual labor, marriage, or, occasionally, sex work. Such arrangements served as an insurance of sort, as those who paid for the children and used them for labor had a vested interest in keeping them healthy and providing food and shelter.[8] Yet children often found themselves in situations that were far from secure. While some children were bought back by their biological parents once the family's financial situation improved,[9] others who were no longer useful to their adoptive family—because of injury, illness, insubordination, or simply because they had become too expensive to feed—could find themselves sold or homeless again.[10]

For its part, the colonial government instituted programs to aid orphaned and abandoned children. As early as 1860, French Catholic orphanages opened in war zones in Cochinchina,[11] and by the interwar years there were orphanages all over Indochina. Yet even with Vietnamese and French social safety nets in place, many children were left to fend for themselves on the streets. Desperate for employment and shelter, homeless children migrated to the cities.

Even children not abandoned or given up for adoption often found themselves homeless in the big city, where they sought employment as domestic servants, boardinghouse boys, or rickshaw pullers to supplement their family's income. Many of the migrant children, like Thi Tuyen, whose story opened this chapter, found refuge in the city's religious edifices, which provided them with some degree of protection. However, even in the churches and pagodas, children remained vulnerable to chilly nights and sexual assault. Outside the church and pagoda gates, migrant children found themselves preyed on by swindlers and criminals. Lured by promises of employment, as well as room and board, many migrant girls were tricked or forced into juvenile sex work.

The problem of unaccompanied migrant children had vexed the Tonkin government since World War I. In 1915, the resident superior of Tonkin warned local administrators of a growing number of homeless children from the Red River Delta who had migrated to Hanoi, Hải Phòng, and Nam Định, where they begged on the streets. At night they slept in churches, pagodas, or abandoned houses; during the day they roamed markets, where they made money by toting food for market customers or pickpocketing. In an attempt to address the problem, the resident superior sent older children to the countryside to work as farmers and placed younger children in the homes of wealthy Vietnamese families, for whom they worked as servants.[12] During the Depression era, the colonial government funded various types of new child-care institutions, including nurseries, day-care centers, and orphanages. These institutions offered day-long, long-term, and, at times, permanent care and taught the children skills that would enable them to earn a living as adults. Boys were placed in apprenticeship programs; girls were taught housekeeping, tailoring, and embroidery, a strategy to give them an alternative to sex work.[13] Despite the programs in place, the volatile economy only led to a proliferation of homeless children desperate for means to support themselves and vulnerable to predatory adults.

The Lure of Youth

Although juvenile sex work was illegal, the demand for adolescent girls in Tonkin was high. Colonial authorities took juvenile sex work seriously, though not as seriously as was dictated by metropolitan law. Under article 334 of the metropolitan French penal code, women were prohibited from selling sex until they were twenty-one years old.[14] The rationale was that sex, particularly paid sex, was corrupting.[15] In Indochina, however, the state set the minimum age for selling sex lower than that of the metropole. Initially, the age limit was decided by each locality, resulting in vastly different age requirements across Indochina. Per laws passed in 1907 and 1908, the minimum age in Hanoi and Hải Phòng was eighteen.[16] While formulating the 1907 law, the mayor of Hanoi had considered lowering the minimum age to fifteen years but later acknowledged that girls that young had likely been exploited or trafficked.[17] The minimum age throughout Cochinchina was eighteen,[18] but within the city of Saigon, girls could register as sex workers at fourteen years old.[19] The February 3, 1921, law instituting a uniform system for regulated sex work in Tonkin required that men be at least twenty-one years old before entering a brothel but did not stipulate a minimum age for women to register as sex workers. The default minimum age for sex workers in the French concessions of Hanoi and Hải Phòng thus remained eighteen. As these laws applied to all residents regardless of race, this meant that French as well as Vietnamese girls could sell sex at a much younger age than would have been permitted in the metropole. This, of course, alarmed colonial administrators.

In 1925, the director of the Administration of Justice for Indochina brought these discrepancies to the attention of the governor-general and called for a uniform age limit for sex workers.[20] Noting that certain areas of Indochina were not in compliance with the age requirements for sex work as stipulated by article 334 of the French penal code, the governor-general called for a modification of the February 3, 1921, law.[21] Yet René Robin, the resident superior of Tonkin, made the argument that on account of the sexual "precociousness" of the "Indochinese races," the minimum age for sex work should be eighteen, and he argued that this should be uniform across Indochina to avoid "inequality among girls of the same race."[22] When Robin and the director of the Administration of Justice for Indochina cited article 204 of the Annamite Penal Code, which required that Vietnamese fathers give children over twenty years old the liberty to make certain decisions for themselves, Dr. Le Roy des Barres called out the inconsistency of the age requirement: "I do not see why girls can prostitute themselves at 18 years old, but boys cannot enter brothels until they are 21 years old."[23] The debate was settled with the decree of October 7, 1926, which set the age of inscription for a Vietnamese woman at eighteen, while the age for clients remained at twenty-one.[24]

Even with the age restriction, juvenile sex work was pervasive in Tonkin during the interwar years. This was due to an eager customer base as well as greedy pimps and madams, for whom juvenile prostitution was quite profitable. For one thing, youth was considered beautiful, especially in the sex industry, where late nights, poor nutrition, frequent illness, and brutal managers tended to age women prematurely. Moreover, young girls tended to defer to adults and were thus easy for madams and pimps to control. Being naive to criminal scams in the city, girls could be easily tricked into sex work, and their lack of familiarity with city geography made them less likely to escape. And, most important, they were profitable: pimps and madams could get away with paying the girls nothing and keeping all their earnings for themselves.

Girls were also attractive for their potential virginity. Evidence from Hải Phòng reveals a high demand for virgins. In 1920, a court there tried a case in which a girl was sold to a man who was looking for a virgin.[25] In 1926, a Hải Phòng court listened to another case in which a man paid ten piastres for a fifteen-year-old's virginity.[26] Virginity was a commodity in that some men found gratification in being a girl's first sexual experience. Clients also erroneously believed that virgins could not carry venereal diseases and thus felt safe having intercourse with them. Yet clients were easily duped. Some juvenile sex workers who claimed to be virgins had likely had sex multiple times but profited from their youthful looks to sell their "virginity." Even if the client landed a bona fide virgin, it was quite possible that she carried a venereal disease, as infections could be transmitted without sexual intercourse.

While the majority of underage sex work occurred in secret locations, registered brothels also illegally housed adolescents. In 1926, the commander of the French military police in Lạng Sơn estimated that three-quarters of registered sex workers were underage but had falsely registered, and he lamented that it was impossible to control this.[27] A few months later, the French resident stationed in Đông Sơn called for an easier way to verify the exact age of registered sex workers. As he explained, this was difficult task, as many sex workers had been abandoned by their family or were orphans, and their home villages were ashamed of their occupation and refused to recognize them and verify their age.[28]

The Vietnamese-language media was clearly disturbed by the prevalence of adolescents selling sex. Journalists were careful to note when clandestine sex workers were underage, emphasizing the girls' state of biological development. They used terms such as "budding girl" (*gái non*)[29] or "girl who has not yet reached maturity" (*gái chưa đến tuổi trưởng thành*).[30] Others described girls by their age, for example, "a girl who had just turned twelve years old" (*gái mới 12 tuổi*)[31] and "juvenile" (*gái vị thành niên*).[32] The articles convey a sense of lost innocence or an irreversible psychological change. In 1939, a mother who had been reunited with her twelve-year-old daughter told the newspaper *Đông Pháp* that the girl had "completely changed" and was wearing makeup and behaving like a debauched girl.[33]

Adolescent Sex Workers

The existing information available on the lives of juvenile sex workers points to their vulnerability. Juvenile sex workers overwhelmingly came from hardship and poverty and, as children, were dependent on adults, even if their bodies had reached sexual maturity. For one thing, they needed shelter and food. Few adolescents could find jobs that paid wages high enough to pay for rent, and, even if they could, landlords were unwilling to rent to minors, especially girls. Moreover, adolescents tended to be emotionally dependent on adults, trusting the adults to act in their best interest. Consequently, youth were easily tricked into sex work. Particularly vulnerable were peasant migrants to the cities and marginalized groups, including ethnic Chinese and métisses.

Newspaper reports reveal that some girls voluntarily sold sex, though this seems to have been the exception. In 1933, the newspaper *Zân Báo* covered a story about a twelve-year-old girl who had been arrested three times for clandestine sex work in Hanoi. While she was managed by two madams, the article portrays her as a willing participant, driven by a desire for wealth and material goods.[34] Similarly, as *Đông Pháp* reported in 1936, sixteen-year-old Đặng Thị Như from Thái Bình Province, whose story opened this book, sold sex of her own volition.[35]

As the historical sources show, the vast majority of adolescent sex workers were made to sell sex either by coercion or circumstance. Orphans girls were most at risk for being forced or tricked into sex work. The loss of family left young girls searching for food and shelter, and pimps and madams took advantage of their dire situation. For example, a fourteen-year-old girl told a Hải Phòng court in 1920 that she had been forced to sell sex when her parents died.[36] In 1923, the same court heard the story of Yoc Ting, who had likewise been coerced into selling sex after the death of her parents. That same year, *Ngọ Báo* covered the case of a twelve-year-old orphan named Nguyễn Thị Lan, who, after the death of her parents, found herself homeless, "wandering the streets of Hanoi" without anyone to care for her. After days of desperately searching for shelter, she met two seemingly kind ladies who offered her employment and a place to stay, but they lured her to a boardinghouse, where they made her perform sex work.[37] In 1939, *Đông Pháp* printed a story about Luong Yime, a seventeen-year-old from Lạng Sơn who had lost both parents and had no relatives to support her. She migrated to Hải Phòng in search of employment but had no way of supporting herself. Forced into selling sex, she received only a meager ration of food and a change of clothes as compensation.[38]

Adopted children—those whose parents had died or were unable to take care of them—were susceptible to the whims of their new families. While some adopted children were brought into families as equals, for the most part they were secondary members whose role, at least in the case of girls, amounted to that of a maid doing menial housework in return for room and board. As a result, when adopted daughters became a burden to families, the families often kicked them out of the house or sold them into sex work. For example, in 1923 a Hải Phòng court heard the case of Lai Fa, a minor whose age was not specified. Her adoptive mother ran an opium den in Hanoi, where she worked serving opium and cleaning up after customers. When she was no longer useful to the business, her adoptive mother sold her to a brothel through a broker.[39] In 1939, *Đông Pháp* reported that a Miss Thị Lan had been arrested for prostituting a thirteen-year-old girl. While in custody, Thị Lan confessed to police that the girl, whose name was Thị Nuôi—Vietnamese for "Adopted"—was her adopted daughter.[40]

Many girls who had run away from home found themselves in the sex industry—out of desperation or by coercion. Unregistered brothels, singing houses, and dance halls—most of which provided food and shelter in exchange for sex work—were one of few choices for girls who needed to survive in the big city.[41] Take, for example, the 1935 case, reported in *Ngọ Báo*, of sixteen-year-old Ngô Thị Yến who ran away from her family in Nam Định. When she arrived in Hải Phòng, she had no money, housing, or support network, so she entered into a debt-bondage prostitution agreement with the owner of a dance hall, who provided her with room and board as part of the agreement.[42] While these girls could have worked in other industries—chiefly domestic servitude—the clandestine sex industry potentially offered better pay and more independence. Moreover, given that domestic servants were vulnerable to rape by their boss families, sex work may well have seemed like a better alternative.

Other runaway girls were tricked into selling sex. In 1920, fifteen-year-old Thi Binh from Nam Định fled her home after a particularly brutal beating by her mother. Along the way, she stopped at a restaurant. The owner mentioned that his wife was on her way to Hạ Lý, a neighborhood in Hải Phòng, and suggested that Thi Binh go with her. The wife offered to find a Chinese husband for Thi Binh, but the girl refused. Nonetheless, she got in the car with the wife. When they arrived, the wife sold her for three piastres to Thi Loc, a brothel owner. The wife had apparently made a business of this, as Thi Binh overheard her tell Thi Loc that she would be bringing her two more underage girls.[43]

In 1926, the fifteen-year-old orphan Ly Cam told a Hải Phòng court about her tragic descent into forced sex work. She was born in Hải Phòng to a Chinese mother and Vietnamese father, both of whom had died when she was very young. After their deaths, a neighboring family adopted her and, per convention at the time, required her to be their servant. One day, while shopping at the market, she lost the ten piastres with which the mother had entrusted her to buy food for that night's dinner. Scared to return to her adoptive family empty-handed, Ly Cam ran away. Like so many orphans, she quickly became desperate for shelter. After wandering the Hải Phòng streets looking for a job that provided room and board, she met Thi Chung, a friendly woman who offered her a place to stay. Soon after welcoming Ly Cam into her home, the woman forced the girl into sex work.[44] The stories did not stop there. A 1940 article published in Đông Pháp told the story of Tchao-Huong. A sixteen-year-old ethnic Chinese girl, she met a woman named Cấu Sam, who promised her a more exciting life. The girl ran away from her parents, only to find herself manipulated into selling sex and forced to steal goods from local shops to be resold for a profit.[45]

Migrants girls were exceptionally vulnerable to being forced or duped into sex work. Most susceptible were those who had migrated alone and arrived in the city with few resources and no place to stay—and who were desperate for employment and naive to the reality of urban crime. Girls like fifteen-year-old Thi Tuyen from Thái Bình, whose 1925 story opened this chapter, came to Hanoi looking for better opportunities but were deceived by false offers of legitimate employment.[46] Other migrant girls fell into sex work after having been separated from their families. In some cases, migrant children were separated from parents or siblings as the family made its way to a big city. Lost and alone, without shelter, food, or survival skills, girls became easy prey for pimps and madams. This was the case for fifteen-year-old Thị Hợi, who was separated from her adoptive family en route from Hải Dương to Hanoi, as reported by Đông Pháp in 1938. Thị Hợi was quick to accept a Chinese woman's offer to shelter her while she looked for her family. The woman, however, sold her to an ả đào singer. Realizing there was profit to be made from Thị Hợi's virginity, the singer, in turn, sold her to an elderly Chinese man.[47]

Migrants girls from China in particular found themselves in dangerous situations. Although precise statistics are unavailable, the surviving records of the Hải Phòng courts indicate that a disproportionate number of girls from China—whether voluntary migrants or victims of trafficking—were forced into sex work. Chinese girls were popular among ethnic Chinese men looking to buy sex, as they could speak the same language and appealed to those looking for endogamous sex. Moreover, as strangers in a new land where they did not speak the local language or know the local geography, Chinese girls were easily taken advantage of and could be manipulated or forced into submitting to madams and pimps. In 1920, a Hải Phòng court heard the case of fourteen-year-old Vong A Kiou, an orphan from Pakhoi, just across the border in China. After her parents died, she was taken in by her aunt. After a few months, her aunt sold her to a neighbor, who in turn transported her to Hải Phòng. They traveled by junk to Tonkin, stopping in Móng Cái and a few other seaside villages along the way. When they arrived in Hải Phòng, Vong A Kiou stayed with a friend of the neighbor, also a Chinese migrant. After a few days, the woman sold her into sex work.[48] Likewise, in 1926, a Hải Phòng court heard the case of La Fa, a Chinese minor whose age was unlisted. The girl migrated to Hải Phòng to accept an opportunity to work as an apprentice to a tailor. When she arrived for work, the tailor forced her into sex work.[49] And in 1939, Đông Pháp reported that a seventeen-year-old Chinese girl from the border town Lạng Sơn was trafficked to Hải

Phòng. There, she was sold to a Chinese man, who forced her into sex work and gave her only minimal food and clothing in return.[50]

Eurasian mixed-race girls were likewise sought after by men looking to buy underage sex, and their precarious social and economic situation left them vulnerable to scams. Many single Vietnamese mothers were abandoned by their French lovers and left to raise their children alone, often with few resources. Such children were often shunned by Vietnamese society as outsiders, leaving them without marriage prospects or employment. Moreover, with their unique looks, young métisses were exoticized and sexualized by Vietnamese and French society alike, creating a market for their prostitution. Since the 1890s, French authorities feared that mixed-race girls were being sold into the sex industry by their mothers or sold into human-trafficking rings.[51] As one administrator warned, "the Vietnamese woman who consents to live with Europeans is a veritable prostitute. Once the European man leaves, she returns to her vice and the child is exposed to debauchery . . . and the girls often go on to become prostitutes"[52] Another administrator claimed mothers would "compromise their child's morality" and "prostitute [their mixed-race daughters] the moment they could."[53] Indeed, this fear, which dominated French policy towards Eurasians from the 1890s through the end of the colonial era, was one of the driving forces behind colonial policies to remove fatherless métis children from their Vietnamese mothers.[54] While this fear was likely overstated, some adolescent métisses were indeed prostituted. In 1922, a Hải Phòng court heard the case of a mixed-race "young girl" whose age was unlisted. She lived with a woman named Miss Hai Vinh who dressed her in European clothing to accentuate her European heritage and partnered with a rickshaw puller to connect the girl to customers.[55] In research for his 1934 reportage story, "Kỹ Nghệ Lấy Tây" [The Industry of Marrying Westerners], journalist Vũ Trọng Phụng also found that some mothers of young métisses made money from prostituting their daughters.[56]

Other adolescents entered the sex trade after being kidnapped and forced to sell sex. Newspapers buzzed with stories of human-trafficking networks that operated in Tonkin (see chapter 3). Rumors spread about mẹ mìn abducting young children by luring, tricking,[57] or drugging them.[58] The mẹ mìn went on to sell the girls to third-party pimps or brothels.[59] Mẹ mìn also found a market for girls with Chinese gangs. As part of a regional human-trafficking network, the gangs transported the girls to China or Hong Kong, where they were "destined to become merchandise to sell to an old Chinese man."[60]

Sadly, in some cases families sold their own children into sex work. This was often a function of poverty or death in families. Family members who had inherited the responsibility of raising a newly orphaned child in the wake of the parents' death sometimes turned to traffickers to relieve them of that responsibility. Such were the 1920 cases of Vong A Kiou, mentioned above, whose aunt sold her to traffickers,[61] and Yoc Ting, whose aunt sold her to a brothel.[62] In rare cases, parents sold their own children to pay debts or taxes. For example, in 1939, *Việt Báo* reported the case of a father who brought his twelve-year-old daughter to a brothel to sell her virginity and used the profits to pay off his debts.[63]

Other girls were tricked into selling sex through bait-and-switch offers for employment. Adults preying on the naiveté of adolescent girls offered them jobs, only to force them sell sex when they showed up for work. In 1935, *Đông Pháp* reported that when seventeen-year-old Ng. Thị Minh migrated from Bắc Ninh to live with her uncle in Hanoi, a neighbor couple befriended her and convinced her to leave her uncle to go work for them. What young Ng. Thị Minh did not now at the time was that the husband-wife team intended to sell her to a brothel.[64] In 1941, *Tin Mới* and *Đông Pháp* reported a story about two fifteen-year-old girls in Hải Phòng who were lured with promises of lucrative jobs selling drinks at a bar for fifteen piastres per month. When they arrived for work, the boss forced them to sell sex in a singing house.[65]

Another common variation of this scheme involved hiring a migrant girl as a domestic servant and then forcing her into juvenile prostitution. The scheme was particularly successful because young migrant girls, most of whom had not lined up safe shelter in the city, were attracted to jobs that enabled them to reside in the houses where they worked. Conversely, the employers were attracted to the young migrant girls because they accepted low salaries and were typically submissive to authority. Peasant girls from the countryside easily found work in the cities with upper-middle class families, for whom they cooked, cleaned, and took care of children. In return, they received room and board along with their meager salary as well as what they thought would be the security of living in a family environment. As mentioned above, live-in servants were vulnerable to predatory bosses, but overall, domestic servitude was a decent starter job for those who arrived in the city with no family support system or knowledge of urban life. And for these reasons, scam artists easily enticed girls with the prospect of domestic work.

In 1937, for example, *Việt Báo* reported a story about seventeen-year-old Trần Thị Lan, who accepted a job as a servant in the home of Nguyễn-Thị Châu, who would take advantage of her vulnerability as a migrant in a big city with no social network. Trần Thị Lan had no way of knowing that Nguyễn-Thị Châu's home was once a registered brothel and now operated as a clandestine brothel. Nguyễn-Thị Châu attempted to force Trần Thị Lan into sex work, but she resisted. Angered by the girl's insubordination, Nguyễn-Thị Châu beat her and took her to the dispensary, where she ruined Trần Thị Lan's reputation by forcing her to register as a sex worker.[66] Later that year, *Việt Báo* reported that when migrating to Hải Phòng to find work, Nguyễn Thị Đào, seventeen, took a job as a maid in Nguyễn Thị Giáp's home. After only a few days of working, Giáp procured her to customers, knowing full well that Nguyễn Thị Đào had no choice but to comply.[67] In 1941, *Đông Pháp* ran a story about a brother and sister from Ninh Bình Province who had made their way to Hạ Long. Unaware of the many fronts for sex work in the black market sex industry, the pair found work as a maid and servant in an ả đào singing house. Eagerly awaiting their paychecks after working for a few months, they found that the owner of the singing house was unwilling to pay them. Instead, the owner forced the fifteen-year-old girl to sell sex.[68]

Marriage promises were a particularly successful scam. In colonial Vietnam, marriage was important to both girls and their parents. In rural areas of colonial-era Tonkin, women were expected to marry by twenty-two years old and produce an heir who would carry on the family line and pay respect to their ancestors.[69] But for girls from impoverished families, marriage was not guaranteed. Marriages arranged by parents were often decided along class lines. Girls with low social status or orphans with no family at all were generally viewed as unsuitable mates and ran the risk of never being paired up with a husband and, by extension, never having children. More fundamentally, young women who could not find husbands sometimes found their very survival on the line. As colonial Tonkin was a patrilineal society, parents fully expected to discontinue financial support as soon as their daughters married.[70] Given the essential role of marriage in women's survival, impoverished girls who had reached sexual maturity easily fell prey to false promises of marriage that ended in prostitution.

Take, for example, the 1920 case of a fourteen-year-old orphan from China. After the girl had spent some time working with a tailor in Hải Phòng, living in her house, running errands for her, and helping her cut fabric and sew patterns, the woman brokered a marriage proposal from a Chinese man. Even though the fourteen-year-old had never met the man, social convention allowed for her to accept the proposal. Little did she know that far from making a romantic gesture, the man had instead paid the tailor for the girl's virginity.[71] Similarly, in 1923, as reported to a Hải Phòng court, a girl whose age was not specified (though she was listed as a minor) was approached by a woman offering to find her a husband. Thrilled at the prospect of marriage, the girl accepted and went with the woman to meet the prospective husband. But the woman never intended to follow through on her promise. Instead, she sold the girl to a brothel.[72]

Girls who had been forced into the sex industry were frequently subjected to extreme violence. Brothel owners and pimps used rape as a weapon to intimidate girls and deter them from resisting the demands of procurers or customers. This was evident in the 1925 case of fifteen-year-old Thi Tuyen, whose story of being brutally raped and sodomized opened this chapter. Sadly, this practice was all too common. In 1937, after luring seventeen-year-old Nguyễn Thị Đào, mentioned above, into working for her with promises of a job as a servant, Nguyễn Thị Giáp brought five men to the home to gang-rape the girl as an initiation into forced prostitution.[73]

In sum, children's naiveté rendered them susceptible to being lured, tricked, or kidnapped. Pimps and madams preyed on poor, orphaned, or adopted children and runaways. They manipulated or forced the girls into the shadowy market for juvenile sex work.

Market Operations

The market for adolescent girls was characterized by secrecy and decentralization. Pimps and madams took extensive measures to hide their operations. Their efforts to connect men looking for sex with adolescent girls were protected by layer upon layer of middlemen to avoid police detection. Moreover, there was no specific location equivalent to an ả đào singing house or dance hall that explicitly marketed underage girls and virgins. Instead, those looking for adolescents had to be in the know.

Juvenile sex workers were controlled by a manager—a pimp or madam—who collected earnings but rarely paid the young workers. Some managers were former sex workers themselves. For example, a Hanoi court heard the case of thirty-five-year-old Nguyễn Thị Mai from Hải Phòng. She herself had worked as a registered sex worker until she aged out of the industry. Her experience meant she was quite familiar with the business of selling sex. Indeed, in 1937, she was arrested for forcing a fourteen-year-old girl into to sell sex.[74] A similar 1938 case reported in *Đông Pháp* concerned Ng Thị-Lan, known as Hai Lan, a registered sex worker who operated from her own home and even dutifully submitted to the venereal exams required by the colonial state. Although her personal operation adhered to the regulation system, she was also holding captive a sixteen-year-old girl whom she had forced to sell sex.[75] Some managers, such as Phùng Thị Hồng, were even repeat offenders. In 1938, Phùng Thị Hồng was arrested for forcing Thị Nuột, a minor whose age was not specified, into selling sex. When police booked Phùng Thị Hồng, they found records of multiple previous arrests for having lured other underage adolescent girls into sex work.[76]

Managers operated secretly from private homes, often using guises to explain their connection to the underage girls who lived with them. Managers often claimed fictitious household or familial relations to account for the presence of the young girls. As *Đông Pháp* reported in 1938, when authorities apprehended Ng Thị-Lan, the registered sex worker mentioned above who had forced a sixteen-year-old girl living in her home to sell sex, Ng Thị-Lan claimed that the girl was her household servant.[77] Similarly, in 1939 *Đông Pháp* reported the case of a woman who had been arrested for prostituting a thirteen-year-old. The woman pleaded innocence, claiming the girl was her adopted daughter.[78]

A recurring element in the sources are tailors who pimped juvenile girls and claimed that the girls were apprentices at their shop. This ruse was particularly effective as most tailor apprentices were in fact adolescent girls who slept at the tailor shop at which they were learning their trade. Moreover, the genuine enthusiasm that many young apprentices felt at the prospect of eventually owning their own shop provided cover for clandestine operations and made the girls easy prey for manipulation and abuse. Such was the case in 1920, when a Hải Phòng court heard the story of fourteen-year-old Vong A Kiou, the Chinese orphan mentioned above, who was brought to Hải Phòng and procured by a tailor.[79] In 1923, the same court tried another case of a Hanoi tailor. She had offered an adolescent girl a job as an apprentice but instead took her to Hải Phòng, where she sold the girl to a brothel.[80]

The surviving historical sources suggest the substantial role that Chinese men and women played in the market for adolescent girls. In 1920, a Hải Phòng court prosecuted a Chinese woman for running a clandestine brothel at which police found two girls, only ten and eleven years old—a case so brutal that the police described the girls as "enslaved."[81]

Similarly, in 1923, a Hải Phòng court heard the case of a Chinese woman who had been arrested for "leading a minor into debauchery" in Hải Phòng.[82] A few years later, in early January 1926, a court in Hải Phòng tried a case in which authorities stopped a Chinese man and woman from trafficking a young girl to China by boat. They caught the woman, but the man jumped into the water and swam away.[83] In 1939, Đông Pháp reported a story about a Chinese man in Hải Phòng who had forced a seventeen-year-old Chinese girl from Lạng Sơn into sex work.[84]

The disproportionate representation of Chinese traffickers and pimps can be attributed to multiple factors. A likely one was the ubiquity of Chinese-run trafficking syndicates (discussed in chapter 3) that sold women and girls between China and Tonkin. Moreover, racial antipathy may have made Vietnamese police more likely to arrest a Chinese man caught with a minor than a Vietnamese man in a comparable situation. Within the Chinese diasporic community, a tight network appeared to develop that connected Chinese men who preferred endogamous sex with ethnic Chinese girls.

Aware that parading underage girls on the street would attract not just customers but also the vice police, pimps and madams relied on middlemen to find clients. Middlemen were typically men and women whose professions required frequent contact with the public. Their success lay not just in their access but also in their street savvy. As discussed in chapter 1, their work as itinerant vendors or rickshaw puller afforded them relationships with diverse locals in the neighborhood, insider knowledge of street life and neighbors' private lives, and connections with crime circles. Middlemen had multiple advantages when it came to avoiding the police, beyond the legitimate jobs that provided cover. Because most were homeless—they slept in their rickshaws or vending carts at night—police could not track them. Moreover, given their familiarity with the streets, they knew the best exit routes to take whenever the police swept them for criminal activity. In Hanoi and Hải Phòng, itinerant flower vendors often played the role of middlemen.[85] Take, for example, the 1944 story in the newspaper Việt Cường about twenty-eight-year-old Ng Thị Lộc, a fifty-nine-year-old itinerant flower vendor in Hải Phòng who was arrested for luring a minor into sex work.[86] More frequently, pimps and madams used rickshaw pullers to find customers. Men looking to pay for sex with young girls made inquiries of rickshaw pullers who were in the know. Rickshaw pullers would then pick up the young girls from their managers and take them to meet the customers. In 1922, a juvenile métisse, whose age was unlisted, told a Hải Phòng court that rickshaw

pullers had played an essential role in forcing her to sell sex by finding customers and transporting her from the madam's house to secret
locations where customers were waiting. Similarly, in 1926, Ly Cam, the
fifteen-year old mentioned above, told the court that a Miss Chung, who
had forced her into sex work, had depended on rickshaw pullers to find
clients and connect her to them.[87]

Once middlemen had fetched underage girls from managers, they
brought the girls to clients at boardinghouses, which served as a nexus
for underage sex work. The young métisse and Ly Cam, both mentioned
above in the context of Hải Phòng court cases, were taken by rickshaw
pullers to meet clients at boardinghouses.[88] Boardinghouse owners and
boardinghouse boys participated in the juvenile sex market market on
multiple levels. Some boardinghouse owners were pimps themselves:
they controlled the operations, housed young girls, provided sexy clothing and heavy makeup, and forced them to take customers in the squalid,
roach-infested rooms.[89] Other boardinghouse owners looked the other
way when pimps and madams rented rooms where sex workers as young
as twelve years old were brought to meet customers.[90] Like rickshaw pullers, boardinghouse boys frequently acted as middlemen to connect prospective customers to pimps. As reported in Đông Pháp in 1935, a boardinghouse boy working on Soeurs Antoines Street in Hanoi was arrested
for his role in an operation to pimp out a seventeen-year-old girl named
Minh. A migrant to Hanoi from Bắc Ninh Province, she was lured by a
husband-wife team who sold her for ten piastres to the boardinghouse
boy. The boy dolled her up with sexy clothes and makeup, secretly found
her customers, and forced her to satisfy them in various boardinghouse
rooms.[91]

There is scant documentation on the men who sought out adolescent
sex workers. From the information that has survived, it appears that
clients came from diverse backgrounds: rich and poor, Chinese, Indian,
European, and Vietnamese. Likewise, we know little about how much
customers paid for sex with underage girls. In her 1926 testimony to a
Hải Phòng court, fifteen-year-old Ly Cam, mentioned above, said that
men paid 0.50 piastres per night to the madam who had forced her to sell
sex. Some clients, however, tipped her 0.20 or 0.30 piastres, money that
she was able to hide from her madam.[92] In 1935, Ngọ Báo reported that
Chinese clients paid 3.20 piastres per night to the madam who controlled
Thị Bảo, the seventeen-year-old girl mentioned in chapter 3 who was
kidnapped in the Djbouti Garden.[93]

The shady actors who prostituted adolescent girls went to extensive measures to hide their criminal activities. They kept young girls locked up in their homes, connected with customers only through middlemen, and brought girls to meet clients at boardinghouses. Only those in the know could find underage sex workers. Hanoi police managed to rescue some of them by conducting frequent surveillance operations at boardinghouses. Typically fettered by colonial privacy laws protecting private businesses from police interference, the vice squad used the menace of juvenile sex work to justify searches for sex workers, whether juvenile or adult.[94] Although it was difficult for police to thwart juvenile prostitution rings, rescue underage sex workers, or arrest perpetrators, some cases were tried in the local courts, and criminals were brought to justice.

Crime and Punishment

Because of the decentralized nature of the historical sources,[95] it is difficult to determine how many arrests were made for juvenile prostitution, how many cases were tried, or how many perpetrators were punished. It seems clear that only a small number of cases were caught by police. What little statistical information is available indicates that in 1926, 180 underage sex workers working in clandestine brothels or working illegally in registered brothels in Hanoi were returned to their parents.[96] A decade later, the 1937–38 fiscal year report of the Hanoi vice squad cites more than twenty cases of traffickers caught "corrupting minors" and "leading them into debauchery."[97]

Authorities learned about juvenile prostitution in a number of ways. Undercover vice police went to both registered and clandestine brothels to search for breaches of the regulation system laws, including juvenile sex work.[98] They also staked out boardinghouses and private homes rumored to be clandestine brothels.[99] For example, in 1933, Ngọ Báo reported a sting in which officer Nguyen Sang witnessed two women taking a ten-year-old girl into a boardinghouse on Lamber Street. The women then stood guard outside the door; when the girl came out, Sang immediately arrested the group.[100] Authorities, as we shall see in chapters 5 and 6, often used the policing of juvenile sex work as a pretext for raids on ả đào houses and dance halls.

Cases of juvenile sex work also came to light when third parties reported them to the police. In a case from 1935, the owner of a registered brothel alerted authorities to a rival operation of illegal juvenile sex work when it threatened her own profits.[101] In a few lucky cases, good Samaritans alerted cases to authorities. In 1941, *Đông Pháp* covered a story in which Lê Tư Thoan, a fruit vendor in Hanoi, was horrified to learn that a woman named Thị Hy, also known as Sen, was prostituting young girls out of her house. The fruit vendor took the case to the police, who uncovered a larger operation and arrested four offenders.[102] Police also learned about cases from brave girls who were fortunate enough to have escaped their forced prostitution and alerted authorities. Thị Ngân, fifteen, and Thị Oanh, seventeen, fled from captors who had lured them with a bait-and-switch employment offer and then forced them into sex work. After providing authorities with essential details about their captors, police arrested three women who ran an ả đào singing house in Thượng Lý.[103]

Concerned parents played an important role in the justice process. Some parents of missing girls notified newspapers, sent out family members to look for them, and petitioned authorities to intervene.[104] When twelve-year-old Thị Thiện disappeared, her mother took it upon herself to search Hanoi's many brothels. Horrified to find Thị Thiện in a brothel on Bichot Street, she marched to the nearest police station and demanded that authorities rescue the young girl and arrest the brothel owners.[105] Similarly, when the parents of fifteen-year-old Thị Ngân and seventeen-year-old Oanh, mentioned above, learned that their daughters had been lured into sex work at an ả đào house, they were determined to bring the perpetrators to justice. They took their case to the police, insisted that authorities arrest the three women who ran the house, and turned to the newspaper *Tin Mới* to publicize their story.[106]

In at least one case, village leaders intervened on behalf of children who had been forced into sex work. This occurred in the case mentioned above involving two siblings who had migrated to Hanoi from Ninh Bình Province, looking for work as servants. Both brother and sister found jobs as servants, only to discover that the house where they worked was a brothel. The owner proceeded to force the sister to sell sex. Upon learning of their situation, the village head of Hoang Long interceded to negotiate their release.[107]

Malefactors found in violation of the 1926 decree, which set the minimum age limit for sex work at eighteen, would be fined one to fifteen francs and/or imprisoned one to five days.[108] From the sources available, it appears that some were punished more severely. That year, a court in Hải Phòng fined Yune A Nang 4.24 piastres and sentenced him to six months in prison for leading a minor into debauchery.[109] In 1935, a court sentenced Trần Thị Lan and a Chinese woman, Ao Chi, with six months in jail for kidnapping and forcing a seventeen-year-old girl to sell sex.[110] In 1940, Trần Thị Hoan was fined five hundred francs and issued a one-year suspended sentence for selling two underage girls. In the same case, ả đào singing house owner Nguyễn Thị Minh, who had forced underage girls to take customers, received a two-year suspended sentence and a fine of two thousand francs.[111] In a 1940 case in which a gang of four women had lured a pair of sixteen- and seventeen-year-old sisters into forced sex work, a court gave the women a one-year suspended sentence and fined them from five hundred to two thousand francs.[112]

In some instances, courts forced those found guilty to pay a sum of money to the parents of the underage girls they had forced or tricked into sex work. Fines ranged from twenty to thirty piastres.[113]In the 1940 case mentioned above, for example, a court ordered the gang of four women who lured two sisters to pay a small settlement to the parents.[114] While court records do not include an explanation for the requirement that parents be paid, there were at least two likely reasons. It may have been compensation for the emotional hardship of almost losing two daughters; it may also have been a payment for the girls' virginity.

Judging from the vice squad and Hải Phòng court records available for 1937 and 1938, in most hearings on leading a minor into debauchery, courts sentenced the guilty to under one year. For example, in 1937 in Hải Phòng, thirty-five-year-old Nguyen Thi Mai was sentenced to one month in prison for leading a fourteen-year-old girl into sex work.[115] The 1938 records from the vice squad include numerous cases: a court imposed a six-month prison term on a thirty-three-year-old woman in Hanoi for leading a sixteen-year-old girl into debauchery; a thirty year-old woman in Hải Phòng was condemned to eight months in prison for kidnapping four girls, aged fourteen, eighteen, and nineteen, with the intent of prostituting them. As the perpetrator was Chinese, the court deported her and instituted an eight-year ban from Tonkin.[116] Also in 1938, a fifty-two-year-old woman was sentenced to six months in prison for kidnapping a fourteen-year-old girl in Hải Phòng with the intent of selling her into the sex industry.[117] That same year, the court ordered a twenty-year-old woman to serve three months for corrupting a minor.[118] In another Hải Phòng case, a twenty-year-old woman was jailed for six months for kidnapping an eleven-year-old girl and forcing her to sell sex.[119] And in Lạng Sơn, two Tonkinese women were condemned to three months in prison for selling a fifteen-year-old girl into sex work.[120]

In certain rare instances, the courts ordered longer sentences. In 1938, the court condemned a forty-nine-year-old Chinese woman to eighteen months in prison and given a fine of five hundred francs and a five-year prohibition from entering Tonkin after serving her sentence.[121] Similarly, *Việt Báo* ran a story in 1940 about the conviction by a Hanoi city court of å đào singing house owner Nguyễn Thị Minh, who was given a two-year suspended sentence and a two-thousand-franc fine for forcing two underage girls to sell sex.[122]

In cases where there were male and female defendants, it appears that the female defendant received the heavier punishment. In 1938, an eighteen-year-old Tonkinese man and woman in Lạng Sơn were found guilty of rape and leading a fourteen-year-old girl into prostitution. The man was condemned to two years in prison and the woman to three years, and the court forced the couple to pay the mother of the victim thirty piastres.[123] That same year, in Nam Định, a couple was found guilty of leading a sixteen-year-old girl into prostitution. The woman, thirty years old, was sentenced to a year in prison, while the man was ordered to serve only eight months.[124] While it is not clear from the vice squad records why male and female defendants were punished differently, any number of explanations are possible. The female defendant may have been the mastermind of the case, she may have played the lead role in luring adolescent girls, or she may have been penalized for failing to live up to the courts' expectation that women be nurturing.

Not all the cases that came to the attention of authorities were punished. Vice squad records from 1938 tell of such cases. In one case, a fifty-year-old Tonkinese woman appeared to be "leading a young girl into debauchery," but police lacked sufficient proof to arrest her.[125] In Lạng Sơn, a Chinese man and a Tonkinese woman tried to sell two Tonkinese girls, aged sixteen and eighteen, to traffickers who had plans to sell them to a brothel in China. For unstated reasons, the vice squad never pursued the case.[126] Others miscreants went unpunished when authorities failed to take the victims seriously. When two adolescent girls, whose age was unlisted—though police noted that they had "not yet reached sexual maturity" (*chưa đến tuổi trưởng*)—told police that they had been forced to sell sex at an å đào singing house on Khâm Thiên Street in Hanoi, police refused to arrest the employer, assuming that the girls had faked the story to seek revenge on their boss.[127] In another case, authorities in Hải Phòng allowed a Chinese man go free even after discovering that he had pimped out a seventeen-year-old girl. Fed up, a journalist covering the case subtly shook readers' confidence in the police when he or she asked rhetorically if authorities were going to put the pimp under surveillance to ensure that he not force any more young girls into prostitution.[128]

Some accused culprits managed to evade the law through elaborate tricks. In one 1941 case, police discovered some young girls during a sting operation at an á đào house, took the girls into custody, and awaited the arrival of their families. When the parents showed up, colonial officials greeted them with all the gravitas befitting the situation. Little did the authorities know that their sentiments were woefully misplaced. The owner of the á đào house, loath to part with her valuable underage property, had arranged for a set of fake parents to claim the girls and then return them to her singing house. Authorities eventually got wind of the scam and arrested the coconspirators.[129] So egregious was the case that it was covered by multiple news outlets.

The market for young girls flourished due to the constant supply of young girls forced into sex work. Poverty in Tonkin caused by colonial economic policy and exacerbated by natural disasters and the Great Depression left many girls orphaned, abandoned, or simply eager to migrate in search of work. Their precarious status as young, desperate female migrants made them easy to exploit.

For the most part, authorities took cases of adolescent sex work seriously. Vice police carefully staked out boardinghouses, and colonial courts tried cases of juvenile sex work and delivered punishment to guilty parties. Yet the market flourished nonetheless. For one thing, underage girls were in high demand. Not only did the idea of having sex with a virgin stoke the male imagination and ego, but customers wrongly assumed that they could protect themselves from venereal diseases by having sex only with virgins.

The success of the market for adolescent girls lay in its secrecy. It was decentralized and only open to those in the know who could find middlemen to connect them to a madam or pimp with an underage girl. As a result, for all the police efforts and court actions, this shady market thrived throughout the interwar years.

CHAPTER 5

Ả Đào Singers

New Ways to Police Female Performance Art

In 1939, provincial authorities raided a group of ả đào singing houses in Thái Bình and forced the singers to "get familiar with the 'duck's beak'" (*làm quen với "mỏ vịt"*), a euphemism for the speculum used in venereal exams. Shortly after the raid, the newspaper *Việt Báo* published an open letter to Head Councilman Thiều signed by Cô Ngà and "The girls of Vũ Tiến neighborhood." The Vũ Tiến neighborhood was an area in Thái Bình Province known for its ả đào singing houses, many of which were rumored to be clandestine brothels. The letter is surprisingly fresh in the way it uses sarcasm and wordplay to challenge authorities on their hypocrisy for ordering the arrest of singers. It begins: "Sir, head of the colonial council, . . . [we] recently received news that you are so worried about our flesh that you felt you had to order us to the hospital immediately." The letter grows increasingly sarcastic: "Oh! What did we do to deserve a person as decent as you, sir? That's so very kind." It even dares to point out authorities' hypocrisy in condemning the very practice in which they were enthusiastically participating: "It's as if our bodies are laid out like fish on a chopping board and any government official who wants to can cut off a bite, so . . . is there anyone left to whom can we can complain?" The letter continues with a metaphor of flesh, food, and sex: "Once they finish the vegetarian serving, they turn to the *mặn* serving . . . and then they blame us for having venereal disease and force us to submit to venereal exams." The word "mặn" refers to salty, meaty food, which is also associated in Buddhism with inciting sexual passion. Local mandarins, the authors disclosed, frequented ả đào singing houses and took "generous servings" without paying. They teased, "If I may say so, sir, these servings are very 'mặn.' Very mặn. Like *nước mắm chắt* [a famously salty fish sauce from Hải Phòng]."[1]

This provocative letter from the ả đào singers in the Vũ Tiến neighborhood revealed a public secret in interwar Tonkin: the art of ả đào singing was often a front for clandestine sex work. Ả đào singing was a popular form of traditional female-sung music. In Vietnamese, the music form is called *hát ả đào*, the singers are called *cô đầu*, and the venue is called *nhà hát ả đào*. To simplify for anglophone audiences, I will refer to "ả đào music," "ả đào singing houses," and "ả đào singers." Ả đào music, dating back in various iterations to the fourteenth century, had historically found an audience with the scholarly gentry. It was held in high esteem through the centuries and associated with the Vietnamese literary revival of the late nineteenth century. In the colonial period, however, the reputation of ả đào entertainment suffered as the social standing of the mandarin class declined with French rule and as Vietnamese newspapers began exposing the link between sex work and ả đào venues. Ả đào venues attracted men who were looking for comfort in traditional culture in this era of dynamic cultural change—at least for the night. So well known was this secret sale of sex that corrupt Vietnamese mandarins frequented ả đào singing houses and regularly hired the singer-sex workers, as evidenced by the letter from the girls of the Vũ Tiến neighborhood.

Surprisingly little is known about the late colonial-era singing houses and the experiences of ả đào singers. Ả đào music has been explored in rich ethnomusicology studies by Barley Norton, Stephen Addis, Hai Tran Quang, and Alineor Anseil as well as a recent important literary analysis by Hoàng Thị Ngọc Thanh.[2] While these ethnomusicology and literary studies do reference the links between the sex industry and ả đào music that developed in the twentieth century, the relationship between the clandestine sex industry and these music venues remains unexplored.

During the late colonial period, sex workers and their managers who were looking to evade the laws governing the colonial regulatory prostitution system used ả đào singing houses as a front for clandestine sex work. While not all singers or waitresses working in the music venues engaged in—or even knew about—sex work, the activities of those clandestine sex workers at the ả đào music houses made the venues a well-known destination for those seeking sex on the sly. On multiple occasions, the colonial government attempted to regulate sex work in á đào venues, but workers easily evaded the law. Clandestine sex work proliferated in á đào singing venues because house owners and singers artfully subverted colonial law and took advantage of its geographic limits. Moreover, local authorities who were in charge of policing á đào singing houses were often their best customers. In the late 1930s, colonial authorities drew on laws designed to combat human trafficking and venereal diseases to police the singing houses while circumventing privacy laws, as evidenced by the letter from the singers in the Vũ Tiến neighborhood.

The Decline of a Craft

It is not clear when á đào music became associated with clandestine sex work. The á đào music tradition, which began as a female form of performance art, dates at least as far back as the early years of the Lê dynasty (1428–1777). Ethnomusicologists Addiss and Norton date the genesis of modern á đào music style to the musical forms called *hát cửa đình* and *hát cửa quyền*. Originally intended for elites, the music was performed mostly at religious and public ceremonies in its early years. Singers took their craft seriously, organizing into guilds and adhering to strict rules governing their diets and chastity. By the end of the fifteenth century, á đào music had become widely popular, with ensembles performing in every district of the northern portion of what is now Vietnam. Economic downturn in the seventeenth and eighteenth centuries led villages to sell the rights of á đào guilds to wealthy male scholars. As a result, á đào music was restricted to elite entertainment.[3]

During the eighteenth and nineteenth centuries, singers were known to be beautiful young women. Most were well educated; some were daughters of scholars. In the villages, they sang at festivals or on special occasions. Their songs held a special place in Vietnamese literature, usually covering topics such as the beauty of the Vietnamese landscape, political satire, the doldrums of the author, or happy times. Singers would eventually marry important men, including scholars or mandarins.[4]

Perhaps hinting at illicit activities associated with á đào houses, in the early nineteenth century, a legal code punished any civil and military officials, as well as the sons of state officials, who so much as entered them.[5] In the mid-nineteenth century, during a Vietnamese literary revival, the musical form became a fashionable source of entertainment among the scholarly elite. Vietnamese literati lent their poems to á đào singers, and local mandarins and elite families hired á đào groups to perform in their homes.[6]

FIGURE 10. Undated pre–World War I postcard showing a professional á đào singing group, which likely did not include sex workers, in Hải Phòng. From author's personal collection.

In the wake of colonization, major changes in political, economic, and social structures precipitated a decline in the reputation of á đào music. First, with the late nineteenth-century French colonization of the northern areas of Vietnam, the colonial government replaced Vietnamese-educated mandarin officials with French-educated counterparts, and mandarins and literati lost their high social standing as a result. Because members of the scholar-gentry patronized the á đào establishments, the decline in their reputation meant that á đào houses in turn lost an important social credential. Second, as cities developed, at the turn of the century á đào houses opened up in urban areas. Singing house owners were women and typically former singers themselves. The rumored link between colonial urbanization and crime contributed to the association between á đào houses and debauchery. Moreover, after World War I, Indochina's turbulent economy, coupled with large-scale migrations to the protectorate's urban centers, sparked a sharp increase in the supply of sex workers, particularly in á đào music venues.[7] As Tonkin's economy recovered in the mid-1930s, the á đào entertainment industry became flooded with customers.

Much to the chagrin of colonial administrators, the 1921 law, designed to apply the regulation system uniformly across French territory, left colonial authorities unable to police clandestine sex work in singing houses. For one thing, the 1921 law could not transgress French

administrative boundaries into suburban areas, where most ả đào singing houses were located. Moreover, the 1921 law only enabled authorities to police registered sex workers, which ả đào singers decidedly were
not. The 1921 definition of prostitution also appears to have applied only
to those whose main profession was prostitution. Women who worked
in ả đào singing houses made every effort to present their profession as
an art form, however sexualized it may have been. Throughout the late
colonial period, as we shall see, there was a constant back-and-forth
between colonial administrators trying to police sex work in ả đào venues and ả đào singers using the guise of art to evade being classified as
sex workers.

Clandestine sex work in late colonial Tonkin was a poorly kept secret
among the public. Ả đào singing houses typically clustered in groups, such
that neighborhoods tended to be associated with the trade. Ả đào houses
colocated in order to take advantage of the business opportunities presented by customers wandering in and out of singing houses. As a result,
entire neighborhoods of ả đào houses sprang up. Boardinghouses soon
followed to provide a space for sex workers and their clients to meet at
night. As will be discussed in the next chapter, in the mid-1930s, dance halls
opened in ả đào neighborhoods, in part to take advantage of the hopping
entertainment business in ả đào neighborhoods.

Until approximately 1930, many lively ả đào neighborhoods existed
within the municipal limits of Hanoi and thus were subject to French
law and scrutiny. Hanoi was home to the most infamous and lucrative
ả đào neighborhoods, including houses in the old quarter on Mã Vỹ, Hà
Trung, and Vĩnh Hồ Streets. While city police could not legally treat ả
đào singing houses as brothels due to the constraints of the 1921 law,
the city slapped the owners of singing houses with heavy taxes, and
police fined them for noise violations and forced them to close early in
the evening.[8]

In the 1930s, most ả đào singing houses "migrated en masse" to the
suburbs, just a few meters outside the legal boundaries of the provincial
capitals, enabling them to avoid city regulations while benefiting from the
customer base of the big cities.[9] This strategy played out in Hanoi and Hải
Phòng, as well as the smaller provincial cities of Ninh Bình and Nam Định.[10]
Moving to the suburbs outside the cities was a savvy business move for ả
đào establishments. Because French law only extended to the city limits,
those areas outside the city fell under the indigenous legal code and taxation
system. Moreover, as Dr. Bernard Joyeux claimed, ả đào singers and their
establishments were protected by the Vietnamese mandarins who governed

the suburbs—and were loyal clients,[11] a fact backed up by the letter from the singers of the Vũ Tiến neighborhood that opened this chapter.[12]

By 1937, the suburban zone outside of Hanoi was home to 183 å đào singing houses with a total of 899 women; in 1938, the numbers rose to 216 houses with 958 women, according to the estimates of Mayor M. H. Virgitti and Dr. Joyeux.[13] That same year, journalist Nguyễn Đình Lạp counted 1,400 women working in å đào singing houses.[14] In 1939, an article in the newspaper *Đông Pháp* counted "up to 2,000 girls" living together "to the beat of the *phách*" (a bamboo drumstick used to strike a small, wooden plank resulting in a beat that was associated with å đào music) in the suburbs.[15]

Some of the more famous locations across the administrative line encircling Hanoi included the neighborhoods of Khâm Thiên, Thai Hà Ap, Bạch Mai, Chùa Mới, and Gia Lâm, where, as Dr. Joyeux characterized the situation, "they can play with full liberty through the early hours of the morning."[16] Khâm Thiên Street, the most popular spot for å đào singing, was ideal for business. Just outside the city limits, it was a twenty-minute walk from the Hanoi train station and situated along the major route from the city to Hà Đông Province. At night, Khâm Thiên "transformed into an animated street" with its multitude of å đào singing houses.[17] As the most famous destination for enjoying å đào singing houses, it was home to the most elegant singers and charged the highest prices. The Ngã Tư Sở neighborhood, on the other hand, was considered the lowest-status area for singers and attracted a lower-class clientele (see table 5.1).

Table 5.1 Statistics for singing houses, 1938

NEIGHBORHOOD	HOUSES	SINGERS
Khâm Thiên	67	335
Vạn Thái	43	215
Ngã Tư Sở	52	260
Chùa Mới	33	165
Kim Liên	10	50
Kim Mã	22	140
Gia Quất and Gia Lâm	30	450
Vĩnh Hồ	23	115
Total	270	1,400

Source: Nguyễn Đình Lạp, "Than niên trụy lạc," 209.

Å đào neighborhoods tended to be seedy places. Left undeveloped by the colonial government, the suburbs were rundown sites of decay and crime. With little running water, limited streetlights, dirt roads, and sparse greenery, suburbs were dusty and dirty. Open sewers left a stench. Å đào singing houses tended to be located along the main roads leading out of the city toward the provinces. Indeed, one of the only reasons for city folk to stop in the suburbs on their way out to the country was to enjoy some illicit entertainment.

As the sun fell over Tonkin each night, the dim, dusty å đào neighborhoods turned lively. Lights from the singing houses refracted in the damp northern Vietnamese air, lending a warm glow to the street. The air outside smelled of roasted peanuts and steamed pork buns, which were common late-night drinking snacks. Wealthy men pulled up in shiny automobiles, a stark contrast to the poverty of the suburbs. Passengers dressed in traditional tunics stepped onto the street, quickly shuffled past shoe shiners and street hawkers, and ducked into å đào singing houses. Higher-end sex workers arrived by rickshaws; others walked to work or lived in quarters above the singing house. In lower-class å đào neighborhoods, singers openly propositioned men on the street. As one police officer described when working the beat in the sketchy Ngã Tư Sở neighborhood, once night fell, the solicitation of clients became intense. Women chased after pedestrians and bicyclists or hired rickshaw pullers to help them hunt down potential clients.[18]

The smell of alcohol and cigarettes greeted pedestrians as they passed å đào singing houses. Most of the suburban å đào houses were two-story buildings: the first floor was for the main performance, and the second floor was reserved for living quarters and private parties—and clandestine sex work. While houses typically had electricity or gas lighting, few had running water. Inside, they were furnished eclectically. An account from 1930 described European furniture jutting up against traditional Vietnamese altars for commemoration of ancestors.[19]

Performances started at eight in the evening, and singers played at an establishment for anywhere from twenty minutes to several hours.[20] The livelier shows lasted to the break of dawn.[21] As the night began, a young singer joined by a player of the long-neck lute (đàn dây) took her place on a low wooden table. Meanwhile, customers chatted noisily as attractive waitresses, many of them boarders at the å đào singing house, "rotated stealthily" among the guests, serving alcohol, lighting cigarettes and opium pipes, targeting their teasing and flirting at the wealthiest and most influential men without neglecting the rest of the customers.[22]

A typical night played out accordingly: With three strikes to a drum, a customer signaled to the performers and audience that he was ready to listen to the music. The attractive young singer adjusted a small wooden plank upon which she stirred up a beat with a phách, took a deep breath, and belted out a tune. The lute player allowed the audience to savor the singer's first few notes and then joined in. The young woman sang poetry, sometimes familiar works of well-known poets such as Nguyễn Du. Other times she sang her own compositions or even a poem that a customer slipped to her only moments before she went on stage. The music was spontaneous and enhanced by audience participation, creating the feel of a personal relationship between performer and participant.[23] When the singing was particularly beautiful or the poetry grew intense, the audience member who called the musicians into action showed his approval by beating the "praise drum" (trống chầu), striking its top when the music was good and its side if it was exceptional.[24] Other audience members dropped bamboo cards (trù) into a bucket to express satisfaction. The sound of the trù hitting the bucket was said to inspire singers because acts that won the most trù were certain to be invited back.[25]

With the exception of singers and bar girls, å đào houses were male spaces. Men gathered "not to listen to the songs, but to drink alcohol, smoke opium, and find a bit of pleasure."[26] Audiences were known to comprise exclusively men rumored to belong to the upper crust of society, including civil servants and members of bourgeois families.[27] A 1938 Đông Pháp report on events at å đào houses, however, reveals a more diverse crowd that drew from all ranks of Vietnamese society, from the poorest of rickshaw pullers to the sons of influential former mandarins.[28] That same year, Roger Charbonnier observed mandarins, scholars, and low-level civil servants frequenting å đào houses.[29] In places such as the Ngã Tư Sở neighborhood that catered to a lower-class clientele, houses reportedly enjoyed few clients at the end of the month, when customers' pockets had run dry before the next month's paycheck arrived.[30]

Å đào establishments appealed to those who felt comfortable in or fetishized the image of traditional Vietnamese culture. Singers played to this image: they drew from traditional poetry for their musical repertoire and eschewed "modern" clothing, although they embraced modern makeup styles. Their look contrasted sharply with that of the taxi dancers who worked in the same neighborhood, with their short, Western-style dresses and caked-on makeup. Of course, the image cultivated by

the á đào singers could hardly be considered an ideological statement—
it was more a matter of appealing to a certain market. All it took for a
sex worker to move from a singing house to a dancing hall was a quick
wardrobe change.

Patrons at á đào singing houses were overwhelmingly Vietnamese or
ethnic Chinese, the latter rumored to be the more generous customers.[31]
Some colonial government sources reference "Chinese singers" who
served an exclusively Chinese clientele. Given that they operated not
only in Tonkin but also in Phnom Penh, it is not clear whether they were
actually singing á đào music, which was indigenous to Tonkin.[32]

Curiously absent from the newspaper reports on á đào music houses
were references to French men; indeed, former á đào singer Ngọc (who
requested I use a pseudonym), who performed in the 1940s, does not recall
seeing French men in the establishments.[33] Dr. Joyeux reasoned that European soldiers remained uninterested in á đào singing because they could
not speak the local language and were unfamiliar with traditional culture.[34] In 1938, another French administrator observed that European men
were more interested in open-air cafés and dance halls, the latter another
venue for clandestine sex work that will be discussed in the next chapter.[35]

Many of the á đào houses capitalized on the sensual nature of the singing. Owners encouraged workers to flirt with customers. Men patronized
a favorite singer, and stories abound about customers falling hopelessly
in love with singers. Customers showed up with gifts of fruit and jewelry to win the affections of their favorite singer,[36] and they grew jealous when á đào singers paid too much attention to other customers.[37]
Some singers parlayed their flirting into marriage proposals, while others engaged in sex work.[38]

Á đào singers' role in the clandestine sex trade was complicated. When
making a point about the ubiquity of sex work in á đào singing neighborhoods, journalist Trọng Lang reported that patrons he interviewed used
the term "brothel girls" more often than "singers" when referring to
the women in á đào houses in the Ngã Tư Sở, Kim Mã, Tám Gian (Vĩnh-
Hào), and Chùa Mới neighborhoods.[39] Yet many singers never sold sex or
exchanged money for sexual favors. Ngọc, the former á đào singer who,
in the 1940s, regularly performed on Khâm Thiên Street, insisted that
she never sold sex herself—nor did she know of any singers who did.[40]
In a 1938 article in *Thời Vụ Báo*, the journalist Ngô Tất Tố, writing under
the pseudonym Xuân Trào, made a distinction between the good girls,
known as *đào trò* ("official" á đào singers), and the bad girls, known as
đào rượu ("drink servers" or "bar girls"). Đào rượu, he explained, "did not

know how to sing a single verse" and, instead, engaged in sex work.[41] But it is more likely that the division was not so clear-cut. Some "official" å đào singers may have occasionally traded sex for money, and some bar girls may have teased and tempted to earn extra tips but never given in to their clients' desires.

Colonial officials were well aware that clandestine sex work was taking place in the å đào houses. The French resident of Ninh Bình called women who worked in å đào houses "pseudo-singers."[42] In 1938, the French resident of Nam Định claimed that there was a direct correlation between the rise in the number of women who claimed to be å đào singers and the decline in the numbers of women registering with police as prostitutes, insinuating that increasing numbers of sex workers were covertly working out of å đào singing houses.[43] The following year, another official complained that brothels were misidentifying sex workers as "singers." By labeling them singers, the brothels could avoid registering them as prostitutes and, in turn, avoid paying the requisite taxes and submitting them to the regulatory prescriptions of the 1921 law.[44] The heads of the Hanoi Prophylactic League, Dr. Joyeux and Mayor Virgitti, asserted that "in reality, there are no longer any singing houses, but veritable bordellos."[45] In a separate study, Dr. Joyeux wrote that "having lost all artistic character, [å đào singers] are no more than common hetaeras. . . . They form a class of luxury hens for indigène men."[46] Writing in 1937, the head of a gendarmerie unit stationed in Sơn Tây insisted "without a shadow of doubt" that å đào singers are "prostitutes disguised under the title of 'singers.'"[47] As Dr. Joyeux told journalist Vũ Trọng Phụng, "å đào houses that are strictly for music no longer exist; instead, they are brothels."[48] Vũ Trọng Phụng, for his part, was careful to point out to his readers that he did not necessarily agree with the doctor's generalization that all å đào singers were sex workers.[49] In 1939, the French resident in Bắc Giang concurred with his counterpart in Ninh Bình that brothel owners have "given the appellation 'singers' to their pensionaries who are in fact prostitutes."[50]

The å đào music industry became famously associated with venereal diseases. When journalist Vũ Trọng Phụng interviewed Dr. Joyeux about sex work happening in å đào establishments, the doctor illustrated his point with a story about the boss of an å đào singing house who had ordered two hundred douche pouches to be used by women on Khâm Thiên Street, asking rhetorically what else the request could be for if not for sex workers.[51] In interviews with Vũ Trọng Phụng, Dr. Henri Coppin, head of the Hanoi Dispensary, suggested that å đào singers may have been the source through which venereal diseases spread to "honest" Vietnamese families."[52] Dr. Le Roy des Barres declared that "in the cities prostitution flourishes, and the majority of singing houses are only infected brothels, in which the artists are singers in name only."[53] The consequence, Dr. Joyeux concluded, was that "the citizens of Hanoi suffer from all those singing establishments with bogus names that encircle the city with a ring of venereal disease germs."[54]

Indeed, venereal diseases were a problem among women who worked in å đào singing houses. Of the twenty-two women who were apprehended for suspicion of clandestine sex work during a 1932 raid on an å đào singing house in Hà Đông, twenty tested positive for a venereal disease.[55] In 1938, after forcing å đào singers to submit to venereal exams, the French resident stationed in Nam Định reported a 90 percent morbidity rate.[56] Just two weeks later, the director of local health services in Hanoi, Dr. Raymond, made the same claim of a 90 percent incidence of a venereal disease among å đào singers.[57] Referring to å đào houses as brothels (nhà lầu xanh), one journalist writing for Đông Pháp in 1938 estimated that 90 percent of the singers at the å đào houses had a venereal disease.[58] A 1943 health inspection report for Hải Phòng noted that although the number of venereal disease cases among registered sex workers was decreasing, the number of infections had increased due to raids on å đào singing houses, "which are considered to be establishments like maisons de tolerance [brothels]."[59]

Judging by the slang terms used in another 1938 Thời Vụ Báo article, å đào houses and venereal disease–infected areas became all but synonymous. The journalist referred to å đào neighborhoods as "gonorrhea villages" (làng lậu) or "syphilis villages" (làng tiêm la). That same journalist also used the euphemism "å đào music village" (làng sênh phách) to refer to the areas of a hospital or dispensary that treated venereal diseases.[60] Another journalist from Thời Vụ Báo, also writing in 1938, derided singers as "maids painted up with excessive makeup and venereal germs."[61]

Understandably, å đào singers had a bad reputation among Tonkin's wives, who worried that their husbands were off philandering under the guise of culture, squandering family resources, and returning home with venereal diseases (see figure 11).[62] In 1930, the Vietnamese wives of mandarins in Hải Dương complained to the colonial government that singers were infecting their husbands.[63] Similarly, in 1937, "we, the inhabitants of the province of Sơn Tây" wrote a letter to the resident superior of Tonkin on behalf of "unhappy wives ruined by the venereal disease transmitted by their husbands, who had themselves been contaminated by singers from the Rue de Đông Tác."[64]

—Mặt kìa | thế mà bảo rang đi dự hội-đồng cứu tế | Cứu ai ? Tế ai...
← O'!! .. Cứu tế phu nữ thất nghiệp mà ! ..

FIGURE 11. "Mặt kìa! Thế mà bảo rằng đi dự hội-đồng cứu tế! Cứu ai? Tế ai?"
"Ơ!! . . . Cứu tế phụ nữ thất nghiệp mà."
"Look at you! You said you are attending an emergency-rescue meeting! Who are you helping? Who are you saving?"
"Uh . . . I'm saving unemployed women."
Credit: *Phong Hóa*, January 13, 1933, 1. (The image does not include the cartoonist's name.)

The singers' reputations in their home villages deteriorated to the extent that their families and other village residents were shamed by the association. In 1926, when authorities attempted to register local å đào singers and issue identity cards, French authorities reported that mandarins from the singers' home villages had refused to verify their identities or recognize them as village members.[65] In a 1938 story in *Thời Vụ Báo*, a journalist reported that daughters often lied to their parents about their real profession in the big city, such as the case of a peasant girl who had migrated to Hanoi and fooled her father into thinking that she was employed as a maid. In reality, she was employed as a singer and clandestine sex worker.[66]

Public opinion of singers likewise deteriorated. "If at one time the singing profession may have been respectable, it has sunk into the lowest form of prostitution" reported Dr. Raymond, who treated sex workers.[67] Alluding to their clandestine activities, Hải Phòng councilman Nguyen Ngoc Phong, also known as Sy Ky, insisted to the mayor that å đào "singers" rarely sing.[68] Roger Charbonnier called singers "charming artists that are actually common prostitutes. . . . Some of the older ones know how to sing. The majority are illiterate and do not understand the meaning of the [poetry in the] songs."[69]

By the late colonial period, the reputation of ả đào music, which was historically a hallmark of elite scholarly culture, had deteriorated. The musical form, once a proud cultural tradition, became associated with clandestine sex work and venereal diseases. The wives of local villagers despised the singers, village officials refused to recognize the singers as village members, and colonial administrators dismissed all ả đào singers as clandestine sex workers.

Singers, Madams, and Clients

An investigation of the actors involved in the business of sex work at ả đào singing houses reveals a diverse group of women who became involved in the sex industry for a variety of reasons. Although some women certainly were empowered through the sex industry, many were vulnerable due to poverty. Madams and clients appeared all too willing to capitalize on their vulnerabilities. The result was rowdy nights and high rates of crime in the singing houses.[70]

Without hearing the voices of the ả đào singers themselves, it is impossible to know what motivated those singers who sold sex voluntarily. A widespread assumption in the historical sources had it that most of the women were motivated by poverty. One French official speculated in 1926 that many of the ả đào sex workers were orphans or migrants from the countryside trying to earn a living in the city.[71] Journalist Trọng Lang recalled that the ả đào singers and sex workers with whom he had spoken in the late 1930s had husbands and even children and were looking to make some extra money for their families.[72] The singers told him that the owner of the brothel at which they worked used promises of food and clothing to recruit impoverished women from the countryside.[73]

Other women were rumored to have been motivated by the lure of riches and an independent lifestyle. Dr. Joyeux and Mayor Virgitti suggested in 1938 that their patients were looking to escape strict parents and traditional Vietnamese culture and were attracted to an ostensibly glamorous life of fancy clothing, jewelry, and makeup.[74] Another journalist writing for Thời Vụ Báo in 1938 asserted that the women who worked in ả đào houses "enjoyed the pampering . . . of a mandarin's son."[75] A 1939 article from Đông Pháp described the singers as "thousands of girls who were past a marriageable age, were neglected by their family, or were duped in love," suggesting they were led to the independent lifestyle not by choice.[76]

But life as an å đào singer was not all glamour and fun. Sadly, some women found themselves tricked into working at å đào singing houses and forced into debt bondage. For example, in 1937, *Việt Báo* reported a story about twenty-year-old Nguyễn Thị Liên, who ran away from her home in Thái Bình Province after her father beat her. When she arrived in Hanoi, she met an old woman who promised her a job as a maid to a woman who, she later learned, was an å đào singer. After accepting a cash advance from the singer, Nguyễn Thị Liên agreed to work off the debt. The singer, who had noticed that Nguyễn Thị Liên was pretty, forced her to sell sex through debt bondage. Nguyễn Thị Liên eventually contracted a venereal disease.[77] In 1939, *Việt Báo* chronicled the case of Ng. Thị Lỳ, a twenty-two-year-old woman who had borrowed fifteen piastres from the owner of an å đào house in Thượng Cát Village. With interest, the debt soon accrued to thirty piastres. The owner required that she pay off the debt by selling sex, forcing her to endure violent customers on a nightly basis.[78]

While many singers were legal adults, å đào houses nonetheless housed underage clandestine sex workers. For those minors looking to—or forced to—circumvent the age regulation instituted by the 1926 law, most å đào houses were willing to hire underage girls to mingle with customers, serve them drinks, flirt, and offer sexual services.[79] Stories circulated of underage girls who were forced into sex work in å đào houses.[80]

Food was scarce among women working in å đào singing houses. Writing about the late 1930s, journalist Trọng Lang noted that women struggled to find the money to buy even a bowl of rice and spinach. One woman with whom he spoke had the look of being strained and fatigued, and he even compared the woman's appearance to that of a stillborn baby. Other interviewees spoke of frequently being sick, some close to death.[81]

Rape and brutality were likewise commonplace. One singer recounted to Trọng Lang a story of being unable to halt a drunk customer's advances. She eventually gave in, and he raped her until three in the morning. In the end, he begrudgingly paid her only two *đồng*, "like you would give a dog," she reflected.[82] In 1941, *Thông Tin* published a story on Thị Chúc, a twenty-one-year-old singer working at an å đào house in Nam Định in 1941. When she accidentally spilled the contents of an opium pipe, Vũ Thị Bảo, the house owner, scolded her in front of customers and other å đào singers. Ashamed of the public scolding, Thị Chúc burst into tears.

The emotional display made customers uncomfortable, and many left as a result. Enraged at the loss of business, Vũ Thị Bảo beat Thị Chúc.[83]

Sadly, some singers attempted suicide. In 1939 *Đông Pháp* reported on two girls who lived in the same ả đào house in Thái Bình and committed suicide by drinking poison.[84] The following year *Tin Mới* printed a story about thirty-year-old named Thị-Đào, a singer at a house on Khâm Thiên Street. Ashamed of her profession and tired of bad working conditions, she attempted to drown herself in Hoàn Kiếm Lake in downtown Hanoi but was rescued by bystanders.[85]

Reports appeared in newspapers about singers who had run away to escape bad conditions. Thị Ty, a country girl from Thái Bình who was tricked into selling sex when she arrived in the big city in 1931, was one of those who fled, *Ngọ Báo* reported.[86] Ng. Thị Lỳ, mentioned above, who worked at the Thượng Cát Village ả đào house in 1939, told *Việt Báo* that her body became deformed from the violent rape after the owner forced her to sell sex nightly in order to pay off the interest on her loan. Eventually she ran away to become a street food vendor.[87]

Some women robbed their bosses as they fled. Take, for example, a 1937 story published in *Việt Báo* about a young, beautiful Eurasian mixed-race singer who ran off with a client after borrowing thirty piastres from an ả đào house owner without ever working off the debt.[88] In 1939, *Việt Báo* ran a story about Oanh and Tuyết, both twenty-two, who worked in an ả đào house on a debt-bondage contract. Oanh owed thirty piastres and Tuyết forty. Oanh ran away without paying off her debt and swiped an additional thirty piastres' worth of jewelry on her way out. Two days later, Tuyết stole thirty-four piastres' worth of jewelry and likewise ran away.[89] In 1941, *Thông Tin* published a story about an ả đào singer named Đào Thị Hồng, who absconded with money and clothing belonging to the owner of an ả đào establishment in Kiến An.[90] That same year *Thông Tin* ran another story about an ả đào house owner who went on a business trip and left the singer Nguyễn Thị Vân Lan in charge of her business. Nguyễn Thị Vân Lan used the opportunity to steal fifty piastres and some clothing.[91] While many women likely stole out of greed, it is possible that they also acted out of desperation, considering that their meager salary afforded few opportunities to save money and their clothing was considered the property of the madam.

Ả đào house owners called on the police to arrest insubordinate sex workers and sometimes brought legal action against singers who left without paying the debts that had tied them to the ả đào house. Per the 1939 *Việt Báo* story mentioned above, after Ng. Thị Lỳ ran away from the ả đào house in Thượng Cát village, the owner of the house got the police to arrest her and hold her in jail until she found a way to pay off her debt.[92] *Tin Mới* published a story in 1940 about ả đào singers who fled an establishment on Ngã Tư Sở Street, just outside of Hanoi. Customers Mr. L. and Mr. M. had requested permission of Thị Đào, the owner, to take ả đào singers Yến and Mùi out on a date. Thị Đào agreed. When it was getting late and the singers still had not returned, Thị Đào grew nervous about the women, who were a valuable source of income, and went looking for the group. Finding them enjoying a meal at a restaurant, she forced Yến to return to the ả đào house, but Mùi escaped and managed to spend the rest of her night with Mr. L. Angry about the loss of potential revenue, Thị Đào found Mr. M. and insisted that he pay forty piastres if his friend did not bring back Múi. Mr. M. led her to Mùi, who was hiding out in Bắc Giang Province.[93] The following year, *Thông Tin* printed a story about Thị Nguyệt, who had absconded from an ả đào house in Kiến An. She eventually settled in Hải Phòng, changed her name, and got married, but the singing house owner had police track her down, take her from her new family, and forcibly return her to the ả đào house where she had been employed.[94]

Some singers likewise appealed to authorities for help. In 1939, *Đông Pháp* reported a story about a group of singers who banded together to notify the vice squad about the ways that singing house owners exploited and brutalized them.[95] The following year, Thị-Đào the aforementioned singer who tried to drown herself in Hoàn Kiếm Lake, left a suicide note at a prayer column in the nearby Ngọc Sơn Temple that read, "My soul has been a victim of great injustice; please have authorities investigate."[96]

But involving the authorities came with risks. In 1937, the gendarmerie in Sơn Tây—who lacked the legal jurisdiction to register singers as sex workers unless, per the 1921 law, they tested positive for a venereal disease on more than one occasion—used complaints about frequent thefts in the ả đào houses on Rue de Hanoi as a justification for photographing singers and recording their identification information. This enabled police to keep tabs on the women without violating the prohibition on registering them as sex workers. Of course, the women who worked in the ả đào houses there were not naive and skipped town whenever they got word that police were coming to photograph them.[97]

Stories appeared in the newspapers about conniving ả đào singers tricking innocent men. In 1939, *Việt Báo* ran a story about Mr. L., a thirty-three-year-old peasant, who fell in love with Thị Phương, a singer at an establishment on Hương Ký Street, hoping to become her husband one day. When she learned of his intentions, Thị Phương accepted his proposal of marriage and requested money to prepare for the wedding. Initially, he gave her fifty piastres, but she sneered at him for being cheap. He then gave her a hundred more piastres and paid for her wedding dress, but, come wedding day, she was nowhere to be found. When Mr. L. discovered that Thị Phương had skipped town with his money, he filed a report with the police, who managed to track her down. Thị Phương told them that Mr. L. was already married and that the money he had given her was to pay for all the alcohol he had drunk.[98]

Judging by newspaper coverage of crime in á đào neighborhoods, the customers at á đào establishments could likewise be unsavory characters. Owners often extended credit to clients and then had to resort to harassment to be repaid; other customers refused to pay at all.[99] Many clients attempted to slip out without paying their bills.[100] Some clients even robbed the á đào singers themselves. In a 1931 story covered by *Ngọ Báo*, five men visited an á đào house on Cầu Lim Street in Ninh Bình Province. At the end of the night, when the owner presented them with their bill, the customers created some confusion as a distraction. Suspecting that the men aimed to stiff him, the owner frisked them and found that they had stolen two gold bracelets and some betel nuts from the singers.[101]

Some customers concocted elaborate scams to rob singers. In 1939, *Việt Báo* reported a story about two Chinese customers who walked into an á đào house flashing big bills to attract pretty singers. The women working at the house were excited, as Chinese men were rumored to be generous. The men partied at the singing house until three in the morning and then spent the night with the singers. When the group woke up, the men invited the singers to go shopping. Together they shopped for furniture, clothing, and jewelry. All the while, the men placed orders for gifts for the singers—including a diamond ring for one lucky woman. The men asked the shop owners to put the merchandise aside so they could pick it up at the end of the day, a common practice in colonial Tonkin. The group then went to a shoe shop, where one of the men tried on a particularly expensive pair. Claiming to be all out of cash from the day's shopping spree, he asked a singer if he could borrow some. She lent him her savings of seventy piastres, whereupon the group went out for dinner. Afterward, the singers suggested they return to the stores to pick up the gifts. The Chinese men distracted them by insisting on taking some photos first and went to their car to fetch their camera. The singers waited patiently at the table, but the men never returned, leaving the singers to foot the bill. As it turned out, not only were the singers out ten piastres for the meal and seventy piastres for the shoes, but the gifts that the men had supposedly ordered for them—including the diamond ring—had never actually been paid for.[102]

In another scam reported a few months later in *Việt Báo*, a group of clients stayed overnight in an å đào singing house, violating a local ordinance forbidding men to spend the night in å đào houses. That night, the clients and singers "had intimate conversation—and a little passion." In the early morning, the men attempted to sneak out while the singers were still sleeping. The singers awoke to the sound of the men leaving and found that their clients had not only stiffed them of the night's bill, but robbed them as well. Five or six of the singers and the madam took off after the men, chasing them across the suburban-city boundary and through Hanoi's streets. Three of the men managed to escape, but a singer caught up with one of the men and snatched his wallet, refusing to return it until his friends had returned the stolen goods and paid their bill.[103] In a 1944 case chronicled in *Việt Cường*, a customer at an å đào establishment on Vĩnh Hồ Street of the Ngã Tư Sở neighborhood spent four consecutive nights listening to Lê Thị Trá, an å đào singer. On the fourth night, he propositioned her to spend the night with him. She accompanied him to a boardinghouse, dressed in her finest clothing. The next morning, she awoke to find herself naked and alone, her dress and jewelry nowhere to be seen. In the humiliating scene that followed, Lê Thị Trá was forced to pay the bill for the room herself and walk back to the å đào establishment wearing nothing but her underwear.[104]

Å đào house owners sometimes resorted to extreme measures to deal with unruly customers. To collect on unpaid bills, some owners seized valuables from customers. This was the case in a 1936 story in *Đông Pháp* about a customer named Lương who was forced to give up his watch when he claimed not to have enough money to pay for his night's escapades.[105] In another case chronicled the following year in *Việt Báo*, Ng. Thị Cả directed her employees to lock up the bicycles of some customers until they paid. The men refused, claiming that the singers had never sung, hinting at blackmail for the illegality of using an å đào singing house as a cover for clandestine sex work. To spite the owner, one of the men pulled his penis out of his pants and made a show of urinating all over her furniture. A fight ensued, and both sides filed reports with the police.[106]

In the late colonial period, it was no secret that many å đào houses were fronts for clandestine sex work. They had a reputation for wild nights, unsavory characters, venereal diseases, and sex on the sly. Yet, as infamous as the ả đào singing houses were, the state struggled mightily to bring them under the regulation codes.

Colonial Attempts to Regulate Sex in Ả Đào Music Venues

The persistence of sex work in many ả đào music venues was related to the larger challenges of regulating the sale of sex. Authorities made many attempts to bring sex work that occurred in ả đào music houses under state control but were hindered by loopholes in the regulatory system and the challenges of managing sex work more generally. The French metropolitan and colonial governments alike attempted to impose order by classifying sex workers and their place of operation, and by writing laws to subject sex workers to regulations.[107] Yet ả đào singers and house owners insisted that they were performance artists and professional musicians, not common prostitutes. While that was an accurate statement for most of the traditionally trained singers, others used the singing profession as a cover for clandestine sex work.

The colonial government attempted to regulate ả đào houses on multiple occasions, but the laws intended to give the government regulation powers actually limited the scope of state authority. In 1926, the governor-general of Tonkin conceded that ả đào singers could not be forced to submit for venereal exams because they were musicians, not prostitutes, according to the strict definition of the 1921 law. Similarly, the vice squad did not have the authority to search ả đào houses for evidence of sex work.[108] That same year, the resident superior of Tonkin lamented that the 1921 law could not be applied to ả đào singers, thus impeding investigations of clandestine sex work. The sentiment was shared by Dr. Raymond, who called on the colonial government to replace the law, which he considered ineffective and incomplete.[109] In response to a 1932 request to outlaw ả đào singing due to the singers' association with sex work, the resident superior of Tonkin reluctantly rejected the request on the grounds that singers were not prostitutes according to the 1921 law.[110] In 1937, the French resident stationed in Sơn Tây complained that it was impossible to "institute certain laws against prostitution because of individual liberty," referring to French laws protecting the privacy of citizens.[111]

The colonial state's inability to bring ả đào houses under regulation for selling sex frustrated local administrators and public health officials alike. In 1934, Hải Phòng councilman Nguyen Ngoc Phong appealed to the mayor: "It's a pity for them as well as Annamite society.... The girls find themselves in misery. Don't all these unhappy girls deserve our concern?"[112] In 1938, the French resident stationed at Nam Định accused the colonial administration of being "duped by the women," calling sex work in å đào houses "a scandal tolerated by the administration."[113] That same year, another colonial doctor complained that in its efforts to protect the virtues of traditional music, the state "feigns to the point of ignoring" the existence of sex work that took place in å đào houses.[114] Dr. Joyeux and Mayor Virgitti warned that Hanoi was "surrounded by a network of virulent venereal disease outbreaks, forming a true 'crown of Venus,' tolerated and accepted by public authorities, and a permanent challenge to French authority and French civilization."[115]

In the 1930s, local officials implemented local-level city planning codes and drew upon public health measures to limit the sex work in å đào houses. Authorities attempted to force singers to register as prostitutes in Nam Định in 1932 and in Hanoi in 1938,[116] but singers refused.[117] In 1937, the vice squad "toured" certain well-known å đào neighborhoods, including Khâm Thiên, Ngã Tư Sở, and Chùa Mới, to catch houses that stayed open past local curfew. Violators were fined a single piastre.[118] This nominal fine failed to deter singing houses from abiding by the curfew; because the profits garnered from customers who stayed after hours far exceeded the fine, there was financial incentive to ignore the law.[119] In Hà Đông, officials banned street solicitation and closed offending å đào singing houses for eight days in July 1938, *Đông Pháp* reported.[120] That August, *Thời Vụ Báo* ran a story about singers caught violating city codes in Nam Định. The singers were fined and forced to undergo pelvic exams. Those who refused to submit or managed to evade exams were slapped with fines ten times greater than those imposed on singers in Hanoi.[121] In September, the French resident stationed at Nam Định proposed to make what he characterized as "fake singers" register with the state, carry identity cards, submit to biweekly venereal exams, and pay taxes on their earnings.[122] That same year, the vice squad in Hanoi staked out boardinghouses in hopes of catching singers in the act of selling sex.[123] In February 1939, police in Bắc Giang forced twenty-eight singers to undergo pelvic exams; doctors found eighteen women infected.[124]

Savvy sex workers artfully evaded the law. In the 1932 Nam Định and 1938 Hanoi cases mentioned above, singers refused orders to register with police.[125] Likewise, in the 1937 case mentioned above, in which houses in well-known á đào neighborhoods were fined one piastre for staying open past curfew, the nominal fine failed to deter singing houses from abiding by the curfew.[126] In Nam Định, clandestine sex workers escaped forced venereal checkups by fleeing the province or pretending to abandon their á đào houses. Đông Pháp covered a story in 1938 about singers who posted "for rent" signs to trick police into thinking their house was vacant while they continued to accommodate customers on the sly.[127] Other singers, also reported in Đông Pháp in 1938, went on strike when authorities in Nam Định mandated that they submit to venereal disease testing and pay taxes on the sale of sex. Still others continued to see clients furtively.[128] In 1938, when authorities in Ninh Bình directed á đào singers to submit to weekly venereal tests, Đông Pháp reported that singers bribed officials to look the other way.[129]

Women who worked in á đào singing houses lobbied authorities to stop treating them as sex workers on grounds that they were female performance artists. In 1935, Ngọ Báo ran a story about authorities in Bắc Ninh who forced all á đào singers on Phủ Từ Street to submit to pelvic exams and closed some of the singing venues. Angry singers marched to the local mandarin's house in protest of being classified anything but singers, only to be arrested and carted off to the dispensary in tears.[130] In 1938, Đông Pháp printed a story about singers from greater Hà Đông Province who collaborated with those from Khâm Thiên Street to call on local officials to abandon venereal testing requirements and to grant their work professional status.[131] Within a month, singer Nguyễn Thị Loan, owner of an á đào house in the Oanh Rợp / Ngã Sáu neighborhood in Nam Định, wrote directly to the resident superior of Tonkin to protest against taxes unfairly imposed on her singers and singing house, a measure enacted after Vietnamese soldiers who were infected with venereal diseases implicated á đào singers in her house as the source of their infection. She argued that he erroneously conflated the singing profession with sex work, which "is designed to satisfy the sexual needs of men." Á đào singers, she explained, "do not make a living in this way because all we sell is singing . . . for men of fine character and noble men of letters." She argued that her singing house employed a diverse group of women—old as well as young, widowed and married as well as single—many of whom, she wrote, would have been unlikely to attract customers looking for sex. Regardless of their age and looks, all her singers, she insisted, had beautiful voices. As proof, she laid out the á đào training process, comparing singers in her establishment to highly respected professional singers in Europe.[132]

Authorities were faced with a dilemma: they needed to prevent singers from spreading venereal diseases, yet registering them as sex workers would offend the women and risk causing them to flee. To avoid angering singers yet prevent infected women from spreading venereal diseases, in 1937, officials in Hà Đông proposed creating a small clinic on Khâm Thiên Street, it would be a doctor's office that would be billed as open to the public but aimed to treat a clientele of á đào singers and taxi dancers. The idea was to allow the women to discreetly seek treatment so as not to incur shame. The hope was that the women would seek treatment of their own will if they did not have to register as sex workers.[133] After all, in the spirit of the Sellier proposal discussed in chapter 2, the goal was to treat venereal diseases and prevent transmission, not to police women's sex lives. In 1939, the French resident stationed in Bắc Giang proposed requiring singers to carry medical booklets to record their medical information and provide proof of negative venereal exam results.[134]

While local governments in Tonkin drew upon city planning and public health codes to attempt to bring order to á đào singing houses, in the late 1930s, high-ranking colonial administrators found the twofold legal traction necessary to bring á đào singing houses under state regulations. In the late 1930s, the colonial government managed to come up with an alternative to the 1921 law. To do so, the resident superior of Tonkin capitalized on two of the most intractable—and widely bewailed—problems of the day: human trafficking (discussed in chapter 3) and the spread of venereal diseases (discussed in chapter 2). Drawing from the rhetoric associated with these two issues, the resident superior of Tonkin crafted laws that enabled the colonial government to police clandestine sex work in á đào houses and dance halls by shifting the focus from *regulation* to *protection*—from regulating the sex lives of unregistered women to protecting singers from exploitative managers and the public from the spread of venereal diseases.

The governor-general drew from the debates surrounding human trafficking. The international movement against trafficking criticized France's tolerance of brothel prostitution on the grounds that it created a market for trafficking. Although France objected to the League of Nation's characterization of registered brothels as sites of trafficking, the governor-general of Indochina nonetheless employed the rhetoric of the antitrafficking movement to make the case for regulating the á đào singing clubs. In September 1938, Governor-General Jules Brévié sent an impassioned letter to the local administrators of the colony, informing them of the League of Nations' call to suppress trafficking. The letter described a typical scenario in which ả đào singing houses were supplied with trafficked women: an elderly woman—a mẹ mìn—lures a young girl from the country with false promises of employment and lends her clothing or offers a cash advance on her salary. The girl is thus tricked into debt bondage and forced to sell sex at an ả đào house until the debt is repaid.[135]

Meanwhile, the governor-general also came under pressure to institute public health measures. In 1938, the resident superior of Tonkin expressed frustration with the limits of the 1921 law defining prostitution. Because police could not regulate singers for sex work, he invoked the Sellier proposal, which called for criminalizing the spread of venereal diseases, to urge police and doctors to pursue singers who had been identified as a source of venereal contagion.[136] Within a few weeks of the governor-general's announcement, Dr. Joyeux and Hanoi's Mayor Virgitti warned of the delicate situation: "These women fear most of all the dishonor of being registered as a prostitute." They advised that the ả đào workers be allowed to maintain their titles as singers and echoed the request of the French resident at Hà Đông that a new dispensary be created on Khâm Thiên Street, where they could be treated close to their workplace while avoiding registering with police as sex workers.[137] A separate report published by the pair suggested using French-trained Vietnamese midwives to conduct venereal exams, the hope being that sex workers would be more likely to let a Vietnamese woman conduct a pelvic exam than a French man. The report suggested requiring those who tested positive to submit to treatment.[138]

The governor-general seemed to have hit on a solution. In an April 1939 letter to the local heads of administration, he acknowledged that although Indochina could not depart from the French regulation system, which was the foundation for the 1921 law, "local considerations" could justify exceptions to the rule. Ả đào singers, as well as taxi dancers (to be discussed in the next chapter), he proposed, could be that exception.[139] As discussed in chapter 3, on May 22, 1939, the resident superior of Tonkin issued a decree to regulate the working conditions of singers and dancers. Its language reflected the concerns and solutions offered by administrators and public health officials. First, the decree included measures to protect singers from human trafficking and exploitative debt contracts. The decree forbade advances in cash, jewelry, or clothing valued at more than two months' worth of salary and forbade interest charged on such advances. Singing houses were forbidden from holding workers against their will, and workers who had taken advances would be allowed to transfer their debts to new singing establishments without accruing interest on said debts. The decree stated that singers must be paid for their work in cash and that salaries could not replaced by room and board only. Those singers said to be apprentices were required to provide evidence of parental consent, a measure taken to prevent juvenile sex work.[140]

A second important point of the decree was the artful balance it achieved in establishing antivenereal measures while avoiding labeling á đào singers or taxi dancers as prostitutes. Administrators were well aware that labeling them as prostitutes—correctly or not—would likely anger them and discourage them from cooperating. The decree mandated that singing houses seek state approval to operate and required all singers and employees to register, verify their identity, and maintain a medical record book. It forbade men from living at such establishments or staying overnight. Under the decree, singers who habitually sold sex would be forced to register as such and enter a state-sanctioned brothel. Houses where women were caught selling sex would be forced to register as brothels and fined three to fifteen francs.[141]

City and provincial level regulations quickly followed the decree. In fact, it was this May 1939 decree that administrators in Thái Bình acted upon only a few months later, in August, when police rounded up singers in the Vũ Tiến neighborhood and forced them to submit to venereal exams, as chronicled in the letter that opened this chapter.[142] A decree of November 22, 1939, required singing houses in Hà Đông to close by one in the morning and forbade men from spending the night.[143] In 1940, local governments in Hải Phòng and Hưng Yên passed ordinances banning customers from staying overnight in á đào houses, and houses that committed two offenses were warned that a third offense would result in obligatory registration as a brothel.[144] *Việt Báo* ran a story in 1940 about a mandate in Thanh Hoá that required venereal exams for all á đào singers after an infected man was believed to have contracted a venereal disease from a singer. The local singers refused to comply until the mayor issued a decree forcing the singers to submit to exams.[145] In 1942, *Đông Pháp* reported that after catching singers soliciting customers on the street in the Tàu Bay and Ngã Tư Sở neighborhoods, authorities "decontaminated" nearby á đào houses by mandating that all singers submit to pelvic exams. When the women refused, authorities fined and shut down the houses for three days.[146] In 1944, after witnessing á đào singers solicit clients, police raided the á đào establishments in the Ngã Tư Sở neighborhood. They found two pregnant women, arrested 144 women, and sent sixty-seven to the local dispensary.[147]

The 1939 decree did manage to protect some singers from exploitive debt contracts and unscrupulous bosses. *Việt Báo* ran a story in 1940 about the conviction by a Hanoi city court of ả đào singing house owner Nguyễn Thị Minh, who was given a two-year suspended sentence and a two-thousand-franc fine for forcing two underage girls to sell sex.[148] Thị Chúc, the singer mentioned above who was beaten by her boss after spilling the contents of an opium pipe in 1941, filed a complaint with the police, accusing her boss of running a brothel.[149] In another case published in *Tin Mới* in 1941, two young women who had been lured by a mẹ mìn and sold to an ả đào house managed to escape, then went to authorities who immediately arrested the offenders and the singing house's owner.[150]

Penalties and stricter enforcement notwithstanding, some singers, customers, and ả đào house owners continued to subvert the regulation system. In November 1939, *Việt Báo* ran a story about a group of customers and singers who ignored the ban on customers staying overnight by turning off all lights in the house.[151] *Tin Mới* reported in 1941 that certain houses in Hưng Yên conned authorities into permitting them to stay open after the state-imposed curfew.[152] One journalist writing for *Việt Báo* in 1939 jokingly predicted that customers would do anything they could to spend the night with singers and find a way around the law, including pretending to be the sons of ả đào singers or house janitors, a job reserved for adolescent boys.[153] Another journalist writing for the same paper that year noted that corrupt mandarins looked the other way when ả đào house parties raged on into the wee hours, leading him to conclude that the locally imposed eleven o'clock curfew on singing houses was merely an "imaginary" law.[154]

Singers steadfastly defended their profession. Some fought back in very public ways that embarrassed authorities. Women such as Dịch-chi, Cô Ngà, and "the girls of Vũ Tiến neighborhood," whose 1939 story opened this chapter, did not hesitate to expose the hypocrisy of officials who espoused moral virtues by day and frequented ả đào clandestine brothels by night.[155] Frustrated by the popular association between ả đào signing and clandestine sex work, ả đào singer Hoàng Liên Bích of the Ngã Tư Sở neighborhood published a letter in *Thông Tin* in 1943, that held ả đào house owners accountable for ruining the musical form's reputation. She lamented that due to the association with sex work, the public now scorned this form of female performance art. Greedy singing house owners, she wrote, took advantage of poor women who would do anything for a few morsels of food and forced girls to "slut around" (đĩ thoã). Of the sixty girls with whom Hoàng Liên Bích spoke, none had been trained in the art of singing. As a result, Hoàng Liên Bích complained, the á đào industry had become a "market for lipstick and powder" (chợ bán son phấn), a euphemism for prostitution. Using another euphemism for prostitution in á đào neighborhoods, the author expressed hope that one day the "opium and flowers neighborhood" (xóm yên hoa) would become a place frequented by respectable ladies and gentlemen.[156]

During the late colonial period, those looking to avoid the constraints of the French regulatory system governing the sex industry used á đào performances as a front for clandestine sex work. Despite authorities' efforts to police clandestine sex work in á đào singing houses, sex workers persisted with relative success for three reasons. For one thing, clandestine sex workers deflected accusations of prostitution through the guise of performance art. Singers, bar girls, establishment owners, and customers were drawn to the nuanced sexuality of á đào music and used the pretext of singing to protect them from laws governing the exchange of physical intimacy for money. Moreover, although unregistered sex work in á đào singing houses was not permitted by law, it was nonetheless in high demand. Singing houses were flooded with customers looking for comfort in traditional culture, including off-duty authorities themselves, as evidenced by the letter that opened this chapter. Finally, authorities had limited legal tools with which to police clandestine sex work in the singing houses. Constrained by the 1921 law that defined prostitution and limited policing action to French territories, colonial and local governments tried to monitor the sex work that went on in á đào houses by imposing city planning ordinances and forcing singers to submit to venereal exams. Yet these measures were largely ineffective. Consequently, clandestine sex work in á đào singing houses proved to be impossible for the colonial state to fully regulate, and clandestine sex work thrived in them.

Yet authorities continued to face the problem plaguing the entire clandestine sex industry—namely, the difficulty of policing sex and sexuality. Singers continued to subvert the system. Their success was not only in their crafty measures but also in their unremitting flow of clients, including administrators who had themselves enacted laws designed to thwart the very prostitution in which they were partaking.

CHAPTER 6

Taxi Dancers

Western Culture and the Urban-Rural Divide

In the mid-1930s, a Western-style ballroom dancing fad took Tonkin's urban areas by storm. Popular in Europe and other parts of Asia, ballroom dancing quickly became a hot trend in cities and their immediate suburbs as well as the outskirts of Tonkin military bases. Youths lined up nightly outside dance halls; inside, patrons danced with their friends or bought tickets to tango, waltz, and foxtrot with professional dancers called taxi dancers. The professionals were young women employed by the dance hall to keep the party going, elevate the level of dance, and encourage men to spend money on drinks. Vietnamese and ethnic Chinese youth joined French, African, Caribbean, and Indian men on the dance floor. Western-style dancing was the only form of entertainment in which it was acceptable—even expected—for Vietnamese men and women to touch one another in public. Hot, sweaty bodies danced the foxtrot, tango dancers held one another close, and patrons shed layers of clothing as they spun and swayed to upbeat tunes. While most patrons came to dance halls for fun and a little flirting, the atmosphere was ripe for selling sex on the sly, and taxi dancers quickly earned a reputation as clandestine sex workers.

Sex work in dance halls exemplified the rural-urban divide that characterized late colonial Vietnam. The success of dance halls relied on an image of urban sophistication and modern style and thus appealed to those who wanted Vietnam to modernize. With their Western music and "modern décor," dance halls provided a temporary escape from the poverty of colonial Tonkin and the traditional norms governing male-female interaction. For one night, patrons could dress up in glamorous Western clothing and forget their problems while partying the night away in an art deco ballroom. Moreover, the purchase of a ticket bought male patrons a chance to dance with—or even spend the night with—the true symbol of modernity: the modern girl, an independent, liberated young woman who was hip to Western fashion and lifestyle. Modern girls embraced Western ideas of leisure and luxury; they also rejected traditional expectations of young women; they were sexually liberal—and many of them sold sex.

Most of the sophisticated modern girls who worked at dance halls were in reality young, impoverished peasant women who had migrated to the city looking to earn extra income. Indeed, the success of the dance hall business model was very much dependent on the countryside. The glamorous image enjoyed by dance halls derived much of its potency from the contrast between urban and rural life, and dance hall owners capitalized on this contrast in marketing their product. By exploiting the labor—particularly intimate labor—of impoverished peasant women, dance halls also profited from the economic disparity between the city and country.

With their public display of physical contact and the rumors of clandestine sex work, dance halls quickly became a matter of concern among journalists and government officials. Vietnamese journalists wrote prolifically about the darker sides of dance halls, blaming capitalism, materialism, Westernization, and the cult of modernity for ruining wholesome, young peasant women and youth more generally. For their part, French colonial administrators were disturbed by the health threat—specifically the risk of venereal diseases—that sex workers in the dance halls posed to their military clientele. As was the case for á đào houses, the colonial government worked with provincial governments to enact a series of local ordinances regulating dance halls.

Rural Poverty and New Urban Cultural Trends

The growing economic disparity and cultural differences between urban and rural areas in the late colonial period gave rise to the all the elements necessary for selling unregistered sex work in dance halls: a labor force, a customer base, a venue, and a seductive image. By the mid-1930s, when the dancing craze came to the protectorate, Tonkin was just beginning to recover from the Great Depression. The rubber and rice markets inched back toward pre-Depression levels, and the economy in urban zones had almost returned to normal. Yet the countryside was slow to recover from the economic crisis, leading migrants from the countryside to flood the cities of Hanoi and Hải Phòng in search of employment. Among them were women who migrated permanently, those who migrated temporarily looking for work between harvests, and those who commuted daily between the countryside and city. As female migrants were typically stuck in low-paying jobs, many opted to earn extra money selling sex on the side.

Meanwhile, in the urban areas, a market for entertainment activities, including dance halls, developed. As the urban economies improved, city folk grew wealthier, and the middle class grew. Members of the urban middle class, with their disposable income, began treating themselves to entertainment, leisure activities, fashion, and material luxuries. At the movies, they admired starlets showing off the latest fashion trends; in the dance halls, they made their own fashion statements, sporting new outfits and flashing expensive jewelry.

Referred to as "the child of Europeanization,"[1] the dance hall trend arose in the context of two political and cultural trends in the late colonial period: modernization and Westernization, also known as Europeanization though also influenced by trends outside Europe, including those from the United States and Argentina. Proponents of modernization looked for solutions to Vietnam's problems and called for changes in many aspects of Vietnamese society, including fashion, romance, and the traditional family structure. Those who favored modernization promoted, among others, individualism, questioned arranged marriages, and embraced the notion of romantic love.[2] Colonial efforts to introduce French culture under the *mission civilisatrice* and through the educational system, as well as intermingling among the young French and Vietnamese adults, resulted in a related Westernization trend. According to one French official, "Youth then seemed drunk with Europeanization and became fanatical about this new religion. Nothing seemed to them more worthy to study, copy, and assimilate to than European culture. It was thanks to this [cultural] revolution that . . . [Western-style] dance took root and succeeded so quickly."[3] The Westernization trend saw some among the city folk adopt Western lifestyles, fashion, and culture.[4]

In the words of journalist Vũ Trọng Phụng, "The encounter between East and West [had] a profound effect on material lives," as it ushered in a new life of theaters, cinemas, modern fashion, perfume, makeup, and dance halls.[5]

The modernization and Westernization trends found visible expression in fashion, and new European-inspired styles became the de facto uniform of dance halls. In the 1920s, urban middle-class men swapped out the traditional tunic for dapper European suits and cut their hair according to European style.[6] One particularly popular hairstyle worn by men in dance halls was a slicked-back style called *le tango*, after the music.[7] Not surprisingly, the most notable changes in fashion occurred among women. Young women in the cities slipped their feet into high heels and abandoned dull-toned clothing for brighter colors and imported fabric. They parted their hair to the side, a style considered sexually suggestive during that era, and wore it bobbed or finger-curled. Following the style of popular Western actresses, they plucked their eyebrows to accentuate the arches. In the 1930s, chic urban young women began wearing clothing that highlighted the female figure. They adopted the *belle poitrine* fashion trend that showed off a smaller waist and fuller breasts, and the more daring among them wore European lingerie, including padded brassieres.[8]

Many young urban woman also flashed unabashed smiles revealing a mouth full of white teeth—a testament to their rejection of the Vietnamese teeth-blackening tradition.[9] Once all their adult teeth had grown in, Vietnamese adolescent girls had their teeth blackened in a rite-of-passage ceremony. The black lacquer applied to the teeth was considered attractive and believed to protect teeth and ward off ghosts or bad spirits. In the early twentieth century, when Vietnamese women who married or cohabited with French men abandoned the practice of lacquering their teeth, white teeth became associated with interracial sex—and, by extension, loose morals and even sex work.[10] By the late 1930s, most middle-class young women in the cities and suburbs had abandoned the teeth-lacquering tradition, but it continued in the countryside. In fact, as evidenced by the literature on dance halls, white teeth would become an easy way to distinguish true city girls from peasant women.[11]

With the rise of the middle class, the development of the entertainment industry, and the growing popularity of Western fashion trends, a new icon appeared in Tonkin cities: the modern girl, who was the star of Tonkin's dance halls. By the 1930s, modern girls had become a global phenomenon, from New York, Paris, and Cairo, to Bombay, Rangoon, Tokyo,

Penang, Singapore, and Tonkin.[12] While there were, of course, variations on how the modern girl developed in each country—for example, the American analogue was the flapper—there were similarities among modern girls across the world. No matter where she lived, the modern girl was independent, she wore Western clothes, high heels, and makeup, and she subscribed to a new set of sexual mores.

The modern girl (*gái tân-thời* or *gái mới*) phenomenon arrived in Tonkin in the mid-1930s.[13] Following the lead of the Modern Girl Research Group, I use "modern girl" as a heuristic device with which to explore a new trend, widely reported in the Tonkin press, in which women eschewed Vietnamese traditions in favor of Western culture and increasingly lived independently of their families. In the cities, they found employment as shop girls, hostesses, bar girls, or taxi dancers. While their socioeconomic position was higher than, say, that of a domestic servant, wet nurse, nanny, or manual laborer, their position was not considered as respectable as a teacher or French-trained midwife, and their morals would continually come under question. Interestingly, notwithstanding the ubiquitous talk of modern girls in the press, films, novels, commercial advertisements, and fashion columns, they represented only a small portion of the urban female population. As the newspaper *Phụ Nữ Tân Văn*, published in Saigon but widely read throughout the Vietnamese-speaking areas of Indochina, reminded readers, modern girls were hardly the norm; the vast majority of Vietnamese women were struggling to survive and did not have the time or money to pay attention to fashion or leisure activities.[14]

Modern girls defied social norms for women, though in a nonpolitical way. Their very existence challenged the Confucian understanding of women's role in society.[15] They were individualistic: as romantics, they preferred to fall in love rather than rely on their parents to arrange their marriage. They enjoyed the new leisure activities that European colonization had introduced to Indochina: they drank alcohol, frolicked at beaches and swimming pools in revealing bathing suits, and spent afternoons sipping coffee in cafés and nights swinging in men's arms in dance halls. They played tennis and other sports. With their form-fitting, flashy attire, modern girls were—at least by traditional Vietnamese standards—the very personification of material and sexual excess.[16]

For the most part, modern girls had a bad reputation in Tonkin. With their penchant for new clothing and a consumer lifestyle, they were denounced as materialistic.[17] As Judith Henchy notes, "While many media images sought to domesticate the bourgeois woman as a passive consumer, [the modern girl] image was exploited as evoking a world of transgression and transition, becoming an icon of modernism's complexities."[18] The press warned they were nothing but demimondaines (*gái giang hồ*)[19] and homewreckers and associated them with sex work.[20] In his reportage investigation of the Hanoi Dispensary, journalist Thao Thao asked rhetorically why so many modern women (*cô tân-thời*) were seen entering the dispensary.[21]

Dancing Comes to Tonkin

In Vietnam, dance halls were made possible by the commercialization of music through the importation of mass-produced recordings and stock arrangements of Western dance music. In the early twentieth century, motion pictures, radio, sound recordings, and sheet music, which had become widely available, exposed consumers throughout the world to Western music.[22] The gramophone, ubiquitous in urban areas of Asia since the end of World War I, brought music to listeners at any time, in any place, without the need to hire a large band. Moreover, the arrival of Western cinema in Tonkin in the early 1930s introduced music that provided the soundtrack for new images of fashion, materialism, and public displays of romantic affection.[23] As a result, Western music became popular throughout Asia.

The business model for Tonkin's dance halls—also known as taxi dancing—had originated in the United States at the turn of the century. The trend spread to Europe in the early 1920s and caught on in most of Asia shortly thereafter. The dancing craze had arrived in Japan by the mid-1920s, and, by the fall of 1928, Shanghai saw the first of its many dance halls open.[24] Initially, the taxi dancers in Shanghai were exclusively Russian women, but, by the 1930s, it was mostly locals who worked at the dance halls. By the end of the decade there were an estimated twenty-five hundred to three thousand taxi dancers in Shanghai alone.[25] With dancing occurring everywhere from fancy hotels to elegant department stores to gritty, mafia-run taxi dance halls, Shanghai's night life grew infamous. City denizens buried their noses in newspaper gossip columns to catch the latest scandal involving dancers and eagerly anticipated the annual crowning of Shanghai's best dancer.[26]

As ships carrying bands to entertain passengers docked in Southeast Asia's main harbors, the dancing craze spread to the region's major port cities, including Singapore, Penang, and Bangkok.[27] Dance halls in Asia quickly became "sites of sexual consumption and courtship."[28] In this era of modernization, youth in many Asian countries went to dance halls looking for fun and flirtation outside of the traditional courtship structure. As Su-Lin Lewis observed in Rangoon, Singapore, Penang, and Bangkok, taxi dancers were objects of male desire and were associated with sex work.[29]

In the early years of the dancing trend in Tonkin, few Vietnamese youth were familiar with Western dance. The Western-style dancing that did exist in Tonkin before the mid-1930s was limited to Vietnamese people who had socialized in European circles, and it took place in private homes.[30] Indeed, research by Jason Gibbs shows that Vietnamese students frequently engaged in dancing while studying in Paris.[31] The short story "Cái hại khiêu-vũ" (The harm of dancing) claims that Western dance was introduced by a Vietnamese student who had returned home after studying abroad in France. The dancing trend, however, would not become popular in Tonkin until the 1930s. In 1933, one of the first dance halls to cater to Vietnamese as well as European participants, Élite Dancing, opened on Khâm Thiên Street, which had already been established as a center for late-night—and illicit—entertainment. That year, the newspaper *Hà Thành Ngọ Báo* published an article introducing this style of dancing to the literate public. Author Tuy-Tinh praised dancing as a rigorous form of exercise, as an art, and as a symbol of modern civilization.[32]

Because few Vietnamese women were familiar with Western dance moves, dance hall owners in Tonkin initially imported professional taxi dancers from Shanghai. Concerned that the dubious reputation of these women threatened the prestige of the local Chinese community, Chinese congregations in Tonkin lobbied the Chinese consulate in 1936 to have them expelled. In response, the vice police arrested more than thirty Chinese taxi dancers working in dance halls in Hanoi, Hải Phòng, and Nam Định and repatriated them to China.[33]

In Tonkin, Western-style dancing was limited to the two major urban areas of Hanoi and Hải Phòng, their immediate suburbs, and the larger provincial capitals. Consequently, the dancing trend developed, for the most part, as an urban phenomenon that reflected the widening cultural gap between city and rural folk, a phenomenon also seen in Japan.[34] As Tonkin's dancing craze was rooted in Westernization, it was popular in areas where European culture was trendy and less popular in the countryside, where Westernization had not taken hold, with the exception being military bases that had high numbers of European soldiers.[35] Khâm Thiên Street, on the suburban edge of Hanoi, was home to dance halls such as Étoile Dancing, Déesa Dancing, Le Casino, La Pagode, Élite, and Féeric, whose French names reflected the Westernization trend out of which they had arisen.[36]

Because Western-style dancing was a new phenomenon in Tonkin, most Vietnamese youth lacked dancing skills. To build a patron base, make money, and train new taxi dancers, dance hall owners opened dance schools.[37] Particularly busy neighborhoods, such as Khâm Thiên Street in 1938, had multiple dance schools.[38] Classes were held in the late afternoon, enabling taxi dancers to sleep late after a long evening of dancing and spending the night with customers. At the schools, taxi dancers trained prospective ones and taught dance classes to middle-class and wealthy young men who aspired to learn Western dance moves—or who wanted to flirt with taxi dancers.[39] Smaller dance halls employed ten to fifteen taxi dancers; larger halls employed as many as seventy-six.[40] Writing in 1939, one journalist estimated that there were two thousand taxi dancers in Hanoi alone.[41]

Soon after dance halls opened in Tonkin, the Hanoi government jumped to collect tax on dancing revenues. As taxes limited profit, those dance halls located inside the city limits moved to Khâm Thiên Street in Hà Đông, just outside the colonial government's taxing jurisdiction.[42] The city government quickly missed the business drummed up by dance halls and reconsidered its decision. But Khâm Thiên Street was already established as an entertainment district with high profits, so the city failed to lure them back into taxing jurisdiction.[43] With the addition of the dance halls, Khâm Thiên Street, already crowded with ả đào singing houses, became a de facto entertainment quarter. Dance halls likewise migrated to the suburbs of Hải Phòng. In 1943, Hải Phòng officials even considered creating an official entertainment quarter in the city's Lạch Tray suburb specifically for ả đào singing houses, dance halls, and the accompanying boardinghouses.[44]

Like the ả đào singing houses in the suburbs, dance halls quickly became associated with clandestine sex work. French authorities more or less assumed that all taxi dancers were clandestine sex workers.[45] In their book on venereal diseases in suburban Hanoi, Mayor Virgitti and Dr. Joyeux called taxi dancing "a new pseudo-artistic means of selling oneself expensively."[46] They told journalist Vũ Trọng Phụng that dance halls were convenient for selling sex and that brothel madams frequently sent sex workers to solicit men there.[47] As Vũ Trọng Phụng famously wrote, "the Bạch My spirit"—the spiritual guardian of sex workers—"has acquired a new type of prostitution, just as women have acquired a new occupation that serves debauchery."[48] And Trọng Lang, who was himself propositioned by taxi dancers, mused, "In the dance clubs, girls go from timidly dancing the fox trot to dancing the debauched dance."[49]

Although modern dance halls appeared very different from traditional ả đào singing clubs, the two businesses were symbiotic. Dance halls used a similar business model in which female entertainment was a cover for sex work and sex was sold in a public setting so as to access a large customer base. By the mid-1930s, most singing houses had a back room dedicated for dancing.[50] Dance halls were typically owned by former ả đào singers or mistresses of Vietnamese mandarins, themselves patrons of ả đào houses.[51] Dance halls opened up in ả đào neighborhoods and were financially profitable largely due to their proximity to the ả đào houses.[52] Entertainment districts formed in which drunken customers could stumble from one establishment to another. In areas such as Khâm Thiên Street outside of Hanoi and the Lạch Tray neighborhood outside of Hải Phòng, they colocated to share customers and employees. By 1938, there were at least six dance halls on Khâm Thiên Street.[53]

Recognizing that dancing was a lucrative industry, ả đào house bosses sent their prettiest women to work in the dance halls.[54] Writers used the vocabulary of the ả đào houses to refer to taxi dancers who sold sex. For example, a 1939 article in Đông Pháp referred to taxi dancers as "đào nhảy," borrowing the "đào" from "cô đào," the Vietnamese term for singers. Given the connection between ả đào singing houses and sex work, in the interwar years, the term "đào" developed negative connotations and came to refer to lower-class singers.[55] Journalist Trọng Lang summed it up: "Dancing girls are singing girls who also dance" (các cô nhảy là cô đầu kiêm nhảy), alluding to the prevalence of sex work among both types of female entertainers.[56]

Inside Dance Halls

Around ten in the evening, young men and women dressed in the latest Western fashions lined up outside the dance halls, hoping to be admitted, while the hottest music from Europe and the Americas pounded from behind the doors.[57] Although dance hall patrons were both male and female, the former far outnumbered the latter. To address the imbalance, dance hall owners employed taxi dancers. The professionals raised the level of the dancing while ensuring that plenty of beautiful women were available to dance with male patrons—women who were comfortable being touched by strangers and performing sex work after hours.

Tonkin's dance halls followed a taxi-dancer ticket system business model. The name, which originated in the early twentieth-century United States, referred to the short turn taxi dancers took with each paying partner, like a quick ride in a taxi. Patrons paid a cover fee to enter the hall—in 1935, the Déesa dance hall charged one đồng[58]—and purchased a booklet of tickets that allowed them to dance with the club's taxi dancers. Each ticket was worth one dance that lasted one song.[59] Taxi dancers greeted patrons at the door and flirted with them in hopes of maximizing the number of tickets they retrieved. At the end of the night, taxi dancers would turn over their tickets to dance hall owners, who would calculate the dancers' pay based on the number of tickets they had submitted.

Inside, the dance halls were elegant, clean, and modern, adorned with art deco motifs and outfitted with the latest lighting technology.[60] To evoke a romantic mood, the halls were dimly lit, with pools of blue, green, and red light adding a note of mystery.[61] Each night, several dozen snazzy songs played on the gramophone. More elegant spaces had house bands, which consisted of three to seven musicians, typically French, Russian, or Philippine.[62] Among the host of Western songs, popular French songs played, including "Après toi je n'aurais plus d'amour" ("After you I'll no longer love"), "C'est à Capri" ("It's in Capri"), and "Si l'on ne s'était pas connu" ("If we'd never known each other"). Particularly crowd-pleasing were songs by the Corsican Tino Rossi,[63] as well as the soundtrack from *Footlight Parade*, a 1933 American film that featured a scene with a white actress in yellow-face as an Asian sex worker set to the song "Shanghai Lil," a hit in Tonkin's dance halls.[64]

On "electric nights" that aimed to recreate the scenes in dance halls of Paris or Shanghai,[65] scores of young men and women embraced one another, "faces wild, eyes mesmerized, mysterious," Nguyễn Đình Lạp recounted, "as the beat of the music moved through them like waves."[66] Couples danced the rumba, the java-java, the boogie, the waltz, the tango (*tăng gô*), and the foxtrot (*phốc tốc*).[67] Taxi dancers not yet paired off with a patron circulated throughout the crowd to serve drinks and flirt with men.[68] Owners of the dance clubs made additional money when taxi dancers convinced patrons to buy them lemonade, favored for its high water content and high profit margin.[69] Some nights lasted until the wee hours of the morning, when taxi dancers and patrons coupled off and discreetly retreated to boardinghouses.

The dance hall was a scene in which to be seen. After all, the dance halls were not only for the act of dancing but also for watching others and showing off one's own moves. Vain patrons checked their hair and makeup in enormous mirrors strategically placed to amplify the effects of the lighting, make the hall appear larger, and give the illusion of a crowd double the size. Plush chairs imported from Europe proved perfect for lounging with—and discreetly touching—a members of the opposite sex while watching the spectacle on the dance floor. In his exposé on debauched youth, journalist Nguyễn Đình Lạp made note of the sexualized way that the new generation interacted with one another in these intimate spaces of the dance halls: "Around the table in the middle of the room, four young men gather around three or four taxi dancers. They touch each other, tug at one another, pat each other. . . . They laugh like firecrackers." Sipping wine, smoking cigarettes perched in extravagant cigarette holders under billows of smoke, they got lost in the night and forgot about the responsibilities of their daily lives.[70] In the crowd, one could hear "the pop of the bottles, the clink of glasses as patrons toasted one another and screamed with joy, 'À l'amour! À la santé de tout! À Venus!'" ("To love! To everyone's health! To Venus!")—the latter toast, of course, being a reference to beautiful women and the sexual charge in the air.[71]

It was not just Vietnamese men who came to show off their trendy suits and flash a little money to attract women. Chinese, European, and African men joined the party too.[72] Indeed, as a nexus for Westernized youth culture and a site of sexual consumption, dance halls were known for interracial mingling. Young Vietnamese women could be seen slow-stepping in the arms of European men.[73] Vietnamese and Chinese youth joined French and Foreign Legion troops on the dance floor, laughing, chatting, and holding their bodies close as the moved to the beat of the music. According to Mayor Virgitti and Dr. Joyeux, French and Foreign Legion soldiers favored dance halls because, with their Western music and culture, they possessed a more familiar cultural context than ả đào singing houses, which catered to a more traditionally Vietnamese aesthetic. Foreigners unfamiliar with the local language or customs came to meet French-speaking Vietnamese women.[74] At the same time, young Vietnamese men and women, who had been exposed to French culture in school and Western music on the radio and films, came to dance halls to revel in the Western ambiance.[75] Given that Tonkin's dance halls attracted such a broad array of clients, most sex workers enjoyed plentiful work—though their incomes rarely reflected the abundance.

Far from being an interracial utopia, however, dance halls were frequently the site of violence that, while not always explicitly racialized, often ended on racial terms. In 1934, *Hà Thành Ngọ Báo* reported, a brawl broke out at the Étoile dance hall after Foreign Legion soldiers tried to leave without paying. When the female manager and a male French-speaking Vietnamese student confronted them on their way out, the Foreign Legion soldiers, angered by the audacity of a Vietnamese man challenging them, punched him.[76] Another violent episode, likewise reported by *Hà Thành Ngọ Báo*, occurred a few months later at the same dance hall. Two drunk French soldiers arrived after hours, only to find out that dance tickets were no longer being sold. Enraged, they grabbed a ticket booklet, tore it in half, pushed the hostess to the ground, and yanked women from nearby tables or from the arms of other men and forced them out to the dance floor, holding their wrists while the women tried to wriggle out from their grip. A fight broke out with Vietnamese men attempting to protect the taxi dancers from the French men, leaving one man paralyzed from a punch that knocked him flat on his back.[77] In 1936, French sailors showed up at a the Hải Phòng dance hall drunk and belligerent. They manhandled women as they danced, and police were called in when they roughed up Germaine, a Vietnamese taxi dancer popular among male patrons.[78]

Hard feelings from romantic rejections also contributed to the violence. In 1939 *Đông Pháp* reported on a jealousy-driven fight that had broken out at Venice Dancing on Sơn Nam Alley, off Khâm Thiên Street. A taxi dancer had rejected multiple advances by a European man, who in turn picked a fight with some of the other soldiers with whom she had been dancing that night. Dance club patrons intervened, but the scuffle only escalated. Broken tables and chairs flew out the dance club door and crashed onto the street, alarming and even injuring some passersby.[79] That same year, *Đông Pháp* also published a story about a man who had left his wife for a taxi dancer-turned-sex-worker. His wife went looking for him, only to find him in the arms of his dancer-lover. The wife confronted the taxi dancer, the women exchanged words, and a violent fight ensued; the police were called to break things up.[80] In 1938, *Đông Pháp* ran a story about an incident in which two Chinese men asked a Vietnamese woman to dance, whereupon a group of French men—whose jealousy likely had racial overtones—started a brawl with them.[81] In 1940, *Tin Mới* ran a story about twenty-three-year-old Đào Thị Ngọc Chinh, who had been abandoned by the French lover she had met in a dance hall. Heartbroken and devastated, she attempted to commit suicide by drowning but was pulled out of the water and resuscitated by bystanders.[82]

At the end of the night, as the music wound down and empty glasses littered the tables and bar, "the only girls left are the sex workers," Trọng Lang wrote.[83] Taxi dancers, who lived in dorms and lacked privacy, took their clients to local boardinghouses to perform sex work for which, according to one 1938 source, they charged one to five piastres per night depending on their presumed desirability.[84] It is apparent from a few anecdotal sources that dance halls offered male as well as female sex workers, but the information available about male sex workers is scant.[85]

Dance halls soon became associated with the spread of venereal diseases. In 1938, journalist Trọng Lang generalized that all taxi dancers were infected.[86] In a study on venereal diseases among soldiers stationed in Tông, a base near Hanoi, military physician Dr. Marcel Piere and Dr. Joyeux likewise asserted that all clandestine sex workers in dance halls carried venereal diseases.[87] In Hải Phòng, a 1943 hygiene inspection report noted that while the official number of venereal disease cases among registered sex workers had decreased, the official number of overall venereal disease cases had actually increased due to raids on dance halls, "which are considered to be establishments like *maisons de tolerance*,"[88] thus insinuating that dance halls had a higher concentration of sex workers (see table 6.1). As dance halls were a popular site for interracial socializing in a Western cultural context, they became the most popular form of prostitution for military men—and, authorities believed, the main source of venereal disease transmission.

Table 6.1 Cases of venereal disease after raids of dance halls

1940	360
1941	840
1942	1,300

Source: "Rapport d'inspection du 28 avril au 1 mai et du 4 au 6 mai 1943, Municipalité de Haiphong," CAOM, RSTNF 1387.

The Life of a Taxi Dancer

While modern girl taxi dancers seemed to embody the latest trends in modernization and Westernization, a careful investigation into the historical sources reveals a different side of the women who worked in dance halls. Although they embraced modern aesthetics, few taxi dancers were actually sophisticated city girls living carefree lives; the majority were peasant girls who had migrated to the city to make ends meet. While it is possible that the historical sources, overwhelmingly written by men and not the modern girls themselves, may have exaggerated taxi dancers' situation as dire either out of ignorance or to deter readers from pursing this lifestyle, the similarities of the disparate stories lead this historian to take the following details of taxi dancers' stories seriously. It is important to understand that, on a whole, the taxi-dancer experience was likely a mix of the two images: carefree fun as well as exploitative work.

Humble origins notwithstanding, professional taxi dancers certainly looked the part of modern girls. Their faces were caked with white powder, their lips glistened with red lipstick, and their teeth sparkled white.[89] They wore slinky, brightly colored dresses, even in the winter cold. They smoked cigarettes and gave off an air of sensuality.[90] Per the stereotype of modern girls, taxi dancers tended to live independently of their families. At times this independence was self-initiated; other times it was an unavoidable consequence of rural-to-urban migration. In his short story "Một thiếu nữ ở Hà Thành" (A young lady in Hà Thành), Vietnamese journalist J. Leiba chronicles the life of Thúy, "who lived alone in Hanoi, with no obligations, a life that young ladies love." Taxi dancers spoke rudimentary French—or learned it on the job so they could banter with French or Foreign Legion soldiers. They did not shy away from flirting or even intimate contact with men, including Westerners.[91] After some time working in the dance halls, many reportedly grew crass, manipulating men for their money and drunkenly singing off key.[92]

Some taxi dancers did fit the image of modern girls in search of exciting lives. Mai, a taxi dancer interviewed by D. Thiêu-Tước in 1936, explained that after being orphaned, she moved to Hanoi with a girlfriend and took a job in a shop, where she was paid only twelve piastres per month. After her friend left to follow her fiancé to Saigon, Mai fell in with a group of modern girls who were preoccupied with their looks. Mai soon found herself infected by her friends' vanity and materialism, a lifestyle that her shopgirl salary could not support. Eventually, she took a job at a dance hall where men doted on her and she could make enough money to buy herself the latest fashions.[93] In 1939, *Việt Báo* printed a story about Thị Đ., from Nam Định, the daughter of a mandarin and the wife of a scholar. Bored by the duties expected of a traditional wife, Thị Đ. left her husband and ran away to Khâm Thiên Street to pursue the glamorous life of a taxi dancer.[94] J. Leiba, in his fiction, described taxi dancers as wanting to lead exciting and independent lives. Many, he wrote, were introduced to dancing through boyfriends who led them into debauchery.[95]

Some lucky women even got into dancing because they actually loved to dance. Trọng Lang likened dancing to opium, noting how some taxi dancers "craved" it.[96] Speaking about taxi dancers, one patron told Trọng Lang that, for them, "dancing is a religion."[97] Their love for the activity sometimes managed to outshine what would otherwise have been unbearable hardships.[98] One poignant example that seemed to leave Trọng Lang shaken was the case of Miss Lương, an ethnic-minority migrant to the city, whose ill-fitting dancing shoes had cut off her circulation to the point that some of her toes needed to be amputated. When Trọng Lang visited her at the hospital, she shared her eagerness to get back to the dance floor and grilled him about the latest hit songs. Weak and with her feet bandaged, she pulled herself out of bed, hobbled across the hospital floor, and attempted to practice her moves. Despite the life-changing injury, she insisted she still loved dancing.[99]

Indeed, taxi dancing was exciting. Besides providing women a chance to practice their language skills when flirting with foreign men, it also allowed them to hobnob with cosmopolitan, middle-class Vietnamese men, many of whom were otherwise unlikely to interact with lower-class women. Taxi dancers also formed deep friendships with one another. They often lived together in dormitories above dance halls or rented rooms together in the 36 Streets section of Hanoi. They spent their nights working together and their days teaching dance, shopping, or double-dating with customers.

Most taxi dancers, however, merely acted the role of free-spirited, sophisticated, urban modern girls. As the extant historical sources reveal, they were, for the most part, peasant women trying to make ends meet. Many came to dancing to escape hardship. When Trọng Lang asked a taxi dancer what led her to the profession, she lamented in a low voice, "Because of circumstances," alluding to poverty and a difficult life before she became a taxi dancer.[100] Another dancer, Miss Th., informed Trọng Lang that women got into the profession to support their younger siblings or to take care of their elderly parents.[101] In 1940, *Đông Pháp* published an article about twenty-four-year-old Trần Thị Tâm from Bắc Giang, who had turned to dancing as a last resort. Originally a shopkeeper, she met a French officer and lived with him at the military base in Tông until he repatriated to France. Unemployed and with no marital prospects, she survived off the money he sent back to her for the first few months. But when the money stopped coming, she became desperate, and the only employment she could find was at a dance hall in Hanoi.[102]

Dancing, for some women, was only a temporary job to earn quick money. By the late 1930s, desperate peasant women moonlighted in dance halls to make it through the gap between harvests. Young women from the countryside came to Hanoi between harvests to sell vegetables and fish at Đồng Xuân Market during the day. At night, these women—reeking of fish—took up part-time work as taxi dancers and occasional sex workers. To hide their rural origins, they pressed their lips together in closed-mouth smiles to avoid revealing their black teeth. Many such women led a double life: they used fake names, they relied on the anonymity of the cities to avoid shame directed at them from fellow villagers, and they never told their family that they danced—or engaged in sex work—for money.[103]

As was the case in many sectors of the clandestine sex industry, some women were tricked into working as taxi dancers and, by extension, sex workers. Such was a 1935 complaint filed to police by Ngô Quốc Lâm, who claimed that a Miss Xuyên, the owner of a dance hall in Hải Phòng, had manipulated his sixteen-year-old daughter, Ngô Thị Yến, into dancing.[104] Similarly, in 1938, Đông Pháp printed a story about Đặng Thị Nuột, mentioned in chapter 3 as the young woman who got lost while traveling to Hải Dương. On her travels, she met Phùng Thị Hồng, who tricked her into selling sex with a bait-and-switch promise of employment. Phùng Thị Hồng overpowered Đặng Thị Nuột, held her down, her cut hair, and scraped the black lacquer off her teeth so she would fit in with the modern crowd, and attempted to sell her to the owner of a dance hall who wanted to prostitute her. The sale fell through when Đặng Thị Nuột turned out to be too clumsy to dance.[105]

Taxi dancers usually signed contracts with dance hall owners. A contract typically required them to greet patrons at the door, dance with male patrons, entice them to buy them drinks, and romance them.[106] The contracts signed between taxi dancers and dance hall owners could be for the short or long term. In 1935, Ngọ Báo covered the case of sixteen-year-old Ngô-Thị Yến, who was locked into a one-year contract.[107] In J. Leiba's fictionalized, yet true-to-life, account of a dance hall, taxi dancers had three-, six-, or twelve-month contracts.[108] Contracts typically

included agreements about room and board. Most taxi dancers boarded
in the dance studios themselves. They lived with other taxi dancers in
dormitory-style conditions upstairs from the dance hall and were served
paltry meals.[109] Those who resided at the dance hall saw their room and
board deducted from their salaries or replacing their salaries altogether.

Dancing house contracts typically included an advance sum of money
with which the taxi dancer was expected to buy fashionable Western
clothing suitable for the European and modernized image of her new
workplace. In 1936, Thị Cúc and Thị Tình were each forced to borrow
fifty piastres to buy clothing.[110] Others, like Ng Thị Đào and and Ng Thị
Thu, signed with a Miss Ý's dance hall on the agreement that they would
get a cash advance of one hundred piastres to pay off a small debt and
buy new clothing.[111] Clothing debt was one way dance hall owners maintained control over their employees.

Dance contracts also covered the cost of dance lessons. As many women
did not know how to dance, they had to take lessons in dance schools
before going to work. Dance hall owners required those who needed dance
lessons to sign long-term contracts obliging them to pay back the money
spent on training them to dance. Women like Ng Thị Đào and Ng Thị Thu,
mentioned above, who quit before the term of the contract expired, were
still required to pay back the money they owed for the lessons.[112]

Unlike the proprietors of other clandestine brothels, dance hall owners allowed their employees a remarkable amount of freedom to come
and go as they pleased.[113] At the end of the night, taxi dancers paired off
with customers and spent the night together in boardinghouses. In the
wee hours of the morning, after collecting money from their respective
clients, taxi dancers retreated back to the dormitories above the dance
halls. They slept late the next day and, upon waking, practiced their
dance moves, taught dance classes, or went on dates, which often led to
sex with dance hall patrons.[114]

While dance hall owners offered a degree of leniency for taxi dancers'
day-to-day activities, the owners frequently exploited contracts, forcing
dancers into debt bondage. In 1936, a taxi dancer lamented to J. Leiba
that by signing a six-month contract, she "naturally gave away [her]
freedom."[115] According to an article that appeared that same year in Ngọ
Báo, the proprietor of the Feéric club on Khâm Thiên Street withheld salaries from employees for as long as eight months, only occasionally giving them a few piastres—all the while forcing them to sign false receipts
that read "paid."[116] The exploitative nature of debt-bondage contracts
sparked outrage in journalist Trọng Lang. He lamented that taxi dancers

were effectively "dancing coolies" (*cu li nhảy*) and condemned dance halls as a "daily prison scene of slaves" where taxi dancers nearly danced themselves to death to pay off their debts.[117]

In rare cases, taxi dancers could get out of their debt-bondage agreements early. As Trọng Lang wrote, "The dancing profession could only be abandoned in two ways: first by dying, second by marrying a rich husband."[118] Some taxi dancers had the remains of their debt paid off by one or more of their customers—likely those seeking marriage or sexual favors in return. In order to marry a taxi dancer, a new husband was required to pay off her debt before she could be released for the nuptials. In many cases, taxi dancers who wanted to marry saw their debts falsely inflated to as much as seventy piastres—a rapacious move by their bosses to capitalize on the impending marriage.[119]

As it was difficult to get out of contracts, some taxi dancers ran away before fulfilling their terms. In 1935, *Ngọ Báo* ran a story about sixteen-year-old Ngô-Thị Yến from Nam Định, mentioned earlier, who had signed a one-year contract. Unable to endure the life of a sex worker, she escaped from the dance hall and attempted to reunite with her family.[120] Likewise, in 1936, *Trung Hoà Báo* reported the story of Thị Cúc and Thị Tình, who had signed a contract to borrow fifty piastres and work for a Miss Tòng, the owner of a dance hall in Hải Phòng. As the debt tied them to a low-paying job with poor working conditions, the pair absconded without repaying the loan. They found work in Nam Định at the popular Palace dance hall, which paid taxi dancers a higher salary.[121]

Ties to the criminal underworld enabled dance hall owners to send henchmen to find women who had broken their contracts. After sixteen-year-old Ngô Thị Yến, whose 1935 story was mentioned above, had a change of heart about dancing, she broke her debt contract and ran home to her family. On the way back to her village, she found shelter with a family friend, who sent word to her parents. Before they could reunite with her, Miss Xuyến, her former boss, had her hunted her down and roughed up.[122] In 1936, when Miss Tòng, mentioned above, realized that Thị Cúc and Thị Tình had skipped town before the terms of their contracts were met, she got word that they were working at Palace dance hall and sent hired thugs to seize and return them. When their new boss at Palace refused to turn over the pair, a bloody fight ensued. Police were called to break up the altercation, and both sides were fined for the violence.[123] In the dance hall where journalist Trọng Lang interviewed taxi dancers, the boss had contacts at the local police headquarters who helped him find runaway employees while he awaited their return with a horsewhip in hand.[124]

Savvy taxi dancers turned to authorities for help. As *Ngọ Báo* reported in 1935, after sixteen-year-old Ngô-thị Yến, whose story was recounted earlier, had been beaten by her former boss, her family was devastated by the extent of her injuries and filed a police complaint against the dance hall boss.[125] As mentioned above, in 1936, the owner of the Feéric dance club made taxi dancers work eight months without pay and forced them to sign false receipts of payment. Enraged by the injustice and imbalance of power, one taxi dancer brought this case to police and filed a lawsuit. The court summoned the owner, who countersued for slander; it is unclear from the historical record what ensued.[126] In another case from 1939, a group of singers and taxi dancers, empowered by number, reported their exploitative bosses to the vice police and the office of labor. Historical records do not indicate whether either office took action.[127]

Beyond the exploitative contracts, work as a professional dancer could be crushing. Journalist Trọng Lang even referred to dancing as "suffering in a new career for Vietnamese women."[128] For one thing, the taxi dancers worked long hours, dancing five to eight hours a night, six nights per week. That typically meant about a few dozen songs per night, until one in the morning on weeknights and two or three on weekends. Dancing required a large initial investment: women had to buy Western clothes, shoes, jewelry, and makeup to cultivate the image of the modern girl, and those who did not already know how to dance had to pay for dance classes. Since most women—especially those from the countryside—had little money to pay for the clothes and dance classes, they had to borrow from dance hall owners and thus became vulnerable to debt-bondage arrangements. Compounding the problem, taxi dancers earned meager salaries—less than ả đào singers.[129] Their earnings were based on the number of tickets they collected for each dance, tips from customers, a commission from customer drink orders, and sex work. Salaries varied, depending on the location of the dance hall, with dance halls on Khâm Thiên Street paying the most.[130] When Trọng Lang investigated the dance halls there, he found that salaries ranged from five to fifteen đồng per month.[131] Taxi dancers with children saw their salaries reduced to three to four đồng per month, as women with children were seen as less sexy. Such salaries were never enough to pay for warm clothing or even new shoes—a frequent necessity in a profession that relies on moving feet.[132]

Taxi dancers rarely had weather-appropriate clothing to keep them warm. While only light clothing was necessary in the hot, sweaty dance halls, but outside the building taxi dancers endured cold, damp Hanoi winters clad in nothing more than a skimpy dress. In his investigation,

Trọng Lang found that they tended to only own only one outfit, and few owned overcoats. One taxi dancer explained that she would have had to borrow from the boss to afford a coat. To avoid falling further into debt with dance hall bosses, many taxi dancers borrowed coats from their male customers. Trọng Lang noticed that one dancer even used the opportunity to fish loose change from their pockets.[133]

Further exacerbating their situation, taxi dancers had to submit to being continually sexualized by men. Their precarious financial situation and ready customer base provided an incentive for taxi dancers to moonlight as clandestine sex workers. Taxi dancers were portrayed in a short story by Bạch Đinh as having to dance "in front of the covetous eyes of powerful men. This is the profession of the forbidden and craving, where men drool over women."[134] Alluding to sex work after hours, Trọng Lang quipped they were girls "who belonged . . . to everyone."[135]

Taxi dancers were subject to violence in dance halls and the affiliated dormitories. One taxi dancer confided to Trọng Lang that she had been raped by the dormitory cook. Although her boss was aware of the situation, he did nothing to punish the cook or prevent it from happening again.[136] Another taxi dancer named Miss T. shared a harrowing story of her boss beating her when he learned she was pregnant.[137] In 1939, Việt Báo published an article about Thị Đ., mentioned earlier, who had migrated to the city to work in a dance hall. Unlike most migrants, Thị Đ. married into a wealthy family and rebelled against traditional expectations of a wife. Enamored of the modern girl trend, she ran away from her family to a dance hall in Hanoi. Unfortunately for her, the dance hall owner got wind of her unusually large savings of one thousand piastres and enthusiastically welcomed her to the establishment even though she was, by all accounts, a terrible dancer. Upon gaining her trust, the dance hall owner beat her up and stole her money and jewelry.[138]

Not surprisingly, the long hours, meager pay, abuse, and lack of warm clothing took a toll on many taxi dancers' well-being. Trọng Lang described the women he interviewed as skinny, with sallow, blotchy skin, lackluster eyes, and "signs of hunger and cold."[139] Taxi dancers who began the night as beautiful young women ended the night worn and haggard, with dark circles under their eyes from lack of sleep and an excess of face powder by way of compensation.[140] In 1936, D. Thiêu-Tước wrote that under all their makeup, the taxi dancers were pale with anemia.[141] What appeared to be the desired *fausse maigre* figure—a narrow build with healthy curves—turned out to be, in many cases, a skinny, sickly figure artificially augmented by a European-style padded bra.[142]

Reportage journalists noted the high rate of illness among taxi dancers. As Trọng Lang recalled, one dancer's fetid breath was symptomatic of a host of health problems: "rot of the intestines, liver, and lungs, exaggerated because of night labor, poor eating, [the presence of] bacteria, and tuberculosis." [143] One of the taxi dancers whom Nguyễn Đình Lạp interviewed for his 1937 work "Thanh Niên Trụy Lạc" (Depraved youth), was clearly sick with a fever and cough. Although she was coughing up blood, she could not afford to rest, for she could not survive without her salary. Other women he interviewed smoked opium to ease the pain brought on by long nights of dancing.[144] Yet sick as some dancers were, they could not afford to take time off, as their salary would have been suspended. To avoid a pay cut, they continued working long hours late into the night even with high fevers.[145] Moreover, those who were sick could rarely afford medication with their measly pay. One woman whom Trọng Lang interviewed suffered from tuberculosis; unable to purchase the necessary medicine with her eight-piastre-per-month salary, she had little choice but to suffer the progression of the disease.[146]

With sex work came the risk of pregnancy. Some taxi dancers were able to get illegal abortions from traditional medical practitioners (in pill or herbal form) or from itinerant midwives; others could not or chose not to abort. Miss T., a taxi dancer, said her boss beat her regularly while she was pregnant with her first child. She confided in Trọng Lang that she was pregnant with a second but continued to dance despite frequent morning sickness; she hid her growing belly by cinching her waist tightly with a belt.[147] Sadly, Trọng Lang would eventually discover that Miss T.'s life had proven so difficult that she committed suicide while still pregnant.[148] For those who carried their pregnancy to term, life became even more difficult. To keep their jobs, they had to return to work within weeks of giving birth. Along with the challenges of being a single mother in a very conservative society, taxi dancers saw their salaries decrease with each child, as mothers were presumed to be less sensual.[149]

The dance hall business model was to offer patrons a night of entertainment and the opportunity to dance—or more—with sophisticated modern girls. Yet instead of hiring independent city girls, dance halls exploited the cheap labor force of impoverished—even desperate—young peasant women migrating to the cities and their suburbs. Many came to dancing out of necessity and found themselves exploited, trapped in unfair contracts, and suffering from poor health. With the frequent reportage press coverage, word spread about the debauchery occurring nightly in dance halls and the ways dance hall proprietors exploited naive young women.

Public Opinion on the Dancing Craze

While dance halls were popular among Tonkin's middle-class urban youth, they became a source of criticism among Vietnamese authors and French authorities alike. There was no shortage of Vietnamese-language literature published on what one journalist called the "dancing epidemic" (*nạn khiêu vũ*).[150] Vietnamese authors criticized the dancing craze for a variety of reasons. For one thing, dance halls were emblematic of the Westernization trends and materialism that were sweeping Tonkin. An anonymous journalist writing in 1936 for *Việt Báo* accused Vietnamese youth of imitating European and American youth "but in a cruder and more animalistic way."[151]

A particularly popular condemnation of the dancing world was the way it corrupted seemingly wholesome peasant women. "The profession of dancing," Trọng Lang warned, "is the ladder that leads innocent country girls to the dregs of society."[152] J. Leiba's short story "Một thiếu nữ ở Hà Thành" (A young lady in Hà Thành) is a critique of the shallow ambition that wrecks the life of a young woman who has come to Hanoi in search of independence.[153] When a young man professes his feelings of true love, she rejects them for the independent, decadent life of a taxi dancer. In his novel *Làm Đĩ* (To whore), Vũ Trọng Phụng dramatizes the way in which dance halls could destroy homes and turn otherwise demure young women into sex workers.[154] Similarly, Nguyễn Đình Lạp's 1938 exposé, "Thanh niên trụy lạc" (Depraved youth), chronicled the bad behavior and excessive drinking and smoking that occurred in dance halls among young men and women alike. He portrayed young men who took advantage of naive young peasant women who had come to the city to work as taxi dancers.[155]

The harshest criticism came from Trọng Lang's 1938 reportage series, later published in book form as *Hà Nội Lầm Than* (Wretched Hanoi). The author interviewed multiple taxi dancers whom he found were being exploited and often abused by dance hall owners. The women he interviewed were in poor health and severely underpaid. Trọng Lang went so far as to accuse the dance hall owners of "enslaving" these taxi dancers.[156] So scathing were his exposés that, as he later revealed, he received death threats from dance hall owners and their henchmen.[157]

Clandestine sex work in dance halls also vexed the colonial government. Authorities' main concern was the role of taxi dancers and dance halls in the spread of venereal diseases among personnel of the French Army, French Navy, and Foreign Legion. After all, dance halls were servicemen's favorite destination for socializing with young Vietnamese women and seeking out sex workers. As military personnel preferred dance halls to å đào singing houses, they were more likely to be infected with venereal diseases by a taxi dancer than by an å đào singer.[158] Mayor Virgitti and Dr. Joyeux went so far as to deem dance halls the "new halls of contamination for Europeans, particularly European troops."[159] "Under an exterior of elegance and cleanliness," Dr. Piere wrote, taxi dancers "hide dirt and shocking and disgusting lesions." As many taxi dancers were in the second, and latent, phase of a syphilis infection, Piere wrote, soldiers and sailors could not easily identify infected women.[160] He deemed taxi dancers the "most dangerous" threat to France's military forces in Tonkin.

As in the case of å đào singing houses, the colonial government tried to legislate ways to police dance halls. Like å đào singers, taxi dancers were not considered sex workers according to the 1921 law defining prostitution, and thus authorities had little policing powers over them. Initially, local governments in the suburbs attempted to exert control through city ordinances imposing limits on the hours that dance halls could operate. For example, those found open after midnight (except on Saturday) were slapped with fines.[161] Those that stayed open to one in the morning paid 0.80 piastres; those that remained open past that time had to pay five piastres.[162] Such fines were negligible in their impact, as dance halls reaped much larger profits if they stayed open.

Eventually, in May 1939, the colonial government introduced a law that enabled the state to restrict the activities of å đào singing houses and dance halls alike, as discussed in chapter 5. Article 1 of the 1939 law required dance hall owners to register all existing dance halls and apply for permission to open new ones. The owners were required to provide identifying information for all of their professional taxi dancers, including their names and home villages. The law also mandated that dance halls close at midnight.[163] To prevent human trafficking and debt bondage, the 1939 law stipulated new rules for recruiting taxi dancers. It carefully demarcated the relationship between dance hall owners and dancers and set limits for dance contracts. No women could be forced to work at dance halls, according to the law.[164] All taxi dancers had to be paid in cash—not with clothing or food—and dancers who boarded in the dormitory could have their rent deducted, but the deductions could amount to only a portion of their salaries. In other words, room and board could not replace salary and leave women to dance without pay. Dance hall owners could offer taxi dancers terminal cash loans but could not force them into debt for borrowing clothing. To prevent the sale of sex, men were banned from staying overnight in the dormitories.[165] And taxi dancers who resided in the dormitories were required to carry a work booklet.[166]

The law also included good-faith measures to protect taxi dancers from unscrupulous bosses. To prevent women from being trafficked or tricked into working at dance halls, the 1939 law required that the recruitment of dancers be supervised by a state-appointed official.[167] The law also required taxi dancers to undergo three months of vocational training—an attempt by the state to ensure that dancers actually danced as opposed to merely sold sex.[168] Such protective measures were paternalistic insofar as they potentially limited taxi dancers' freedom or drove them further into debt by forcing them to pay for the vocational training themselves. The measures also left taxi dancers vulnerable to corrupt officials demanding bribes or expensive talent managers who effectively acted as middlemen.[169]

Taxi dancers and dance hall owners alike bristled at the 1939 law. According to an article published in *Việt Báo* that year, dancers complained about the requirement that dance halls close at midnight. With customers only starting to arrive at ten o'clock, the establishments were losing much-needed revenue, and the taxi dancers were missing out on collecting dance tickets and valuable tips. The customers themselves were not happy with the law insofar as it limited their fun.[170] Dance halls such as Casino, Honkong, and Vogue on Khâm Thiên Street petitioned the local government to allow them to stay open until one on weeknights and three on Friday and Saturday nights.[171] Other dance halls simply ignored the 1939 law. In 1940, the provincial administration issued repeated warnings to dance hall owners reminding them not to hire minors without parental consent, to require taxi dancers to carry their work booklet, to limit the loans provided to dancers, and to forbid patrons from staying in dorms overnight.[172]

Given the drunken patrons, rowdy nights, interracial interactions, exploitive labor practices, and rumors of sex work and venereal disease transmission, it is no surprise that dance halls were frowned upon by Vietnamese writers and French health-care professionals. As dance halls were not registered brothels and were mostly located outside colonial jurisdiction, the colonial state had little authority to regulate them. As with sex work in á đào singing houses, the colonial government drew on the 1939 law to prevent trafficking and instituted local-level regulations to limit activities inside dance halls and increase policing power. Yet the popularity of dance halls among French military personnel protected the halls from excessive policing. Colonial authorities refrained from policing dance halls with the zeal that they applied to á đào singing houses in large measure to keep the troops happy. As a result, sex work continued largely unfettered in Tonkin's dance halls.

Clandestine sex work in Tonkin dance halls was the product of two colliding socioeconomic developments—one urban, one rural. In the city itself, which had recovered more quickly from the Great Depression than had the countryside, urban middle-class youth began to enjoy material goods and an abundance of leisure activities. Dance halls were a particularly salient expression of the cosmopolitan, consumer-driven youth culture that swept Tonkin during the 1930s. Young men and women of diverse ethnicities, decked out in the latest European fashions, piled into dance halls where they smoked, drank, and danced to Western music until the wee hours of the morning. Driven by the allure of the modern and the taboo, the halls developed a nearly cult-like following.

Meanwhile, a very different trend characterized Tonkin's rural areas, which were much slower to recover from the ravages of the Depression. Persistent poverty drove peasant women into the cities and suburbs, where they, too, were drawn to the many dance halls—not as customers but as workers eager for a paycheck. The dance halls, the epitome of urban sophistication and luxury, thus owed their existence not just to the urban Tonkin's economic boom but to the impoverished countryside. As for the glamorous, free-spirited modern girls who served as the primary workforce of dance halls—and the primary attraction for male customers—they were, for the most part, an illusion.

The decadent and carefree atmosphere of the dance halls themselves was likewise—at least to a certain extent—an illusion. Drunken fights broke out between jealous men, racial anxieties bruised fragile male egos, and frauds and scammers preyed on naive men and women. This atmosphere inevitably took its toll on the taxi dancers, who had to harden themselves to survive as hustlers or risk being taken advantage of. After hours, many were subjected to financial manipulation, intimidation, and all manner of physical and emotional abuse. As a result, Tonkin's dance halls became the object of scorn by Vietnamese journalists and colonial authorities alike.

Conclusion

Patterns of Clandestine Sex Industries into the Postcolonial Era

Tonkin's flourishing black market for sex during the interwar years owed its success in large part to French colonial rule. Colonial rule gave rise to sites of tension—economic disparity, an urban-rural divide, an uneven distribution of colonial law, and cultural shifts—and it was within them that the black market thrived. During the interwar years, the volatile capitalist economy imposed by the French, along with new cultural trends, spawned two divergent yet symbiotic groups: a customer base of relatively affluent and middle-class urbanites looking for a good time and a labor force of impoverished rural women looking for income. Desperate to support themselves and their families or disenchanted with the expectations traditionally assigned to young women—or, more often, a combination of both—this population of women increasingly turned to clandestine sex work.

The colonial state's blind spots allowed this market to flourish. For one thing, colonial officials miscalculated the unintended effects of their strictly regulated "tolerance" system. Unwilling to risk their reputations by officially registering with the police, to limit their profits by paying taxes, or to submit to invasive gynecological exams, many sex workers went underground. Moreover, the colonial state had inadequate means of policing these workers. The terms of Tonkin's protectorate status placed geographical limits on the reach of French law, and the 1921 law that implemented uniform regulations across the French concessions defined sex work narrowly. The narrow definition combined with French privacy laws and limited jurisdiction reduced police powers to pursue leads on clandestine sex work.

Moreover, without denying the authoritarian role of the colonial state, it is important to note that in marginalizing certain colonized populations—in this case impoverished Vietnamese women—the French colonial state lost much of its ability to monitor and control them. The vice squad could not track the many young women and girls who were slipping in and out of urban areas—whether taking shelter in pagodas, being taken in by well-meaning or malicious madams, or being forced or manipulated into sex work. Police failed to identify the many rickshaw drivers and itinerant vendors who served as undercover intermediaries for juvenile prostitution rings. Doctors were not permitted to perform venereal exams or quarantine women in the dispensaries located within the French concessions without reason—though some did anyway. Police and customs officials were largely unsuccessful in their efforts stop kidnappers and traffickers from transporting women to China or selling them to local brothels.

Nonetheless, authorities sought alternative means of restricting the black market. The governor-general capitalized on two serious concerns of the time—venereal diseases and human trafficking—to make the case for policing ả đào singing houses, dance halls, and boardinghouses. The colonial government also collaborated with provincial governments to institute local-level ordinances to impede business operations, including limiting hours of operation, instituting heavy taxes on entertainment spots, and prohibiting customers from sleeping at the venues overnight.

Despite numerous regulations and ordinances, as well as exhaustive policing efforts, sex workers easily sidestepped the reach of the government and found ways to make money in an informal economy. They took advantage of the uneven distribution of colonial power. They dodged colonial regulations by leaving the French-administered cities to operate in the suburbs, just outside of the reaches of the vice squad. When local ordinances imposed restrictions on hours of operation or prohibited men from spending the night, they boldly ignored the law in favor of profit. They skipped town when police attempted to register them or conduct venereal exams. When local authorities shuttered their clandestine brothels, they simply moved to another location—or pretended to have moved—and continued to sell sex furtively. As marginal actors in society—female children, unmarried women, migrants, runaways, orphans, or victims of kidnapping—black market sex workers were able to operate below police radar and engage in money-making endeavors unencumbered by legal constraints.

Yet, while their invisibility to the law did afford these women and girls a certain agency, it also put them at risk. Mẹ mìn kidnappers and Chinese trafficking gangs profited from selling women and girls. Owners of dance halls and singing houses encouraged—or even forced—employees to accept extended debt-bondage contracts. Pimps and madams often withheld sex workers' salaries and brutalized insubordinate women. Venereal infections often went untreated, leading to serious health repercussions.

The stories of the women and girls in this book reveal a close relationship between choice and coercion. Taken individually, it is tempting to reduce these people's experiences to a binary of either agency or victimhood. But placing their stories within the context of larger historical trends such as mass poverty, migration, and cultural change reveals that this binary is misleading. Here, I draw from the insightful work of Elisa Camiscioli, who complicates the binary of coercion and choice in her research on French women who traveled to Argentina in the early twentieth century.[1] By applying Camiscioli's analysis to the case of Tonkin, it is more helpful to understand the black market sex industry of the interwar years as a place where degrees of coercion and choice often coexisted in a single experience. Some women came to the black market looking for independence, which they found—to a degree—by entering into a debt-bondage contract. Indeed, some of them entered such contracts understanding that they would have to give up a degree of their freedom in order to gain their long-term independence or to give their family economic independence. Other women were trafficked into the sex industry but continued to sell sex even when they were no longer coerced. Of course, others were raped, beaten, and held against their will.

The decadent, entertainment-focused clandestine sex industry described in this book gradually came to an end by the mid-1940s. From 1940 to 1975, Vietnam was in a nearly constant state of war. With the Japanese invasion of Southeast Asia in 1940, daily life changed dramatically in Tonkin—especially for the black market sex industry. In June 1940, France capitulated to Germany, and the fascist Vichy government soon took control of the colony. Meanwhile, Japan expanded its reach in the Pacific. In September 1940, Japan occupied Indochina, meeting little resistance from the French colonial government. The Japanese troops, for their part, maintained relative peace and allowed the colonial government to maintain its administrative control over the protectorate. Yet, within less than two years, the war began heating up in Tonkin. In early 1942, Allied forces bombed cities as well as industrial and military facilities. Hải Phòng was hit repeatedly, driving its residents to flee to the countryside. In 1943 and 1944, the border towns of Lào Cai and Cao Bằng, both party towns known for clandestine sex work, were bombed and their residents evacuated. By winter 1944–45, Tonkin had descended into famine, leaving more than four hundred thousand victims. On the night of March 8–9, 1945, the Japanese military staged a *coup de force*, seizing complete control of Tonkin. Allied forces responded by increasing their bombing through the summer.[2]

With the violence and famine associated with World War II, the clandestine sex industry changed. Residents of Hanoi and Hải Phòng fled to the countryside to escape the bombings, thereby decreasing the size of the urban customer base. While unregistered sex work certainly continued—and may have even increased—during the war, the market was no longer an entertainment-focused industry as it had been during the interwar years. Decadent forms of leisure such as dance halls and ả đào singing houses were, for the most part, a rarity in the context of wartime atrocities. Moreover, the hostilities of wartime made the European culture of dance halls less appealing than it once had been. Local musicians no longer set Vietnamese lyrics to Western music,[3] and, one by one, formerly popular dance halls closed down. By the end of the decade, the few remaining dance halls would be run by the French military rather than enterprising Vietnamese.

The black market sex industry continued to wane in the face of political upheaval and further military conflict. The Japanese surrendered in August 1945; in September, Hồ Chí Minh declared the emergence of an independent, communist-ruled Vietnam known as the Democratic Republic of Vietnam (DRV). Within a few weeks, however, French troops returned to reclaim the colony. Initially the French government and Hồ Chí Minh's DRV attempted to negotiate a settlement, but war between the two broke out in fall 1946.

In the late 1940s, medical discoveries and changes in metropolitan law made clandestine sex work less of a pressing concern for the colonial state, which was still fighting to maintain control of Indochina. Whereas during the interwar years the threat of venereal diseases motivated the colonial state to find new tools with which to control clandestine sex work, the discovery of antibiotics mitigated the threat that venereal diseases posed. Meanwhile, the colonial regulation system began to fall out of favor as abolitionists in the metropole called for ending the laws governing state-sanctioned brothels. On April 13, 1946, the Marthe Richard Law—named after a former sex worker turned abolitionist—ended the brothel system in the metropole, though the sale of sex itself remained legal and regulated. Though the Marthe Richard Law was never applied to the protectorate, the abolitionist ideas behind it eroded enforcement of the regulation system.[4]

As war continued in Indochina during the late 1940s and early 1950s, clandestine sex workers set up shop near military encampments to profit from the built-in customer base. Rumors began to spread during the First Indochina War that the DRV was deliberately sending women who carried venereal diseases to spread the infection among French soldiers, triggering anxiety among military and colonial officials alike. Although the French military now had antibiotics with which to treat venereal diseases, outbreaks were still problematic. To prevent further contagion, authorities developed a closely monitored brothel system with which to service military personnel. The French military hired local sex workers and imported women from the French North African colonies to Tonkin an effort to appeal to troops from North Africa. In this system, with its bordels militaire de compagne, sex workers were required to travel with military units and to submit to regular venereal exams in order to prevent the spread of infection among troops.

Whereas colonial officials aimed to control the sale of sex for public health reasons, their communist counterparts sought to eradicate the sale of sex for moral ones. Beginning in 1946, the areas of Tonkin that had come under communist control underwent rather stark cultural reforms. As had been the case when the communists took over Shanghai, communist forces in Tonkin put an end to sites deemed bastions of capitalist decadence and debauchery.[5] In 1946, the DRV levied heavy taxes on ả đào houses and the area's few remaining dance halls.[6] One by one, dance halls and singing houses closed due to both the tax burden and pressure from police.[7]

Fighting continued until the spring of 1954, when the Geneva Accords ended French colonial rule in Vietnam and allowed for the temporary division of the country at the seventeenth parallel, with the DRV governing the North and the Republic of Vietnam (RVN) governing the South. Historians know little about the sex industry under the DRV. After independence, the DRV banned the sale of sex and excoriated ả đào house owners and singers for sexualizing cultural tradition, and local police in

Hanoi and the surrounding provinces shut down the å đào venues one by one. Singers refrained from teaching the craft of å đào to their daughters so as to protect them from the bad reputation that might result—even if this meant letting the tradition die out.[8] The infamous Khâm Thiên Street, long past its days as a vibrant neighborhood for clandestine sex work in singing houses and dance halls, was destroyed by US forces during the 1973 Christmas bombings. Not until 2009—when the United Nations Educational, Scientific, and Cultural Organization recognized ca trù, a music form closely related to å đào, as an intangible cultural heritage—would the reputation of this musical tradition be at least partially restored.[9]

In the South, during the US-Vietnam War (1964–75), the sale of sex continued to be banned under the RVN, but an entertainment-based black market sex industry once again began to flourish. This occurred in spaces of tension similar to those seen during the interwar years, including a volatile capitalist economy, demographic shifts, rapid urbanization, and the introduction of new cultural trends. US military and economic aid resulted in an influx of money to the cities while the countryside remained poor, exacerbating the type of economic disparity experienced during the 1930s. The pattern of migration likewise echoed that of the interwar period. From 1963 to 1975, ten million people fled the fighting in the countryside or were forced to evacuate to cities.[10] The urban labor force became saturated, and, as had happened before, many migrant women supported themselves with sex work. The cult of individualism that had arisen during the colonial period remained popular, and new American cultural trends swept the cities, transforming them into sites of cultural experimentation. As in the interwar years, a generation of rebellious youth emerged. Urban, young Vietnamese men and women experimented with sex, drugs, and rock and roll. Bars and go-go clubs opened to cater to Western military personnel and Vietnamese with a taste for American culture.[11] Pretty young women, typically migrants from rural war zones, squeezed into microminis, sequined bustiers, and patent leather boots, painted on frosted eyeshadow and heavy mascara, and girated to songs such as "We Gotta Get out of This Place" by the Animals, a favorite song among American GIs. The city of Saigon alone buzzed with more than a thousand bars and a hundred night clubs where clandestine sex work was prevalent.[12] The titillation factor in these establishments was much more overt than it had been at dance halls during the 1930s; between songs, go-go dancers plopped themselves down on GIs' laps, openly propositioning the soldiers, and allowing the men to grope them in public.

The entertainment-focused sex industry in the South came to an end in the spring of 1975, when the People's Army of Vietnam (PAVN) defeated the South. By the end of April, the PAVN had seized Saigon, declaring North and South Vietnam reunified under communist control. The communist government implemented a Soviet-style planned economy and denounced sex workers as traitors for sleeping with enemy soldiers. Police rounded up suspected sex workers and sent them to reeducation camps, where they were taught the supposed evils of sex work, treated for sexually transmitted infections, and given vocational training.[13]

Sex work remained illegal under a unified Vietnam. Yet the extreme poverty resulting from the country's new planned economic system meant that a black market persisted, albeit in a less obvious form. Then, in 1986, the state announced the introduction of the Đổi Mới economic reforms and a new policy of economic liberalism that was open to foreign trade and capitalist investment.[14] Despite being condemned by the state as a "social evil" (tệ nạn xã hội), sex work once again become a booming industry that was again a very public secret. As urban economies improved and a leisure and entertainment culture was revived, karaoke-ôm (karaoke with "hugs") bars popped up in urban and rural areas alike. These bars catered to government officials, businessmen from elsewhere in Asia, and, as the economy improved, the average man. In the cities, bars opened to capitalize on the new forms of wealth flooding Vietnam from international investments. Kimberly Kay Hoang's research on Ho Chi Minh City's early twenty-first-century sex industry shows an industry in which specialized bars catered to Asian businessmen, to wealthy returning Vietnamese (Việt kiều), and to Western tourists. "Social evils" such as sex work, drugs, and gambling and Western products such as Coca-Cola soared in popularity.

This brief look at the decades beyond the interwar years highlights the reemergence of similar patterns in the way sex was sold in interwar Tonkin, mid-century South Vietnam, and post–Đổi Mới Vietnam. Each of these eras' sex industries were public secrets, as they were, for the most part, entertainment-focused. Moreover, each emerged out of similar social tensions: economic disparity, cultural change, and an urban-rural divide. The spaces of tension described in this book, particularly those that developed in the context of volatile economies, fostered clandestine sex work. In the case of interwar Tonkin, unequal distribution of the law across geographic spaces invited subjects to find creative ways to evade policing. Economic disparity in all three eras created both a population of workers desperate to get out of poverty and a customer base eager to spend money on illicit entertainment. Cultural changes brought about by increased contact with the West—whether through colonialism, the Vietnam War, or globalism—encouraged women to reconsider the traditional gendered expectations of their role in family and society. So powerful were the forces driving the black market sex industry in twentieth- and twenty-first-century Vietnam that even innumerable attacks by a wide range of actors—from colonial vice squads and health officials to the communist state's cultural cleansing and campaign against "social evils"—could not dampen its appeal or diminish its success.

NOTES

Abbreviations

CAOM   Centre des archives nationales d'outre mer
CGI   Gouverneur général d'Indochine
MH   Marie Ville de Hanoi
RF   Résidence de France
RSA   Résidence supérieure d'Annam
RST   Résidence supérieure du Tonkin
RSTNF   Résidence supérieure du Tonkin, Nouveaux Fonds
VNNA 1 Vietnam National Archives, Center 1, Hanoi, Vietnam
VNNA 2 Vietnam National Archives, Center 2, Ho Chi Minh City, Vietnam

Introduction

1. "Ra Hanoi tìm việc, một thiếu nữ bị bán làm gái hồng lâu," *Đông Pháp*, September 9, 1936.

2. Nguyễn Vinh Phúc, ed. *Lịch Sử Thăng Long Hà Nội*, 265–67.

3. Joyeux and Virgitti, "Le péril vénérien," 1.

4. Goscha, *Vietnam*, 83.

5. See article CCCXL of the Gia Long legal code. According to P. L. F Philastre, the code was adopted from a Chinese legal code that deposes officials in cases when they or their sons when they commit moral infractions, including visiting public singers. Philastre, *Études sur le droit*, 546–48.

6. See, e.g., the Contagious Disease Acts passed in Britain. Philippa Levine, *Prostitution, Race, and Politics*.

7. For an excellent discussion of the international concern about the relationship between sex work and venereal disease, see Levine, *Prostitution, Race, and Politics*. Areas outside of the French concessions were governed by Vietnamese law per the decree of April 28, 1886, for the city of Hanoi. Joyeux, *Le péril vénérien*.

8. Charbonnier, "Contribution à l'étude."

9. Limoncelli, *Politics of Trafficking*.

10. Tạ Thị Thúy, *Việc nhượng đất, khẩn hoang ở bắc kỳ từ 1919 đến 1945*; Ngo Vinh Long, *Before the Revolution*, 14–15.

11. Ngo Vinh Long, *Before the Revolution*, 123–24.

12. Ngo Vinh Long, 129.

13. Dao The Tuan, "La transition agraire au Vietnam," 458.

14. Brocheux and Hémery, *Indochina*, 255; Truong Chinh and Vo Nguyen Giap, *Peasant Question*, 86.

15. While population statistics quantifying female migration do not exist, there is ample qualitative evidence of female migration. For an excellent study of *longue durée* population movement, see Langlet-Quach Thanh Tâm, "La repartition spatiale de la population," 169–193; Nguyễn Văn Cư, *Hà Nội Xưa và Nay*, 308–12.

16. Any quantifying measures taken of migrants during the colonial period failed to take into account the transient nature of migration. During the interwar years, peasants moved around the countryside or into the cities not only permanently but also temporarily for a few months between growing seasons—or even moved between rural and urban areas on a daily basis—yet snapshot measurements of population statistics could not reflect this transient nature. Moreover, many of the migrants failed to register with the state or settled just outside the city limits in the suburbs.

17. Dang Xuân Duong and Lê Hông Kê, "La population de Hanoi," 246.

18. Murray, *Development of Capitalism*; Goscha, *Vietnam*; Zinoman, *Vietnamese Colonial Republican*, 256.

19. Nguyễn Văn Khánh and Phạm Kim Thanh, "Mấy nhận xét về kinh tế hàng hoá ở Hà Nội thời kỳ thức dân pháp đô hộ và tạm chiếm."

20. BĐP, "Một Việc nên Chú Ý: Vấn đề phủ nữ thất nghiệp," *Báo Đông Pháp*, September 9, 1931.

21. Marr, *Vietnamese Tradition on Trial*; Trinh Van Thao, *L'école française en Indochine*, 39; Nguyễn Văn Ký, *La société vietnamienne*, 51–54; Bezancon, *Une colonisation educatrice?*; Tran, *Post-Mandarin*; Goscha, *Vietnam*, 345.

22. Sato, *New Japanese Woman*; Feng, *New Woman*; Ikeya, *Refiguring Women*.

23. Brocheux and Hémery, *Indochina*, 238; Goscha, *Vietnam*, 351.

24. Marr, *Vietnamese Tradition on Trial*.

25. This reportage was originally published in the *Báo Ích Hữu* newspaper in 1938. Nguyễn Đình Lạp, "Thanh niên trụy lạc."

26. For excellent discussions of the new trends sweeping urban Tonkin, see Marr, *Vietnamese Tradition on Trial*; Jamieson, *Understanding Vietnam*; Nguyễn Văn Ký, *La société vietnamienne*. On abusive in-law relationships, see Nhất Linh, *Đoạn Tuyệt*, and Phan Trọng Thưởng, Nguyễn Cừ, and Nguyễn Hữu Sơn, *Phóng Sự Việt Nam*, vols. 1–3.

27. Vũ Trọng Phụng, *Làm đĩ*, 7.

28. Nguyễn Đình Lạp, "Thanh niên trụy lạc," 208.

29. Vũ Trọng Phụng, *Làm đĩ*, 87–89.

30. Zinoman, *Vietnamese Colonial Republican*, 148–49.

31. Thao Thao, "Gái Trụy Lạc . . . ," *Việt Báo*, illegible date, presumably February 23, 1937.

32. Trọng Lang, *Hà Nội lầm than*.

33. Bodros, "Le péril vénérien"; Bouvier and Riou, *Instruction technique*; Charbonnier, *Contribution à l'étude*; Coppin, "La prostitution"; Gaide, *Le peril vénérien*; Grenierboley and Nguyen Dinh Diep, "La consulation de Kham Thien"; Joyeux, *Le péril vénérien*, 453–675; Joyeux, "Le dispensaire antivénérien"; Joyeux and Virgitti, "Le péril vénérien"; Le Roy des Barres, "Les maladies vénériennes"; Martial, "La prophylaxie des maladies vénériennes."

34. See, e.g., the eleven articles republished in Baudrit, *Bétail humain*; League of Nations, *Records of International Conference*; League of Nations, *Commission of Enquiry into Traffic*; League of Nations, *Commission d'dnquête*."

35. Jamieson, *Understanding Vietnam*, 102–3.

36. The leading studies of Vietnamese print culture are McHale, *Print and Power*, and Peycam, *Birth of Vietnamese Political Journalism*. For a rich discussion of reportage journalism, see Zinoman, *Vietnamese Colonial Republican*, 148–49; Jaimeson, *Understanding Vietnam*; Marr, *Vietnamese Tradition on Trial*; Tran, *Post-Mandarin*; and Nguyen, "Self-Reliant Literary Group."

37. See, e.g., stories published in Phan Thưởng Trọng, Nguyễn Cừ, and Nguyễn Hữu Sơn, *Phóng sự Việt Nam*, vols. 1, 2, and 3. For an outstanding study of Vietnamese reportage writings on prostitution, see Tran, *Post-Mandarin*.

38. The elimination of the mandarin education system in 1919 led to a new generation of journalists trained in quốc ngữ and French as well as a broader audience. Vietnamese writers educated under the French system began to investigate the lives of women and write to an audience that included women. Tran, *Post-Mandarin*.

39. Nguyen-Vo, *Ironies of Freedom*; Hoang, *Dealing in Desire*.

40. Stur, *Beyond Combat*; Sun, "Where the Girls Are." Nguyễn Bảo Trang is currently completing a dissertation at Giessen University.

41. Tracol-Huynh, "Shadow Theatre of Prostitution"; Tracol-Huynh, "Between Stigmatization and Regulation"; Tracol-Huynh, "Encadrer la sexualité"; Tracol-Huynh, "Entre ombre et lumière"; Tracol-Huynh, "La prostitution au Tonkin colonial"; Tran, *Post-Mandarin*; Malarney, "Introduction."

42. Tracol-Huynh, "Shadow Theatre of Prostitution"; Roustan, "Mousmés and French Colonial Culture."

43. Đặng Thị Vân Chi, "Báo chí tiếng Việt và vấn đế mại dâm dưới thời Pháp thuộc."

44. Lê Thị Hồng Hải. "Mại dâm và quản lý mại dâm ở Việt Nam trong thời kỳ Pháp thuộc."

45. See chapter 1 of Hoang, *Dealing in Desire*.

46. Rodriguez, "L'administration de la prostitution."

47. Cherry, "Down and Out in Saigon."

48. Lessard, *Human Trafficking in Colonial Vietnam*.

49. Martinez, "'La Traite des Jaunes.'"

50. Limoncelli, *Politics of Trafficking*.

51. European sex workers were typically women from Central Europe, called *valaques*, who came to Tonkin in the early years of French colonization of Tonkin. They were expelled in 1915. In 1938, only one European woman was registered as a prostitute, but she no longer practiced; instead, she worked as an intermediary between clients and clandestine French and mixed-race sex workers. According to Roger Charbonnier, the colonial government in Tonkin avoided registering European sex workers "at all costs." Those Europeans who sold sex on the black market were typically married women who were looking to earn income beyond their husband's salary. Charbonnier, "Contribution à l'étude," 11–12, 19.

52. Charbonnier, 11–12.

1. The Geography of Vice

1. Papin, *Histoire de Hanoi*, 227–28; Goscha, *Vietnam*, 83–84, 223.

2. Trung Tâm Lưu Trữ Quốc Gia 1, *Lịch sử Hà Nội qua tài liệu lưu trữ tập I*, 89–90; Brocheux and Hémery, *Indochina*, 76–77, 85; Papin, *Histoire de Hanoi*, 225.

3. See, e.g., "Dụ dỗ gái tơ làm nghề mại dâm, hai người đàn bà bị bắt," *Đông Pháp*, July 2, 1937; "Gái tơ mà giá đáng có vài hào thôi ư?," *Đông Pháp*, July 31, 1937; "Hai cô gái quê bị gạt vào nhà ả đào, nửa đêm lội qua ao trốn đi bị bắt ở phố Hàng-Đậu," *Việt Báo*, April 16, 1939; and "Không để cho khách được thoả tình, một con em nhà thị-Oanh bị cắt tóc," *Đông Pháp*, July 20, [year unclear, early 1940s].

4. "French Indo-China," 70; Ng Shui Meng, *Population of Indochina*, 15.

5. Dao The Tuan, "La transition agraire au Vietnam," 459.

6. Grendreau, Dô Tiên Dung, and Pham Dô Nhât Tân, "Les migrations internes," 196.

7. This statistic included Hải Dương, Vĩnh Yên, Sơn Tây, Hà Nam, and Ninh Bình; it did not include Quảng Yên, Bắc Giang, or Phú Thọ. Gourou, *Les paysans du Delta Tonkinois*, 144, 160.

8. Ng Shui Meng, *Population of Indochina*, 18–19.

9. "French Indo-China," 74.

10. Li Tana, *Peasants on the Move*, 3, 21.

11. Henry, *Économie agricole de l'Indochine*, 27.

12. Lainez, "Human Trade in Colonial Vietnam," 21–35.

13. Hardy, *Red Hills*, 76–79.

14. Brocheux and Hémery, *Indochina*, 261–62.

15. "L'Agent (illegible)" to the Commissioner of Vice Squad, June 17, 1921, VNNA 1, MH 257.

16. Tạ Thị Thúy, *Việc nhượng đất, khẩn hoang ở bắc kỳ từ 1919 đến 1945*; Papin, *Histoire de Hanoi*, 214, 247; Brocheux and Hémery, *Indochina*, 123.

17. Marcel Piere and Bernard Joyeux, "Contribution à l'étude des maladies vénériennes au Camp de Tong (Tonkin) et plus spécialement dans l'effectif Européen," 1938, VNNA 1, MH 2593.

18. In 1897, the colonial government introduced the colonial taxation system to directly tax villages in individuals. In 1923, the colonial government introduced the État Civil, a civil registration system to track individuals. The system followed with a 1925 property tax code. Consequently, the colonial state taxed individuals directly. As Pierre Brocheux and Daniel Hémery have argued, the combination of the État Civil and the tax code led to individuation. Brocheux and Hémery, *Indochina*, 91, 99.

19. Brocheux and Hémery, 259.

20. Gourou, *Les paysans du Delta Tonkinois*, 573; Ng Shui Meng, *Population of Indochina*, 20.

21. Piere and Joyeux, "Contribution à l'étude."

22. Brocheux and Hémery, *Indochina*, 255.

23. Charbonnier, "Contribution à l'étude," 12.

24. Department of Railways, *Official Guide to Eastern Asia*.

25. Papin, *Histoire de Hanoi*, 225.

26. Department of Railways, *Official Guide to Eastern Asia*, 140.

27. Phạm Xanh, "Hà Nội Trong Tiến Trình Lịch Sử Tư Tưởng Nước Nhà 30 Năm Đầu Thế Kỷ XX," 497.

28. Papin, *Histoire de Hanoi*, 224; Gouvernement général de l'Indochine, *Annuaire statistique de l'Indochine, 1930–1931*, 51; Dang Xuân Duong and Lê Hồng Kê, "La population de Hanoi," 246.

29. Saigon was the economic powerhouse of Indochina. Ng Shui Meng, "Population of Indochina," 40.

30. Charbonnier, "Contribution à l'étude," 14.

31. Joyeux, *Le péril vénérien*, 26.

32. Charbonnier, "Contribution à l'étude," 14. Thao Thao gives the same statistics for clandestine sex workers in 1937. Thao Thao, "Gái Trụy Lạc...," *Việt Báo*, presumably February 23, 1937.

33. Vann, "White City on a Red River," 97.

34. Vann, 93.

35. Vann, "Sex and the Colonial City," 412.

36. Joyeux, *Le péril vénérien*, 27.

37. "Hai cô gái quê bị gạt vào nhà á đào, nửa đêm lội qua ao trốn đi bị bắt ở phố Hàng-Đậu," *Việt Báo*, April 16, 1939.

38. Joyeux, *Le péril vénérien*, 34.

39. Xuân Chào, "Gặp Đâu Nói Đấy: Giêm thuấ 'nhẩy' tăng giá điện," *Thời vụ báo*, February 22, 1938.

40. Papin, 253.

41. Vann, "White City on a Red River," 84, 159; Papin, *Histoire de Hanoi*, 248.

42. Department of Railways, *Official Guide to Eastern Asia.*

43. Charbonnier, "Contribution à l'étude," 26.

44. Joyeux, *Le péril vénérien*, 34.

45. Department of Railways, *Official Guide to Eastern Asia.*

46. Nguyễn Vinh Phúc, *Lịch Sử Thăng Long Hà Nội*, 267–68.

47. For an excellent study of modern-day roving street vendors, see Jensen, Peppard, and Vũ Thị Minh Thắng, *Women on the Move.*

48. For more information itinerant vendors and contraband alcohol, see Sasges, *Imperial Intoxication*, 141.

49. Hahn, "Rickshaw Trade in Colonial Vietnam," 47–85.

50. "Text ramentié par la résidence supérieure," n.d., presumably late 1937 or early 1938, CAOM, RSTNF 3856.

51. Hahn, "Rickshaw Trade in Colonial Vietnam," 47–85. See also Nguyễn Công Hoan, *Người Ngựa và Ngựa Người*, and Tam Lang, "Tôi kéo xe," 17–72.

52. Nguyễn Công Hoan, *Người Ngựa và Ngựa Người*, 37–47.

53. See Vũ Trọng Phụng, *Lục Xì.*

54. At the turn of the century, the city ordered the destruction of shacks, but with each economic crisis, the city saw more being built. By 1930, they amounted to approximately 15 percent of the houses in the city. Papin, *Histoire de Hanoi*, 249; Vann, "White City on a Red River," 212.

55. See the negotiations between Kinh and the boardinghouse owner in Nguyễn Đình Lạp, "Than niên trụy lạc," 205.

56. "Réunion du conseil municipal de Hanoi, session du mois d'août séance du 25 août 1922," VNNA 1, MH 289.

57. "Projet de lute antivénérienne à Hanoi," 1934, CAOM, RSTNF 3856.

58. Nguyễn Đình Lạp, "Thanh niên trụy lạc," 210.

59. Virgitti and Joyeux, *Le péril vénérien*, 18.

60. To RST and Mayor of Hanoi, VNNA 1, RST 78667–01.

61. "Le Commissaire central de police à M. l'administrateur Maire de la Ville Hanoi," August 22, 1922, VNNA 1, MH 289.

62. "Réunion du conseil municipal de Hanoi, session du mois d'août séance du 25 août 1922," VNNA 1, MH 289.

63. "Rapport sur le fonctionnement du service des mœurs du 1er janvier au 31 décembre 1926," VNNA 1, RST 78667.

64. René Robin to MH, April 6, 1927, VNNA 1, RST 78667.

65. Testimony of Minh Huong, August 1926, VNNA 1, Tribunal Haiphong 867.

66. Charbonnier, "Contribution à l'étude," 24; Virgitti and Joyeux, Le péril vénérien, 17.

67. "Le Commissaire central de police à M. l'administrateur Maire de la Ville Hanoi," August 22, 1922, VNNA 1, MH 289.

68. René Robin to MH, April 6, 1927, VNNA 1, RST 78667.

69. The most famous literary case of this was Huyền, the protagonist of Vũ Trọng Phụng's Làm đĩ. She followed her lover to Saigon, where she stayed in a boarding house. When she ran out of money, the owner forced her into prostitution to pay the debt. Vũ Trọng Phụng, Làm đĩ.

70. Thao Thao, "Gái Trụy Lạc . . . ," Việt Báo, presumably February 23, 1937.

71. "Le Commissaire central de police à M. l'administrateur Maire de la Ville Hanoi," August 22, 1922, VNNA 1, MH 289.

72. "Le Commissaire central de police."

73. Mayor Hanoi to RST, November 5, 1926, VNNA 1, RST 78667.

74. René Robin to MH, April 6, 1927, VNNA 1, RST 78667.

75. VNNA 1, MH 5755.

76. "Projet de lute antivénérienne à Hanoi," 1934, CAOM, RSTNF 3856.

77. "Texte ramentié par la résidence supérieure," n.d., presumably late 1937 or early 1938, CAOM, RSTNF 3856.

78. In 1914, the colonial government began grouping brothels together; by 1920, the state had developed a reserved quarter outside the city center. Miller, "'Romance of Regulation,'" 384.

79. Miller, 385–86.

80. Aalbers and Sabat, "Remaking a Landscape of Prostitution," 112–28.

81. Joyeux, Le péril vénérien, 54; Charbonnier, "Contribution à l'étude," 58–59.

82. "Dr. Joyeux à M. les membres de la commission du quartier réserve," December 22, 1931, VNNA 1, RST 78667–1. The municipal council, however, rejected the idea. "Sous-commission de prophylaxie des maladies vénériennes, procès-verbal de la 9ème séance, 12 janvier 1934," CAOM, RSTNF 3856.

83. Mayor of Hanoi to RST, March 4, 1932, VNNA 1, MH 2591.

84. Miller, "'Romance of Regulation,'" 387.

85. "Sous-commission de prophylaxie des maladies vénériennes, procès-verbal de la 9ème séance, 12 janvier 1934," CAOM, RSTNF 3856; "Sous-commission de prophylaxie des maladies vénériennes, procès-verbal de la 9ème séance, 30 janvier 1934," CAOM, RSTNF 3856.

86. "Commission de prophylaxie des maladies vénériennes, procès-verbal de la 2ème séance, 2 mai 1943," CAOM, RSTNF 3856.

87. Mayor of Hanoi to RST, March 4, 1932, VNNA 1, MH 2591.

88. "Sous-commission de prophylaxie des maladies vénériennes, procès-verbal de la 9ème séance, 12 janvier 1934," CAOM, RSTNF 3856.

89. "Commission de prophylaxie des maladies vénériennes, procès-verbal de la 2ème séance, 2 mai 1943," CAOM, RSTNF 3856.

90. Papin, *Histoire de Hanoi*, 235.

91. Vann, "White City on a Red River," 217–18.

92. This speaks to Erik Harms's argument of "edginess" in early twenty-first-century margins of Ho Chi Minh City. In the suburb of Hóc Môn, Harms found residents skillfully deployed the division between traditional and modern, city and country for their profit. Erik Harms, *Saigon's Edge*.

93. Vann, "White City on a Red River," 217.

94. Vann, 217. See also Merriman, *Margins of City Life*.

95. "L'Inspecteur général de l'hygiène et de la santé publique à Directeur des finances de l'Indochine," November 4, 1936, VNNA 1, MH 2593.

96. "Extrait de l'Avenir du Tonkin," February 21, 1938, CAOM, RSTNF 3856.

97. After 1939, Mixed Air Group 595 joined the base.

98. Condoms and other forms of birth control were banned in France until 1967.

99. Virgitti and Joyeux, *Le péril vénérien*, 19–20; "Hai cô đầu kiện chủ tại phò thanh-tra lao động và nhờ 1 5ng phó bang-trưởng Khách che chở," *Đông Pháp*, July 19, 1938.

100. "Các chủ nhà Khiêu vũ ở phố Khâm thiên xin cho lui giờ nhẩy đến 3 gời sáng," *Việt Báo*, November 3, 1939.

101. Nguyễn Vinh Phúc, *Phố và Đường Hà Nội*, 284–85; Lê Thước, Vũ Tuân Sán, Vũ Văn Tín, Trần Huy Bá and Nguyễn Văn Minh, *Lược Sử Hà Nội*, 261.

102. Giang Quân, *Khâm Thiên—Gương Mặt Cuộc Đời*, 44–45.

103. Virgitti and Joyeux, *Le péril vénérien*; Lê Thước, Vũ Tuân Sán, Vũ Văn Tín, Trần Huy Bá and Nguyễn Văn Minh, *Lược Sử Hà Nội*, 261.

104. Giang Quân, *Khâm Thiên—Gương Mặt Cuộc Đời*, 49–50.

105. Hoàng Cao Khải was the viceroy of Tonkin. The French government granted him this territory after his work in helping them capture the revolutionary Phan Đình Phùng. Nguyễn Vinh Phúc, *Phố và Đường Hà Nội*, 542–43.

106. "Dỗ gái vị thanh-niên làm nghề bất chính bốn người bị bắt," *Đông Pháp*, November 24, 1935; "Ngã Tư Sở lại xuất hiện cái tệ chị em ra đường kéo khách," *Thông Tin*, November 14, 1943; M. de Pereyra to RST, February 24, 1944, VNNA 1, MH 2596; Virgitti and Joyeux, *Le péril vénérien*, 22.

107. Virgitti and Joyeux, *Le péril vénérien* 23; Nguyễn Vinh Phúc, *Phố và Đường Hà Nội*, 45–48.

108. Virgitti and Joyeux, *Le péril vénérien* 25.

109. Hội Đồng Lịch Sử Thành Phố, *Địa Chí Hải Phòng*, 8; "Rapport d'inspection du 28 avril au 1 mai et du 4 au 6 mai 1943, Municipalité de Haiphong," CAOM, RSTNF 1387; Hội Đồng Lịch Sử Hải Phòng, *Lược Khảo Đường Phố Hải Phòng*, 19–20.

110. Hội Đồng Lịch Sử Hải Phòng, 19–20; J. Gauthier "Hai Phong, Port du Tonkin," n.d. (likely 1937), CAOM, Guernut 28. See also Brocheux and Hémery, *Indochina*.

111. A second geographical problem facing Hải Phòng was its unique river tides. The Cửa Cấm River only had one period of high tide per day, and during the colonial period low tide was too shallow for most boats. Ships, therefore, either had to stop quickly or remain at the mouth of the river to avoid the silting problems and to time the tides. J. Gauthier, "Hai Phong, Port du Tonkin," n.d. (likely 1937), CAOM, Guernut 28; Brocheux and Hémery, *Indochina*, 131; Department of Railways, *Official Guide to Eastern Asia*, 131.

112. Department of Railways, *Official Guide to Eastern Asia*, 132.

113. Department of Railways, 133–34.

114. Hải Phòng connected by water to Hanoi, Hưng Yên, and Sơn Tây on the Red River; Nam Định on the Lạch Giang River; Ninh Bình on the Đáy River; Thái Bình on the Trà Lý River; Hải Dương on the Thái Bình River; Đáp Cầu and Phủ Lạng Thương on the Thương River; Việt Trì and Tuyên Quang on the River Claire; and Hòa Bình on the Black River.

115. Ng Shui Meng, *Population of Indochina*, 41.

116. Hội Đồng Lịch Sử Hải Phòng, *Lược Khảo Đường Phố Hải Phòng*, 20.

117. Ng Shui Meng, *Population of Indochina*, 41.

118. Ng Shui Meng, 41–42.

119. Hội Đồng Lịch Sử Thành Phố, *Địa Chí Hải Phòng*, 9; Hội Đồng Lịch Sử Hải Phòng, *Lược Khảo Đường Phố Hải Phòng*, 20, 25.

120. "Bureau d'hygiène de Haiphong, rapport annuel de 1934," VNNA 1, RST 78750.

121. Bodros, "Le péril vénérien," 676–77.

122. "Bureau d'hygiène de Haiphong, rapport annuel de 1934," VNNA 1, RST 78750.

123. "Rapport d'inspection du 28 avril au 1 mai et du 4 au 6 mai 1943, Municipalité de Haiphong," CAOM, RSTNF 1387.

124. "Rapport d'inspection."

125. "Dỗ gái vị thành niên làm nghề mại dâm ba thiếu-phụ bị bắt," *Đông Pháp*, November 19, 1941.

126. Department of Railways, *Official Guide to Eastern Asia*, 132.

127. Avenue de Belgique is currently Lê Lợi Street. Hội Đồng Lịch Sử Hải Phòng, *Lược Khảo Đường Phố Hải Phòng*, 140.

128. "Bureau d'hygiène de Haiphong, rapport annuel de 1934," VNNA 1, RST 78750; "Trừ tiệt bọn mại dâm," *Ngọ Báo*, December 12, 1933; "Dỗ gái vị thành niên làm nghề mãi dâm ba thiếu-phụ bị bắt," *Đông Pháp*, November 19, 1941.

129. "Đường phố không phải nơi chào khách của gái bán phấn buôn hương," *Tin Mới*, July 22, 1940.

130. Duy Tan Road and Route de Lạch Tray run south out of the city; Hội Đồng Lịch Sử Hải Phòng, *Lược Khảo Đường Phố Hải Phòng*, 398–99.

131. Rue de la Marine is currently Hạ Lý Road along the Tam Bạc River. "Dỗ gái vị thành niên," *Việt Cường*, June 8, 1944.

132. "Rapport d'inspection du 28 avril au 1 mai et du 4 au 6 mai 1943, Municipalité de Haiphong," CAOM, RSTNF 1387.

133. Dr. Bodros, director of the Bureau of Hygiene, to the mayor of Hai Phong, September 17, 1932, CAOM, RSTNF 3856.

134. Dr. Bodros to mayor of Hai Phong.

135. "Bureau de hygiène de Haiphong, Rapport sur l'année 1930, " VNNA 1, RST 78750"; "Bureau d'hygiène de Haiphong, Rapport annuel de 1934," VNNA 1, RST 78750.

136. M. Paquin, mayor of Haiphong, to RST, May 26, 1920, CAOM, RSTNF 3897.

137. "Bureau d'hygiène de Haiphong, Rapport sur l'année 1930," VNNA 1, RST 78750; "Bureau d'hygiène de Haiphong, Rapport annuel de 1934," VNNA 1, RST 78750.

138. "Rapport d'inspection du 28 avril au 1 mai et du 4 au 6 mai 1943, Municipalité de Haiphong," CAOM, RSTNF 1387.

139. "Các cô bồi bàn ở các trà thất cũng phải đi khám bệnh," *Đông Pháp*, August 1, 1942.

140. "Một người dỗ đàn bà con gái bán sang Tàu vừa bị bắt," *Đông Pháp*, November 7, 1938; "Mẹ mìn," *Trung Hoà Nhật Báo*, April 8, 1933.

141. "Một mụ Khách chuyên dỗ người vừa sa lưới pháp luật," *Trung Hoà Nhật Báo*, July 26, 1938.

142. "Hai mụ buôn người bị bắt," *Trung Hoà Báo*, August 22, 1936.

143. "Nạn mất người," *Trung Hoà Nhật Báo*, January 19, 1928.

144. "Dỗ trẻ con đem bán," *Trung Hoà Nhật Báo*, March 27, 1930.

145. "Một tổ buôn người bị khám phá," *Việt Báo*, August 21, 1936.

146. Brocheux and Hémery, *Indochina*, 131.

147. "Dỗ người đem bán bị bắt," *Trung Hoà Nhật Báo*, October 22, 1932.

148. "Lại mất con gái," *Trung Hoà Nhật Báo*, August 30, 1928.

149. Nguyên Hồng, *Bước đường viết văn*, 16–18; Hội Đồng Lịch Sử Hải Phòng, *Lược Khảo Đường Phố Hải Phòng*, 362–65; "Chỉ vì tên "Bà Ba" mà ba bà bị bắt," *Đông Pháp*, January 28, 1939; "Tổ buôn người ở vườn Hoa Djibouti: Ba mụ buôn bán trẻ con sa lưới pháp luật," *Việt Báo*, September 15, 1941; Hội Đồng Lịch Sử Thành Phố, *Địa Chí Hải Phòng*, 9.

150. Nguyên Hồng, *Bước đường viết văn*, 16–18.

151. Hội Đồng Lịch Sử Hải Phòng, *Lược Khảo Đường Phố Hải Phòng*, 354–55.

152. "Chỉ vì một tên "bà ba" mà ba bà bị bắt," *Đông Pháp*, January 28, 1939; "Tổ buôn người ở vườn Hoa Djibouti: Ba mụ buôn bán trẻ con sa lưới pháp luật," *Việt Báo*, September 15, 1941.

153. "Quyền dỗ gái non làm nghề mại dâm," *Ngọ Báo*, October 5, 1935.

154. Department of Railways, *Official Guide to Eastern Asia*, 136.

155. RST to RF Quang Yen, December 1, 1932, CAOM, RSTNF 3856.

156. Department of Railways, *Official Guide to Eastern Asia*, 137.

157. See, e.g., cases of trafficking women: "Trốn ở bên Tàu về," *Ngọ Báo*, July 5, 1931; "Một tổ buôn người bị khám phá," *Việt Báo*, August 21, 1936; and "Chỉ vì một tên "bà ba" mà ba bà bị bắt," *Đông Pháp*, January 28, 1939.

158. "Mẹ mìn dỗ 5 người con gái," *Trung Hoà Nhật Báo*, August 2, 1930.

159. "Buôn Người," *Trung Hoà Báo*, December 24, 1936.

160. "Khám phá được một đảng buôn người," *Ngọ Báo*, September 25, 1935.

161. See Vũ Trọng Phụng, "Kỹ Nghệ Lấy Tây."

162. RST to RF Quang Yen, December 1, 1932, CAOM, RSTNF 3856.

163. RF Lao Kay to RST, April 13, 1933, CAOM, RSTNF 3987.

164. Henri Delevaux to RST, March 30, 1932, CAOM, RSTNF 3987.

165. "Le Général de division Verdier à RST," May 17, 1934, CAOM, RSTNF 3987.

166. "Le Commandant du 1er territoire militaire to Capitaine délègue à Dinh Lap," January 18, 1937, CAOM, RSTNF 4402.

167. Virgitti and Joyeux, *Le péril vénérien*, 23–24.

168. Charbonnier, "Contribution à l'étude," 13.

169. Charbonnier, 17.

170. RF Yen Bay to RST, May 1924, CAOM, RSTNF 3897; "Note de Service," signed Buhrer, February 19, 1936, CAOM, RSTNF 3897.

171. Vũ Trọng Phụng, *Kỹ nghệ lấy tây*.

172. RF Quang Yen to RST, March 14, 1936, CAOM, RSTNF 3987.

173. Dr. Augier to RF Sontay, January 16, 1934, CAOM, RSTNF 3856.

174. "Rapport de 1 janvier–31 decembre, 1926, Service des Mœurs," VNNA 1, RST 78667.

175. Hilaire to Monet, April 11, 1924, CAOM, RSTNF 3987; "Commission de prophylaxie des maladies vénériennes, procès verbal de la 1ère séance: 8 janvier 1934," CAOM, RSTNF 3856.

176. See Firpo, *The Uprooted*.

177. Dr. Augier to RF Sontay, January 16, 1934, CAOM, RSTNF 3856.

178. "Rapports annuels des provinces du Tonkin sur l'assistance médicale," 1931, VNNA 1, S03 9.

179. Pinault to RF Quang Yen, April 9, 1936, CAOM, RSTNF 3987.

180. Augier to RF Sontay, January 16, 1934, CAOM, RSTNF 3856.

181. Livrets de travail were required for sex workers under the decision of February 10, 1936. RF Quang Yen to RST, March 14, 1936, CAOM, RSTNF 3987; Philippot to RST, March 24, 1936, CAOM, RSTNF 3987.

182. "Dr. Millous to Général de division commandant supérieur des troupes du group d'Indochine," January 16, 1939, CAOM, RSTNF 3856.

183. Piere and Joyeux, "Contribution à l'étude."

184. Piere and Joyeux.

185. Piere and Joyeux.

186. Piere and Joyeux.

187. Piere and Joyeux.

188. Piere and Joyeux.

189. Piere and Joyeux.

190. Son Tay to RST, November 25, 1937, CAOM, RSTNF 3897; Patrouillault to RF Sontay, December 4, 1937, CAOM, RSTNF 3897.

191. Piere and Joyeux, "Contribution à l'étude."

192. "Các nhà cô đầu và tiệm nhảy có lẽ không được chứa đàn ông ngủ đêm," *Đông Pháp*, March 29, 1939.

193. Tagliacozzo, *Secret Trades*.

194. Sûreté to RSTNF, July 23, 1938, VNNA 1, RST 76594.

195. "Le commandant du 2ème territoire miliaire à RST," July 8, 1941, CAOM, RSTNF 2153.

196. Hải-Ngọc, "Việc trừ hạng gái ngang," *Ngọ Báo*, June 27, 1931.

197. "Le commandant du 2ème territoire miliaire à RST," July 8, 1941, CAOM, RSTNF 2153.

198. Hải-Ngọc, "Việc trừ hạng gái ngang."

199. Hải-Ngọc.

200. Hải-Ngọc.

2. Venereal Diseases

1. "Gouvernement générale d'Indochine, inspection générale des services sanitaires, rapport annuel d'ensemble 1928," VNNA 1, Inspection générale de l'hygiène et de la santé publique S03 4.

2. "Rapport sur le fonctionnement du service de l'assistance médicale au Tonkin pendant l'année 1928," VNNA 1, RST 32032.

3. "Gái giang hồ ở Quảng-yên đều phải bắt lên nhà thương khám vi trùng," Việt Báo, August 25, 1939.

4. General Billote, quoted in "Commission de Prophylaxie des Maladies Vénériennes, Procès Verbal de la 1ère Séance," January 8, 1934, CAOM, RSTNF 3856.

5. For an excellent discussion of gendered discourse about venereal disease, see Spongberg, Feminizing Venereal Disease.

6. Miller, "'Romance of Regulation,'" 1.

7. Areas outside of the French concessions were governed by Vietnamese law per the decree of April 28, 1886, for the city of Hanoi. Joyeux, Le péril vénérien.

8. Dr. Bernard Joyeux, "Projet de lute antivénérienne à Hanoi," 1934, CAOM, RSTNF 3856.

9. A. Le Roy des Barres, "Les maladies vénériennes au Tonkin," 144; Joyeux, Le péril vénérien, 16.

10. Dr. Raymond to RST, September 19, 1938, CAOM, RSTNF 3987.

11. General of Division Lombard to GGI, February 8, 1916, CAOM, RSTNF 3856.

12. Minister of War to the General Commander Superior of Troops, Group Indochina, December 20, 1916, CAOM, RSTNF 3856.

13. "Assistance médicale de Thai Binh rapport annuel de 1919," CAOM, RSTNF 4011.

14. Hill, "Strangers in a Foreign Land," 275.

15. M. Maquin, Mayor of Haiphong, to RST, May 26, 1920, CAOM, RSTNF 3897.

16. "RST, direction locale de la santé, rapport annuel 1920," VNNA 1, RST 32024.

17. "RST direction sociale de la santé, assistance médicale du Tonkin, rapport annuel de 1921," VNNA 1, RST 32025.

18. "Rapport annuel d'ensemble sur le fonctionnement de l'Inspection générale des Services sanitaires et médicaux de l'Indochine (1928)," VNNA 1, Inspection générale de l'hygiène et de la santé publique de l'Indochine S03 4.

19. "Comité local d'hygiène du Tonkin séance du mardi 2 mars 1920," VNNA 1, RST 32024.

20. The earliest iteration of the French regulation system dates to 1802, when the city of Paris established venereal disease clinics to inspect sex workers. Miller, "'Romance of Regulation,'" 6.

21. Decree of February 3, 1921, printed in Joyeux, Le péril vénérien, 184–89; Charbonnier, "Contribution à l'étude," 37–38.

22. Decree of February 3, 1921, 184–89; Charbonnier, "Contribution à l'étude," 37–38.

23. Article 34 of the decree of February 3, 1921, printed in Joyeux, *Le péril vénérien*, 184–89.

24. Thao Thao, "Gái Trụy Lạc . . . ," *Việt Báo*, unclear date (presumably February 23, 1937).

25. Charbonnier, "Contribution à l'étude."

26. RF Nam Định to RST, September 5, 1938, CAOM, RSTNF 746.

27. Hải-Ngọc, "Việc trừ hạng gái ngang," *Ngọ Báo*, June 27, 1931.

28. "8.000 người ở Hà Nội đến nhà thương để chữa bệnh giang-mai," *Đông Pháp*, November 7, 1941.

29. "Rapport annuel des provinces du Tonkin, 1933," VNNA 1, Inspection générale de l'hygiène et de la santé publique de l'Indochine S03 10.

30. "Assistance médicale province de Yen Bay, rapport annuel de 1930," VNNA 1, Inspection générale de l'hygiène et de la santé publique de l'Indochine S03 8; "Rapport, 1931," VNNA 1, Inspection générale de l'hygiène et de la santé publique de l'Indochine S03 9.

31. "Assistance médicale province de Yen Bay, rapport annuel de 1930"; "Rapport annuel et statistiques des maladies indigènes et Européens, hospitalisé à l'ambulance de Lao Kay de l'année 1922," VNNA 1, Direction locale de la santé du Tonkin Q6 92. Ethnic Thổ women in Cao Bằng were the exception, and they were listed among clandestine prostitutes. Hải-Ngọc, "Việc trừ hạng gái ngang," *Ngọ Báo*, June 27, 1931.

32. "Assistance médical de Ha Nam, rapport médical annuel d'année 1923," CAOM, RSTNF 4021.

33. Phan-Thất-Thời, "Bịnh hoa liễu hại mạng người," *Văn Minh*, January 11, 1927.

34. "Kết quả của trụy lạc: Vì mắc bệnh tình, một thiếu niên đâm đầu xuống ao tự tử," *Việt Báo*, September 12, 1941.

35. Response from Do Van Nam, representative from Minh Huế (Cochinchina), November 7, 1937, CAOM, Guernut 22.

36. Vũ Trọng Phụng, *Lục Xì*, 31.

37. Syphilis is a bloodborne infection that gets filtered into the baby's bloodstream through the umbilical cord, thus affecting the baby's development.

38. "Rapport sur le fonctionnement du service de l'assistance médicale au Tonkin pendant l'année 1928," VNNA 1, RST 32032.

39. Vũ Trọng Phụng, *Lục Xì*, 31. As the cervix blocks out vaginal tract infections, gonorrhea is acquired in the process of birth, as the baby passes through the birth canal.

40. Response from Do Van Nam, representative from Minh Huế (Cochinchina), November 7, 1937, CAOM, Guernut 22.

41. E.g., there was the story of a deformed premature baby that was the result of both husband and wife having a venereal disease. "Một cái quái thai vì nọc bệnh phong tình," *Đông Pháp*, October 8, 1941.

42. "Ông Nguyễn Duy Uông nói tại hội quán Afana về bệnh phong tình," *Trung Hoà Báo*, February 18, 1939.

43. "8.000 người ở Hà Nội đến nhà thương để chữa bệnh giang-mai," *Đông Pháp*, November 7, 1941.

44. "Rapport annuel d'ensemble sur le fonctionnement de l'inspection générale des services sanitaires et médicaux de l'Indochine (1928)," VNNA 1, Inspection générale de l'hygiène et de la santé publique de l'Indochine S03 4.

45. "Rapport sur le fonctionnement du service de l'assistance médicale au Tonkin pendant l'année 1928," VNNA 1, RST 32032; Miller, "'Romance of Regulation,'" 270, 277.

46. "Việc bài-trừ nạn hoa-liễu," Thời Vụ Báo, February 22, 1938.

47. Joyeux, "Projet de lute antivénérienne à Hanoi."

48. "Trừ tiệt bọn mại dâm," Ngọ Báo, December 12, 1933.

49. See, e.g., "Tìm ra 1 nhà chuyên chứa gái mại dâm," Đông Pháp, August 13, 1938.

50. Q. G., "Trước khi để ý đến bọn cô đầu. Hãy nên để ý đến một bọn người ăn mày," Quốc Gia Nhật Báo, July 20, 1939.

51. "Nghề mãi dâm," Ngọ Báo, February 26, 1933.

52. "Bùi thị-Mùi đã bị làm án về tội dỗ gái làm nghề mãi dâm," Đông Pháp, August 12, 1938.

53. "Rapports annuel des provinces du Tonkin sur l'assistance médicale, 1930," VNNA 1, Inspection générale de l'hygiène et de la santé publique de l'Indochine S03 8.

54. Vũ Trọng Phụng, Lục Xì, 91.

55. Thao Thao, "Gái Trụy Lạc . . . ," Việt Báo, February 19, 1937.

56. Dr. Marcel Pierre and Dr. Bernard Joyeux, "Contribution à l'étude des maladies vénériennes au Camp de Tong (Tonkin) et plus spécialement dans l'effectif Européen," n.d. (1937 or 1938), VNNA 1, MH 2593.

57. GGI to Governor of Cochinchina, RST, RSA, RS Kouang-Tcheou-Wan, October 31, 1930, CAOM, RSTNF 3856.

58. Ligue prophylactique de la ville de Hanoi, "Réponse au projet de lutte contre les maladies vénériennes présenté par l'inspecteur général de l'hygiène et de la santé publiques," VNNA 1, MH 2593.

59. "Observations, remarques et conclusions sur le fonctionnement du Service de Contrôle médical et de Règlementation de la Prostitution surveillée à Hanoi (1er Janvier au 1er Septembre 1933)," VNNA 1, MH 2592.

60. Joyeux, "Projet de lute antivénérienne à Hanoi."

61. Joyeux, Le péril vénérien, 45.

62. Joyeux, "Projet de lute antivénérienne à Hanoi."

63. Vũ Trọng Phụng, Lục Xì, 90.

64. "Rapports annuels des provinces du Tonkin sur l'assistance médicale (1930): Hôpital de Nam Dinh," VNNA 1, Inspection générale de l'hygiène et de la santé publique de l'Indochine S03 8.

65. "Procès-verbal de la réunion de la commission des maladies vénériennes," May 2, 1938, VNNA 1, MH 2593.

66. General Billotte, "Note de service," June 1, 1931, CAOM, RSTNF 3987.

67. "Rapport Médical Annuel 1923, Yen Bay," CAOM, RSTNF 4021.

68. Charbonnier, "Contribution à l'étude," 44.

69. Response from Do Van Nam, representative from Minh Hue (Cochinchina), November 7, 1937, CAOM, Guernut 22; "Công cuộc bài trừ bệnh hoa liễu," Thông Tin, March 24, 1943; "Rapports annuels des provinces du Tonkin sur l'assistance

médicale (1931)," VNNA 1, Inspection générale de l'hygiène et de la santé publique de l'Indochine S03 9.

70. "Công cuộc bài trừ bệnh hoa liễu," *Thông Tin*, March 24, 1943.
71. "Sous-commisison de prophylaxie des maladies vénériennes, procès-verbal de la 9ème séance," January 12, 1934.
72. "Công cuộc bài trừ bệnh hoa liễu," *Thông Tin*, March 24, 1943.
73. "Cơ quan bài trừ hoa liễu," *Việt Báo*, August 18–19, 1936.
74. VNNA 1, RST 48294; "RST direction locale de la santeé assistance médicale du Tonkin, rapport annuel de 1923," VNNA 1, RST 32027.
75. "Procès-verbal de la réunion de la commission des maladies vénériennes," May 2, 1938, VNNA 1, MH 2593.
76. Letter RF Lang Son to RST, September 2, 1926, CAOM, RSTNF 2897; Letter, "Le maréchal de logis chef de gendarmerie Certifions de commissaire de police à RF Langson," January 29, 1926, CAOM, RSTNF 3897.
77. "Một nhà chứa lậu ở Khâm Thiên bị khám hai người đàn bà bị bắt," *Đông Pháp*, October 22, 1941.
78. The first dispensary was located on Hàng Cân Street. In 1902, the dispensary moved to Hàng Long Street. In 1918, it was temporarily moved into a shrine behind the mayor's office before moving to the courthouse site. Thao Thao, "Gái Trụy Lạc . . . ," *Việt Báo*, February 19, 1937; Vũ Trọng Phụng, *Lục Xì*, 29–30; Charbonnier, "Contribution à l'étude," 40.
79. Charbonnier, "Contribution à l'étude," 41–44.
80. Thao Thao, "Gái Trụy Lạc . . . ," *Việt Báo*, February 19, 1937.
81. Thao Thao, "Gái Lục Sì . . . ," *Việt Báo*, February 15–16, 1937.
82. "Sous-commission de prophylaxie des maladies vénériennes, procès-verbal de la 9ème séance," January 12, 1934, CAOM, RSTNF 3856.
83. "Observations, remarques et conclusions sur le fonctionnement du Service de Contrôle Médical et de Règlementation de la Prostitution surveillée à Hanoi (1er Janvier au 1er Septembre 1933)," VNNA 1, MH 2592.
84. "Rapport annuel sur le fonctionnement du service municipal d'hygiène de Hanoi en 1930," VNNA 1, MH 5754.
85. Joyeux, *Le péril vénérien*, 40.
86. "Sous-commission de prophylaxie des maladies vénériennes, procès-verbal de la 9ème séance," January 12, 1934, CAOM, RSTNF 3856.
87. Vũ Trọng Phụng, *Lục Xì*, 85.
88. Malarney, "Introduction," 12.
89. Vũ Trọng Phụng, *Lục Xì*, 72.
90. Joyeux, *Le péril vénérien*, 40.
91. "Le commissaire de police du 1ère arrondissement à m. le commissaire central de police Hanoi," April 11, 1917, VNNA 1, MH 704.
92. Report to Sûreté, February 18, 1935, VNNA 1, MH 824.
93. Inspector of Vice Squad to Police Commissioner, March 21, 1935, VNNA 1, MH 824.
94. RST, Process Verbal, February 12, 1935, VNNA 1, MH 824.
95. Letter, Police Commissioner to Mayor of Hanoi, March 22, 1935, VNNA 1, MH 824.

96. "Province de Ninh Binh, Rapport annuel 1921," CAOM, RSTNF 4019.

97. "RST direction locale de la santé, assistance médicale du Tonkin, rapport annuel de 1923," VNNA 1, RST 32027.

98. "Rapport sur les statistiques sanitaires de l'infirmerie de la garnison à Mongcai (1922)," VNNA 1, Direction locale de la santé du Tonkin Q6 84.

99. "RST direction locale de la santé, assistance médicale du Tonkin, rapport annuel de 1923," VNNA 1, RST 32027.

100. RF Ninh Binh to RST, April 21, 1926, CAOM, RST 3897.

101. "RST, assistance médicale du Tonkin, rapport annuel de 1926," VNNA 1, RST 32030.

102. Dr. Raymond explains that they took this measure because the 1921 law was inapplicable to the unregistered women of Sept Pagodes. Letter, Dr. Raymond to RST, December 27, 1939, CAOM, RSTNF 3856.

103. "Cô phải vì cô đào bị đi khám vi-trùng, mà cái nhà trong xóm Bình Khang đóng của," Ngọ Báo, March 13, 1935.

104. "Đại-biểu cô đào yết-kiến quan võ-hiển," Việt Báo, May 30, 1937.

105. "Muốn tránh nạn đi khám bệnh và theo chị em phố Rợp, chị em Ngã Sáu quyết định đình nghiệp," Đông Pháp, August 13, 1938; "Nay mai cô đầu ở Ninh Bình sẽ phải đi khám bệnh," Đông Pháp, October 5, 1938.

106. "Procès-verbal," May 3, 1926, VNNA 1, Tribunal Hai Phong 1982.

107. "Dụ dỗ gái tơ làm nghề mại dâm, hai người đàn bà bị bắt," Đông Pháp, July 2, 1937.

108. "Gái giang hồ ở Quảng-yên đều phải bắt lên nhà thương khám vi trùng," Việt Báo, August 25, 1939.

109. Hải-Ngọc, "Việc trừ hạng gái ngang," Ngọ Báo, June 27, 1931.

110. "Trừ tiệt bọn mại dâm," Ngọ Báo, December 12, 1933.

111. "Note de service," Signed Buhrer, February 19, 1936, CAOM, RSTNF 3987.

112. Letter, "vợ lính tây" to "Monsieur quan thông sự," n.d., March 1936CAOM, RSTNF 3987.

113. Letter, RF Quang Yen to RST, March 14, 1936, CAOM, RSTNF 3987; Letter from General of the Division, March 24, 1936, CAOM, RSTNF 3987.

114. "Note de service, le colonel Hihaus, commandant d'armes au médecin charge du service médical du détachement du 5ème étranger à Việt Trì," January 6, 1939, CAOM, RSTNF 3856; Local Director of Health Services to Director of Health Services for Troops, January 14, 1939, CAOM, RSTNF 3856.

115. Dr. Raymond to RST, December 27, 1939, CAOM, RSTNF 3856.

116. "Province de Hoa Binh, assistance médicale au Tonkin, année 1933 rapport annuel," VNNA 1, Inspection générale de l'hygiène et de la santé publique de l'Indochine S03 10.

117. Dr. Gide to Chef de Battalion Sept Pagodes, February 23, 1939, CAOM, RSTNF 3856.

118. "Officier de la légion d'honneur à le commandant du 1èr territoire militaire," February 19, 1938, CAOM, RSTNF 3991.

119. "Nguyen Van Tran dit An Tan à Lieutenant Colonel," December 19, 1937 (French-language version of letter), CAOM, RSTNF 3991.

120. "Nguyen Van Tran dit An Tan à Lieutenant Colonel."

121. "Nguyen Van Tran dit An Tan à Lieutenant Colonel."

122. "Nguyen Van Tran dit An Tan à Lieutenant Colonel."

123. Letter, February 1938, CAOM, RSTNF 3991.

124. "Rapport annuel sur le fonctionnement du service municipal d'hygiène de Hanoi en 1930," VNNA 1, MH 5754.

125. Letter, February 1938, CAOM, RSTNF 3991.

126. RST to Military Commander in Mongcai, February 1938, CAOM, RSTNF 3991.

127. Letter from Dr. Theil, December 18, 1937, CAOM, RSTNF 3991.

128. Letter from Captain Martin in Tiên Yên, December 22, 1937, CAOM, RSTNF 3991.

129. An Tan to RST, January 17, 1938, CAOM, RSTNF 3991.

130. Joyeux, *Le péril vénérien*, 53–54.

131. RF Quảng Yên to Commander of Forces in Quảng Yên, March 10, 1936, CAOM, RSTNF 3987.

132. "Note de Service," signed Billotte, June 1, 1931, CAOM, RSTNF 3987.

133. "Observations, remarques et conclusions sur le fonctionnement du Service de Contrôle médical et de Règlementation de la Prostitution surveillée à Hanoi (1er Janvier au 1er Septembre 1933)," VNNA, 1 MH 2592; Taraud, *La prostitution coloniale*, 341–46.

134. Miller, "'Romance of Regulation,'" 11.

135. Miller, 12–13.

136. Charbonnier, "Contribution à l'étude," 49–50.

137. Joyeux, *Le péril vénérien*, 51–52; Vũ Trọng Phụng, *Lục Xì*, 13–14.

138. Vũ Trọng Phụng, *Lục Xì: Phóng Sự*, 34–35.

139. Vũ Trọng Phụng, 34–35.

140. "Discussion de Dr. de Raymond," n.d. (likely 1930), CAOM, RSTNF 3856.

141. "Note" by RST, July 1, 1932, CAOM, RSTNF 746.

142. Joyeux, *Le péril vénérien*, 51–52.

143. Vũ Trọng Phụng, *Lục Xì*, 35–37.

144. Charbonnier, "Contribution à l'étude," 54.

145. Charbonnier, 37.

146. Charbonnier, 46.

147. Charbonnier, 46.

148. "Một hội đồng bài trừ bệnh hoa liễu đã thành lập," *Trung Hoà Nhật Báo*, December 16, 1933; "Hội-đồng bài trừ bệnh hoa-liễu đã định ba cách đề phòng các thứ bệnh tình," *Đông Pháp*, January 21, 1939.

149. "Một hội đồng bài trừ bệnh hoa liễu đã thành lập," *Trung Hoà Nhật Báo*, December 16, 1933.

150. Inspector General of Public Health Services to President of the Prophylactic League of Hanoi, November 13, 1936, VNNA 1, MH 2593; "Commission de prophylaxie des maladies vénériennes, procès verbal de la 1ère séance: 8 jan 1934," CAOM, RSTNF 3856.

151. Vũ Trọng Phụng, *Lục Xì*, 9.

152. "Commission de prophylaxie des maladies vénériennes, procès verbal de la 1ere séance: 8 jan 1934," CAOM, RSTNF 3856.

153. The renewed abolitionist movement began with the 1934 Stravinsky Affair, which exposed the corrupt relationship between brothel owners and politicians. Miller, "'Romance of Regulation,'" 447.

154. "Note pour monsieur le directeur des bureau Milliès Lecroix," January 1938, RSTNF 3897; RST to Director of Bureaus, January 3, 1938, CAOM, RSTNF 746.

155. Dr. Terrisse to RF Hà Đông, May 19, 1937, CAOM, RSTNF 3856.

156. RF Hà Đông to the Local Director of Health, June 15, 1937, CAOM, RSTNF 3856; RF Hà Đông to RST, June 16, 1937, CAOM, RSTNF 3856.

157. "Đỗ Vân Nam, Représentative de Canton de Minh Hue, présente respectueusement à la commission d'enquête d'outre mer," November 7, 1937, CAOM, Guernut 22.

158. Bilange, Fourniau, and Ruscio, *Rapport de mission*, 164.

159. "Procès-verbal de la réunion de la commission des maladies vénériennes," May 2, 1938, VNNA 1, MH 2593.

160. Vũ Trọng Phụng, *Lục Xì*, 20, 46–47.

161. Ligue prophylactique de la ville de Hanoi, "Réponse au projet de lutte contre les maladies vénériennes présenté par l'inspecteur général de l'hygiène et de la santé publiques," n.d. (presumably spring 1938), VNNA 1, MH 2593; "Projet de lutte contre les maladies vénériennes," n.d. (presumably 1938), VNNA 1, MH 2593.

162. Vũ Trọng Phụng had initially requested permission to write about the dispensary before the Guernut Mission and was denied access. When Godart and the Guernut Mission arrived in Indochina, he was permitted to tag along to their tour of the dispensary. But after Vũ Trọng Phụng published his first few articles, the mayor attempted to terminate his access on the grounds that the articles he published were inaccurate and too negative. Indeed, Vũ Trọng Phụng later admitted that he had fabricated parts of *Lục Xì*. Zinoman, *Vietnamese Colonial Republican*, 36.

163. Vũ Trọng Phụng, *Lục Xì*, 51.

164. Vũ Trọng Phụng, 52–53.

165. Vũ Trọng Phụng, 54.

166. Thao Thao, "Gái Truy Lạc . . . ," *Việt Báo*, February 19, 1937.

167. Vũ Trọng Phụng, *Lục Xì*, 51.

168. Thao Thao, "Gái Truy Lạc . . . ," *Việt Báo*, February 21, 1937.

169. Vũ Trọng Phụng, *Lục Xì*, 150.

170. Vũ Trọng Phụng, 150.

171. Thao Thao, "Gái Truy Lạc . . . ," *Việt Báo*, February 21, 1937,.

172. Vũ Trọng Phụng, *Lục Xì*, 52.

173. Thao Thao, "Gái Truy Lạc . . . ," *Việt Báo*, February 21, 1937.

174. Vũ Trọng Phụng, *Lục Xì*, 150.

175. Thao Thao, "Gái Truy Lạc . . . ," *Việt Báo*, n.d. (presumably February 23, 1937).

176. "Projet de lutte contre les maladies vénériennes," n.d. (likely 1938), VNNA 1, MH 2593.

177. "Việc bài-trừ nạn hoa-liễu," *Thời Vụ Báo*, February 22, 1938.

178. Letter, "l'Inspecteur général de l'hygiène et de la santé publique à M. le directeur des finances de l'Indochine," November 4, 1936, VNNA 1, MH 2593.

179. Letter, "Le ministre des colonies à GGI," December 12, 1936, CAOM, RSTNF 3856.

180. "Rapport de l'inspecteur générale de l'hygiène et de la santé publique: Assistance et œuvres sociales en Indochine," 1937, CAOM, Guernut 22.

181. "Note d'ensemble sur les problèmes essentiels évoqués par les vœux d'ordre social," n.d. (likely 1937), CAOM, Guernut 22.

182. "Viện Dân biểu với việc bài trừ bệnh hoa liễu," *Đông Pháp*, January 31, 1939.

183. "Note pour monsieur le chef de bureau," by RST, October 25 or 29, 1938, CAOM, RSTNF 746.

184. "Hội-đồng bài trừ bệnh hoa-liễu đã định ba cách đề phòng các thứ bệnh tình," *Đông Pháp*, January 21, 1939.

185. Virgitti and Joyeux, *Le péril vénérien*, 30–33.

186. "Thái-bình: Chị em xóm Vũ-tiên gửi bức thư ngỏ cho ông hội Thiều," *Việt Báo*, August 30, 1939.

187. "Vì muốn bài trừ bệnh hoa liễu nên các cô đào phải khám bệnh," *Đông Pháp*, August 13, 1940; "Thanh Hoa: Các cô-đào phải khám bệnh, đã khám 21 cô trong tám nhà hát, 18 cô có bệnh," *Việt Báo*, August 13, 1940.

188. "Một nhà chứa lậu ở Khâm Thiên bị khám hai người đàn bà bị bắt," *Đông Pháp*, October 22, 1941.

189. "Các cô bồi bàn ở các trà thật cũng phải đi khám bệnh," *Đông Pháp*, August 1, 1942.

3. Unfree Labor

1. "Không muốn ở mãi trong bể trầm luân," *Đông Pháp*, January 7, 1940.
2. Parreñas, *Illicit Flirtations*.
3. "Không muốn ở mãi trong bể trầm luân," *Đông Pháp*, January 7, 1940.
4. Murray, *Development of Capitalism*, 410.
5. Lasker, *Human Bondage in Southeast Asia*, 157–58.
6. Reid, "Introduction," 8–10; Jacobsen, "Debt Bondage in Cambodia's Past," 32–43.
7. Henry, *Économie agricole de l'Indochine*, 38–39.
8. Jacobsen, *Sex Trafficking in Southeast Asia*, 72.
9. Thank you to Elisa Camescioli for wisdom on this issue.
10. Jacobsen, *Sex Trafficking in Southeast Asia*, 90.
11. Andaya, "From Temporary Wife to Prostitute," 11–34.
12. Lasker, *Human Bondage in Southeast Asia*, 159.
13. Hershatter, *Dangerous Pleasures*, 196–99; Gronewold, *Beautiful Merchandise*, 70.
14. "Không muốn ở mãi trong bể trầm luân," *Đông Pháp*, January 7, 1940.
15. "Mấy cô gái nhảy vay tiền trước của chủ rồi 'nhảy' đi mất," *Đông Pháp*, January 10, 1937.
16. "Một thiếu nữ 19 tuổi trốn nhà đi làm cô đào rượu bị chú bắt về," *Việt Báo*, November 7, 1939.
17. "Không muốn ở mãi trong bể trầm luân," *Đông Pháp*, January 7, 1940.
18. "Nam Định: Hai chủ nhà khiêu vũ với hai vũ nữ ra sở Cẩm," *Trung Hoà Báo*, May 6, 1936.
19. "Mấy cô gái nhảy vay tiền trước của chủ rồi "nhảy" đi mất," *Đông Pháp*, January 10, 1937.

20. "Không muốn ở mãi trong bể trầm luân," *Đông Pháp*, January 7, 1940.

21. "Hai cô đầu kiện chủ tại phò thanh-tra lao động và nhờ 1 5ng phó bang-trưởng Khách che chở," *Đông Pháp*, July 19, 1938.

22. "Đầu tỵ vào nhà pha," *Ngọ Báo*, November 11, 1931.

23. "Cô Đào quỵt tiền hay chủ ép người ở tiếp khách?," *Đông Pháp*, July 18, 1936.

24. P. V., "Không trả được tiền xe, hai thiếu-nữ bị gán vào nhà ả đầu," *Việt Báo*, August 22, 1936.

25. Thao Thao, "Gái Trụy Lạc . . . ," *Việt Báo*, February 23, 1937.

26. "Nam Định: Hai chủ nhà khiêu vũ với hai vũ nữ ra sở Cẩm," *Trung Hoà Báo*, May 6, 1936.

27. "Cô Đào quỵt tiền hay chủ ép người ở tiếp khách?," *Đông Pháp*, July 18, 1936.

28. "Hai cô đầu kiện chủ tại phò thanh-tra lao động và nhờ 1 5ng phó bang-trưởng Khách che chở," *Đông Pháp*, July 19, 1938.

29. "Ra Hanoi tìm việc, một thiếu nữ bị bán làm gái hồng lâu," *Đồng Pháp*, September 9, 1936.

30. "Một thiếu nữ 19 tuổi trốn nhà đi làm cô đào rượu bị chú bắt về," *Việt Báo*, November 7, 1939.

31. "Mấy cô gái nhảy vay tiền trước của chủ rồi 'nhẩy' đi mất," *Đông Pháp*, January 10, 1937.

32. Ransmeier, *Sold People*, 313.

33. Lessard, *Human Trafficking in Colonial Vietnam*, xv.

34. For more information on the land route to China, see Lessard, "'Cet Ignoble Trafic,'" 1–34; Peters, "Colonial Cholon"; Muller, "Prostitution and Human Trafficking"; and Jacobsen, *Sex Trafficking in Southeast Asia*, 112.

35. As Dian Murray has shown, there was a long history of pirates on the coast of the South China Sea, and Giang Binh (Chiang p'ing) was the eighteenth-century headquarters. Murray, *Pirates of the South China Coast*; Martinez, "'La Traite des Jaunes,'" 204–21; Tagliacozzo, *Secret Trades, Porous Borders*.

36. "Voeu n21 relatif à la traite des jaunes," by Nguyen Xuan Ty, People's Representative from Haiphong, September 13, 1938, VNNA 1, RST 76594.

37. French Vice Consulate in Pakhoi to Resident General, January 23, 1888, VNNA 1, RST 3384.

38. Tagliacozzo, *Secret Trades, Porous Borders*; Lessard, "'Cet Ignoble Trafic,'" 27.

39. RF Bắ Kạn to RST, May [illegible date] 1904, VNNA 1, RST 8857.

40. During the French Revolution in 1794, slavery was abolished in France and its territories, though it was reestablished in the territories in 1802. In 1817, France banned the slave trade, but the ban did not go into effect until 1826. In 1848, the state abolished slavery in all French territories.

41. Sasges, *Imperial Intoxication*, 26.

42. RF Bac Kan to RST, May 14, 1904, VNNA 1, RST 46677.

43. The 1815 Code of Gia Long made it illegal to take or seduce a person for later sale or slavery (article 244), to use violence to take women or children, sell them, or make them slaves (article 237), to hold lost children for sale, marriage, or concubinage (article 77), or to encourage debauchery among young girls (268 decree 16). In 1883, the Annamite penal code made it illegal to steal a child (articles 354–57), to take a woman or a child of the opposite sex (article 138), to sell or trade children

(article 140), or to take a minor out of Tonkin without parental consent (article 141). "Rapport annuel à la Société des Nations au sujet de la traite des femmes et des enfants en Indochine, année 1922," 1923, CAOM, GGI 17763.

44. Letter to the Procurer General of the Court of Hanoi, December 24, 1938, VNNA 1, RST 76594. While the surviving historical documents do not indicate that any French citizens were caught trafficking women and girls, if they had been involved in trafficking schemes they would have been tried under French law.

45. The decree of December 12, 1905, imposed fines and prison sentences on traffickers. "Ministère des affaires étrangères de Belgique," decree, December 12, 1905, 49–51, VNNA 2, RSA 446; Francis Pressense, League of Human Rights, to Minister of Colonies, October 22, 1906, VNNA 2, RSA 446; RSA to GGI, March 23, 1907, VNNA 2, RSA 446.

46. For example, the boats at the local naval station were not fast enough to chase the Chinese traffickers. The resources of the *inspecteur de la garde indigène* and the *chef de post des îles Go-Ton* were also insufficient. League of Human Rights, section Haiphong, to GGI, December 12, 1910, VNNA 1, GGI 5020.

47. League of Nations, *Records of International Conference*, 11, 54; Boris and Berg, "Protecting Virtue, Erasing Labor," 24; Leppanen, "Movement of Women," 523–33.

48. Limoncelli, *Politics of Trafficking*.

49. For a brilliant analysis of the moral panic about white slavery, see Camiscioli, "Coersion and Choice," 483–507.

50. Donovan, *White Slave Crusades*, 30–31; Rupp, *Worlds of Women*, 150–52.

51. Signing countries included France, Britain, the German Empire, Italy, the Netherlands, Portugal, Russia, Sweden, Norway, and Switzerland. The treaty was ratified on January 18, 1905, and promulgated in Indochina on February 19, 1905. "International Agreement for the Suppression of the 'White Slave Traffic,' May 18, 1904, 35 Stat. 1979, 1 L.N.T.S. 83, Entered into Force 18 July 1905," *Journal officiel de la république française* 49 (February 19, 1905): 1205, VNNA 2, RSA 1310.

52. GGI to Local Heads of Administration, July 1, 1938, CAOM, RSTNF 746; O'Callaghan, *Yellow Slave Trade*, 130–32.

53. League of Nations, *Records of International Conference*, 15–16, 78.

54. League of Nations, 11, 54; Boris and Berg, "Protecting Virtue, Erasing Labor," 24; Leppanen, "Movement of Women," 523–33.

55. League of Nations, *Records of International Conference*, 127–28; Lessard, *Human Trafficking in Colonial Vietnam*, 123–24.

56. League of Nations, *Records of International Conference*, 66, 71.

57. League of Nations, *Commission d'enquête*, 38.

58. Miller, "'Romance of Regulation,'" 3; Limoncelli, *Politics of Trafficking*.

59. "Service de la Sûreté, Rapport annuel année 1923, Réponses au questionnaire de la Société des nations relative à la traite des femmes et des enfants," CAOM, GGI 17763; "Rapport annuel à la Société des Nations au sujet de la traite des femmes et des enfants en Indochine, 1924," CAOM, GGI 17763.

60. Baudrit, "Bétail humain," 119.

61. "Rapports journaliers de la police municipale en novembre 1940 et janvier 1942," VNNA 1, MH 2517; "Rapports journaliers de la police municipale en 1942," VNNA 1, MH 552.

62. "Nạn Mất Con," *Trung Hoà Nhật Báo*, March 14, 1929; "Sao Dạo Này Nhiều Người Mất Con Thế ?," *Ngọ Báo*, April 27, 1928.

63. See, e.g., "Một Đứa Dỗ Người Đã Bị Bắt," *Trung Hoà Nhật Báo*, July 9, 1932.

64. "Sao Lắm Mẹ Mìn Thế?," *Trung Hoà Nhật Báo*, November 23, 1928.

65. League of Nations, *Commission d'enquête*, 17.

66. Thank you to Andrew Morris, Brad Davis, David Chen, Cecelia Chen, and Johanna Ransmeier for helping me with the Chinese etymology.

67. Henriot, *Prostitution and Sexuality in Shanghai*, 171; Hershatter, *Dangerous Pleasures*, 182; Ransmeier, *Sold People*.

68. "Buôn Người," Ngày Nay, February 10, 1935.

69. "Sao Lắm Mẹ Mình Thế?," *Trung Hoà Nhật Báo*, November 23, 1928.

70. "Buôn Người," Ngày Nay, February 10, 1935.

71. Hoàng Đạo Thúy, *Phố phường Hà Nội xưa*, 204.

72. "Buôn Người," Ngày Nay, February 10, 1935.

73. The newspapers presented the mẹ mìn as ethnically Vietnamese, although journalists reported one case of a Chinese mẹ mìn. Newspapers, however, did report two cases of mẹ mìn in their twenties. "Một Mụ Khách Chuyên Dỗ Người Vừa Sa Lưới Pháp Luật," *Trung Hoà Báo*, July 26, 1938; "Lạng Sơn: Dỗ người đem bán," *Hà Thành Ngọ Báo*, May 23, 1928.

74. "Chỉ vì một tên "bà ba" mà ba bà bị bắt," *Đông Pháp*, January 28, 1939.

75. "Mẹ mìn dỗ con gái," *Ngọ Báo*, July 24, 1931.

76. There was one case where the kidnapper threatened to use force. "Dụ dỗ con nít," *Trung Lập Báo*, July 12, 1924.

77. "Hai mẹ con định về quê bốc mà mẹ, mẹ mìn đã dỗ mất con," *Việt Báo*, December 16, 1936.

78. "Âm con chủ đi bán bị bắt được quả tang," *Đuốc Nhà Nam*, June 16, 1936.

79. Hoàng Đạo Thúy, *Phố phường Hà Nội xưa*, 204.

80. "Bắt một mụ dỗ người," *Đông Pháp*, August 25, 1936.

81. "Ninh Bình: Có lẽ là quân mẹ mìn?," *Ngọ Báo*, April 3, 1936.

82. "Buôn Người," Ngày Nay, February 10, 1935.

83. "Buôn Người," *Trung Hoà Nhật Báo*, April 23, 1924.

84. "Mẹ mìn," *Trung Hoà Nhật Báo*, April 8, 1933.

85. When they regained consciousness, they realized that they "had been caught by the mẹ mìn" and eventually escaped. "Một mụ Khách chuyên dỗ người vừa sa lưới pháp luật," *Trung Hoà Nhật Báo*, July 26, 1938.

86. "Những quân buôn người," *Trung Hoà Nhật Báo*, July 12, 1924.

87. "Dỗ người đem bán," *Trung Hoà Nhật Báo*, May 5, 1931.

88. "Đầu tỵ vào nhà pha," *Ngọ Báo*, November 31, 1931.

89. "Dụ dỗ gái tơ làm nghề mại dâm, hai người đàn bà bị bắt," *Đông Pháp*, July 2, 1937.

90. "Bùi thị-Mùi đã bị lên án về tội dỗ gái làm nghề mại dâm," *Đông Pháp*, August 12, 1938.

91. "Quyến dỗ gái non làm nghề mại dâm," *Ngọ Báo*, October 5, 1935.

92. "Ra tỉnh tìm việc, một cô gái bị quyến rũ làm nghề mãi dâm," *Việt Báo*, August 7, 1937.

93. "Hai chú cháu dỗ gái vị thanh-niên làm nghề mại dâm đã bị bắt," *Đông Pháp*, August 12, 1938.

94. "Dỗ gái vị thành niên làm nghề mại dâm ba thiếu-phụ bị bắt," *Đông Pháp*, November 19, 1941; "Ba mụ đàn bà bị bắt về tội dỗ gái vị thành niên," *Tin Mới*, November 19, 1941; "Dỗ gái vị thành niên làm nghề mại dâm ba thiếu-phụ bị bắt," *Đông Pháp*, November 19, 1941.

95. "Bảy cô gái Tàu bị dỗ sang Cholon để rước khách," *Việt Báo*, July 3, 1937.

96. "Ba mụ đàn bà bị bắt về tội dỗ gái vị thành niên," *Tin Mới*, November 19, 1941; "Dỗ gái vị thành niên làm nghề mãi dâm ba thiếu-phụ bị bắt," *Đông Pháp*, November 19, 1941.

97. Ra Hanoi tìm việc, một thiếu nữ bị bán làm gái hồng lâu," Đồng Pháp, September 9, 1936.

98. "Mẹ mìn dỗ 5 người con gái," *Trung Hoà Nhật Báo*, August 2, 1930.

99. "Buôn thịt bán người," *Trung Hoà Nhật Báo*, October 6, 1923.

100. Sûreté to RST, July 23, 1938, VNNA 1 RST 76594.

101. "Những quân buôn người," *Trung Hoà Nhật Báo*, July 12, 1924; "Buôn thịt bán người," *Trung Hoà Nhật Báo*, October 6, 1923.

102. For more information on Southeast Asian concepts of and views toward piracy, see Young, "Roots of Contemporary Maritime Piracy."

103. Black Flag rebels traded Vietnamese women in exchange for guns to fight the French. Lessard, *Human Trafficking in Colonial Vietnam*; Marsot, *Chinese Community in Vietnam*, 42–43; Camp Davis, *Imperial Bandits*.

104. Barrett, "Transnational Webs," 228–30.

105. Billingsley, *Bandits in Republican China*, 35.

106. Ransmeier, *Sold People*.

107. Marr, *Vietnamese Tradition on Trial*, 154–55.

108. Ng Shui Meng, *Population of Indochina*; Robequain, *Economic Development of French Indo-China*, 43.

109. Whereas French law required other foreigners to have a passport, a visa, police verification of their identity, a medical certificate, and a work contract or a deposit for a return ticket, Chinese merely had to possess a passport. Marsot, *Chinese Community in Vietnam*, 110.

110. Decree of December 13, 1913, found in Marsot, 113.

111. Marsot, 116–25.

112. With the Great Depression hitting Indochina's Chinese population especially hard, many ethnic Chinese returned to China. Then the 1937 Japanese attack on China resulted in a flood of migrants from China looking to escape wartime violence and economic turbulence. Marsot, 52–53, 100.

113. League of Nations, *Commission d'enquête*, 29.

114. Transcripts from September 8, 1920, VNNA 1, Tribunal Haiphong, 1300–1.

115. Ransmeier, *Sold People*; Henriot, *Prostitution and Sexuality*, 165–67.

116. Baudrit, "Bétail humain," 97–130.

117. "Mẹ mìn dỗ 5 người con gái," *Trung Hoà Nhật Báo*, August 2, 1930.

118. "Trốn ở bên Tàu về," *Ngọ Báo*, July 5, 1931.

119. "La Traite des fillettes annamites," *Le Courrier Saigonnais*, September 7, 1906; Field, *Shanghai's Dancing World*, 107.

120. RST to GGI, March 24, 1938, VNNA 1, RST 7659.

121. "Lại bắt được mẹ mìn," *Trung Hoà Nhật Báo*, March 19, 1936.

122. "Buôn Người," *Trung Hoà Báo*, December 24, 1936.

123. Metropolitan Penal Code, article 344, paragraph 7, modified July 24, 1937, and article 344, modified for Indochina to apply to indigenous and assimilated Asians (Decree of December 31, 1912); "Traite des femmes et des enfants," n.d. (likely 1938), VNNA 1, RST 76594.

124. "Voeu n21 relatif à la traite des jaunes" by Nguyen Xuan Ty, representative from Haiphong, September 13, 1938, VNNA 1, RST 76594.

125. Sûreté to RST, July 23, 1938, VNNA 1, RST 76594.

126. January 1926: 01Yune A Nang. VNNA 1, Tribunal Haiphong 867–01.

127. Report regarding July 1937–June 1938, Sûreté to RST, July 23, 1938, VNNA 1, RST 76594.

128. Lasker, *Human Bondage in Southeast Asia*, 163.

129. Lasker, 160–61.

130. Jacobsen, "Debt Bondage in Cambodia's Past"; Délaye, "Esclavage et représentations coloniales"; Dyson, *States, Debt, and Power*, 69; "The Wish List of the Vietnamese People (1925)," 222–23; Miers, *Slavery in the Twentieth Century*, 121–30.

131. Lasker, *Human Bondage in Southeast Asia*, 162–63.

132. Minister of Foreign Affairs to Minister of Colonies, December 31, 1938, CAOM, RSTNF 746.

133. GGI to Heads of Local Administration, September 15, 1938, CAOM, RSTNF 746.

134. "Note pour le RST," September 30, 1938, CAOM, RSTNF 746.

135. "Note pour le RST."

136. "Le problème de la regimentation de la prostitution devant la commission des questions sociales de la Société des Nations," December 29, 1938, CAOM, RSTNF 746.

137. Minister of Foreign Affairs to Minister of Colonies, December 31, 1938, CAOM, RSTNF 746.

138. Brévié to Local Heads of Administration, April 11, 1939, CAOM, RSTNF 746.

139. RST, Decree of May 22, 1939, CAOM, RSTNF 746; "Quan Thống Sứ đã ký nghị định về luật-lệ của nhà hát ả đào và tiệm khiêu-vũ," *Đông Pháp*, May 27, 1939.

4. Adolescent Sex Work

1. Court hearing, May 22, 1925, VNNA 1, Tribunal Haiphong 1831.

2. Tạ Thị Thúy, *Việc nhượng đất, khẩn hoang ở bắc kỳ từ 1919 đến 1945*; Ngo Vinh Long, *Before the Revolution*, 14–15.

3. Brocheux and Hémery, *Indochina*, 255; Truong Chinh and Vo Nguyen Giap, *Peasant Question*, 86.

4. For an excellent study on maternity programs, see Nguyen, *Childbirth, Maternity, and Medical Pluralism*.

5. For more on village-level social relief programs, see Ngô Vĩnh Long, *Before the Revolution*, 92–97, and Nguyen-Marshall, *In Search of Moral Authority*, 26–30.

6. Ngô Vĩnh Long, *Before the Revolution*, 92–97.

7. Van Nguyen-Marshall, *In Search of Moral Authority*, 26–30; Ngô Vĩnh Long, 92–97.

8. Ransmeier, *Sold People*.

9. Baudrit, *Bétail humain*, 131.

10. Tavernier, *La famille annamite*, 70–71.

11. Vaudon, *Les filles de Saint-Paul*, 16–31, 75.

12. RST to Head Residents of the Provinces, June 24, 1915, VNNA 1, MH 205858; Central Commissioner of Tonkin to President of the Central Commission of Hanoi City, July 7, 1915, VNNA 1, MH 205858.

13. Marquis, *L'oeuvre humaine*, 22; Hoang Trong Phu Tong Do, "Les oeuvres de protection de la maternité et de l'enfance de la province de Hadong," in *Congrès international pour la protection de l'enfance*, 499.

14. GGI to Heads of Local Administration (except Cochinchina), December 19, 1925, CAOM, RSTNF 3987.

15. On Western approaches toward childhood sexuality, see Egan and Hawkes, "Imperiled and Perilous," 355–67.

16. Article 27 of the Decree of April 25, 1907, City of Hanoi, VNNA 1, MH 2574; Article 27 of the Decree of April 21, 1908, City of Hải Phòng, VNNA 1, RST 1989.

17. Mayor of Hanoi to RST, April 29, 1907, VNNA 1, RST 1986.

18. Decree of March 1, 1915, Cochinchina, CAOM, RSTNF 3987.

19. Director of the Administration of Justice in Indochina to GGI, November 20, 1925, CAOM, RSTNF 3987.

20. Director of the Administration of Justice in Indochina to GGI, November 20, 1925, CAOM, RSTNF 3987.

21. GGI to Heads of Local Administration (except Cochinchina), December 19, 1925, CAOM, RSTNF 3987.

22. René Robin to GGI, February 27, 1926, CAOM, RSTNF 3987.

23. Dr. Le Roy des Barres, January 29, 1926, CAOM, RSTNF 3987.

24. Decree of October 7, 1926, printed in Joyeux, *Le péril vénérien*.

25. Court Hearing, September 8, 1920, VNNA 1, Tribunal Haiphong 1300-01.

26. VNNA 1, Tribunal Haiphong 867.

27. Gaucher to French Resident at Langson, August 23, 1926, CAOM, RSTNF 3897.

28. Signed French Resident at Dongson, September 24, 1926, CAOM, RSTNF 3987.

29. "Quyền dỗ gái non làm nghề mãi dâm," *Ngọ Báo*, October 5, 1935.

30. "Dỗ gái chưa đến tuổi trưởng thành vào nhà hát," *Ngọ Báo*, December 12, 1933.

31. "Gái mới 12 tuổi đã làm nghề mãi dâm," *Ngọ Báo*, April 7, 1933.

32. "Dỗ gái vị thành niên làm nghề mãi dâm một người bị bắt," *Đông Pháp*, August 20, 1938.

33. "Định dỗ con gái ngươi làm nghề bất chính," *Đông Pháp*, November 11, 1939.

34. "12 Tuổi mà đã làm đĩ," *Zân Báo*, April 13, 1933.

35. "Ra Hanoi tìm việc, một thiếu nữ bị bán làm gái hồng lâu," *Đông Pháp*, September 9, 1936.

36. Court hearing, September 8, 1920, VNNA 1, Tribunal Haiphong 1300-01.

37. "Gái mới 12 tuổi đã làm nghề mãi dâm," *Ngọ Báo*, April 7, 1933.

38. "Một Hoa-kiều bị bắt vì ép gái vị thành-niên làm nghề mãi dâm," *Đông Pháp*, March 22, 1939.

39. "Chuong Chi dite Sey Chia," October 21, 1923, VNNA 1, Tribunal Haiphong 1610.

40. "Thị Lan bị phạt 8 tháng tù về tôi dỗ gái vị thành niên làm nghề mại dâm," *Đông Pháp*, May 12, 1939.

41. "Can tội dỗ gái, Cầu-Sam trốn vào nhà thương Khách để làm lạc đường nhà chuyên trách," *Đông Pháp*, August 14, 1940.

42. "Ông Ngô Quốc Lâm thưa cô Xuyên, chủ một tiệm nhảy ở Haiphong, về tội dỗ con gái ông đi làm 'gái nhảy,'" *Ngọ Báo*, February 11, 1935.

43. Court hearing, February 17, 1920, VNNA 1, Tribunal Haiphong 1300.

44. VNNA 1, Tribunal Haiphong 867.

45. "Can tội dỗ gái, Cầu-Sam trốn vào nhà thương Khách để làm lạc đường nhà chuyên trách," *Đông Pháp*, August 14, 1940.

46. Court hearing, May 22, 1925, VNNA 1, Tribunal Haiphong 1831.

47. "Một cô bé 15 tuổi bị dỗ làm nghề mãi-dâm," *Đông Pháp*, July 6, 1938.

48. Court hearing, September 8, 1920, VNNA 1, Tribunal Haiphong 1300-1301.

49. "Chuong Chi dite Sey Chia," October 21, 1923, VNNA 1, Tribunal Haiphong 1610.

50. "Một Hoa-kiều bị bắt vì ép gái vị thành-niên làm nghề mại dâm," *Đông Pháp*, March 22, 1939.

51. Montagne to Paris, November 10, 1903, CAOM, GGI 7701; Montagne to Paris, January 29, 1904, CAOM, GGI 7701.

52. "Note," February 29, 1904, CAOM, GGI 7701.

53. Sambuc, "Notes et documents," 208–9.

54. Firpo, *The Uprooted*, 28–29.

55. Interview with Nguyen Thi Su, February 19, 1922, VNNA 1, Tribunal Haiphong 1550.

56. Vụ Trọng Phụng, "Kỹ Nghệ Lấy Tây."

57. "Dỗ người đem bán bị bắt," *Trung Hoà Nhật Báo*, October 22, 1932.

58. For example, two mẹ mìn were arrested for drugging a fifteen-year-old girl in Hà Đông and taking her to Mường Mán to eventually sell her to a prostitute, who would in turn pimp her out. "Suýt nữa phải tay mẹ mìn," *Trung Hoà Nhật Báo*, June 16, 1932.

59. "Quyền dỗ gái non làm nghề mại dâm," *Ngọ Báo*, October 5, 1935; "Buôn Người," *Trung Hoà Báo*, December 24, 1936; Firpo, "La traite des femmes," 113–24.

60. Firpo, "La traite des femmes," 113–24; "Mẹ mìn dỗ 5 người con gái," *Trung Hoà Nhật Báo*, August 2, 1930.

61. Court hearing, September 8, 1920, VNNA 1, Tribunal Haiphong 1300-1301.

62. Court hearing, October 21, 1923, VNNA 1, Tribunal Haiphong 1610.

63. "Cô bé 12 tuổi ấy bị đấu một chỗ để 'làm tiền'?" *Việt Báo*, November 11, 1939.

64. "Dỗ gái vị thanh-niên làm nghề bất chính bốn người bị bắt," *Đông Pháp*, November 24, 1935.

65. "Ba mụ đàn bà bị bắt về tội dỗ gái vị thành niên," *Tin Mới*, November 19, 1941; "Dỗ gái vị thành niên làm nghề mãi dâm ba thiếu-phụ bị bắt," *Đông Pháp*, November 19, 1941.

66. "Ép người đi làm gái chứa không được lại mấy đội con gái bắt vào nhà Lục-sì," *Việt Báo*, January 6, 1937.

67. "Ra tỉnh tìm việc, một cô gái bị quyến rũ làm nghề mại dâm," *Việt Báo*, August 7, 1937.

68. "Hai anh em ra tỉnh tìm việc, em mới 15 tuổi bị ép làm nghề mại dâm," *Đông Pháp*, September 27, 1941.

69. In the 1930s, the average age of marriage for women was sixteen to twenty years old. Nguyễn Văn Ký, *La société vietnamienne*, 274.

70. While parents gave their daughters to the new husband's family, they still maintained contact with their daughters.

71. Court hearing, September 8, 1920, VNNA 1, Tribunal Haiphong 1300-1301.

72. "Chuong Chi dite Sey Chia," October 21, 1923, VNNA 1, Tribunal Haiphong 1610.

73. "Ra tỉnh tìm việc, một cô gái bị quyến rũ làm nghề mại dâm," *Việt Báo*, August 7, 1937.

74. VNNA I, Cour d'Appel de Hanoi 10809.

75. "Dỗ gái vị thành-niên làm nghề mại-dâm một người bị bắt," *Đông Pháp*, August 20, 1938.

76. "Hai chú cháu dỗ gái vị thanh-niên làm nghề mãi dâm đã bị bắt," *Đông Pháp*, August 12, 1938

77. "Dỗ gái vị thành niên làm nghề mại dâm một người bị bắt," *Đông Pháp*, August 20, 1938.

78. "Thị Lan bị phạt 8 tháng tù về tội dỗ gái vị thành niên làm nghề mại dâm," *Đông Pháp*, May 12, 1939.

79. Court Hearing, September 8, 1920, VNNA 1, Tribunal Haiphong 1300-1301.

80. "Chuong Chi dite Sey Chia," October 21, 1923, VNNA 1, Tribunal Haiphong 1610.

81. Court Hearing, September 8, 1920, VNNA 1, Tribunal Haiphong 1300-1301.

82. "Chuong Chi dite Sey Chia," October 21, 1923, VNNA 1, Tribunal Haiphong 1610.

83. VNNA 1, Tribunal Haiphong 867-01.

84. "Một Hoa-kiều bị bắt vì ép gái vị thành-niên làm nghề mại dâm," *Đông Pháp*, March 22, 1939.

85. "Bốn người bị thưa về tội dỗ gái vị thành niên làm nghề mái dâm," *Đông Pháp*, November 3, 1941.

86. "Dỗ gái vị thành niên," *Việt Cường*, June 8, 1944.

87. VNNA 1, Tribunal Haiphong 867.

88. VNNA 1, Tribunal Haiphong 867.

89. "Dỗ gái vị thanh-niên làm nghề bất chính bốn người bị bắt," *Đông Pháp*, November 24, 1935.

90. "Gái mới 12 tuổi đã làm nghề mại dâm," *Ngọ Báo*, April 7, 1933.

91. "Dỗ gái vị thanh-niên làm nghề bất chính bốn người bị bắt," *Đông Pháp*, November 24, 1935.

92. VNNA 1, Tribunal Haiphong 867.

93. "Quyền dỗ gái non làm nghề mại dâm," *Ngọ Báo*, October 5, 1935.

94. Police Commissioner to Mayor of Hanoi, August 22, 1922, VNNA 1, MH 289.

95. Records for the Sûreté and the Tonkin police were organized separately. Few of the archives remain. During the time that I was researching at VNNA 1, few Hanoi court records were available. While I was able to access files from the Hải Phòng courts, the records were incomplete.

96. Vice Squad Report, 1 January–31 December 1926, VNNA 1, RST 76594.

97. Vice Squad Report, July 1937–June 1938, July 23, 1938, VNNA 1, RST 76594.

98. "Một Hoa-kiều bị bắt vì ép gái vị thành-niên làm nghề mại dâm," *Đông Pháp*, March 22, 1939.

99. Police Commissioner to Mayor of Hanoi, August 22, 1922, VNNA 1, MH 289.

100. "Gái mới 12 tuổi đã làm nghề mại dâm," *Ngọ Báo*, April 7, 1933.

101. "Dỗ gái vị thanh-niên làm nghề bất chính bốn người bị bắt," *Đông Pháp*, November 24, 1935.

102. "Bốn người bị thưa về tội dỗ gái bị thành niên làm nghề mãi dâm," *Đông Pháp*, November 3, 1941.

103. "Ba mụ đàn bà bị bắt về tội dỗ gái vị thành niên," *Tin Mới*, November 19, 1941.

104. Firpo, "La traite des femmes," 113–24.

105. "Định dỗ con gái người làm nghề bất chính," *Đông Pháp*, November 11, 1939.

106. "Ba mụ đàn bà bị bắt về tội dỗ gái vị thành niên," *Tin Mới*, November 19, 1941.

107. "Hai anh em ra tỉnh tìm việc, em mới 15 tuổi bị ép làm nghề mã dâm," *Đông Pháp*, September 27, 1941.

108. Decree of October 7, 1926, found in Joyeux, *Le péril vénérien*.

109. VNNA 1, Tribunal Haiphong 867-01.

110. "Quyền dỗ gái non làm nghề mại dâm," *Ngọ Báo*, October 5, 1935.

111. "Tại tòa án, Hanoi: Quyến dũ gái vị thành niên," *Việt Báo*, August 30, 1940.

112. "Dỗ gái vị thành niên định cho làm nghề mại dâm," *Đông Pháp*, August 30, 1940.

113. Vice Squad Report July 1937–June 1938, July 23, 1938, VNNA 1, RST 76594.

114. "Dỗ gái vị thành niên định cho làm nghề mại dâm," *Đông Pháp*, August 30, 1940.

115. VNNA 1, Cour d'Appel de Hanoi 10809.

116. Sûreté to RST, July 23, 1938, VNNA 1, RST 76594.

117. Sûreté to RST, July 23, 1938.

118. Sûreté to RST, July 23, 1938.

119. Sûreté to RST, July 23, 1938.

120. Sûreté to RST, July 23, 1938.

121. Sûreté to RST, July 23, 1938.

122. "Tại tòa án, Hanoi: Quyến dũ gái vị thành niên," *Việt Báo*, August 30, 1940.

123. Sûreté to RST, July 23, 1938, VNNA 1, RST 76594.

124. Sûreté to RST, July 23, 1938.

125. Sûreté to RST, July 23, 1938.

126. Sûreté to RST, July 23, 1938.

127. "Dỗ gái chưa đến tuổi trưởng thành vào nhà hát," *Ngọ Báo*, December 12, 1933.

128. "Một Hoa-kiều bị bắt vì ép gái vị thành-niên làm nghề mại dâm," *Đông Pháp*, March 22, 1939.

129. "Dỗ gái vị thành niên làm nghề mãi dâm ba thiếu-phụ bị bắt," *Đông Pháp*, November 19, 1941, 3; "Ba mụ đàn bà bị bắt về tội dỗ gái vị thành niên," *Tin Mới*, November 19, 1941.

5. Ả Đào Singers

1. "Thái Bình: Chị em xóm Vũ Tiên gửi bức thư ngỏ cho ông hội Thiều," *Việt Báo*, August 30, 1939.

2. Addiss, "Hat A Dao," 18–31; Tran Quang Hai, "Review Essay," 128–33; Norton, "Singing the Past," 27–56; Hoàng Thị Ngọc Thanh, "Người ả đào qua các tư liệu từ thế kỷ XIX đến giữa thế kỷ XX (Kỳ 8)."

3. Addiss, "Hat a Dao," 19–20; Norton, "Singing the Past," 27–56; Tran, "Commodification of Village Songs," 141–57.

4. Charbonnier, "Contribution à l'étude," 26–27; Nguyễn Văn Ký, *La société vietnamienne*, 300–301.

5. See article CCCXL of the Gia Long Code. According to P. L. F Philastre, the code was adopted from a Chinese legal code that deposes officials in cases when they or their sons commit moral infractions, including visiting public singers. Philastre, *Études sur le droit*, 546–48.

6. Addiss, "Hat A Dao," 21–22.

7. Tracol-Huynh, "Prostitutes, Brothels," 176–93.

8. Joyeux, *Le péril vénérien*, 34.

9. Joyeux, 34.

10. RF Ninh Binh to RST, April 21, 1926, CAOM, RSTNF 3987; RF Ninh Binh to RST, April 21, 1926, CAOM, RSTNF 3897; Decree from Mayor of Nam Dinh, April 12, 1922, CAOM, RSTNF 3856.

11. Vũ Trọng Phụng, *Lục Xì*, 120.

12. "Thái Bình: Chị em xóm Vũ Tiên gửi bức thư ngỏ cho ông hội Thiều," *Việt Báo*, August 30, 1939.

13. Joyeux and Virgitti, "Le péril vénérien," 26.

14. Nguyễn Đình Lạp, "Thanh niên trụy lạc," 204.

15. "Các nhà cô đầu và tiệm nhảy có lẽ không được chứa đàn ông ngủ đêm," *Đông Pháp*, March 29, 1939.

16. Joyeux, *Le péril vénérien*, 12.

17. Joyeux, 34.

18. RST to de Pereyra, February 24, 1944, VNNA 1, MH 2596.

19. Joyeux, *Le péril vénérien*, 34.

20. Ngọc, interview with author, May 4, 2013, Hanoi.

21. "Lại thêm một chuyện quan viên chén khướt ở nhà cô đầu, không có tiền chi, phải viết văn tự nợ," *Đông Pháp*, July 27, 1938; "2 Cô đầu đuổi bắt 3 quan viên ngót 1 cây số lại bắt hụt," *Tinh Mới*, (unclear date) 1940; "Lấy Đồng-hồ chi chầu hát, một quan viên mới ra thoát nhà cô đầu," *Đông Pháp*, July 23, 1936.

22. "Lấy Đồng-hồ chi chầu hát, một quan viên mới ra thoát nhà cô đầu," *Đông Pháp*, July 23, 1936; Ngọc, interview with author, May 4, 2013, Hanoi.

23. Norton, "Singing the Past," 27–56.

24. Audience interaction and expressions of approval are found in other forms of East Asian music—tor example, the *changgo* drummer in Korean *p'ansori* music. Email communication with Barley Norton, July 5, 2013.

25. Ngọc, interview with author, May 4, 2013, Hanoi; Norton, "Singing the Past," 27–56. Today, *ca trù* music is popularly understood to be the musical descendent of *á đào* music. Although ca trù and á đào music are technically different in style, in the late colonial period they shared similar performative measures. "Nhiều nhà cô đào bị phạt vì để cho các quan viên đập trống quá giờ," *Việt Báo*, September 9, 1937.

26. Charbonnier, "Contribution à l'étude," 28.

27. Joyeux, *Le péril vénérien*, 12; Ngọc, interview with author, May 4, 2013, Hanoi; Joyeux and Virgitti, "Le péril vénérien," 4.

28. In the late 1930s, a typical night at a hát á đào house cost customers four piastres; drinks and sexual favors cost extra. "Lại thêm một chuyện quan viên chén khướt ở nhà cô đầu, không có tiền chi, phải viết văn tự nợ," *Đông Pháp*, July 27, 1938.

29. Charbonnier, "Contribution à l'étude," 28.

30. "Cô đào và quan viên đem nhau đi tìm tổ uyên-ương nào?," *Việt Báo*, September 4, 1937.

31. "Quan viên bịp cô đào: Hai người Tàu tự xưng là Vinh và Lâm vào nhà 48 phố Ngã-tư-Trung hiền để làm siêu lòng bà chủ và cô em," *Việt Báo*, July 7, 1939.

32. Guillemain to Governor of Colonies and RST, July 6, 1932, CAOM, RSTNF 3987; RST to GGI, March 11, 1938, CAOM, FM Indo NF 2367 (2).

33. Ngọc, interview with author, May 4, 2013, Hanoi.

34. Vũ Trọng Phụng, *Lục Xì*, 128.

35. "Note pour m. le chef de bureau," October 25, 1938, CAOM, RSTNF 746.

36. Virgitti and Joyeux, "Les maisons de chanteuses," 81–86.

37. "Lấy Đồng-hồ chi chầu hát, một quan viên mới ra thoát nhà cô đầu," *Đông Pháp*, July 23, 1936.

38. Joyeux and Virgitti, "Le péril vénérien," 9.

39. Trọng Lang, "Hà Nội Lầm Than," in Phan Trọng Thưởng, Nguyễn Cừ, and Nguyễn Hữu Sơn, *Phóng Sự Việt Nam*, vol. 3, 133.

40. Ngọc, interview with author, May 4, 2013, Hanoi.

41. Xuân Trào, "Cô đầu tức là thợ hát," *Thời vụ báo*, July 7, 1938.

42. RF Ninh Binh to RST, April 21, 1926, CAOM, RSTNF 3897.

43. RF Nam Định Lotzer to RST, September 5, 1938 CAOM, RSTNF 746.

44. Pettelat to RF Bắc Giang, February 25, 1939, CAOM, RSTNF 746.

45. Joyeux and Virgitti, "Le péril vénérien," 4.

46. Joyeux, *Le péril vénérien*, 12.

47. Patrouillault to RF Sontay, December 4, 1937, CAOM, RSTNF 3897.

48. Vũ Trọng Phụng, *Lục Xì*, 121–22.

49. Vũ Trọng Phụng, 119.

50. RF Bac Giang to RST, February 25, 1939, CAOM, RSTNF 746.

51. Vũ Trọng Phụng, *Lục Xì*, 24–25.

52. Vũ Trọng Phụng, 119.

53. A. Le Roy des Barres, "'Les maladies vénériennes au Tonkin,' extrait de ce bulletin avril 1927," in Joyeux, *Le péril vénérien*, 145.

54. Vũ Trọng Phụng, *Lục Xì*, 24.

55. RF Ninh Binh to RST, April 21, 1926, CAOM, RSTNF 3897.

56. RF Nam Dinh to RST, September 5, 1938, CAOM, RSTNF 746.

57. Raymond to RST, September 19, 1938, CAOM, RSTNF 3987.

58. "Nay mai cô đầu ở Ninh Bình sẽ phải đi khám bệnh," *Đông Pháp*, October 5, 1938.

59. "Rapport d'inspection du 28 avril au 1 mai et du 4 au 6 mai 1943. Munici-palité de Haiphong," CAOM, RSTNF 1387.

60. "Sênh phách," referring to the phách stick that hát ả đào singers used to beat a rhythm, is an old way of referring to ả đào music. "Vậy còn cô đào Hà Nội thì sao?," *Thời Vụ Báo*, August 12, 1938.

61. "Cô đào không bằng con sen," *Thời Vụ Báo*, September 27, 1938.

62. Nguyễn Văn Ký, *La société vietnamienne*, 217.

63. "Rapports annuels des provinces du Tonkin sur l'assistance médicale (1930)," VNNA 1, Inspection Générale de l'Hygiène et de la Santé Publique de l'Indochine S03 8.

64. RF Sontay to RST, November 25, 1937, CAOM, RSTNF 3897.

65. Douguet to RF, September 24, 1926, CAOM, RSTNF 3987. The author of this source does not cite the location of the village.

66. "Cô đào không bằng con sen," *Thời Vụ Báo*, September 27, 1938.

67. Raymond to RST, September 19, 1938, CAOM, RSTNF 3987.

68. Nguyen Ngoc Phong dite Sy Ky to Mayor Haiphong, June 8, 1934, CAOM, RSTNF 3856.

69. Charbonnier, "Contribution à l'étude," 28.

70. Patrouillault to RF Sontay, December 4, 1937, CAOM, RSTNF 3897.

71. Douguet to RF, September 24, 1926, CAOM, RSTNF 3987.

72. Trọng Lang, "Hà Nội Lầm Than," 132.

73. Trọng Lang, 131.

74. Joyeux and Virgitti, "Le péril vénérien," 7.

75. "Cô đào không bằng con sen," *Thời Vụ Báo*, September 27, 1938.

76. "Các nhà cô đầu và tiệm nhảy có lẽ không được chứa đàn ông ngủ đêm," *Đông Pháp*, March 29, 1939.

77. "Trút lốt con sen làm cô đào, Thị Liên mắc bệnh hoa liễu, bị đuổi lại bị bắt nợ," *Việt Báo*, September 5, 1937.

78. "Một cô đào rượu đã phải từ giã phách đàn để làm nghề bán cháo lòng cũng không được yên thân?," *Việt Báo*, February 8, 1939.

79. "Dỗ gái chưa đến tuổi trưởng thành vào nhà hát," *Ngọ Báo*, December 12, 1933; "Tại tòa án, Hanoi: Quyến dũ gái vị thành niên," *Việt Báo*, August 30, 1940.

80. "Ra Hanoi tìm việc, một thiếu nữ bị bán làm gái hồng lâu," *Đồng Pháp*, September 9, 1936. See also "Ba mụ đàn bà bị bắt về tội dỗ gái vị thành niên," *Tin Mới*, November 19, 1941.

81. Trọng Lang, "Hà Nội Lầm Than," 129–31.

82. Trọng Lang, 133.

83. "Nam Định: Vì làm mất một món khách, một cô đầu rượu bị vùi hoa dập liễu," *Thông Tin*, August 13, 1941.

84. "Chán cảnh yên-hoa hai cô đầu uống thuốc độc chết," *Đông Pháp*, March 6, 1939.

85. "Một đào hát Khâm-Thiên nhẩy xuống hồ Gươm tự-tử nhưng vớt lên được," Tin Mới, July 7, 1940.

86. "Đầu Ty vào nhà pha," *Ngọ báo*, November 11, 1931.

87. "Một cô đào rượu đã phải từ giã phách, đàn để làm nghề bán cháo lòng cũng không được yên thân?," *Việt Báo*, February 8, 1939.

88. "Cô đào và quan viên đem nhau đi tìm tổ uyên-ương nào?," *Việt Báo*, September 4, 1937.

89. "Một nhà hát hai cô đào bỏ trốn," *Việt Báo*, November 15, 1939.

90. "Tuy đã thay dạng dạng đổi tên đào nương ấy vẫn không thoát khỏi tay nhà chuyên trách," *Thông Tin*, August 18, 1941.

91. "Hà Đông: Một cô đầu ăn cắp tiền và quần áo của chủ rồi trốn đi," *Thông Tin*, August 10, 1941.

92. "Một cô đào rượu đã phải từ giã phách đàn để làm nghề bán cháo lòng cũng không được yên thân?," *Việt Báo*, February 8, 1939.

93. "Quan Viên Đem Cô Đầu Ngã Tư-Sở trốn lên Bắc Giang," *Tin Mới*, July 19, 1940.

94. "Tuy đã thay dạng đổi tên đào nương ấy vẫn không thoát khỏi tay nhà chuyên trách," *Thông Tin*, August 18, 1941.

95. "Các nhà cô đầu và tiệm nhẩy có lẽ không được chứa đàn ông ngủ đêm," *Đông Pháp*, March 29, 1939.

96. "Một đào hát Khâm-Thiên ngẩy xuống hồ Gươm tự-tử nhưng vớt lên được," Tin Mới, July 7, 1940.

97. Patrouillault to RF Sontay, December 4, 1937, CAOM, RSTNF 3897.

98. "Một ông lang bị một cô đào hứa làm vợ lẽ để lừa hai chuyến mất 120p," *Việt Báo*, August 3, 1939.

99. "Lại thêm một chuyện quan viên chén khướt ở nhà cô đầu, không có tiền chi, phải viết văn tự nợ," *Đông Pháp*, July 27, 1938.

100. "2 Cô đầu đuổi bắt 3 quan viên ngót 1 cây số lại bất hụt," *Tin Mới*, March 15, 1940; "Lấy Đồng-hồ chi chầu hát, một quan viên mới ra thoát nhà cô đầu," *Đông Pháp*, July 23, 1936.

101. Âm-Sơn, "Thế mà thú cô đầu! Đi hát không tiền, lại còn nhờ đồ nữ trang của chị em," *Ngọ Báo*, April 17, 1931.

102. "Quan viên bịp cô đào: Hai người Tàu tự xưng là Vinh và Lâm vào nhà 48 phố Ngã-tư-Trung hiền để làm siêu lòng bà chủ và cô em," *Việt Báo*, July 7, 1939.

103. "Bốn quan viên cố ngủ lấy một đêm cuối cùng nữa ở nhà ả đào để sáng ngày ra gây thành một tấn náo kịch," *Việt Báo*, November 24, 1939.

104. "Quan viên bóc lột cô đào trong phòng trọ," *Việt Cường*, February 23, 1944.

105. "Lấy Đồng-hồ chi chầu hát, một quan viên mới ra thoát nhà cô đầu," *Đông Pháp*, July 23, 1936.

106. "Nam quan viên bị các cô đào loạn đả lại bị trói cả một đêm," *Việt Báo*, September 12, 1937.

107. For a thorough study of the French regulation system, see Corbin, *Women for Hire*.

108. René Robin to RF Ninh Binh, June 18, 1926, CAOM, RSTNF 3897.

109. "Note pour m. le chef de bureau," from RST, May 15, 1926, CAOM, RSTNF 3987; Dr. Raymond to RST, September 19, 1938, CAOM, RSTNF 746.

110. "Note" from RST, July 1, 1932, CAOM, RSTNF 746.

111. RF Son Tay to RST, December 14, 1937, CAOM, RSTNF 3897.

112. Nguyen Ngoc Phong, also known as Sy Ky, to Mayor Haiphong, June 8, 1934, CAOM, RSTNF 3856.

113. RF Nam Định to RST, September 5, 1938, CAOM, RSTNF 746.

114. Dr. Raymond to RST, 1938, CAOM, RSTNF 3987.

115. Joyeux and Virgitti, "Le péril vénérien," 29.

116. "Note pour M. le Chef de Bureau," October 25, 1938, CAOM, RSTNF 746.

117. "Note pour M. le Chef de Bureau," October 25, 1938.

118. "Nhiều nhà cô đào bị phạt vì để cho các quan viên đập trống quá giờ," *Việt Báo*, September 9, 1937.

119. "Nhiều nhà cô đào bị phạt vì để cho các quan viên đập trống quá giờ."

120. "Mấy nhà hát cô đầu bị phạt 8 hôm không được mở cửa," *Đông Pháp*, July 19, 1938.

121. "Vậy còn cô đào Hà Nội thì sao?," *Thời Vụ Báo*, August 12, 1938.

122. RF at Nam Định Lotzer to RST, September 5, 1938, CAOM, RSTNF 746.

123. Charbonnier, "Contribution à l'étude," 29.

124. RF Bắc Giang to Police Commissioner, February 25, 1939, CAOM, RSTNF 746.

125. "Note pour M. le Chef de Bureau," October 25, 1938, CAOM, RSTNF 746.

126. "Nhiều nhà cô đào bị phạt vì để cho các quan viên đập trống quá giờ," *Việt Báo*, September 9, 1937.

127. "Chị em dưới xóm hồng-lâu đã dọn nhà đi gần hết," *Đông Pháp*, August 17, 1938.

128. "Muốn tránh nạn đi khám bệnh và theo chị em phố Rợp, chị em Ngã Sáu quyết định đình nghiệp," *Đông Pháp*, August 13, 1938.

129. "Nay mai cô đầu ở Ninh Bình sẽ phải đi khám bệnh," *Đông Pháp*, October 5, 1938.

130. "Có phải vì cô đào bị đi khám vi-trùng, mà cái nhà trong xóm Bình Khang đóng cửa," *Ngọ Báo*, March 13, 1935.

131. P. V., "Không trả được tiền xe, 2 thiếu-nữ bị gán vào nhà ả-đầu." *Đông Pháp*, August 17, 1938.

132. Nguyễn Thị Loan to RST, September 1, 1938, CAOM, RSTNF 746.

133. RF Ha Dong to Director of Local Health Service, June 15, 1937, CAOM, RSTNF 3856; RF Ha Dong to RST, June 16, 1937, CAOM, RSTNF 3856; RST to Head of Bureau, (date illegible; presumably October 25 or 29, 1938), CAOM, RSTNF 746.

134. RF Bac Giang to Police Commissioner of Bac Giang, February 25, 1939, CAOM, RSTNF 746.

135. GGI to Heads of Local Administration (excluding Kouang-Tcheou-Wan), September 15, 1938, CAOM, RSTNF 746.

136. RST to Director of Bureau, January 3, 1938, CAOM, RSTNF 746.

137. "Note pour M. le chef de bureau," October 25, 1938, CAOM, RSTNF 746.

138. Joyeux and Virgitti, "Le péril vénérien," 30–32.

139. GGI Jules Brevié to Heads of Local Administration, April 11, 1939, CAOM, RSTNF 746.

140. RST, Decree of May 22, 1939, CAOM, RSTNF 746; "Nhà cô đào ở các xóm không được chứa quan viên ở lại qua đêm nữa!," *Việt Báo*, September 29, 1939.

141. RST, Decree of May 22, 1939, CAOM, RSTNF 746; "Một việc cải cách nhân đạo: Quan Thống-sứ Bắc Kỳ đã ký nghị định về luật lệ của các nhà hát ả đào và tiệm khiêu vũ," *Trung Hòa Báo*, May 30, 1939.

142. "Thái Bình: Chị em xóm Vũ Tiên gửi bức thư ngỏ cho ông hội Thiều," *Việt Báo*, August 30, 1939.

143. "Bốn quan viên cố ngủ lấy một đêm cuối cùng nữa ở nhà ả đào để sáng ngày ra gây thành một tấn náo kịch," *Việt Báo*, November 24, 1939.

144. "Hải Phong: Lại một nhà cô đầu nữa bị truy-tố chứa quan viên ngủ lại đêm," *Đông Pháp*, January 5, 1940; "Hưng Yên: Các nhà hát đã được lệnh không được để quan viên ngủ đêm," *Tin Mới*, July 8, 1940.

145. "Vì muốn bài trừ bệnh hoa liễu nên các cô đào phải khám bệnh," *Đông Pháp*, August 13, 1940 "Thanh Hoa: Các cô-đào phải khám bệnh, đã khám 21 cô trong tám nhà hát, 18 cô có bệnh," *Việt Báo*, August 13, 1940.

146. "Cô đào ra đường kéo khách, 4 nhà hát bị đóng cửa," *Đông Pháp*, July 30, 1942.

147. "Confidential," de Pereyra to RST, February 24, 1944, VNNA 1, MH 2596.

148. "Tại tòa án, Hanoi: Quyến dũ gái vị thành niên," *Việt Báo*, August 30, 1940.

149. "Nam Định: Vì làm mất một món khách, một cô đầu rượu bị vùi hoa dập liễu," *Thông Tin*, August 13, 1941.

150. "Ba mụ đàn bà bị bắt về tội dỗ gái vị thành niên," *Tin Mới*, November 19, 1941.

151. "Bốn quan viên cố ngủ lấy một đêm cuối cùng nữa ở nhà ả đào để sáng ngày ra gây thành một tấn náo kịch," *Việt Báo*, November 24, 1939.

152. "Hưng Yên: Các nhà hát đã được lệnh không được để quan viên ngủ đêm," *Tin Mới*, July 8, 1940.

153. "Nhà cô đào ở các xóm không được chứa quan viên ở lại qua đêm nữa!," *Việt Báo*, September 29, 1939.

154. "Thái Nguyên: Cô đào vẫn được tiếp khách đánh trống đến 12 giờ," *Việt Báo*, 1939.

155. "Thái Bình: Chị em xóm Vũ Tiên gửi bức thư ngỏ cho ông hội Thiều," *Việt Báo*, August 30, 1939.

156. "Ý kiến của chị Hoàng Liên Bích, Ngã Tư sở," *Thông Tin*, April 25, 1943.

6. Taxi Dancers

1. Joyeux and Virgitti, *Le péril vénérien*, 15.

2. The most thorough study of the modernist movement is Martina Thucnhi Nguyen's work on Tự Lực Văn Đòan "The Self-Reliant Literary Group (Tự lực văn đòan): Colonial Modernism in Vietnam, 1932–1941."

3. Joyeux and Virgitti, *Le péril vénérien*, 15–16.

4. Although the trend was frequently refered to as "Europeanization," a more accurate description would be "Westernization," as many of the trends in question came not only from Europe but also from the United States or Argentina.

5. Vũ Trọng Phụng, *Làm đĩ*, 6.

6. By the 1930s, suits were the norm for urban middle-class men; peasants and the poor maintained traditional Vietnamese clothing. Nguyễn Văn Ký, *La société vietnamienne*, 244–47.

7. Nguyen, "Wearing Modernity," 109.

8. The most notable and enduring change was the new Lemur tunic, a variation on the traditional *áo dài*. Though influenced by European styles, it was a purely Vietnamese fashion statement; French women never wore it. Nguyen, 85–86, 100.

9. Tân Khách, "Gái mới," *Phong Hoá*, July 21, 1933.

10. Cô Ngã, "Mốt" *Vịt Đực*, August 17, 1938.

11. Nguyên Xuân Hiên, "Betel-Chewing in Vietnam," 504–7; McLeod and Nguyen, *Culture and Customs of Vietnam*, 129; Nguyễn Văn Ký, *La société vietnamienne*, 233–34.

12. Modern Girl Around the World Research Group, "The Modern Girl around the World: A Research Agenda and Preliminary Findings," 245–94. On modern girls: Peiss, "Girls Lean Back Everywhere," 347–53; Lewis, *Cities in Motion*, 246–52; Healey, "Modernity, Identity, and Constructions," 96–121; Ikeya, *Refiguring Women*, 96–119.

13. Thao Thao, "Gái Lục Sì . . . ," *Việt Báo*, February 15–16, 1937.

14. "Phong Trào 'Theo Mới,'" *Phụ Nữ Tân Văn*, March 22, 1934.

15. McHale, "Printing and Power," 189; Henchy, "Vietnamese New Women," 133.

16. McHale, "Printing and Power," 189.

17. Vũ Trọng Phụng, *Lục Xì*, 135.

18. Henchy, "Vietnamese New Women," 133.

19. The term *giang hồ* refers to people who were independent of their families or, by the twentieth century, social butterflies. The term had positive connotations when describing men as adventurers but carried a negative connotation for women, as society expected them to remain with their family.

20. Ng Vương, "Gái giang-hồ: những người ấy chỉ đáng thương hại," *Đông Pháp*, November 2, 1940.

21. Thao Thao, "Gái Lục Sì . . . ," *Việt Báo*, February 15–16, 1937.

22. Lewis, *Cities in Motion*, 232; Gibbs, "West's Songs, Our Songs," 74.

23. Gibbs, "The West's Songs, Our Songs," 64.

24. Atkins, *Blue Nippon*, 59; Ambaras, *Bad Youth*, 160; "Variété: Les salles de danse à Changhai," *L'éveil économique de l'Indochine*, June 21, 1931.

25. Wakeman., *Policing Shanghai, 1927–1937*, 108.

26. Field, *Shanghai's Dancing World*; Field, "Selling Souls in Sin City," 107.

27. Lewis, *Cities in Motion*, 236–38.

28. Lewis, 236–38.

29. Lewis, 236–38.

30. E.g., in 1929, Hanoi's famous L'Hôtel du Coq d'Or was reconstructed to include a dance hall that was popular among Europeans. "La reconstruction d'un grand hôtel de Hanoi: L'Hôtel du Coq d'Or," *L'éveil économique de l'Indochine*, June 30, 1929; Joyeux and Virgitti, *Le péril vénérien*, 13.

31. Tuy-Tinh, "Tôi nhảy, chị nhảy, chúng ta nhảy . . . ," *Hà Thành Ngọ Báo*, September 30, 1933; Trần Văn Lý, "Cái Hại Khiêu-Vũ," *Trung Hoà Báo*, June 19, 1937; Gibbs, "Điệu Rumba trên dòng Cửu Long."

32. Tuy-Tinh, "Tôi nhảy, chị nhảy, chúng ta nhảy . . . ," *Hà Thành Ngọ Báo*, September 30, 1933.

33. "Hơn 30 vũ nữ Trung Hoa bị đuổi về Tầu," *Ngọ Báo*, June 16, 1936.

34. For the case of Japan, see Atkins, *Blue Nippon*, 73.

35. Joyeux and Virgitti, *Le péril vénérien*, 16; Vũ Trọng Phụng, *Lục Xì*, 122–28; Marcel Piere and Bernard Joyeux, "Contribution à l'étude des maladies vénériennes au Camp de Tong (Tonkin) et plus spécialement dans l'effectif Européen," 1938, VNNA 1, MH 2593.

36. Joyeux and Virgitti, *Le péril vénérien*, 21, 26; Nguyễn Văn Ký, *La société vietnamienne*, 296.

37. This is an interesting reversal of the American trend, where the need for extra income led dance school owners to sell dance turns, which ultimately developed into dance halls.

38. Joyeux and Virgitti, *Le péril vénérien*, 21, 26; Nguyễn Văn Ký, *La société vietnamienne*, 296.

39. Trọng Lang, *Hà Nội lầm than*, 30; Joyeux and Virgitti, *Le péril vénérien*, 15.

40. From Rigal, November 25, 1939, VNNA 1, MH 2954; Joyeux and Virgitti, *Le péril vénérien*, 26.

41. "Các nhà cô đầu và tiệm nhảy có lẽ không được chứa đàn ông ngủ đêm," *Đông Pháp*, March 29, 1939.

42. Xuân Chào, "Gặp Đâu Nói Đấy: Giảm thuế "nhẩy" tăng giá diện," *Thời Vụ Báo*, February 22, 1938.

43. "Hanoi: Giảm thuế cho các tiệm khiêu vũ," *Trung Hoà Báo*, March 3, 1938.

44. "Rapport d'inspection du 28 avril au 1 mai et du 4 au 6 mai 1943, Municipalité de Haiphong," CAOM, RSTNF 1387.

45. Vũ Trọng Phụng, *Lục Xì*, 109–10, 122–28.

46. Joyeux and Virgitti, *Le péril vénérien*, 16.

47. Vũ Trọng Phụng, *Lục Xì*, 127–28.

48. Vũ Trọng Phụng, 122.

49. Trọng Lang, *Hà Nội lầm than*, 40, 46.

50. Joyeux and Virgitti, *Le péril vénérien*, 16.

51. Joyeux and Virgitti, 21.

52. Vũ Trọng Phụng, *Lục Xì*, 126–27.

53. Joyeux and Virgitti, *Le péril vénérien*, 26; Nguyễn Văn Ký, *La société vietnamienne*, 296.

54. Joyeux and Virgitti, *Le péril vénérien*, 16.

55. "Cuộc đại náo trong một tiệm nhảy ở Khâm Thiên," *Đông Pháp*, June 26, 1939. When used for a woman, the word "đào" itself has its etymological origin in a historical singer's name. During the colonial period, "đào" specifically referred to ả đào singers. Today "đào" can be used as either an insult to women—not limited to prostitution or singing—or as a term of endearment.

56. Trọng Lang, *Hà Nội lầm than*, 14.

57. "Các chủ nhà Khiêu vũ ở phố Khâm thiên xin cho lui giờ nhẩy đến 3 giờ sáng," *Việt Báo*, November 3, 1939.

58. "Bước chân dịp dàn (Bước chân nhịp nhàng) xuyên qua mấy tiệm khiêu vũ," *Ngày Nay*, February 20, 1935.

59. "Đêm qua . . . Một người đi khiêu vũ bị hai người lính đánh trong nhà Etoile Dancing," *Hà Thành Ngọ Báo*, April 16, 1934. A similar model was seen in Japanese dance halls. Atkins, *Blue Nippon*, 69.

60. Piere and Joyeux, "Contribution à l'étude des maladies vénériennes," 1938, VNNA 1, MH 2593.

61. Nguyễn Đình Lạp, "Thanh niên trụy lạc," 212.

62. Indeed, Filipino musicians brought American music all over Southeast Asia. Gibbs, "West's Songs, Our Songs," 74.

63. Gibbs, 68.

64. See reference in J. Leiba, "Một thiếu nữ ở Hà Thành," in Phan Trọng Thưởng, Nguyễn Cừ, Nguyễn Hữu Sơn, *Phóng Sự Việt Nam, 1932-1945*, vol. 2, 1224, and Trọng Lang, *Hà Nội lầm than*, 52.

65. Trọng Lang, *Hà Nội lầm than*, 14.

66. Nguyễn Đình Lạp, "Thanh niên trụy lạc," 214, 212.

67. Bạch Đinh, "Những tiệm nhảy ở trước cửa Bồ Đề," 1239–41.

68. Piere and Joyeux, "Contribution à l'étude des maladies vénériennes," 1938, VNNA 1, MH 2593.

69. Trọng Lang, *Hà Nội lầm than*, 17.

70. Nguyễn Đình Lạp, "Thanh niên trụy lạc," 212.

71. Nguyễn Đình Lạp, 213.

72. E.g., see "Cuộc đại náo trong một tiệm nhảy ở Khâm Thiên," *Đông Pháp*, June 26, 1939.

73. Joyeux and Virgitti, *Le péril vénérien*, 14.

74. Joyeux and Virgitti, 16.

75. Trọng Lang, *Hà Nội lầm than*, 25.

76. "Tại Etoile Dancing" *Hà Thành Ngọ Báo*, March 20, 1934.

77. "Đêm qua . . . Một người đi khiêu vũ bị hai người lính đánh trong nhà Etoile Dancing," *Hà Thành Ngọ Báo*, April 16, 1934.

78. "Extrait du rapport journalier de la police municipal de Haiphong du 15 au 16 juin (1936)," CAOM, RSTNF 3856.

79. "Cuộc đại náo trong một tiệm nhảy ở Khâm Thiên," *Đông Pháp*, June 26, 1939.

80. "Một cô gái nhảy bị thưa về tội quyến rũ chồng người và còn hàng-hung đánh vợ người nữa," *Đông Pháp*, July 28, 1939.

81. "Một người Hoa-kiều bị lính Tây đánh ở tiệm nhảy," *Đông Pháp*, July 9, 1938.

82. "Thất vọng vì tình một cô vũ nữ nhảy xuống sông Tam bạc," *Tin Mới*, July 17, 1940.

83. Trọng Lang, *Hà Nội lầm than*, 25.

84. Police Commissioner to Mayor Hanoi, August 22, 1922, VNNA 1, MH 289; Piere and Joyeux, "Contribution à l'étude des maladies vénériennes," 1938, VNNA 1, MH 2593.

85. Piere and Joyeux, "Contribution à l'étude des maladies vénériennes," 1938, VNNA 1, MH 2593.

86. Trọng Lang, *Hà Nội lầm than*, 20.

87. Piere and Joyeux, "Contribution à l'étude des maladies vénériennes," 1938, VNNA 1, MH 2593.

88. "Rapport d'inspection du 28 avril au 1 mai et du 4 au 6 mai 1943, Municipalité de Haiphong," CAOM, RSTNF 1387.

89. "Ông Ngô Quốc-Lâm thưa cô Xuyến, chủ một tiệm nhảy ở Haiphong, về tội dỗ con gái ông đi làm 'gái nhảy,'" *Ngọ Báo*, February 11, 1935; "Một Chuyện Ngắn: Để Viết Hà Nội Lầm Than, Cũng một lối về phóng sự truy lạc," *Thông Tin*, July 18, 1943.

90. Trọng Lang, *Hà Nội lầm than*, 16.

91. Leiba, "Một thiếu nữ ở Hà Thành (Đời thực của một cô gái sống một mình giữa cảnh phồn hoa gió bụi)," 1224.

92. Trọng Lang, *Hà Nội lầm than*, 15.

93. D. Thiều-Tước, "Mai Vũ-Nữ," *Ngọ Báo*, April 5, 1936.

94. "Một tiểu thư trốn cảnh gia đình để đi làm gái nhảy bị lừa hết cả tiền bạc và tư trang gần 1.000$00," *Việt Báo*, October 20, 1939.

95. Leiba, "Một Khúc 'Hà Mãn Tử não nùng,"1234; Leiba, "Một thiếu nữ ở Hà Thành (Đời thực của một cô gái sống một mình giữa cảnh phồn hoa gió bụi)," 1223-31.

96. Trọng Lang, *Hà Nội lầm than*, 40.

97. Trọng Lang, "Để Viết Hanoi Lầm Than (1937)," *Thông Tin*, August 15, 1943, 2, 3.

98. Trọng Lang, "Để Viết Hanoi Lầm Than: Một Mối U Tình, Hay Là Quả Cam Thối!," *Thông Tin*, August 1, 1943, 3, 4.

99. Trọng Lang, *Hà Nội lầm than*, 38.

100. Trọng Lang, 19.

101. Trọng Lang, 31.

102. "Bị bí kế sinh nhai, cô Tâm đành phải trở về nghề cũ làm gái nhảy," *Đông Pháp*, March 10, 1940.

103. Trọng Lang, *Hà Nội lầm than*, 33, 45.

104. "Ông Ngô Quốc Lâm thưa cô Xuyến, chủ một tiệm nhảy ở Haiphong, về tội dỗ con gái ông đi làm "gái nhảy," *Ngọ Báo*, February 11, 1935.

105. "Hai chú cháu dỗ gái vị thanh-niên làm nghề mại dâm đã bị bắt," Đông Pháp, August 12, 1938.

106. Trọng Lang, *Hà Nội lầm than*, 24.

107. "Ông Ngô Quốc-Lâm thưa cô Xuyến, chủ một tiệm nhảy ở Haiphong, về tội dỗ con gái ông đi làm 'gái nhảy,'" *Ngọ Báo*, February 11, 1935.

108. Leiba, "Một thiếu nữ ở Hà Thành (Đời thực của một cô gái sống một mình giữa cảnh phồn hoa gió bụi)," 1223-31.

109. Trọng Lang, *Hà Nội lầm than*, 18.

110. "Nam Định: Hai chủ nhà khiêu vũ với hai vũ nữ ra sở Cẩm," *Trung Hoà Báo*, May 6, 1936.

111. "Mấy cô gái nhảy vay tiền trước của chủ rồi "nhẩy" đi mất," *Đông Pháp*, January 10, 1937

112. "Mấy cô gái nhảy vay tiền trước của chủ rồi "nhẩy" đi mất."

113. Trọng Lang, *Hà Nội lầm than*, 20.

114. Trọng Lang, 21, 22, 27; Leiba, "Một thiếu nữ ở Hà Thành (Đời thực của một cô gái sống một mình giữa cảnh phồn hoa gió bụi)," 1223-31.

115. Leiba, "Một Khúc 'Hà Mãn Tử' não nùng,"1234.

116. "Có phải chủ tiệm nhảy Fééric không trả tiền lương cho vũ nữ không?," *Ngọ Báo*, May 5, 1936.

117. Trọng Lang, *Hà Nội lầm than*, 30, 25-26.

118. Trọng Lang, 64.

119. Trọng Lang, 21.

120. "Ông Ngô Quốc-Lâm thưa cô Xuyến, chủ một tiệm nhảy ở Haiphong, về tội dỗ con gái ông đi làm 'gái nhảy,'" *Ngọ Báo*, February 11, 1935.

121. "Nam Định: Hai chủ nhà khiêu vũ với hai vũ nữ ra sở Cẩm," *Trung Hoà Báo*, May 6, 1936.

122. "Ông Ngô Quốc-Lâm thưa cô Xuyến, chủ một tiệm nhảy ở Haiphong, về tội dỗ con gái ông đi làm 'gái nhảy,'" *Ngọ Báo*, February 11, 1935.

123. "Nam Định: Hai chủ nhà khiêu vũ với hai vũ nữ ra sở Cẩm," *Trung Hoà Báo*, May 6, 1936.

124. Trọng Lang, *Hà Nội lầm than*, 20.

125. "Ông Ngô Quốc-Lâm thưa cô Xuyến, chủ một tiệm nhảy ở Haiphong, về tội dỗ con gái ông đi làm 'gái nhảy,'" *Ngọ Báo*, February 11, 1935.

126. "Có phải chủ tiệm nhảy Fééric không trả tiền lương cho vũ nữ không?," *Ngọ Báo*, May 5, 1936; "Về vụ vũ nữ Hoà kiện ông chủ tiệm Fééric," *Hà Thành Ngọ Báo*, May 14, 1936.

127. "Các nhà cô đầu và tiệm nhảy có lẽ không được chứa đàn ông ngủ đêm," *Đông Pháp*, March 29, 1939.

128. Trọng Lang, *Hà Nội lầm than*, 14, 64.

129. "Các nhà cô đầu và tiệm nhảy có lẽ không được chứa đàn ông ngủ đêm," *Đông Pháp*, March 29, 1939.

130. Trọng Lang, *Hà Nội lầm than*, 21.

131. Trọng Lang, 21, 28, 34.

132. Trọng Lang, 35.

133. Trọng Lang, 14, 20, 22, 24.

134. Bạch Đinh, "Những tiệm nhảy ở trước cửa Bồ Đề," 1240.

135. Trọng Lang, *Hà Nội lầm than*, 16.

136. Trọng Lang, 21.

137. Trọng Lang, 55.

138. "Một tiểu thư trốn cảnh gia đình để đi làm gái nhảy bị lừa hết cả tiền bạc và tư trang gần 1.000$00," *Việt Báo*, October 20, 1939.

139. Trọng Lang, *Hà Nội lầm than*, 16.

140. D. Thiêu-Tước, "Mai Vũ-Nữ," *Ngọ Báo*, April 5, 1936.

141. D. Thiêu-Tước was an alias for Dương Thiệu Tước, who would go on to become a famous songwriter and classical guitar teacher. D. Thiêu-Tước, "Mai Vũ-Nữ," *Ngọ Báo*, April 5, 1936.

142. Trọng Lang, *Hà Nội lầm than*, 46.

143. Trọng Lang, 18.

144. Nguyễn Đình Lạp, "Than niên trụy lạc," 213, 224.

145. D. Thiêu-Tước, "Mai Vũ-Nữ," *Ngọ Báo*, April 12, 1936; Trọng Lang, *Hà Nội lầm than*, 37.

146. Trọng Lang, *Hà Nội lầm than*, 28.

147. Trọng Lang, 58.

148. Trọng Lang, 55, 58.

149. Taxi dancers with three or four children only earned five dong per month. Trọng Lang, *Hà Nội lầm than*, 34, 49–50, 55–57.

150. Trần Văn Lý, "Cái Hại Khiêu-Vũ," *Trung Hoà Báo*, June 19, 1937. On literature, see "Hai con đường," *Thời Vụ Báo*, July 18, 1939; Trần Văn Lý, "Cái hại khiêu-vũ," *Trung hoà báo*, June 19, 1937; Trần Văn Lý, "Cái Hại Khiêu-Vũ," *Trung Hoà Báo*, June 19, 1937; and Bạch Đinh, "Những tiệm nhảy ở trước cửa Bồ Đề," 1239–43.

151. "Cơ quan bài trừ hoa liễu," *Việt Báo*, August 18–19, 1936.

152. Trọng Lang, *Hà Nội lầm than*, 13.

153. Hà Thành is another name for Hanoi. Leiba, "Một thiếu nữ ở Hà Thành (Đời thực của một cô gái sống một mình giữa cảnh phồn hoa gió bụi)," 1223–31.

154. Vũ Trọng Phụng, *Làm đĩ*.

155. This reportage was originally published in *Báo Ích Hữu* newspaper in 1938. Nguyễn Đình Lạp, "Than niên trụy lạc," 203–92.

156. Trọng Lang, *Hà Nội lầm than*, 25.

157. Trọng Lang, "Một Chuyện Ngắn: Để Viết Hà Nội Lầm Than, Cùng một lối về phóng sự truy lạc," *Thông Tin*, July 18, 1943.

158. "Note pour M. le Chef de Bureau," October 25, 1938, CAOM, RSTNF 746.

159. Joyeux and Virgitti, *Le péril vénérien*, 16–17.

160. Piere and Joyeux, "Contribution à l'étude des maladies vénériennes," 1938, VNNA 1, MH 2593.

161. Trọng Lang, *Hà Nội lầm than*, 28.

162. "Hanoi: Giảm thuế cho các tiệm khiêu vũ," *Trung Hoà Báo*, March 3, 1938.

163. The decree was announced in March 1939 and approved by the resident superior of Tonkin on May 22, 1939. "Các nhà cô đầu và tiệm nhảy có lẽ không được chứa đàn ông ngủ đêm," *Đông Pháp*, March 29, 1939; "Quan Thống Sứ đã ký nghị định về luật-lệ của nhà hát ả đào và tiệm khiêu-vũ," *Đông Pháp*, May 27, 1939; "Các chủ nhà Khiêu vũ ở phố Khâm thiên xin cho lui giờ nhẩy đến 3 giờ sáng," *Việt Báo*, November 3, 1939.

164. "Một việc cải cách nhân đạo: Quan Thống-sứ Bắc Kỳ đã ký nghị định về luật lệ của các nhà hát ả đào và tiệm khiêu vũ," *Trung Hòa Báo*, May 30, 1939.

165. "Các nhà cô đầu và tiệm nhảy có lẽ không được chứa đàn ông ngủ đêm," *Đông Pháp*, March 29, 1939.

166. "Các nhà cô đầu và tiệm nhảy có lẽ không được chứa đàn ông ngủ đêm," *Đông Pháp*, March 29, 1939; "Quan Thống Sứ đã ký nghị định về luật-lệ của nhà hát ả đào và tiệm khiêu-vũ," *Đông Pháp*, May 27, 1939; "Một việc cải cách nhân đạo: Quan Thống-sứ Bắc Kỳ đã ký nghị định về luật lệ của các nhà hát ả đào và tiệm khiêu vũ," *Trung Hòa Báo*, May 30, 1939.

167. "Quan Thống Sứ đã ký nghị định về luật-lệ của nhà hát ả đào và tiệm khiêu-vũ," *Đông Pháp*, May 27, 1939.

168. "Các nhà cô đầu và tiệm nhảy có lẽ không được chứa đàn ông ngủ đêm," *Đông Pháp*, March 29, 1939.

169. Rhacel Salazar Parreñas found a similar effect in her study of Philippine entertainers working in Tokyo in the early twenty-first century. In enacting paternalistic laws designed to protect Filipinas from sex trafficking, the Japanese and Philippine governments inadvertently forced Filipinas into debt to pay for the middlemen protection. Parreñas, *Illicit Flirtations*; "Các nhà cô đầu và tiệm nhảy có lẽ không được chứa đàn ông ngủ đêm," *Đông Pháp*, March 29, 1939.

170. "Nhà cô đào ở các xóm không được chứa quan viên ở lại qua đêm nữa!," *Việt Báo*, September 29, 1939.

171. "Các chủ nhà Khiêu vũ ở phố Khâm thiên xin cho lui giờ nhẩy đến 3 gời sáng," *Việt Báo*, November 3, 1939.

172. "Các Tiệm nhảy và nhà hát ở Khâm Thiên, Vạn Thái . . . đã phải tuân đúng thể lệ mới ngày 22 Mai 1939," *Việt Báo*, March 28, 1940.

Conclusion

1. Camiscioli, "Coercion and Choice."

2. Tạo Văn and Moto Furuta, *Nạn Đói Năm 1945*.

3. Gibbs, "West's Songs, Our Songs," 73.

4. Brothels were not eliminated until 1946. Registration of prostitutes ended in 1960. Miller, "'Romance of Regulation,'" 2.

5. When the communists took over Shanghai in 1949, they shut down plea-sure industries, including dance halls, claiming a campaign for "healthy enter-tainment." Field, *Shanghai's Dancing World*, 16. For an excellent study on DRV cultural politics, see Ninh, *A World Transformed*.

6. Marr, *Vietnam*, 353.

7. Ngọc, interview with author, May 4, 2013, Hanoi.

8. Ngọc, interview with author, May 4, 2013, Hanoi. Ả đào music was present in Saigon through the end of the US-Vietnam War because of the northerners who had moved down, but it was not associated there with clandestine prostitution.

9. Ngọc, interview with author, May 5, 2013, Hanoi. As Barley Norton has shown, the ca trù music revival of the post–Đổi Mới era is closely related to changes in Vietnamese historical memory and patriotic nostalgia. Norton, "Singing the Past," 29–30. Most recently, Nguyễn Kiều Anh, an eighteen-year-old contestant on *Vietnam's Got Talent*, a television show based on the model of *American Idol*, sang an extract from "Truyện Kiều" in ca trù form. Yến Tiểu, "Thiếu nữ 18 tuổi hát ca trù ấn tượng tại Got Talent," *VN Express/Báo Nhanh Việt Nam*, December 17, 2012, http://giaitri.vnexpress.net/tin-tuc/truyen-hinh/thieu-nu-18-tuoi-hat-ca-tru-an-tuong-tai-got-talent-2402987.html.

10. Sun, "Where the Girls Are," 66–87.

11. Stur, *Beyond Combat*, 57–61.

12. Sun, "Where the Girls Are," 72.

13. Nguyễn-võ Thu-hương, *Ironies of Freedom*, 4.

14. Nguyễn-võ Thu-hương, 4.

BIBLIOGRAPHY

Archives

Centre des Archives Nationales d'Outre Mer, Aix-en-Provence, France
Vietnam National Archives, Center 1, Hanoi, Vietnam
Vietnam National Archives, Center 2, Ho Chi Minh City, Vietnam
Vietnam National Archives, Center 4, Đà Lạt, Vietnam

Newspapers

Báo Ích Hữu
Đông Pháp Thời Báo
Đuốc Nhò Nam
Hà Thành Ngọ Báo
Le Courrier Saïgonnais
Ngày Nay
Ngọ Báo
Phong Hoá
Phụ Nữ Tân Văn
Quốc Gia Nhật Báo
Thanh Niên Đông Pháp
Thời Vụ Báo
Thông Tin
Tin Mới
Trung Hoà Báo
Trung Hoà Nhật Báo
Trung Lập Báo
Văn Minh
Việt Báo
Việt Cường
Việt Dân Tuần Báo
Vịt Đực
Zân Báo

Published Sources

Aalbers, Manuel B., and Magdalena Sabat. "Remaking a Landscape of Prostitution: The Amsterdam Red Light District." *City* 16, no. 1–2 (February–April 2012): 112–28. https://doi.org/10.1080/13604813.2012.662372.

Addiss, Stephen. "Hat A Dao, the Sung Poetry of North Vietnam." *Journal of the American Oriental Society* 93 (1973): 18–31. https://doi.org/10.2307/600514.

Aldrich, Robert. *Greater France: A History of French Overseas Expansion*. New York: Palgrave, 1996.

Ambaras, David. *Bad Youth: Juvenile Delinquency and the Politics of Everyday Life in Modern Japan*. Berkeley: University of California Press, 2006.

Andaya, Barbara Watson. "From Temporary Wife to Prostitute: Sexuality and Economic Change in Early Modern Southeast Asia." *Journal of Women's History* 9, no. 4 (1998): 11–34. https://doi.org/10.1353/jowh.2010.0225.

Andrews, Bridie. *The Making of Modern Chinese Medicine, 1850–1960*. Vancouver: University of British Columbia Press, 2014.

Ariès, Philippe, and André Béjin. *Western Sexuality: Practice and Precept in Past and Present Times*. New York: Basil Blackwell, 1985.

Atkins, E. Taylor. *Blue Nippon: Authenticating Jazz in Japan*. Durham, NC: Duke University Press, 2001.

Au, Sokhieng. *Mixed Medicines: Health and Culture in French Colonial Cambodia*. Chicago: University of Chicago Press, 2011.

Bạch Đinh. "Những tiệm nhảy ở trước cửa Bồ Đề." In Phan Trọng Thưởng, Nguyễn Cừ, and Nguyễn Hữu Sơn, *Phóng Sự Việt Nam*, vol. 2, 1239–41.

Ballantyne, Tony, and Antoinette Burton, eds. *Bodies in Contact: Rethinking Colonial Encounters in World History*. Durham, NC: Duke University Press, 2005.

Bard, Christine. *Les femmes dans la société française au 20e siècle*. Paris: Armand Colin, 2004.

Barrett, Tracy C. "Transnational Webs: Overseas Chinese Economic and Political Networks in Colonial Vietnam, 1870–1945." PhD diss., Cornell University, 2007.

Baudrit, André. *Bétail humain: La traite des femmes et des enfants en Indochine et en Chine de sud suivi de onze documents sur l'esclavage (1860–1940)*. Paris: Connaissances et Savoirs, 2008.

——. "Bétail humain: Rapt, vente, infanticide dans l'Indochine française et dans la Chine du sud." In *Bétail humaine: La traite des femmes et des enfants en Indochine française et en Chine du sud, suivi de onze documents sur l'dsclavage (1860–1940)*, edited by Pierre Le Roux and Nicolas Lainez, 97–130. Paris: Connaissances et Savoirs, 2008.

Bell, Shannon. *Reading and Writing the Prostitute Body*. Bloomington: Indiana University Press, 1994.

Bernheimer, Charles. *Figures of Ill Repute: Representing Prostitution in Nineteenth-Century France*. Durham, NC: Duke University Press, 1997.

Bezançon, Pascale. *Une colonisation éducatrice? L'expérience indochinoise (1860–1945)*. Paris: L'Harmattan, 2002.

Bilange, Francois, Charles Fourniau, and Alain Ruscio, eds. *Rapport de mission en Indochine 1er Janvier–14 Mars 1937*. Paris: L'Harmattan, 1994.

Billingsley, Phil. *Bandits in Republican China.* Stanford, CA: Stanford University Press, 1988.

Blanchard, Pascal, and Sandrine Lemaire, eds. *Culture coloniale: La France conquise par son empire, 1871-1931.* Paris: Éditions Autrement, 2003.

Bodros, Paul. "Le péril vénérien et la prostitution à Haiphong," *Bulletin de la Société médico-chirurgicale de l'Indochine* (June 1930): 676–83.

Boittin, Jennifer Anne. "Two Stories of Gabrielle or Passion, Mobility and the Governance of White Prestige in Colonial Senegal." In *Histories of French Sexuality: Enlightenment to the Present,* edited by Nina Kushner and Andrew Israel Ross (pages forthcoming). Lincoln: University of Nebraska Press, 2020.

Boris, Eileen, and Heather Berg. "Protecting Virtue, Erasing Labor: Historical Responses to Trafficking." In *Human Trafficking Reconsidered: Rethinking the Problem, Envisioning New Solutions,* edited by Kimberly Kay Hoang and Rhacel Salazar Parreñas, 19–40. New York: International Debate Education Association, 2014.

Bouvier, E. J., and M. V. Riou. *Instruction technique sur le traitement des maladies vénériennes.* Hanoi: Imprimerie Taupin, 1941.

Brocheux, Pierre. *Une histoire économique du Viet Nam 1850-2007.* Paris: Indes Savantes, 2009.

Brocheux, Pierre, and Daniel Hémery. *Indochina: An Ambiguous Colonization, 1858-1954.* Berkeley: University of California Press, 2009.

Bullough, Vern, and Bonnie Bullough. *Women and Prostitution: A Social History.* Amherst, NY: Prometheus Books, 1987.

Camiscioli, Elisa. "Coercion and Choice: The 'Traffic in Women' between France and Argentina in Early Twentieth Century." *French Historical Studies* 42, no. 3 (August 2019): 483–507. https://doi.org/10.1215/00161071-7558357.

——. *Reproducing the French Race: Immigration, Intimacy, and Embodiment in the Early Twentieth Century.* Durham, NC: Duke University Press, 2009.

Cao Tự Thanh, and Lê Thị Hoàng Mai, eds. *Phụ nữ Việt Nam trong lịch sử tập 2: Phụ nữ Việt nam thời Pháp thuộc (1862-1945).* Hanoi: NXB Phụ Nữ, 2012.

Charbonnier, Roger. "Contribution à l'étude de la prophylaxie antivénérienne à Hanoi." PhD diss., Faculté de médecine de Paris, 1938.

Cherry, Haydon Leslie. "Down and Out in Saigon: A Social History of the Poor in a Colonial City, 1860-1940." PhD diss., Yale University, 2011.

Congrès international pour la protection de l'enfance, section IX: Comité colonial national de l'enfance. Paris: Imprimerie Beurq, 1933.

Conklin, Alice L. *A Mission to Civilize: The Republican Idea of Empire in France and West Africa, 1895-1930.* Palo Alto, CA: Stanford University Press, 1997.

Coppin, Henri, "La prostitution, la police des mœurs et le dispensaire municipal à Hanoi." *Bulletin de la Société médico-chirurgicale de l'Indochine* (June 1925): 243–71.

Corbin, Alain. *Women for Hire: Prostitution and Sexuality in France after 1850.* Cambridge, MA: Harvard University Press, 1996.

Đặng Thị Vân Chi. "Báo chí tiếng Việt và vấn đế mại dâm dưới thời Pháp thuộc." *Nghiên cứu Gia Đình và Giới* 1 (2008): 34–42. http://chuyencuachi.blogspot.com/2011/04/bao-chi-tieng-viet-va-van-e-mai-dam.html.

——. *Vấn đề phụ nữ trên báo chí tiếng Việt trước năm 1945.* Hanoi: NXB Khoa Học Xã
    Hội, 2007.

Dang Xuân Duong and Lê Hông Kê. "La population de Hanoi." In Gubry, *Population
    et développement au Viêt-Nam*, 242–61.

Dao The Tuan. "La transition agraire au Vietnam comme changement
    d'institutions." In *Développement et transition vers l'économie de marché:
    Ouvrage extrait des troisième journées*, edited by Agence francophone pour
    l'enseignement supérieur et la recherche, 457–71. Québec: Éditions de
    l'Agence, 1998.

Davis, Bradley Camp. *Imperial Bandits: Outlaws and Rebels in the China-Vietnam Bor-
    derlands.* Seattle: University of Washington Press, 2017.

Délaye, Karine. "Esclavage et représentations coloniales en Indochine de la sec-
    onde moitié du XIXe au début du XXe siècle." *Outre-mer* 89, nos. 336–37
    (2002): 283–319. https://www.persee.fr/doc/outre_1631-0438_2002_num_
    89_336_3994.

Department of Railways. *An Official Guide to Eastern Asia.* Vol. 5. Tokyo: Depart-
    ment of Railways, 1920.

Đinh Xuân Lâm, ed. *Đại Cương Lịch Sử Việt Nam Tập II.* Hanoi: NXB Giáo Dục, 2000.

Đỗ Quang Hưng, ed. *Lịch Sử Báo Chí Việt Nam, 1865–1945.* Hanoi: NXB Đại Học Quốc
    Gia Hà Nội, 2000.

Doãn Kế Thiện. *Hà Nội Cũ.* Hanoi: NXB Hà Nội, 2015.

Donovan, Brian. *White Slave Crusades: Race, Gender, and Anti-Vice Activism,
    1887-1917.* Urbana: University of Illinois, 2006.

Downer, Lesley. *Women of the Pleasure Quarters: The Secret History of the Geisha.* New
    York: Broadway Books, 2001.

Dutton, George. "Advertising, Modernity, and Consumer Culture in Colonial
    Vietnam." In *The Reinvention of Distinction: Modernity and the Middle Class in
    Urban Vietnam*, edited by Van Nguyen-Marshall and Lisa B. W. Drummond,
    21–42. Dorrecht: Springer, 2012.

Dyson, Kenneth. *States, Debt, and Power: 'Saints' and 'Sinners' in European History and
    Integration.* London: Oxford University Press, 2014.

Egan, Danielle R., and Gail L. Hawkes. "Imperiled and Perilous: Exploring the His-
    tory of Childhood Sexuality." *Journal of Historical Sociology* 21, no 4 (2008):
    355–67. https://doi.org/10.1111/j.1467-6443.2008.00341.x.

Eisen Bergman, Arlene. *Femmes du Vietnam.* Paris: Éditions des femmes, 1975.

Ezra, Elizabeth. *The Colonial Unconscious: Race and Culture in Interwar France.* Ithaca,
    NY: Cornell University Press, 2000.

Feng, Jin. *The New Woman in Early 20th Century Chinese Fiction.* West Lafayette, IN:
    Purdue University Press, 2004.

Field, Andrew D. "Selling Souls in Sin City: Shanghai Singing and Dancing Host-
    esses in Print, Film, and Politics, 1920–1949." In *Cinema and Urban Culture
    in Shanghai, 1922-1943*, edited by Yingjin Zhang, 99–127. Stanford, CA: Stan-
    ford University Press, 2002.

Field, Andrew David. *Shanghai's Dancing World: Cabaret Culture and Urban Politics,
    1919-1954.* Hong Kong: Chinese University Press, 2010.

Firpo, Christina. "La traite des femmes et enfants dans le Vietnam colonial
    (1920–1940)." *Le Vingtième siècle* 120 (2013): 113–24. Retrieved from http://
    www.jstor.org/stable/42773635.

——. "Sex and Song: Clandestine Prostitution in Tonkin's A Dao Music Houses, 1920–1940." *Journal of Vietnamese Studies* 11, no. 2 (2016): 1–36. https://doi.org/10.1525/vs.2016.11.2.1.

——. *The Uprooted: Race, Childhood, and Imperialism*. Honolulu: University of Hawai'i Press, 2016.

Foucault, Michel. *The History of Sexuality: An Introduction, Vol 1*. New York: Vintage Press, 1990.

"French Indo-China: Demographic Imbalance and Colonial Policy." *Population Index* 11, no. 2 (April, 1945): 68.

Gaide, Lauriol. *Le peril vénérien en Indochine*. Hanoi: Imprimerie d'Extrême Orient, 1931.

Giang Quân. *Khâm Thiên—Gương mặt cuộc đời*. NXB Hà Nội, 1997.

Gibbs, Jason. "Điệu Rumba trên dòng Cửu Long: Bolero—một dạng ca khúc phổ thông Việt Nam," Talawas.org, September 22, 2005.

——. "The West's Songs, Our Songs: The Introduction and Adaptation of Western Popular Song in Vietnam before 1940." *Asian Music* 35, no. 1 (2003): 57–84. www.jstor.org/stable/4098472.

Goscha, Christopher. *Vietnam: A New History*. New York: Basic Books, 2016.

Gourou, Pierre Gourou. *Les paysans du Delta Tonkinois: Étude de géographie humaine*. Paris: Mouton, 1965.

Gouvernement général de l'Indochine. *Annuaire statistique de l'Indochine, 1930-1931*. Vol. 3. Hanoi: Imprimerie d'Extrême-Orient, 1932.

Grandjean, Philippe. *L'Indochine face au Japon, 1940-1945: Decoux-de Gaulle, un malentendu fatal*. Paris: L'Harmattan, 2004.

Granier, Solène. *Domestiques indochinois*. Paris: Vendémiaire, 2014.

Grendreau, Francis, Dô Tiên Dung, and Pham Dô Nhât Tân. "Les migrations internes." In Gubry, *Population et développement au Viêt-Nam*, 195–217.

Grenierboley, Dr., and Nguyen Dinh Diep. "La consultation de Kham Thien 1937 ou premier essai local de décentralisation de la lutte antivénérienne." *Bulletin de la Société médico-chirurgicale de l'Indochine* (March 1938): 299–300.

Gronewold, Sue. *Beautiful Merchandise: Prostitution in China 1860-1936*. New York: Harrington Park Press, 1985.

Gubry, Patrick, ed. *Population et développement au Viêt-Nam*. Paris: Karthala, 2000.

Guillien, Raymond. *Consultation sur le régime des entreprises de pousse-pousse à Hanoi*. Hanoi: Imprimerie G. Taupin, 1939.

Hanh, H. Hazel. "The Rickshaw Trade in Colonial Vietnam, 1883–1940." *Journal of Vietnamese Studies* 8, no. 4 (Fall 2013): 47–85. https://doi.org/0.1525/vs.2014.8.4.47.

Hardy, Andrew. *Red Hills: Migrants and the State in the Highlands of Vietnam*. Honolulu: University of Hawai'i Press, 2003.

Harms, Erik. *Saigon's Edge: On the Margins of Ho Chi Minh City*. Minneapolis: University of Minnesota Press, 2011.

Healey, Lucy. "Modernity, Identity, and Constructions of Malay Womanhood." In *Modernity and Identity: Asian Illustrations*, edited by Alberto Gomes, 96–121. Bundoora: La Trobe University Press, 1994.

Henchy, Judith. "Vietnamese New Women and the Fashioning of Modernity." In *France and "Indochina": Cultural Representations*, edited by Katherine Robson and Jennifer Yee, 121–38. Lanham, MD: Lexington Books, 2005.

Henriot, Christian. *Prostitution and Sexuality in Shanghai: A Social History 1849–1949*. Cambridge: Cambridge University Press, 2001.

Henry, Yves. *Économie agricole de l'Indochine*. Hanoi: Gouvernement général de l'Indochine, 1935.

Hershatter, Gail. *Dangerous Pleasures: Prostitution and Modernity in Twentieth Century Shanghai*. Berkeley: University of California Press, 1997.

Hill, Kim Loan. "Strangers in a Foreign Land: Vietnamese Soldiers and Workers in France during World War I." In *Vietnam: Borderless Histories*, edited by Nhung Thuyet Tran and Anthony Reid, 256–89. Madison: University of Wisconsin Press, 2006.

Hoàng Đạo Thúy. *Phố phường Hà Nội xưa*. Hà Nội: NXB Văn Hoá-Thông Tin, 2000.

Hoang, Kimberly Kay. *Dealing in Desire: Asian Ascendancy, Western Decline, and the Hidden Currencies of Global Sex Work*. Berkeley: University of California Press, 2015.

Hoang, Kimberly Kay, and Rhacel Salazar Parreñas, eds. *Human Trafficking Reconsidered: Rethinking the Problem, Envisioning New Solutions*. New York: International Debate Education Association, 2014.

Hoàng Thị Ngọc Thanh, "Người ả đào qua các tư liệu từ thế kỷ XIX đến giữa thế kỷ XX (Kỳ 8)." *Văn Hóa Nghệ An* (2012). http://www.vanhoanghean.com.vn/chuyen-muc-goc-nhin-van-hoa/nhung-goc-nhin-van-hoa/nguoi-a-dao-qua-cac-tu-lieu-tu-the-ky-xix-den-giua-the-ky-xx-ky-8.

Hội Đồng Lịch Sử Hải Phòng, ed. *Lược Khảo Đường Phố Hải Phòng*. Haiphong: NXB Hải Phòng, 1993.

Hội Đồng Lịch Sử Thành Phố, ed. *Địa Chí Hải Phòng*. Vol. 1. Haiphong: NXB Xí Nghiệp, 1990.

Ikeya, Chie. *Refiguring Women, Colonialism, and Modernity in Burma*. Honolulu: University of Hawai'i Press, 2011.

Jacobsen, Trude. "Debt Bondage in Cambodia's Past—and Implications for its Present." *Studies in Gender and Sexuality* 15, no. 1 (2014): 32–43. https://doi.org/10.1080/15240657.2014.877727.

——. *Sex Trafficking in Southeast Asia: A History of Desire, Duty, and Debt*. New York: Routledge, 2017.

Jaimeson, Neil L. *Understanding Vietnam*. Berkeley: University of California Press, 1993.

Jensen, Rolf, Donald M. Peppard Jr., and Vũ Thị Minh Thắng. *Women on the Move: Hanoi's Migrant Roving Street Vendors*. Hanoi: Women's Publishing House, 2013.

Joyeux, Bernard. "Le dispensaire antivénérien municipal et la ligue prophylactique de la ville de Hanoi." *Bulletin de la Société médico-chirurgicale de l'Indochine* (January 1937): 109–32.

——. *Le péril vénérien et la prostitution à Hanoi: État actuel—bibliographie réglementation*. Hanoi: Imprimerie d'Extrême-Orient, 1930.

Joyeux, Bernard, and Henri Virgitti. "Le péril vénérien dans la zone suburbaine de Hanoi." *Bulletin de la Société médico-chirurgicale de l'Indochine* (January 1937): 73–108.

Khoa Lịch Sử Đại học quốc Gia Hà Nội, ed. *Với Thăng Long Hà Nội*. Hanoi: NXB Thế Giới, 2011.

Lainez, Nicolas. "Human Trade in Colonial Vietnam." In *Wind over Water: Migration in an East Asian Context*, edited by David Haines, Keiko Yamanaka, Shinji Yamashita, 21–35. New York: Berghahn Books, 2015.

Langlet-Quach Thanh Tâm. "La repartition spatiale de la population." In Gubry, Patrick, *Population et développement au Viêt-Nam*, 169–93.

Lasker, Bruno. *Human Bondage in Southeast Asia*. Westport, CT: Greenwood Press, 1950.

Le Manh Hung. *The Impact of World War II on the Economy of Vietnam, 1939-1945*. London: Eastern University Press, 2004.

Lê Thị Hồng Hải. "Mại dâm và quản lý mại dâm ở Việt Nam trong thời kỳ Pháp thuộc." *Nghiên cứu Gia Đình và Giới* 4 (2013): 55–66.

Lê Thước, Vũ Tuân Sán, Vũ Văn Tỉn, Trần Huy Bá and Nguyễn Văn Minh. *Lược Sử Hà Nội*. Hanoi: NXB Văn Hóa Thông Tin, 1964.

League of Nations. *Commission d'enquête sur la traite des femmes et des enfants en Orient*. Geneva: Édition de la Société des nations, 1934.

——. *Commission of Enquiry into Traffic in Women and Children in the East*. Geneva: Édition de la Société des nations, 1932.

——. *Records of the International Conference on Traffic in Women and Children (Meetings Held from June 30th to July 5th, 1921)*. Geneva: Imprimerie Albert Kundig, 1921.

Legg, Stephen. *Prostitution and the Ends of Empire: Scale, Governmentalities, and Interwar India*. Durham, NC: Duke University Press, 2014.

Leiba, J. "Một Khúc 'Hà Mãn Tứ' não nùng." In Phan Trọng Thưởng, Nguyễn Cừ, Nguyễn Hữu Sơn, *Phóng Sự Việt Nam*, vol. 2, 1233–37.

——. "Một thiếu nữ ở Hà Thành (Đời thực của một cô gái sống một mình giữa cảnh phồn hoa gió bụi." In Phan Trọng Thưởng, Nguyễn Cừ, Nguyễn Hữu Sơn, *Phóng Sự Việt Nam*, vol. 2, 1223–31.

Leppanen, Katarina. "Movement of Women: Trafficking in the Interwar Era." *Women's Studies International Forum* 30 (2007): 523–33. https://doi.org/10.1016/j.wsif.2007.09.007.

Le Roux, Pierre, Jean Baffie, and Gilles Beullier, eds. *The Trade in Human Beings for Sex in Southeast Asia*. Bangkok: White Lotus Press, 2010.

Le Roux, Pierre, and Nicolas Lainez, eds. *Bétail humaine: La traite des femmes et des enfants en Indochine et en Chine du sud (1860-1940)*. Paris: Connaissances et savoirs, 2008.

Le Roy des Barres, A. "Les maladies vénériennes au Tonkin." *Bulletin de la Société médico-chirurgicale de l'Indochine* (April 1927): 150–67.

Lessard, Micheline. "'Cet Ignoble Trafic': The Kidnapping and Sale of Vietnamese Women and Children in French Colonial Indochina, 1873-1935." *Journal of French Colonial History* 10 (2009): 1–34. https://doi.org/10.1353/fch.0.0019.

——. *Human Trafficking in Colonial Vietnam*. London: Routledge, 2015.

Levine, Philippa, ed. *Gender and Empire*. London: Oxford University Press, 2004.

——. *Prostitution, Race, and Politics: Policing Venereal Disease in the British Empire*. New York: Routledge, 2003.

Lewis, Su Lin. *Cities in Motion: Urban Life and Cosmopolitanism in Southeast Asia, 1920-1940*. London: Cambridge University Press, 2016.

Li Tana. *Peasants on the Move: Rural-Urban Migration in the Hanoi Region.* Singapore: Institute of Southeast Asian Studies, 1996.

Limoncelli, Stephanie A. *The Politics of Trafficking: The First International Movement to Combat the Sexual Exploitation of Women.* Stanford, CA: Stanford University Press, 2010

Malarney, Shaun Kingsley. "Introduction: Vũ Trọng Phụng and the Anxieties of 'Progress.'" In *Lục Xì: Prostitution and Venereal Disease in Colonial Hanoi*, by Vũ Trọng Phụng, translated by Shaun Kingsley, 1–40. Honolulu: University of Hawai'i Press, 2011.

Marquis, Edouard. *L'oeuvre humaine de la France en Cochinchine.* Saigon: Imprimerie du Théâtre, 1936.

Marr, David G. *Vietnam: State, War, and Society (1945-1946).* Berkeley: University of California Press, 2013.

——. *Vietnamese Tradition on Trial, 1920-1945.* Berkeley: University of California Press, 1984.

Marsot, Alain G. *The Chinese Community in Vietnam under the French.* New York: Edwin Mellen Press, 1993.

Martial, J. E. "La prophylaxie des maladies vénériennes dans une garnison du Tonkin (Langson)." *Annales de médicine et de pharmacie coloniales* 35 (1937): 464–95.

Martinez, Julia. "'La Traite des Jaunes': Trafficking in Women and Children across the China Sea." In *Many Middle Passages: Forced Migration and the Making of the Modern World*, edited by E. Christopher, C. Pybus, and M. Rediker, 204–21. Berkeley: University of California Press, 2007.

McClintock, Anne. *Imperial Leather: Race, Gender and Sexuality in the Colonial Contest.* London: Routledge, 1995.

McHale, Shawn. *Print and Power: Confucianism, Communism, and Buddhism in the Making of Modern Vietnam.* Honolulu: University of Hawai'i Press, 2004.

——. "Printing and Power: Vietnamese Debates over Women's Place in Society, 1918-1934," in *Essays into Vietnamese Pasts*, edited by Keith Taylor and John Whitmore, 173–94. Ithaca, NY: Cornell University Press, 1995.

McLeod, Mark W., and Nguyen Thi Dieu. *Culture and Customs of Vietnam.* London: Greenwood Press, 2001.

Merriman, John M. *The Margins of City Life: Explorations on the French Urban Frontier, 1815-1851.* New York: Oxford University Press, 1991.

Midgley, Claire, ed. *Gender and Imperialism.* Manchester: Manchester University Press, 1998.

Miers Suzanne. *Slavery in the Twentieth Century: The Evolution of a Global Problem.* New York: Altamira Press, 2003.

Miller, Julia Christine Scriven. "'The Romance of Regulation': The Movement against State-Regulated Prostitution in France, 1871-1946." PhD diss., New York University, 2000.

Ministère des affaires étrangères de Belgique. *Documents relatifs à la répression de la traite des esclaves.* Brussels: Hayez, imprimeur des académies royales de Belgique, 1906.

Modern Girl Around the World Research Group, ed. "The Modern Girl around the World: A Research Agenda and Preliminary Findings." *Gender and History* 17: 2 (2005): 245–94. https://doi.org/10.1111/j.0953-5233.2006.00382.x

Monnais-Rousselot, Laurence. *Médecine et colonisation: L'aventure Indochinoise 1860–1939*. Paris: CNRS Éditions, 1999.

Morcom, Anna. *Illicit Worlds of Indian Dance: Cultures of Exclusion*. London: Hurst, 2013.

Morlat, Patrice. *Indochina années vingt: Le rendez-vous manqué, la politique indigène des grands commis au service de la mise en valeur*. Paris: Les Indes savantes, 2005.

——. *La répression coloniale au Vietnam: 1908–1940*. Paris: l'Harmattan, 1990.

Muller, Greg. "Prostitution and Human Trafficking for Sex in Colonial Cambodia." In *The Trade in Human Beings for Sex in Southeast Asia*, edited by Pierre Le Roux, Jean Baffie, and Gilles Beullier. Bangkok: White Lotus Press, 2010.

Murray, Alison. *Pink Fits: Sex, Subcultures and Discourses in the Asia-Pacific*. Clayton: Monash Asia Institute, 2001.

Murray, Dian. *Pirates of the South China Coast, 1790–1810*. Stanford, CA: Stanford University Press, 1987.

Murray, Martin J. *The Development of Capitalism in Colonial Indochina (1870–1940)*. Berkeley: University of California Press, 1980.

Ng Shui Meng. *The Population of Indochina: Some Preliminary Observations*. Field Report Series no. 7. Singapore: Institute of Southeast Asian Studies, 1974.

Ngô Tất Tố. *Tắt Đèn*. Hanoi: NXB Văn Học, 2006.

Ngo Vinh Long, *Before the Revolution: Vietnamese Peasants under the French*. Boston: MIT Press, 1973.

Ngo Vinh Long, Paul Grace, Susan Koff, and Nancy Nichols, eds. *Vietnamese Women in Society and Revolution, vol 1: The French Colonial Period*. Cambridge, MA: Vietnam Resource Center, 1974.

Nguyễn An Nhân. *Nam nữ bí mật chỉ nam*. Hanoi: Phu Van Duong, 1932.

Nguyễn Công Hoan. *Người Ngựa Ngựa Người: Tập truyện ngắn*. Hanoi: NXB Văn Học 2016.

Nguyễn Đình Lạp. "Thanh niên trụy lạc." In Phan Trọng Thưởng, Nguyễn Cừ, and Nguyễn Hữu Sơn, *Phóng Sự Việt Nam*, vol. 2, 203–92.

Nguyễn Du, *The Tale of Kiều: A Bilingual Edition*. Translated by Huỳnh Sanh Thông. New Haven, CT: Yale University Press, 1983.

Nguyên Hồng. *Bước đường viết văn*. Hanoi: NXB Văn Học, 1970.

Nguyễn Khánh Toàn, ed. *Lịch Sử Việt Nam, tập II, 1858–1945*. Hanoi: NXB Khoa Học Xã Hội, 2004.

Nguyen, Martina Thucnhi. "The Self-Reliant Literary Group (Tu Luc Van Doan): Colonial Modernism in Vietnam, 1932–1941." PhD diss., University of California, Berkeley, 2012.

——. "Wearing Modernity: Lemur Nguyễn Cát Tường, Fashion, and the 'Origins' of the Vietnamese National Costume." *Journal of Vietnamese Studies* 11, no. 1 (2016): 76–128. https://doi.org/10.1525/jvs.2016.11.1.76.

Nguyễn Ngọc Tiến. *5678 Bước chân quanh Hồ Gươm: khảo cứu*. HCM City: NXB Trẻ, 2015.

Nguyễn Thành. *Từ điển thư tịch báo chí Việt Nam*. Hanoi: NXB Văn Hóa-Thông Tin, 2001.

Nguyen, Thuy Linh. *Childbirth, Maternity, and Medical Pluralism in French Colonial Vietnam, 1880–1945*. Rochester, NY: University of Rochester Press, 2016.

Nguyễn Văn Cư. *Hà Nội Xưa và Nay*. Hanoi: Nhà Xuất Bản Văn Nhân, 2015.

Nguyễn Văn Khánh, and Phạm Kim Thanh. "Mấy nhận xét về kinh tế hàng hoá ở Hà Nội thời kỳ thực dân pháp đô hộ và tạm chiếm." In Khoa Lịch Sử Đại học quốc Gia Hà Nội, *Với Thăng Long Hà Nội*, 546–56. NXB Thế Giới, 2011.

Nguyễn Văn Ký. *La société vietnamienne face à la modernité: Le Tonkin de la fin du XIXe siècle à la seconde guerre mondiale*. Paris: L'Harmattan, 1995.

Nguyễn Vinh Phúc, ed. *Lịch Sử Thăng Long Hà Nội*. Hanoi: NXB Thời Đại, 2010.

——. *Phố và Đường Hà Nội*. Hanoi: NXB Giao Thông Vận Tải, 2010.

Nguyên Xuân Hiên. "Betel-Chewing in Vietnam: Its Past and Current Importance." *Anthropos* 101 (2006): 499–518.

Nguyen-Marshall, Van. *In Search of Moral Authority: The Discourse on Poverty, Poor Relief, and Charity in French Colonial Indochina*. New York: Peter Lang, 2008.

Nguyễn-Võ Thu-Hương. *The Ironies of Freedom: Sex, Culture, and Neoliberal Governance in Vietnam*. Seattle: University of Washington Press, 2008.

Nhất Linh. *Đoạn Tuyệt: Tiểu-Thuyết*. Saigon: Đời Nay, 1971.

Ninh, Kim N. B. *A World Transformed: The Politics of Culture in Revolutionary Vietnam, 1945-1965*. Ann Arbor: University of Michigan Press, 2002.

Norton, Barley. "Singing the Past: Vietnamese Ca Tru, Memory and Mode." *Asian Music* 36 (2005): 27–56. https://doi.org/10.1353/amu.2005.0023.

O'Callaghan, Sean. *The Yellow Slave Trade*. London: Anthony Blond, 1968.

Osborne, Milton E. *The French Presence in Cochinchina and Cambodia: Rule and Response (1859-1905)*. Ithaca, NY: Cornell University Press, 1969.

Pappin, Philippe. *Histoire de Hanoi*. Paris: Fayard, 2001.

Parenteau, René, and Luc Champagne, eds. *La conservation des quartiers historiques en Indochine*. Paris: Éditions Karthala, 1997.

Parreñas, Rhacel Salazar. *Illicit Flirtations: Labor, Migration, and Sex Trafficking in Tokyo*. Palo Alto, CA: Stanford University Press, 2011.

Peiss, Kathy. "Girls Lean Back Everywhere." In *The Modern Girl around the World: Consumption, Modernity, and Globalization*, edited by Modern Girl Around the World Research Group, 347–53. Durham, NC: Duke University Press, 2008.

Peletz, Michael G. *Gender Pluralism: Southeast Asia since Early Modern Times*. New York: Routelege, 2009.

Peters, Erica J. *Appetites and Aspirations in Vietnam: Food and Drink in the Long Nineteenth Century*. New York: Altamira Press, 2012.

——. "Colonial Cholon and Its 'Missing' Métisses, 1859–1919." *Intersections: Gender and Sexuality in Asia and the Pacific* 21 (2009). http://intersections.anu.edu.au/issue21/peters.htm.

Peycam, Philippe M. F. *The Birth of Vietnamese Political Journalism, Saigon 1916-1930*. New York: Columbia University Press, 2012.

Phạm Xanh. "Hà Nội Trong Tiến Trình Lịch Sử Tư Tưởng Nước Nhà 30 Năm Đầu Thế Kỷ XX." In Khoa Lịch Sử Đại học quốc Gia Hà Nội, *Với Thăng Long Hà Nội*. Hanoi: NXB Thế Giới, 2011.

Phan Đình Phùng and Nguyễn Vinh Phúc. *Phố và Đường Hà Nội*. Hanoi: NXB Giao Thông Vận Tải, 2010.

Phan Thưởng Trọng, Nguyễn Cừ, and Nguyễn Hữu Sơn, eds. *Phóng sự Việt Nam, 1932-1945*. Vol. 1. Hanoi: NXB Văn Học, 2000.

——. *Phóng sự Việt Nam, 1932-1945*. Vol. 2. Hanoi: NXB Văn Học, 2000.

——. *Phóng sự Việt Nam, 1932-1945*. Vol. 3. Hanoi: NXB Văn Học, 2000.

Philastre, P. L. F. *Études sur le droit annamite et chinois: Le Code annamite*. Vol. 2. Taipei: Ch'eng-wen Publishing Company, 1967.

Philips, Richard. *Sex, Politics, and Empire: A Postcolonial Geography*. Manchester: Manchester University Press, 2004.

Pomfret, David M. "'Child Slavery' in British and French Far-Eastern Colonies 1880-1945," *Past and Present* 201, no. 1 (2008). https://doi.org/10.1093/pastj/gtn017.

Proschan, Frank. "Eunich Mandarins, *Soldats Mamzelles*, Effeminate Boys, and Graceless Women: French Colonial Constructions of Vietnamese Genders." *GLQ* 8, no. 4 (2002): 435-67. https://www.muse.jhu.edu/article/12220.

——. "Syphilis, Opiomania, and Pederasty: Colonial Constructions of Vietnamese (and French) Social Diseases." *Journal of the History of Sexuality* 11, no. 4 (2002): 610-36. https://doi.org/10.1353/sex.2003.0043.

Protschky, Susie, and Tom van den Berge, eds. *Modern Times in Southeast Asia, 1920s-1970s*. Leiden: Brill, 2018.

Quétel, Claude. *The History of Syphilis*. Baltimore: Johns Hopkins University Press, 1990.

Ransmeier, Johanna Sirera. "'No Other Choice': The Sale of People in Late Qing and Republican Beijing, 1870-1935." PhD diss., Yale University, 2008.

——. *Sold People: Traffickers and Family Life in North China*. Cambridge, MA: Harvard University Press, 2017.

Reid, Anthony. "Introduction: Slavery and Bondage in Southeast Asian History." In *Slavery, Bondage and Dependency in Southeast Asia*, edited by Anthony Reid, 1-43. New York: St. Martin's, 1983.

Reynolds, Siân. *France between the Wars: Gender and Politics*. London: Routledge, 1996.

Ringdal, Nils Johan. *Love for Sale: A World History of Prostitution*. New York: Grove, 1997.

Robequain, Charles. *The Economic Development of French Indo-China*. London: Oxford University Press, 1944.

Roberts, Mary Louise. *Civilization without Sexes: Reconstructing Gender in Postwar France, 1917-1927*. Chicago: University of Chicago Press, 1997.

Rodriguez, Marie-Corine. "L'administration de la prostitution." In *Vietnamese Society in Transition: The Daily Politics of Reform and Change*, edited by John Kleinen, 223-32. Amsterdam: Het Spinhuis, 2001.

Roustan, Frédéric. "Mousmés and French Colonial Culture." *Journal of Vietnamese Studies* 7, no. 1 (Winter 2012): 52-105. https://doi.org/10.1525/vs.2012.7.1.52.

Rupp, Leila J. *Worlds of Women: The Making of an International Women's Movement*. Princeton, NJ: Princeton University Press, 1997.

Sambuc, Henri. "Notes et documents: Enquête sur la question des métis." *Revue Indochinoise* 19 (February 1913) : 201-9.

Sasges, Gerard. *Imperial Intoxication: Alcohol and the Making of Colonial Indochina*. Honolulu: University of Hawai'i Press: 2017.

Sato, Barbara. *The New Japanese Woman: Modernity, Media, and Women in Interwar Japan*. Durham, NC: Duke University Press, 2003.

Schneider, William H. *Quality and Quantity: The Quest for Biological Regeneration in Twentieth-Century France.* London: Cambridge University Press, 1990.

Scott, George Ryley. *The History of Prostitution.* Middlesex: Senate, 1996.

Scott, James. *The Art of Not Being Governed.* New Haven, CT: Yale University Press, 2010.

Spongberg, Mary. *Feminizing Venereal Disease: The Body of the Prostitute in Nineteenth Century Medical Discourse.* New York: New York University Press, 1997.

Stallybrass, Peter, and Allon White. *The Politics and Poetics of Transgression.* Ithaca, NY: Cornell University Press, 1986.

Stoler, Ann Laura. *Carnal Knowledge and Imperial Power.* Berkeley: University of California Press, 2002.

Stur, Heather Marie. *Beyond Combat: Women and Gender in the Vietnam War Era.* London: Cambridge University Press, 2011.

Sun, Sue. "Where the Girls Are: The Management of Venereal Disease by United States Military Forces in Vietnam." *Literature in Medicine* (Spring 2004) 23, no 1: 66–87. https://doi.org/10.1353/lm.2004.0013.

Surkis, Judith. *Sexing the Citizen: Morality and Masculinity in France, 1870–1920.* Ithaca, NY: Cornell University Press, 2006.

Tạ Thị Thúy. *Việc nhượng đất, khẩn hoang ở bắc kỳ từ 1919 đến 1945.* Hanoi: NXB Thế Giới, 2001.

Tagliacozzo, Eric. *Secret Trades, Porous Borders: Smuggling and States along a Southeast Asian Frontier, 1865–1915.* New Haven, CT: Yale University Press, 2005.

Tai, Hue Tam Ho. *Radicalism and the Origins of the Vietnamese Revolution.* Cambridge, MA: Harvard University Press, 1992.

Tam, Lang. "Tôi kéo xe." In Phan Trọng Thưởng, Nguyễn Cừ, and Nguyễn Hữu Sơn, *Phóng Sự Việt Nam,* vol. 1, 17–72.

Tạo Văn and Moto Furuta. *Nạn Đói Năm 1945: Việt Nam: Những chứng tích lịch sử.* Hanoi: Viện Sử Học Việt Nam, 1995.

Taraud, Christelle. *La prostitution coloniale: Algérie, Tunisie, Maroc (1830–1962).* Paris: Payot, 2003.

Tavernier, Émile. *La famille annamite.* Saigon: Éditions Nguyen Van Cua, 1927.

Thạch Lam. *Hà Nội 36 phố phường.* Hanoi: NXB Văn Học 2005.

"The Wish List of the Vietnamese People (1925)." In *Colonialism Experienced: Vietnamese Writings on Colonialism, 1900–1931,* edited by Truong Buu Lam, 208–27. Ann Arbor: University of Michigan Press, 2000.

Thomas, Martin. *The French Empire at War, 1940–45.* Manchester: Manchester University Press, 1998.

Tracol-Huynh, Isabelle. "Between Stigmatization and Regulation: Prostitution in Colonial Northern Vietnam." *Culture, Health and Sexuality* 12 (2010): S73–S87. https://doi.org/10.1080/13691051003706561.

——. "Encadrer la sexualité au Viêt-Nam colonial: Police des mœurs et réglementation de la prostitution (des années 1870 à la fin des années 1930)." *Genèses* 86, no 1. (2012): 55–77. https://www.jstor.org/stable/26196744.

——. "Entre ombre et lumière: Lieux et espaces prostitutionnels à Hanoi pendant la colonisation (1885–1914)." *Histoire Urbaine* 49, no. 2 (2017): 75–96. https://www.cairn.info/revue-histoire-urbaine-2017-2-page-75.htm.

——. "La prostitution au Tonkin colonial, entre races et genres." *Genre, sexualité et société* 2 (Fall 2009). https://journals.openedition.org/gss/1219.

——. "Prostitutes, Brothels, and the Red Light District: The Management of Prostitution in the City of Hanoi from 1870s to 1950," in *Translation, History and Arts: New Horizons in Asian Interdisciplinary Humanities Research*, edited by J. I. Meng and Atsuko Akai, 176–93. Newcastle: Cambridge Scholars Publishing, 2013.

——. "The Shadow Theatre of Prostitution in French Colonial Tonkin: Faceless Prostitutes under the Colonial Gaze." *Journal of Vietnamese Studies* 7, no. 1 (2012): 10–51. https://doi.org/ 10.1525/vs.2012.7.1.10.

Tran, Ben. *Post-Mandarin: Masculinity and Aesthetic Modernity in Colonial Vietnam.* New York: Fordham University Press, 2017.

Trần Huy Liệu. *Lịch Sử Tám Mươi Năm Chống Pháp quyển II Tập Hạ.* Hanoi: NXB Sử Học 1961.

——. *Xã Hội Việt Nam trong thời Pháp Nhật, quyển I.* Hanoi: NXB Văn Sử Địa, 1957.

——, ed. *Lịch Sử Thủ Đô Hà-Nội.* Hanoi: NXB Sử Học, 1960.

Tran, Nhung Tuyet. "The Commodification of Village Songs and Dances in Seventeenth and Eighteenth-Century Vietnam," in *State, Society and the Market in Contemporary Vietnam*, edited by Hue Tam Ho-Tai and Mark Sidel, 141–57. New York: Routledge, 2012.

Tran, Quang Anh Richard. "From Red Lights to Red Flags: A History of Gender in Colonial and Contemporary Vietnam." PhD diss., University of California, Berkeley, 2011.

Tran Quang Hai. "Review Essay: Recent Recordings of Vietnamese Music." *Asian Music* 11 (1980): 128–33.

Trần Trọng Kim, *Việt Nam Sử Lược.* Hanoi: NXB Văn Hóa Thông Tin, 1999.

Trần Văn Giàu. *Chống Xâm Lăng: Lịch sử Việt Nam từ 1858 đến 1898.* HCM City: NXB Thành Phố Hồ Chí Minh, 2001.

Trinh Van Thao. *L'école française en Indochine.* Paris: Broché, 2000.

Trọng Lang. *Hà Nội lầm than.* Hanoi: NXB Hội Nhà Văn, 2015.

Trung Tâm Lưu Trữ Quốc Gia 1, ed. *Bảng Đối Chiếu tên phố cũ ra phố mới và tên phố mới ra phố cũ Thành Phố Hà Nội Hanoi: Toà Thị Chính, 1951: Lịch sử Hà Nội qua tài liệu lưu trữ tập I.* Hanoi: NXB Văn Hóa-Thông Tin, 2000.

——, ed. *Lịch sử Hà Nội qua tài liệu lưu trữ, tập I: Địa giới hành chính Hà Nội từ 1873 đến 1954.* Hanoi: NXB Văn Hóa-Thông Tin, 2000.

Truong Chinh and Vo Nguyen Giap. *The Peasant Question (1937-1938).* Translated by Christine Pelzer White. Ithaca, NY: Cornell University Press, 1974.

Tuyển Tập Truyện Ngắn Hiện Thực 1930-1945. Hanoi: NXB Văn Học, 2003.

Vann, Michael. "Sex and the Colonial City: Mapping Masculinity, Whiteness, and Desire in French Occupied Hanoi." *Journal of World History* 28, nos. 3–4 (2017): 395–435.

——. "White City on a Red River: Race, Power, and Culture in French Colonial Hanoi." PhD diss., University of California, Santa Cruz, 1999.

Vaudon, Chanoine Jean. *Les filles de Saint-Paul en Indo-Chine.* Chartres: Procure des Soeurs de Saint-Paul, 1931.

Việt Sinh. "Hà Nội Ban Đêm." In Phan Trọng Thưởng, Nguyễn Cừ, and Nguyễn Hữu Sơn, *Phóng Sự Việt Nam*, vol. 2, 685–705.

Vietnamese Women in Society and Revolution 1. The French Colonial Period. Cambridge, MA: Vietnam Resource Center, 1974.

Virgitti, M. H., and B. Joyeux, *Le péril vénérien dans la zone suburbaine de Hanoi.* Hanoi: Imprimerie d'Extrême-Orient, 1938.

——. "Les maisons de chanteuses à Hanoi." *Revue du paludisme et de médecine tropicale* 5 (1947): 81–86.

——. *Quelques oeuvres sociales dans la ville de Hanoi.* Hanoi: Imprimerie d'Extrême-Orient, 1938.

Vũ Bằng. *Bốn mươi năm nói láo.* Hanoi: NXB Hồng Đức, 2013.

Vũ Kiêm Ninh. *Cổng làng Hà Nội xưa và nay.* Hanoi: NXB Văn Hoá Thông Tin, 2007.

Vũ Trọng Phụng. *Dumb Luck: A Novel.* Translated by Peter Zinoman and Nguyen Cam. Ann Arbor: University of Michigan Press, 2002.

——. "Kỹ Nghệ Lấy Tây." In *Kỹ Nghệ lấy tây và cơm thầy cơm cô: Phóng sự.* Hà Nội: NXB Văn Học, 2004.

——. *Làm đĩ.* Hanoi: NXB văn Học, 2015.

——. *Lục Xì: Phóng Sự (1937).* Hanoi: Nhà Xuất Bản Văn Học, 2004.

——. *Số Đỏ.* Hanoi: NXB Văn Học, 2002.

Wakeman, Frederic. *Policing Shanghai, 1927-1937.* Berkeley: University of California Press, 1996.

Warren, James Francis. *Ah Ku and Karayuki-San: Prostitution in Singapore 1870-1940.* Singapore: National University of Singapore Press, 2003.

——. *Pirates, Prostitutes, and Pullers: Explorations in the Ethno- and Social History of Southeast Asia.* Crawley: University of Western Australia Press, 2008.

Yee, Jennifer. "Recycling the 'Colonial Harem'? Women in Postcards from French Indochina." *French Cultural Studies* 15, no. 1 (2004): 5–19. https://doi.org/10.1177/0957155804040405.

Young, Adam J. "Roots of Contemporary Maritime Piracy in Southeast Asia." In *Piracy in Southeast Asia: Status, Issues, and Responses,* edited by Derek Johnson and Mark Valencia, 1–33. Singapore: International Institute of Asian Studies, 2005.

Zinoman, Peter. *Vietnamese Colonial Republican: The Political Vision of Vũ Trọng Phụng.* Berkeley: University of California Press, 2014.

Zheng, Tiantian. *Red Lights: The Lives of Sex Workers in Postsocialist China.* Minnesota: University of Minnesota Press, 2009.

Index

Note: Page references in *italics* refer to illustrative matter.

Aalbers, Manuel, 36
abortion, 4, 182
abuse: at dispensaries, 73, 78–79; in domestic settings, 12; in sex work industry, 2, 108–12, 128, 181, 183, 186. *See also* debt bondage; rape
ả đào music, 137, 138–39, 142–43, 147–48, 224n60, 234n8
ả đào singers: debt-bondage agreements of, 1, 90, 95–96, 97, 106, 149; sex work by, 14, 19, 137–38, 144–45; venereal disease and, 75, 87–89, 145–48. *See also* sex work, overview
ả đào singing houses: business of, 148–51; description of, 142–44; education reform and, 11; policing and punishment of, 110–11, 131–32, 139–41, 150–51, 154–61, 192, 222n5; popular locations for, 41, 55–56, 136–37, 140–41, 144; statistics on, *141*; theft and scams at, 151–54. *See also* boardinghouses; brothels; sex work, overview
adolescent sex work. *See* juvenile sex work
adoption, 98, 113, 116–17, 121–22, 127
Agency to Eradicate Venereal Disease, 71
agriculture, 8–9
anal sex, 5, 52, 69–70
antitrafficking movement, 8, 15, 92, 100–101, 110, 157, 211n153. *See also* human trafficking
Anti-Venereal Disease League, 86
Ao Chi, 133
Argentina, 93, 164, 189, 227n4
arsenic benzene, 70

Bạch Đinh, 181
Bạch Mai neighborhood, Hanoi, 39–40, 86, 141
Bắc Ninh, 74–75

bai mayi, 103
ballroom dancing, 162
Barrett, Tracy, 107
bars and nightclubs, 54, 55, 75, 81, 87, 88, 192, 193. *See also* ả đào singing houses; dance halls
Baudrit, André, 15, 101, 108
bellhops. *See* boardinghouse boys
Billotte, Gaston, 59
birth control, 4, 36, 70, 201n98
birth defects, 8, 59, 60, 61, 67–68, 88, 206n39, 206n41
bismuth, 70
black market sex industry in Vietnam, overview, 1–19, 187–94. *See also* ả đào singing houses; dance halls; geography of vice; human trafficking; juvenile sex work; sex work, overview; sex work regulation laws
Blanchon, Adolphe, 73
blindness, 67
boardinghouse boys, 34, 36, 115, 130
boardinghouses, 2, 7, 14, 21, 33–35, 130, 140. *See also* brothels; juvenile sex work; sex work, overview
Bodros, Paul, 45, 46
booklets, medical, 53–54, 63–64, 76, 87, 157, 171, 185
border towns, 56–58, 98. *See also* human trafficking; sex work, overview
Brévié, Jules, 110–11, 158
brothels, 4, 92, 108–12, 159, 191. *See also* ả đào singing houses; boardinghouses; dance halls; human trafficking; sex work, overview
Bùi Thị Bảo, 50

Camiscioli, Elisa, 93, 189
Cao Bằng, 57, 65

---

250   **INDEX**

capitalism. *See* materialism
ca trù, 192, 223n25, 234n9
Cầu Giáy neighborhood, Hanoi, 39, 42
Cấu Sam, 122
centre d'attractions (proposed), 36–37, 45
chancroids, 59, 61, 72, 87. *See also* venereal diseases
Charbonnier, Roger, 7, 30, 65, 70–71, 148
chattel slavery, 93, 100
Cherry, Haydon, 16
childbirth: poverty and, 116; venereal disease and birth defects, 8, 59, 60, 61, 67–68, 88, 206n39, 206n41. *See also* pregnancy
children. *See* juvenile sex work
China: dance halls in, 20, 108, 167–68, 234n5; Kuomintang (KMT), 34; migrant rights in Vietnam of, 107, 216n109; piracy from, 98, 106–7, 213n35; trafficking and sex industry in, 15, 91–92, 98–99, 102–3, 106–8, 128–29
Chinese Quarter (neighborhood), Hải Phòng, 46
cholera, 9
Chung, Miss, 34
clothing: debt bondage and, 95, 158, 178, 184–85; ill health and, 180, 181; theft of, 150, 153; trends in, 124, 163, 165, 166, 227n6, 227n8
cô đầu. *See* ả đào singers
Commerce d'Abrasin, 57
Commission for Disease Prophylaxis, 37, 59
Commission of Social Questions, 110
Committee for the Hygiene of Tonkin, 63
"Commodified Women's Bodies in Vietnam and Beyond" (*Journal of Vietnamese Studies*), 16
communal land, 8–9, 27, 115–16
Conference of Central Authorities of Eastern Countries on the Traffic of Women and Children, 110
Confucian traditions, 11, 166
Cô Ngà, 136, 160
contraception, 4, 36, 70, 201n98
Convention of Nanking (1930), 107
Crédit Populaire program, 109–10

dance halls: business of, 170–74, 177–80; modern music at, 162–63, 167, 171; reputation of, 182–86; rise in popularity of, 167–70; venereal disease and, 174, 184; violence and abuse at, 173–74, 179, 181, 183, 186; works on, 13–14, 169–70,

183. *See also* bars and nightclubs; boardinghouses; brothels; sex work, overview; taxi dancers
Đặng Thị Như, 1, 106, 120
Đặng Thị Nuột, 105, 177
Đặng Thị Vân Chi, 16
đào, as term, 229n55
đào rượu, 144–45
Đào Thị Ngọc Chinh, 174
Đào Thị Yến, 104
đào trò, 144
debt bondage, 90–98; of ả đào singers, 1, 90, 95–96, 97, 106, 149, 158; at boardinghouses, 35; of peasant farmers, 9, 27; scholarship on, 18; of taxi dancers, 97, 178–79, 184–85. *See also* abuse; human trafficking; poverty; sex work, overview
Delevaux, Henri, 51–52
depraved youth journalism, 12
Dịch-chi, 136, 160
Đinh Thị Hiếng, 96, 97
dispensaries, 71, 86, 157, 158. *See also* Hanoi Dispensary
Djibouti Garden, Hải Phòng, 49, 94, 130
Đội Con Gá, 6
Đổi Mới reforms, 193
domestic work, 49, 90, 113, 117, 122, 125, 166. *See also* migration and women's work; sex work, overview
Đỗ Văn Nam, 66–67
Đỗ Vân Nam, 83
D. Thiêu-Tước, 181

economic depression, 9, 10, 28, 45, 135, 164, 186, 216n112. *See also* poverty
economic geography. *See* geography of vice
education system, 11, 164, 197n38
environmental disasters, 9, 24, 28, 135. *See also* migration and women's work
Europeanization. *See* Westernization
European Quarter (neighborhood), Hải Phòng, 45–46
European sex workers, 18, 64, 197n51
export industry, 8–9, 27, 28, 44

famine, 9, 26–28. *See also* poverty
First Indochina War, 19, 191. *See also* war
flooding, 9, 28
flower vendors, 21, 129
food scarcity, 9, 26–28, 149. *See also* poverty
Franco-Annamite school system, 11

Frass, Madame, 73–74

French colonial administration, overview, 5–6, 8–9, 23–24, 189–91

French League of Human Rights, 100

French Quarter neighborhood, Hanoi, *30,* 31–32

gái mới, 166. *See also* modernity

gái tân-thời, 166. *See also* modernity

geography of vice: border towns, 56–58; Hải Phòng, 43–47; Hanoi, 28–37; Hanoi's suburbs, 37–43; maritime networks of trafficking, 47–51; military bases, 51–56; Red River Delta, 24–28; Tonkin, overview, 22–24

Gia Lâm neighborhood, Hanoi, 39, *40,* 42–43, *141*

Gia Long legal code (1812), 6, 213n43

giang hồ, 167, 228n19

giáp (organization), 116

Gia Quất neighborhood, Hanoi, 43, *141*

Gibbs, Jason, 168

Godart, Justin, 83, 84

gonorrhea, 67, 72, 74, 206n39. *See also* venereal diseases

Great Depression, 9, 10, 28, 45, 135, 164, 186, 216n112

Guernut Mission, 83, 84

Gulf of Tonkin. *See* Tonkin, geographic and administrative overview

Haemophilus ducreyi, 59. *See also* venereal diseases

Hải Phòng, geographic and administrative overview, 43–47, 202n111, 202n114. *See also* Lạch Tray neighborhood, Hải Phòng

Hai Vinh, Miss, 124

Hạ Long Bay, 23, 47, 106

Hanoi, geographic and administrative overview, 28–43. *See also names of specific neighborhoods*

Hanoi Dispensary: consolidation of, 81; disease cases in, 72; investigation of, 14, 27, 65, 83–85, 167; regulation of, 73. *See also* dispensaries; venereal diseases

Hà Nội Lầm Than (Trọng Lang), 183

Hanoi Ophthalmological Hospital, 67, 86

Hanoi Prophylactic League, 69

Hanoi suburbs, geographic and administrative overview, 37–43

hát ả đào. *See* ả đào music

hát cửa đình music, 138

hát cửa quyền music, 138

Henchy, Judith, 166–67

Henriot, Christian, 102, 108

Hershatter, Gail, 103

Hoang, Kimberly Kay, 15, 16, 193

Hoàng Cao Khải, 42, 201n105

Hoàng Liên Bích, 161

Hoàng Thị Tự, 103

Hồ Chí Minh, 19

homelessness, 114, 117–18, 121. *See also* poverty

homosexual sex work, 4, 69

Hồn Gai, 50

Hợp Thiện, 37

human trafficking, 10, 20, 22; maritime networks of, 47–51; by mẹ mìn, 20, 48–49, 102–6, 124, 160, 215n73; policing of, 108–12; scholarship on, 16; state regulation on, 8, 99–102; statistics on, 101; to/from China, 91–92, 98–99, 102–3, 106–8. *See also* antitrafficking movement; debt bondage; juvenile sex work; sex work, overview

Human Trafficking in Colonial Vietnam (Lessard), 16

hunger, 9, 26–28. *See also* poverty

import-export industry, 8–9, 27, 28, 44

India, 110

Indigenous Hospital, 81. *See also* Hanoi Dispensary

Indigenous Quarter (neighborhood): Hải Phòng, 45; Hanoi, 30–31, 71

individualism, 10, 11–14, 164, 192

Indochina Council for the Eradication of Venereal Disease, 82

infant mortality, 67, 116. *See also* birth defects

infectious diseases. *See* venereal diseases

Jacobsen, Trude, 94

Japan, 167, 189–90

Journal of Vietnamese Studies, 16

Joyeaux, Bernard, 35–36, 37, 41, 52, 68, 81, 140–41, 169

juvenile sex work, 19, 21; in ả đào singing houses, 14, 160; age of, 115, 119–20; laws on, 6, 118–19; market operations of, 127–31, 135; policing and punishment of, 114–15, 131–35; poverty and, 114, 115–18, 125; virginity and, 119, 126–27; worker stories, 1, 48–49, 113–14, 120–27. *See also* human trafficking; sex work, overview

karaoke-ôm bars, 193
Khâm Thiên neighborhood, Hanoi,
    38, 40–42; destruction of, 192;
    entertainment work in, 13, 141, 144,
    168–70, 176; exploitation by business
    owners on, 178; medical centers in, 86,
    157, 158; regulation of, 83, 87, 155–56,
    180, 185; sex work in, 134, 145; singing
    houses in, *141*; violence in, 173. *See also*
    Hanoi, geographic and administrative
    overview
kidnapping. *See* human trafficking
Kim Mã neighborhood, Hanoi, 39, *40*, 42,
    141, 144
K'intcheou, China, 98–99
Kỹ nghệ lấy tây (Vũ Trọng Phụng), 53,
    124

Lạch Tray neighborhood, Hải Phòng,
    170
Lainez, Nicolas, 15, 16
Làm Đĩ (Vũ Trọng Phụng), 13–14, 183,
    200n69
Lan, Miss, 35
land theft and land management
    transformation, 8–9, 27, 115–16. *See also*
    poverty
League of Nations, 92, 100–101, 109–12,
    157
Leiba, J., 176, 178, 183
Le Roy des Barres, A., 63, 80, 82, 119, 146
Lessard, Micheline, 16, 98, 99
Lê Thị Cúc, 90, 91, 93, 95, 97, 178, 179
Lê Thị Hồng Hải, 16
Lê Thị Trá, 153
Lê Tư Thoan, 132
Lewis, Su-Lin, 168
L'Hôtel du Coq d'Or, Hanoi, 228n30
Limoncelli, Stephanie, 16, 100
Li Tana, 26
literacy, 11, 17
literary movements, 11–12
livret de travail, 53–54
Lục Xì (Vũ Trọng Phụng), 16, 211n162
Lương, Miss, 176
Lương Thị Xuân, 103
Ly Cam, 122, 130

Mai, 175
Mai Lam boardinghouse, Hanoi, 40
Mai Vien boardinghouse, Hanoi, 40
Malarney, Shaun Kingsley, 16
male sex workers, 174

Mãn (ethnic group), 71
maritime networks of trafficking,
    47–51, 98–99. *See also* transportation
    infrastructure
market vendors, 21, 34, 132
Marr, David, 12
marriage: of á đào singers, 138; cultural
    practices of, 11, 12, 94, 126, 220n69;
    laws on, 76, 213n43; poverty and, 116,
    126; taxi dancers and, 179
Marthe Richard Law (1946), 191
Martinez, Julia, 16
materialism, 10, 11, 13–14, 85, 167, 175,
    183
McHale, Shawn, 15
medical booklets, 53–54, 63–64, 76, 87,
    157, 171, 185
medical centers, 71, 86, 157, 158. *See also*
    Hanoi Dispensary
medicine used for venereal diseases,
    70–74, 190–91
mẹ mìn, 20, 48–49, 102–6, 124, 160,
    215n73. *See also* human trafficking
mercuric chloride, 70
me tây, 53–54, 76
migration and women's work, 2, 8–10,
    20–21, 24–27, 93–94, 105, 125–26, 175.
    See also debt bondage; domestic work;
    human trafficking; rural-to-urban
    migration; sex work, overview
military bases, 46–47, 51–56, 74–80. *See*
    also soldiers; war
Miller, Julia Christine Scriven, 68
Minh, 130
Minh Huong, 34
mission civilisatrice, 11, 164
mixed-race girls and families, 124
modernity, 10, 11, 14, 38, 163–67. *See also*
    Westernization
Móng Cái, 50–51, 74
Morocco, 36, 37, 39, 80
Mường (ethnic group), 66, 71
music: á đào, 137, 138–39, 142–43, 147–48,
    224n60; ca trù, 192, 223n25, 234n9; hát
    cửa đình, 138; hát cửa quyền, 138; from
    Philippines, 229n62; Western-style,
    162–63, 167, 171. *See also* dance halls

New European Quarter neighborhood,
    Hanoi, 32
Ngã Tư Sở / Vĩnh Hồ neighborhood,
    Hanoi, 39, *40*, 42, *141*, 143
Ngô Quốc Lâm, 177

Ngô Tất Tố, 144
Ngô Thị Yến, 122, 177, 179
Ng. Thị Bình, 105
Ng Thị Đào, 95, 97, 178
Ng Thị-Lan, 128
Ng Thị Lộc, 129
Ng. Thị Lỳ, 149, 150–51
Ng Thị Thu, 95, 97, 178
Ng Thị Tình, 95, 97, 178, 179
Nguyễn Bảo Trang, 16
Nguyễn Đình Lạp, 12, 13, 141, 171, 172, 183
Nguyên Hồng, 49–50
Nguyen Ngoc Phong, 147–48, 155
Nguyễn Thị Ch., 95
Nguyễn-Thị Châu, 126
Nguyễn Thị Giáp, 127
Nguyễn Thị Hải, 77–78
Nguyen Thi Lieu, 113–14
Nguyễn Thị Lợi, 48–49
Nguyễn Thị Mai, 127–28
Nguyễn Thị Minh, 133, 160
Nguyễn Thị Na, 68
Nguyễn Thị Vân Lan, 150
nhà dưỡng tế program, 116
nhà hát ả đào. *See* ả đào singing houses
nhà xăm. *See* boardinghouses
nightclubs. *See* ả đào singing houses; bars and nightclubs; dance halls
1921 law. *See* sex work regulation laws

Oanh, 132, 150
opium: dens for, 18, 40, 46, 54, 55–56, 121; French monopolies on, 98; men's use of, 42, 142, 143; prohibition on, 73; women's use of, 84, 182
orphanages, 117
overpopulation, 2, 24–26. *See also* migration and women's work; population statistics

Pak Hoi, China, 98–99, 108
Patenôtre Treaty (1884), 5, 23, 63
Peters, Erica, 16
Philippines, 229n62, 233n169
phóng sự journalism, 11–12, 15
phúng (organization), 116
Phùng Thị Hồn, 128
Phùng Thị Hồng, 177
physical geography. *See* geography of vice
Piere, Marcel, 55, 69, 174, 184
piracy, 98, 106–7, 213n35
place. *See* geography of vice

Police des Moeurs, 6
political geography. *See* geography of vice
Popular Front, 82–83, 110
population statistics, 7, 10, 26, 29, 44–45, 83, 196nn15–16. *See also* overpopulation
poverty, 2–3; housing and, 33, 199n54; juvenile sex work and, 114, 115–18, 125; land transition and, 8–9, 27, 115–16; sex work as escape from, 14, 24, 102, 193; taxi dancers and, 163–65, 176–77. *See also* debt bondage; economic depression; food scarcity; sex work, overview
pregnancy, 4, 70, 85, 160, 181, 182. *See also* childbirth
prostitution, legal definition of, 5, 184. *See also* juvenile sex work; sex work, overview

quarantine, 3, 7, 14, 61, 64, 65, 72, 85, 188. *See also* venereal diseases
quốc ngữ, 11, 197n38

railway, 24
Ransmeier, Johanna Sirera, 98, 103
rape, 10, 52, 105, 114, 122, 127, 134, 149. *See also* abuse
Red River Delta, 24–28, 65–66. *See also* Tonkin, geographic and administrative overview
René Robin Hospital, 86, 91
reportage journalism, 11–12
reproductive economy, 98
research methods, 17–18
reserved quarters for sex work, 30, 36–37, 45–46, 79, 200n78. *See also names of specific neighborhoods*
revolutionaries, 34
rickshaw pullers, 21, 32–33, 96–97, 115, 129–30. *See also* transportation infrastructure
Robin, René, 35, 118–19
Rodriguez, Marie-Corrine, 16
Roustan, Frédéric, 16
rural-to-urban migration, 2, 8–10, 20–21, 196nn15–16. *See also* migration and women's work
rural–urban divide, 13, 162–63, 186

Sabat, Magdalena, 36
Salazar Parreñas, Rhacel, 91, 233n169
Sầm Công neighborhood, Hanoi, 31
sanitation, 35–36

Self-Strengthening Literary Group
(Tự Lực Văn Đoàn), 11–12
Sellier, Henri, 82, 85
sex education, 79, 84, 193, 194
sexual violence, 10, 52, 105, 114, 122, 127,
134, 149. *See also* abuse
sex work, overview, 1–19, 187–94. *See
also* ả đào singing houses; dance halls;
geography of vice; human trafficking;
juvenile sex work; sex work regulation
laws
sex work regulation laws, 2, 61–64,
187–88; on ả đào singing houses and
dance halls, 139–40, 154, 158–59,
184–85, 195n5; age requirements
in, 118–19; amendments to, 6, 154;
definition of prostitution in, 5; regional
jurisdiction of, 50, 51, 79; registration
requirements of, 6, 85, 184. *See also* sex
work, overview; venereal diseases
slavery, 93, 100, 213n43
Slavery Commission, 109
soldiers: with ả đào singers and taxi
dancers, 42, 173–74; venereal diseases
and, 60–62, 69–71, 184, 191–92. *See also*
dance halls; military bases; sex work,
overview; war
Stur, Heather, 16
suicide, 12, 66, 150, 151
Sun, Sue, 16
syphilis, 65–67, 69, 72, 206n37. *See also*
venereal diseases
Syria, 80

Tagliocozzo, Eric, 56
taxation, 8, 31, 169, 198n18
taxi dancers: debt-bondage agreements of,
97, 178–80; description of life as, 175–81;
escape from poverty of, 14, 19, 163–65,
176–77; ill health of, 181–82; as modern
girls, 162–63, 165–67; reputation of,
182–86; rise in popularity of, 167–70;
venereal disease and, 87–89, 158. *See also*
dance halls; sex work, overview
Tchao-Huong, 122
teeth-lacquering traditions and
modernity, 12, 165, 175, 177
Thái Hà Ấp neighborhood, Hanoi, 42
thanh niên trụy lạc journalism, 12
Thao Thao, 14, 35, 65, 72, 84, 85
theft, 10, 150, 152
Thị Bảo, 105, 130
Thi Binh, 122
Thị Chúc, 149–50, 160, 178

Thi Chung, 122
Thị Cúc, 179
Thị Đ., 176
Thị Đào, 151
Thị Hoà, 48–49
Thị Hợi, 123
Thị Hy, 132
Thị Lan, Miss, 121
Thị Lăng, 104
Thị Ngân, 106, 132
Thị Nguyệt, 151
Thị Nuột, 128
Thin Zel boardinghouse, 34
Thị Oanh, 106, 132
Thị Phương, 152
Thị Thiện, 132
Thị Thuật, Miss, 90, 91
Thị Tình, 178, 179
Thi Tuyen, 113–14, 123, 127
Thị Ty, 150
Thu Huong Nguyen Vo, 15
Tô Ân, 85–86
tolerance system. *See* sex work regulation
laws
Tông, 54–56
Tonkin, geographic and administrative
overview, 5–6, 22–24. *See also names of
specific areas*
Tracol-Huynh, Isabelle, 16
trafficking. *See* human trafficking
Tran, Ben, 16
transportation infrastructure, 24, 28–29,
70. *See also* maritime networks of
trafficking; rickshaw pullers
Trần Thị Hoan, 133
Trần Thị Lan, 126, 133
Trần Thị Tâm, 176–77
Trần Văn Téo, 48
Treaty of Huế (1884), 5, 23
Trịnh Thị Ý, 97
Trọng Lang: on incentives of sex workers,
14, 148; on rape incident, 149; on taxi
dancers, 174, 176, 178–79, 180–81, 182,
183
Trương Thị Lan, 103
tuberculosis, 116, 182
Tự Lực Văn Đoàn (Self-Strengthening
Literary Group), 11–12
Tuyết, Miss, 85
typhoon, 43

unemployment, 10
unfree labor, 91, 108–12. *See also* debt
bondage; human trafficking

United Nations Educational, Scientific, and Cultural Organization (UNESCO), 192
urban geography. *See* geography of vice
urban-rural divide, 13, 162–63, 186

valaques, 197n51
Vann, Michael, 30
venereal diseases, 18, 59–61; 1921 law and registration of, 61–64; 1938 study on, 7; ả đào singers and, 75, 87–89, 145–47, 158; boardinghouses and, 34–35; chancroids, 59, 61, 72, 87; dance halls and, 174, 184; effects of, 8, 66–68; gonorrhea, 67, 72, 74, 206n39; informal regulatory reform and, 79–89; mandatory quarantine for, 3, 14; quarantine for, 3, 7, 61, 64, 65, 72, 85, 188; rural collaborative efforts against, 74–79; state identification and prevention program on, 2, 6, 18, 158–59, 191; statistics on, 35, 47, *62, 63,* 72, 83; syphilis, 65–67, 69, 72, 206n37; transmission patterns in Tonkin of, 62, 64–70; treatment centers for, 71–74, 83–84, 86, 157, 158, 205n20, 208n78; treatments used for, 70–71, 190–91. *See also* Hanoi Dispensary

Việt Nam Quốc Dân Đảng (VNQDĐ), 34
violence. *See* abuse; rape; war
virginity, 119, 126–27
Virgitti, M. H., 41, 52, 82, 87, 141
Vong A Kiou, 108, 123, 128
Vũ Thị Tý, 104
Vũ Tiến neighborhood, Thái Bình, 136–37
Vũ Trọng Phụng: on dance halls, 13–14, 169–70, 183; on infant death and birth defects, 67; *Kỹ nghệ lấy tây,* 53, 124; on treatments for venereal disease, 69; on venereal disease and dispensaries, 16, 84, 211n162

war, 19, 45, 189–93. *See also* military bases; soldiers
Westernization, 10, 11, 164–67, 169, 183, 227n4. *See also* modernity
"white slavery," 100. *See also* human trafficking; slavery

Yên Thái neighborhood, Hanoi, 31
Yoc Ting, 121
youth cultural changes, 11–12, 164–65. *See also* modernity; Westernization
Yune A Nang, 132–33

Zinoman, Peter, 14

STUDIES OF THE WEATHERHEAD EAST ASIAN INSTITUTE COLUMBIA UNIVERSITY

Selected Titles

(Complete list at http://weai.columbia.edu/publications/studies-weai/)

Fighting for Virtue: Justice and Politics in Thailand, by Duncan McCargo. Cornell University Press, 2020.

Beyond the Steppe Frontier: A History of the Sino-Russian Border, by Sören Urbansky. Princeton University Press, 2020.

Pirates and Publishers: A Social History of Copyright in Modern China, by Fei-Hsien Wang. Princeton University Press, 2019.

The Typographic Imagination: Reading and Writing in Japan's Age of Modern Print Media, by Nathan Shockey. Columbia University Press, 2019.

Down and Out in Saigon: Stories of the Poor in a Colonial City, by Haydon Cherry. Yale University Press, 2019.

Beauty in the Age of Empire: Japan, Egypt, and the Global History of Aesthetic Education, by Raja Adal. Columbia University Press, 2019.

Mass Vaccination: Citizens' Bodies and State Power in Modern China, by Mary Augusta Brazelton. Cornell University Press, 2019.

Residual Futures: The Urban Ecologies of Literary and Visual Media of 1960s and 1970s Japan, by Franz Prichard. Columbia University Press, 2019.

The Making of Japanese Settler Colonialism: Malthusianism and Trans-Pacific Migration, 1868–1961, by Sidney Xu Lu. Cambridge University Press, 2019.

The Power of Print in Modern China: Intellectuals and Industrial Publishing from the End of Empire to Maoist State Socialism, by Robert Culp. Columbia University Press, 2019.

Beyond the Asylum: Mental Illness in French Colonial Vietnam, by Claire E. Edington. Cornell University Press, 2019.

Borderland Memories: Searching for Historical Identity in Post-Mao China, by Martin Fromm. Cambridge University Press, 2019.

Sovereignty Experiments: Korean Migrants and the Building of Borders in Northeast Asia, 1860–1949, by Alyssa M. Park. Cornell University Press, 2019.

The Greater East Asia Co-Prosperity Sphere: When Total Empire Met Total War, by Jeremy A. Yellen. Cornell University Press, 2019.

Thought Crime: Ideology and State Power in Interwar Japan, by Max Ward. Duke University Press, 2019.

Statebuilding by Imposition: Resistance and Control in Colonial Taiwan and the Philippines, by Reo Matsuzaki. Cornell University Press, 2019.

Nation-Empire: Ideology and Rural Youth Mobilization in Japan and Its Colonies, by Sayaka Chatani. Cornell University Press, 2019.

Fixing Landscape: A Techno-Poetic History of China's Three Gorges, by Corey Byrnes. Columbia University Press, 2019.

The Invention of Madness: State, Society, and the Insane in Modern China, by Emily Baum. University of Chicago Press, 2018.

Japan's Imperial Underworlds: Intimate Encounters at the Borders of Empire, by David Ambaras. Cambridge University Press, 2018.

Heroes and Toilers: Work as Life in Postwar North Korea, 1953–1961, by Cheehyung Harrison Kim. Columbia University Press, 2018.

Electrified Voices: How the Telephone, Phonograph, and Radio Shaped Modern Japan, 1868–1945, by Kerim Yasar. Columbia University Press, 2018.

Making Two Vietnams: War and Youth Identities, 1965–1975, by Olga Dror. Cambridge University Press, 2018.

Playing by the Informal Rules: Why the Chinese Regime Remains Stable Despite Rising Protests, by Yao Li. Cambridge University Press, 2018.

Raising China's Revolutionaries: Modernizing Childhood for Cosmopolitan Nationalists and Liberated Comrades, by Margaret Mih Tillman. Columbia University Press, 2018.

Buddhas and Ancestors: Religion and Wealth in Fourteenth-Century Korea, by Juhn Y. Ahn. University of Washington Press, 2018.

Idly Scribbling Rhymers: Poetry, Print, and Community in Nineteenth-Century Japan, by Robert Tuck. Columbia University Press, 2018.

China's War on Smuggling: Law, Economic Life, and the Making of the Modern State, 1842–1965, by Philip Thai. Columbia University Press, 2018.

Forging the Golden Urn: The Qing Empire and the Politics of Reincarnation in Tibet, by Max Oidtmann. Columbia University Press, 2018.

The Battle for Fortune: State-Led Development, Personhood, and Power among Tibetans in China, by Charlene Makley. Cornell University Press, 2018.

Aesthetic Life: Beauty and Art in Modern Japan, by Miya Elise Mizuta Lippit. Harvard University Asia Center, 2018.

Where the Party Rules: The Rank and File of China's Communist State, by Daniel Koss. Cambridge University Press, 2018.

Resurrecting Nagasaki: Reconstruction and the Formation of Atomic Narratives, by Chad R. Diehl. Cornell University Press, 2018.

China's Philological Turn: Scholars, Textualism, and the Dao in the Eighteenth Century, by Ori Sela. Columbia University Press, 2018.

Making Time: Astronomical Time Measurement in Tokugawa Japan, by Yulia Frumer. University of Chicago Press, 2018.

Mobilizing without the Masses: Control and Contention in China, by Diana Fu. Cambridge University Press, 2018.

Post-Fascist Japan: Political Culture in Kamakura after the Second World War, by Laura Hein. Bloomsbury, 2018.

China's Conservative Revolution: The Quest for a New Order, 1927–1949, by Brian Tsui. Cambridge University Press, 2018.

Promiscuous Media: Film and Visual Culture in Imperial Japan, 1926–1945, by Hikari Hori. Cornell University Press, 2018.

The End of Japanese Cinema: Industrial Genres, National Times, and Media Ecologies, by
    Alexander Zahlten. Duke University Press, 2017.
The Chinese Typewriter: A History, by Thomas S. Mullaney. MIT Press, 2017.
Forgotten Disease: Illnesses Transformed in Chinese Medicine, by Hilary A. Smith.
    Stanford University Press, 2017.
Borrowing Together: Microfinance and Cultivating Social Ties, by Becky Yang Hsu.
    Cambridge University Press, 2017.
Food of Sinful Demons: Meat, Vegetarianism, and the Limits of Buddhism in Tibet, by
    Geoffrey Barstow. Columbia University Press, 2017.
Youth for Nation: Culture and Protest in Cold War South Korea, by Charles R. Kim.
    University of Hawai'i Press, 2017.

CPSIA information can be obtained
at www.ICGtesting.com
Printed in the USA
LVHW111726031120
670608LV00022B/286/J